Law Dictionary

by

Steven H. Gifis

Associate Professor of Law
Rutgers, The State University
of New Jersey, School of Law
Newark

Barron's Educational Series, Inc.
Woodbury, New York

All inquiries should be addressed to:
Barron's Educational Series, Inc.
113 Crossways Park Drive
Woodbury, New York 11797

Library of Congress Catalog Card No. 74-18126

International Standard Book No. 0-8120-0543-0

Library of Congress Cataloging in Publication Data

Gifis, Steven H.
  Law dictionary.

   1. Law—United States—Dictionaries.   I. Title.

KF156.G53   340'.03   74-18126

ISBN 0-8120-0543-0

19 20 21 22 23

Preface

Professions tend to insulate themselves from lay understanding by the development of specialized jargon. The legal profession has achieved this insulation so successfully that the uninitiated is overwhelmed by the incomprehensibility of his or her advocate's prose. Despite the increasing pervasiveness of law into every facet of American life, the special language of the law remains a barrier to nonlawyers. To the extent that this promotes the economic health of the profession, maintains its aura, and prevents unauthorized practice of the law, it may be regarded as a virtue. And the jargon does communicate in a unique way the tradition and stability that the society looks to its legal system to maintain.

The lawyer's language is replete with words having particular meanings. Thus, a lawyer "moves" to "evict a holdover tenant" when his or her client wants to kick the tenant out. The lawyer seeks to "partition a co-tenancy" gone sour and to "compel an accounting" to the "aggrieved party." A client's home is destroyed by earthquake and the insurance company refuses to pay. An attorney asks if the "risk" of earthquake is included in the insured's policy and, if not, whether "representations" were made to the homeowner that would support an action to "reform" the policy or that might create an "estoppel" against the company's denial of "liability." A merchant finds an umbrella in a coat rack; the attorney asks whether it has been "abandoned" or "mislaid" and explains to the merchant the "duty" which the law imposes upon a "finder" of "lost property."

Words and phrases are the tools of the lawyer's trade. Whether the lawyer is drafting a contract, negotiating a settlement, preparing a pleading, filing a tax return, attesting a will, closing a title, or arguing a motion in court, the audience is usually another lawyer. The legal communication process depends upon shared understandings of the professional language. The law school graduate taking a bar examination is counseled to "make noises like a lawyer." The successful bar applicant will not conclude that "the case should be thrown out of court;" rather, in the language of lawyers, he or she will write, "the plaintiff's action on motion should be dismissed for failure to state a cause of action upon which relief can be granted," or "for want of prosecution," or "for failure to join an indispensible party," etc.

Some of the law's reliance upon ancient or archaic terminology and Latin expression is giving way to more modern forms. But criminals still have *mens rea,* gifts are made *inter vivos,* cases still refer to legatees and *scienter,* and attorneys persist in the fiction of contracts which are written "under seal." The earlier cases upon which so much of our law is based are replete with old "forms of action" and peculiar words. They continue to confound experienced attorneys and judges, who sometimes resort to a law dictionary for an explanation. But the effect of this new jargon upon beginning law students is more than confounding. It is discouraging, frustrating, and even frightening. The first-year law student, having survived the competition for admission, now wonders with considerable anxiety whether the law can be mastered when it cannot even be comprehended. The ask, it is hoped, may be eased by the massive repository of legal terms known as a law dictionary.

But the classic law dictionary weighs several pounds and contains hundreds of pages of elaborate definitions. It is a good library aid and research tool, especially helpful on rarely used legal terms. But, in my own experience as a law student, I found such dictionaries too awkward, bulky, and comprehensive to be useful study aids. It was not possible to have it with me when I was reading cases; rather, it primarily adorned the bookshelf, and was rarely consulted. When a word perplexed me, I passed it by, hoping it was unimportant or that its significance would appear in the context of the whole case. On occasion I did resort to a law dictionary, but it was always the library copy — not my own, which was safely resting at home. Few lawyers have an unabridged dictionary within ready reach even if they have one in their private law library. They are just not convenient.

The answer to convenience, of course, is an abridged paperback law dictionary. Those available, up to the present, have been written for the laymen. This dictionary, however, is intended as a portable, useful, study aid for the law student or anyone else who, in a professional way, comes in contact with unfamiliar legal jargon and wants a comprehensible explanation which will permit a basic understanding of the word or phrase. It is hoped that first-year law students in particular will use the book constantly in their reading of cases and will find new legal terms becoming clearer in a matter of moments and becoming a permanent part of their legal vocabulary after several references.

I have been guided by this study aid focus in selecting the entries and defining those selected. First-year law students will find most of the basic terms that they will come upon in their assignments. When I am asked in class by a student what a term means, I generally try to answer the question if I am able, with a simple explanation and an example of its legal significance. I have found that these bits of legal wisdom encourage the kind of analytical questioning that is the mark of the able advocate and have therefore utilized this practice in my law dictionary to help make it stimulating as well as informative. Thus, despite its compact size this dictionary has a considerable encyclopedic dimension, an element which I consider essential for a good law dictionary.

There is always a danger that the legal significance will change, and the definition will become inaccurate or misleading. As Samuel Johnson has observed, "Definitions are hazardous." The definitions rely heavily upon cases and authority. A deliberate effort has been made to insure that the definitions are accurate both from an historical perspective and in light of very recent developments in the law, permitting further research.

Where a treatise or hornbook has been used, the student is encouraged to go to the cited source for a fuller explanation when his interest is sufficiently aroused. In instances where the pronouns *he* and *him* appear in definitions, they have been used to conform with standard law prose. It should be understood that in every case, except where specifically stated, these references apply to both men and women. The goal of these definitions is general familiarity; no effort has been made to include all of the competing definitions.

This is the first edition of this dictionary, and I welcome critical evaluations and suggestions. As for the errors which will undoubtedly be discovered, I can only repeat what Mr. Bouvier said in the preface to his law dictionary in 1839:

"To those who are aware of the difficulties of the task, the author deems it unnecessary to make any apology for the imperfections which may be found in the work. His object has been to be useful: if that has been accomplished in any degree, he will be amply rewarded for his labor."

Reader's comments should be sent to Barron's Educational Series, 113 Crossways Park Drive, Woodbury, New York 11797.

Steven H. Gifis

Hopewell, New Jersey

Acknowledgments

A work of this nature by necessity involves many persons and many sources. I am deeply indebted to a staff of second-year law students at Rutgers—The State University, School of Law, Newark, who contributed dedicated and careful labor to this dictionary: Alan Bowman, Ken Gunning, Ross London, Keith Roberts, Eric Winther, and Saul Zimmerman. Mr. London also acted as staff supervisor. Mr. Roberts served as my chief editorial assistant and to him I owe a special thanks for tireless hours of painstaking attention to detail. Research assistance on a less regular basis was also provided by Michael Dore, Joseph Finnin, Barry Moskowitz, Norman Solomon, and David Watkins. A number of first-year law students assisted in the proof-reading and citation checking necessary to prepare the manuscript for publication. To all of them I extend my thanks for their contribution.

I have been especially gratified, on both a personal and professional level, by the contributions of Professors Alfred Slocum and John Payne of the Law School, whose very substantial commitment of time and scholarly resources to the energy-consuming task of critical evaluation contributed greatly to the quality of the manuscript.

Portions of the manuscript also were read by Gregory Reilly, Class of 1973, and I am also indebted to him for many valuable suggestions.

I am particularly indebted to my wife, Susan Pollard Gifis, Esquire, for her assistance, criticisms, and enduring affection throughout a project which often appeared interminable.

The preparation of the manuscript was the work of my secretary, Ms. Arlene Woodyard, assisted by Mrs. Sherry Zimmerman. Together they typed and re-typed thousands of manuscript pages from handwritten scratches without complaint and with great skill.

This project was partially supported by research funds provided by the Law School. I take this opportunity to express my sincere appreciation.

Treaties and hornbooks often proved more helpful than case authority for many entries and I did not hesitate to draw upon them. I am, therefore, very much indebted to the various legal publishers who have generously extended permissions to quote from their copyright publications. I commend all of my sources to the student for further study.

Finally the author is very much indebted to the editorial staff of Barron's Educational Series, Inc. for their expert criticisms, stylistic suggestions, and continuing patience throughout the enterprise. A special note of thanks must go to Ms. Janet Robertson who had the task of trying to produce a measure of consistency and technical accuracy to the manuscript.

The author is indebted for the generous permission granted him by the following publishers to quote portions of their publications throughout this book.

We also acknowledge permission to quote from the American Law Institute *Model Penal Code* (p.o.d. 1962).

Reproduced with permission from *Survey of the Law of Real Property,* Second Edition, by Smith and Boyer, Copyright © 1971 by West Publishing Company.

Reproduced with permission from *Introduction to the Law of Real Property,* by Moynihan, Copyright © 1962 by West Publishing Company.

Constitutional Law, by B. Schwartz, Copyright © Macmillan Publishing Co., Inc., 1972.

Rollin M. Perkins, *Criminal Law,* 2nd Ed. Copyright © 1969, The Foundation Press, Inc. Reprinted with permission of the publisher.

Civil Procedure (1965), James. Boston: Little, Brown and Company, 1965.

Various definitions draw from portions of *Restatements of the Law* published by the American Law Institute. We gratefully acknowledge permission to reprint from those various *Restatements* as indicated in appropriate entries. The copyright date for various restatements are as follows:

Agency [2d] © 1933 [1958]
Conflicts [2d] © 1934 [1971]
Contracts © 1932
Judgments © 1942
Property © 1936
Foreign Relations Law of the United States © 1962
Torts [2d] © 1934, 1938, 1939 [1965, 1966]
Trusts [2d] © 1935 [1957]
Restitution © 1937

Pronunciation Guide

The decision as to which Latin words, maxims, and expressions should be included in this dictionary, in view of the thousands which the user might encounter, was necessarily a somewhat arbitrary one; but an earnest effort has been made to translate and, where appropriate, to illuminate those terms and phrases considered likely to be crucial to a full understanding of important legal concepts. Hopefully, there are no significant omissions and we have erred only on the side of overinclusiveness.

Each of the Latin and French words and phrases—at least those which continue to be recognized as such and have not become, functionally, a part of the English language—includes a phonetic spelling designed to assist the user in the pronunciation of terms which are probably unfamiliar to her or him. The purpose in providing this pronunciation guide, however, emphatically has not been to indicate "the correct" mode of pronouncing the terms; rather, the goal has been to afford the user a guide to an acceptable pronunciation of them. In the case of Latin words, therefore, neither the classic nor the ecclesiastical pronunciation has been strictly followed; instead, the phonetic spellings provided herein reflect the often considerable extent to which pronunciation has been "Anglicized" and/or "Americanized," partly through widespread legal usage.

Of course, such a system is anything but uniform, and adoption of it is clearly hazardous from the standpoint of general acceptance as well as that of scholarship. Many, if not most, of these terms have alternative pronunciations in common usage throughout the English-speaking legal world, and there has been some deference to classical or ecclesiastical pronunciation and, hopefully, to consistency. Thus, the choices made here, while in most cases meant to reflect the most commonly accepted pronunciation, inevitably have been the product of the author's personal preferences.

The phonetic symbols employed herein were drawn from what the author perceives as a commonly recognized and understood "system." The following guide should be of some assistance in interpreting them.

Vowels

ă as in ăt
ä as in ärmy
à as in arrive
ā as in āpe
ähn (meant to approximate French nasal sound for which there is no English equivalent)

ĕ as in ĕgg
ē as in ēvil
ė as in earn
ĭ as in ĭll
ī as in īce

ŏ as in ŏx
ô as in orgy
ō as in ōpen

ŭ as in ŭp
û as in ûrge
ū as in dūty

Consonants

g as in gas

j as in jump or as the "g" in rouge or bourgeois

Key to Effective Use of This Dictionary

Alphabetization. The reader should note carefully that all entries have been alphabetized letter by letter rather than word by word. Thus *ab initio,* for example, is located between *abeyance* and *abortion,* rather than at the beginning of the listings. In the same manner, *actionable* appears before, not after, *action ex delicto.*

Cross References: **Boldface type** has been used within the text of the definitions and at the end of them, to call attention to terms which are defined in the dictionary as separate entries, and which should be understood and, if necessary, referred to specifically, in order to assure the fullest possible comprehension of the word whose definition has been sought in the first instance.

Terms emphasized in this manner include many which appear in the dictionary only in a different form or as a different part of speech. For example, although the term "alienate" may appear in boldface in the text of a definition, it will not be found as a separate entry, since it is expected that the reader can readily draw the meaning of that term from the definition given for the word "alienation;" likewise, the reader coming across the word "estop" printed in boldface should not despair upon discovering that it is not in fact an entry here, but should instead refer to the term "estoppel."

Also, the reader must not assume that the appearance of a word in regular type precludes the possibility of its having been included as a separate entry, for by no means has every such word been printed in boldface in every definition. Terms emphasized in this manner include primarily those an understanding of which was thought to be essential or very helpful in the reader's quest for adequate comprehension. Many terms which represent very basic and frequently used concepts, such as "property," "possession," and "crime," are often printed in regular type. Furthermore, boldface is used to emphasize a word only the first time that that word appears in a particular definition.

Sub-Entries: Words printed in SMALL CAPITALS include:

1) Those whose significance as legal concepts was not deemed sufficiently substantial to warrant their inclusion in the dictionary as separate entries, though some explanation or illumination was thought desirable, and

2) those which, though important, are most logically and coherently defined in the context of related or broader terms.

Words emphasized in this manner have been either separately and individually defined in the manner of "subcategories" or have been defined or illustrated, implicitly or explicitly, within the text of the definition of the main entry.

Citations: All citations have been abbreviated in order to facilitate the reading of the definitions and in the interests of space economy. Case names, court, and year of decision have been generally omitted. National reporter cites have generally been given without the corresponding state reporter cite. A complete list of abbreviations used in the citations appears on the following pages. Citations to authorities other than cases are given with the last name of the author, title, page(s) or sections(s), year. No special typeface has been used to designate such authorities.

Table of Abbreviations

A [2d]	Atlantic Reporter [second series]
A.B.A. D.R.	American Bar Association, Code of Professional Responsibility, Disciplinary Rule
A.D.	Appellate Division, New York (Supreme Court)
A.L.R. [2d, 3d]	American Law Reports [second, third series]
Am. Dec.	American Decisions
Am. Jur. [2d]	American Jurisprudence [second series]
Barb.	Barbour's Supreme Court Reports, New York
Barn. & Ald.	Barnewall and Alderson's English King's Bench Reports
Bisph. Eq.	Bispham's Equity
Bl. Comm.	Blackstone's Commentaries [* pages refers to original pagination]
Cal. Rptr. [2d]	California Reporter [second series]
C.J.	Corpus Juris
C.J.S.	Corpus Juris Secundum
C.P.L.R.	New York Civil Practice Law and Rules
Cyc.	Cyclopedia of Law and Procedure
Dall.	Dallas' Pennsylvania and United States Reports
Del. Ch.	Delaware Chancery Reports
Edw.	Edward's New York Reports
Eng. Rep.	English Reports
F. [2d]	Federal Reporter [second series]
Fed. Cas.	Federal Cases
Fed. R. Civ. Proc.	Federal Rule of Civil Procedure
Fed. R. Crim. Proc.	Federal Rule of Criminal Procedure
F.R.D.	Federal Rules Decisions
F. Supp.	Federal Supplement
Greenl.	Greenleaf's Reports
Hale P.C.	Hale's Pleas of the Crown
Hen.	King Henry
How. Prac.	Howard's New York Practice Reports
Hun.	Hun's New York Supreme Court Reports
L.E. [2d]	United States Supreme Court Reports, Lawyer's Edition [second series]
L.Q. Rev.	Law Quarterly Review
Metc.	Metcalf's Massachusetts Reports

N.E. [2d]	North Eastern Reporter [second series]
N.J. Eq.	New Jersey Equity Reports
N.J.L.	New Jersey Law Reports
N.J.S.[A].	New Jersey Statutes [Annotated]
N.J. Super.	New Jersey Superior Court Reports
N.Y. Bus. Corp. L.	New York Business Corporation Law
N.Y.S. [2d]	New York Supplement [second series]
N.W. [2d]	North Western Reporter [second series]
Ohio Dec.	Ohio Decisions
Ohio N.P., N.S.	Ohio Nisi Prius, New Series
P. [2d]	Pacific Reporter [second series]
Pet.	Peter's United States Supreme Court Reports
Pick.	Pickering's Massachusetts Reports
Q.B.	Queen's Bench
S. Ct.	Supreme Court Reporter
S.E. [2d]	South Eastern Reporter [second series]
Serg. & R.	Sergeant and Rawle's Pennsylvania Reports
So. [2d]	Southern Reporter [second series]
Stat.	United States Statutes at Large
Steph. Comm.	Stephen's Commentaries on English Law
S.W. [2d]	South Western Reporter [second series]
U.C.C.	Uniform Commercial Code
U.S.	United States Reports
U.S.C.[A].	United States Code [Annotated]
U.S.L.W.	United States Law Week
Wall.	Wallace's United States Supreme Court Reports
Wend.	Wendell's New York Reports
Wheat.	Wheaton's United States Supreme Court Reports
W.L.R.	Weekly Law Reports [Great Britain]

ABANDONMENT knowing relinquishment of one's right or claim to property without any future intent to again gain title or possession; "in law, is defined to be the relinquishment or surrender of rights or property by one person to another. It includes both the intention to abandon and the external act by which the intention is carried into effect . . . there must be the concurrence of the intention to abandon and the actual relinquishment." 164 S.W. 2d 225, 228. One who abandons his newspaper in a barbershop gives up all right and title to it; one who merely forgets to take his newspaper from the barbershop does not legally abandon it. A subsequent finder of property not legally abandoned must make reasonable effort to restore it to the true owner and must relinquish it to him upon demand.

ABATABLE NUISANCE see **nuisance**.

ABATEMENT generally, a lessening, a reduction; also a complete termination of a **cause of action**; "in the sense of common law [it] is an entire overthrow or destruction of the suit, so that it is quashed or ended. But, in the sense of a **court of equity**, an abatement signifies only a present suspension of all proceedings in the **suit**. . . . At common law a suit, when abated, is absolutely dead. But a suit in **equity**, when abated is . . . merely in a state of suspended animation, and it may be revived." 93 S.W. 164, 166. An ABATEMENT OF A LEGACY is the reduction in the amount or the extinction of a **legacy** to a **beneficiary** by the payment of debts owed by the grantor of that legacy, i.e., a **decedent**. An ABATEMENT OF TAXES is a rebate or diminution of taxes previously assessed and/or paid.

ABDUCTION broadly, the criminal or tortious act of "taking and carrying away by force." This taking may be by means of **fraud**, persuasion, or open violence. Its object may be a child, ward, wife, etc. At common law, a wife could not maintain a civil action for abduction of her husband. In its most exclusive sense abduction is restricted to the taking of females for the purpose of marriage, concubinage, or **prostitution**. 60 A. 601, 603. In private or civil [as opposed to criminal] law, abduction is the act of taking away a man's wife by violence or by persuasion. 54 P. 847. Compare **kidnapping**.

ABET see **aid and abet**.

ABEYANCE in property, the condition of a **freehold** or **estate in fee** when there is no presently existing person in whom it **vests**. Generally, an undetermined or incomplete state of affairs.

AB INITIO *(äb ĭn-ī'-shē-ō)*—Lat: from the first act. 219 F. Supp. 274, 276. Most commonly used in reference to the validity of **statutes**, **estates**, **trespassers**, marriages, and **deeds**; e.g., the unlawful marriage is **void** "ab initio"; the insurance policy is valid "ab initio."

ABORTION the premature termination of a pregnancy. An intentionally induced abortion was at common law a **misdemeanor** and in American law a **felony** in most jurisdictions unless performed to save the life of the mother. See Perkins, Criminal Law 139-149 (2d ed. 1969). The right of a woman to have an abortion during the early stages of her pregnancy without criminal sanctions applied to her or those who perform the abortion and to have it free of unreasonable governmental restraint has now been established as part of a constitutional right of personal privacy. During the first trimester the state cannot constitutionally interfere with the ABORTION DECISION which must be left to the medical judgment of the woman's physician. During the second trimester, the state may regulate the abortion procedure in ways that are reasonably related to maternal health. During the last trimester (the stage subsequent to viability) the state "in promoting its interest in the potentiality of human life may if it chooses, regulate, and even proscribe, abortion except where it is necessary, in appropriate medical judgment, for the preservation of the life or health of the mother." 410 U.S. 113, 163-64. Subject to these constitutional guidelines, abortion may still be a criminal offense and is often grouped with other **homicide** offenses, though it usually carries a lesser maximum penalty. See, e.g., N.Y. Penal Law §§125.00, 125.05, 125.40-.60 (defining homicide as conduct which causes the death of a person or an unborn child with which a female has been pregnant for more than twenty-four weeks; defining justifiable abortion; creating two degrees of abortion with lesser felony designations; and proscribing self-abortion during the post-twenty-four-weeks period).

ABRIDGE to lessen, to shorten, to condense; a condensation of the whole, not a mere partition of the whole.

ABROGATE (ABROGATION) "to annul, destroy, revoke, or cancel; to put an end to; to do away with; to set aside," 209 N.E. 2d 172, 174; to make a law void by legislative repeal.

ABSCOND to travel covertly out of the **jurisdiction** of the courts, or to conceal oneself in order to avoid their **process.** 62 N.W. 217, 218. An absconding **debtor** is one who, with intent to avoid his **creditors,** conceals or withdraws himself from within the relevant jurisdiction for the purpose of going beyond the reach of process. An absconding debtor successfully evades the **service** of process. 32 A. 7.

ABSQUE HOC *(äb'-skwā hŏc)* — Lat: but for this; apart from this; if it had not been for this. Technical word used in **pleading.** See **traverse** (SPECIAL TRAVERSE).

ABSTENTION a policy adopted by the federal courts whereby the **district court** may decline to exercise its **jurisdiction** and defer to a state court the resolution of a federal constitutional question, pending the outcome in a state court proceeding of state law **issues** that might avoid a serious constitutional question. When the court defers decision in this manner, it retains jurisdiction and will decide the federal constitutional question if the plaintiff is not satisfied with the state court outcome. Where resolution of the federal constitutional question is dependent upon, or may be materially altered by, the determination of an uncertain issue of state law, abstention may be proper in order to avoid unnecessary friction in federal-state relations, interference with

important state functions, tentative decisions on questions of state law, and premature constitutional **adjudication.** 380 U.S. 578, 539.

A second variant of abstention (and a form of abstention required by some statutes) occurs when the federal court refuses to exercise jurisdiction altogether because the issues presented seem to the court more appropriate for state court resolution. In these instances the abstaining federal court actually "relinquishes" its jurisdiction to the state courts and the doctrine is more appropriately termed RELINQUISHMENT. An example of this form of abstention is the refusal of the federal courts in the interests of **comity** to enjoin state court criminal proceedings. See 401 U.S. 37.

ABSTRACT OF RECORD a complete history in short, abbreviated form of the **case** as found in the **record.** Its purpose is "to bring before the **appellate court** in abbreviated form an accurate and authentic history of all the **proceedings** in the case as they were had in the course of the **trial** below." 164 S.W. 2d 201, 207. "It would have to be complete enough to show that the questions presented for review [by the appellate court] have been properly preserved in the case." 231 S.W. 70.

ABSTRACT OF TITLE a short history of **title** to land; "a summary or epitome of the facts relied on as evidence of **title,** [which] must contain a note of all **conveyances,** transfers, or other facts relied on as evidences of the **claimant's** title, together with all such facts appearing of record as may impair title. . . . it should contain a full summary of all **grants, conveyances, wills** and all records and judicial proceedings whereby the title is in any way affected, and all **encumbrances** and **liens** of record, and show whether they have been released or not." 107 N.E. 180, 183. See **chain of title.**

ABUSE OF DISCRETION a legal appellate review technique for reviewing the exercise of **discretion** by trial courts and administrative agencies and persons; a rationale used by reviewing courts to upset determinations made by trial courts when such determinations are wholly inconsistent with the facts and circumstances before the court and the deductions that can reasonably be made from the facts and circumstances. See 251 N.E. 2d 468, 471. Any "unreasonable, unconscionable [or] arbitrary action taken without proper consideration of the facts and law pertaining to the matter submitted." 458 P. 2d 336, 338. Honest, but erroneous judgments do not constitute "abuse of discretion." See 38 A. 626.

The "abuse of discretion" standard of review is also used in administrative settings. Thus where an agency has discretionary authority to revoke a license, the extent of that discretion is limited, and a serious or gross abuse of that discretion will provoke correction by a reviewing court. Administrative officials such as prosecutors have a very broad discretion and it is generally very difficult to upset their exercise of discretion on the grounds of arbitrary, capricious, or unfair decision-making. Davis, Administrative Law §§ 28.04, 28.06 (3rd ed. 1972). See **discretion**.

ABUSE OF PROCESS employment of the criminal or civil **process** for a use other than one which is intended by law; "the improper use of process after it has been issued, that is, a perversion of it." 32 A. 2d 413, 415. "Malicious use of civil process has to do with the wrongful initiation of such process, while abuse of civil process is concerned with a perversion of a process after it is issued." Id.

ABUT [ABUTTING] to adjoin; to cease at point of contact; to touch boundaries; to border on; "[i]n its primary meaning 'abutting' implies a closer proximity than does the term 'adjacent,' and whether the latter is to be interpreted as lying near to or actually adjoining depends largely on the context in which it is used." 129 P. 163, 164.

ACCELERATION the hastening of the time for enjoyment of an **estate** or a property right which would otherwise have been postponed to a later time. This term is applied to both the **vesting** of a **remainder** due to the premature termination of a **preceding estate** and to clauses, commonly found in **mortgage** agreements (called ACCELERA-

TION CLAUSES), stipulating that an entire debt may be regarded as due upon the default of a single **installment**, or other duty of the borrower.

ACCELERATION CLAUSE a provision in a **contract** or document establishing that upon the happening of a certain event, a party's expected interest in the subject property will become prematurely **vested**. For example, "a stipulation in a **mortgage** that, if the **mortgagor** shall fail to pay any **note** or **installment** of **interest**, or neglect to pay taxes or special assessments, the entire indebtedness shall become due, and payable, or that the **mortgagee** may at his option declare it to be due and payable," 9 S.W. 2d 3, 4; however, "equitable principles may be invoked to relieve a mortgagor from acceleration of the maturity of the debt and from **foreclosure** of the mortgage." 118 F. Supp. 401, 411. In law of contracts, such a clause is found often in installment contracts and can cause an entire debt to become due upon failure to pay an installment as agreed and can cause a **judgment** for the installment barring an **action** for the balance of the debt. Corbin, Contracts §950 (1952).

ACCEPTANCE act of voluntarily receiving something or of a voluntary agreement to certain terms or conditions; implies the right to reject. In contracts, acceptance is consent to the terms of an offer which creates a binding **contract**. In property, it is an element essential to completion of a **gift inter vivos**; however, it is generally presumed if the gift is beneficial. See 36 A. 2d 288, 289. "Acceptance" by a bank of a **check** or other **negotiable instrument** is a formal procedure whereby the bank promises to pay the **payee** named on the check. "Acceptance" is the **drawee's** [bank's] signed engagement to honor the **draft** [negotiable instrument] as presented. It must be written on the draft and may consist of the drawee's signature alone. It becomes operative when completed by **delivery** or notification. U.C.C. §3-410(1).

ACCESSORY one who aids or contributes in a secondary way or assists in or contributes to crime as a subordinate. See 216 So. 2d 829, 831. Mere silence or approval of the commission of crime does not incur accessorial liability. 81 Mo. 483. An accessory does acts which **facilitate** others in the commission or attempted commission of crime or in avoiding apprehension for crime. Compare **accomplice**; **aid and abet**; **conspiracy**.

ACCESSORY AFTER THE FACT those who receive, comfort or assist a felon knowing that he has committed a **felony** or is sought in connection with the commission or attempted commission of a felony. See 234 A. 2d 284, 285. The term thus applies to one who obstructs justice by giving comfort or assistance to a criminal offender in an attempt to hinder or prevent his apprehension or punishment. 378 F. 2d 540.

ACCESSORY BEFORE THE FACT one who procures, counsels, or commands the deed perpetrated, but who is not present, actively or constructively, at such perpetration. See 282 A. 2d 154.

ACCOMMODATION INDORSEMENT see indorsement.

ACCOMMODATION MAKER [PARTY]

one who signs a **note** as acceptor, **maker**, or **indorser** without recovering value therefore, or any compensation, benefit, or **consideration** directly or indirectly by way of the transaction of which the note is a part. The accommodation maker, as **surety**, remains **liable** for the note, even though he receives no consideration. See 87 N.W. 2d 299, 302. He is, in effect, gratuitously obligating himself to guarantee the debt of the accommodated party. The transaction must be one primarily for the benefit of the **payee**. See 264 N.W. 875, 876. If he is obliged to honor his accommodation contract he "has a right of recourse on the instrument against" the accommodated party. U.C.C. §3-415(5).

ACCOMPLICE an individual who voluntarily engages with another individual in the commission or attempted commission of a crime, see 165 N.E. 2d 814; one who is liable for the identical offense charged against the **defendant**, see 233 P. 2d 347; one who knowingly, voluntarily, or purposefully

and with common intent with the principal offender unites in the commission or attempted commission of a crime. Mere presence combined with knowledge that crime is about to transpire, without active mental or physical contribution, does not make one an accomplice. Id. 348, 349. For example, undercover agents are not accomplices. See 478 S.W. 2d 450, 451; 473 S.W. 2d 19, 20. Essential to accomplice liability is a shared, common **mens rea** and criminal purpose between **agent** and **principal**. Compare **accessory**; **aid and abet**; **conspiracy**.

ACCORD agreement; "an agreement whereby one of the parties undertakes to give or perform, and the others to accept, in satisfaction of a **claim, liquidated** [certain] or in dispute, and arising either from **contract** or from **tort**, something other than or different from what he is, or considers himself, entitled to." 408 P. 2d 712, 713. "**Satisfaction** takes place when the accord is executed," 193 A. 2d 601, 602; after which there has been an "**accord and satisfaction**." See **novation**; **settlement**.

ACCORD AND SATISFACTION payment of money, or other thing of value usually less than the amount owed, in exchange for **extinguishment** of the **debt**. It amounts to "something other than strict **performance** or payment. It is doing that by the **covenantor** which the **covenantee** accepts in lieu of a performance of the terms of the covenant." 224 A. 2d 662, 666. There must exist an agreement, actual or implied, that the acceptance of the smaller sum is meant to discharge the obligation to pay the larger sum.

ACCRETION the adding on or adhering of something to property; a means by which a property owner gains ownership of something additional. It usually refers to "the gradual and imperceptible addition of sediment to the shore by the action of water; it is created by operation of natural causes." 198 P. 2d 769, 772. It differs from **avulsion** which "is a sudden and perceptible loss or addition to land by the action of water." 161 F. Supp. 25, 29.

In the law of **succession**, accretion is said to take place when a co-**heir** or co-legatee dies before the property **vests**, or when he rejects the **inheritance** or **legacy**, or when he omits to comply with a **condition**, or when he becomes incapable of taking. The result is that the other heirs or legatees can share in his part. See 2 P. 418, 440.

In situations involving a **trust**, the term refers to any addition to the principal or income that results from an extraordinary occurrence, that is, an occurrence which is forseeable but which rarely happens. See 213 N.W. 320, 322 and 148 F. 2d 503, 506. See **alluvion**; **avulsion**; **reliction**.

ACCRUE generally, to accumulate, to happen, to come into fact or existence; as to a **cause of action**, to come into existence as an enforceable claim. The time that a cause of action accrues determines for how long a plaintiff may wait to bring a suit under the **statute of limitations**.

ACCUSATION a **charge** against a person or corporation; "in its broadest sense it includes **indictment**, **presentment**, **information** and any other form in which a charge of crime or offense can be made against an individual," 151 A. 2d 127, 129; formal charge of having committed a criminal offense, made against a person in accordance with established legal **procedure** and not involving the **grand jury**.

ACCUSE to directly and formally institute legal **proceedings** against a person, charging that he has committed an offense cognizable at law, i.e., to **prosecute**; to charge with an offense judicially or by public **process**. See 73 So. 225, 228.

ACCUSED person against whom a criminal proceeding is initiated. See 73 So. 225, 228. "Accused" and "defendant" refer to one who is held to answer for an offense at any stage of the proceedings, or against whom a complaint in any lawful manner is made, charging an offense including all proceedings from the order of arrest to final execution. A defendant is not accused until charged with the offense or until he becomes subject to actual restraint by **arrest**. See 509 P. 2d 549, 551.

A COELO USQUE AD CENTRUM *(ä kō-ā'-lō ūs'-kwä äd sĕn'-trŭm)*—Lat: from the sky [heavens] all the way to the center of the earth. It is a very old property maxim which marked the boundaries within which an owner owned his property. This is no longer true because the owner of property in modern times owns subject to the rights of airplanes. See Smith and Boyer, Survey of the Law of Property 171 (2d ed. 1971).

ACQUIT to set free or judicially discharge from an **accusation** of suspicion of guilt. See 65 N.Y.S. 1062, 1065. An individual is acquitted when it has been determined, at the close of **trial**, whether by **jury** or by court, that the person has been absolved of the charges which were the bases of the **action**; a **verdict** of "not guilty" acquits the defendant and prevents his retrial under the principles of **double jeopardy**.

In older **contract** terminology, "to acquit" meant to release from a **debt**, duty or charge. See 26 Wend. 383, 400.

ACQUITTAL one who is acquitted receives an acquittal, which broadly means that the individual is released or discharged without any further prosecution for the same act or transaction.

ACT see **overt act**.

ACTIO *(äk'-tē-ō)* doing, performance, action, activity; also, **proceedings**, **lawsuit**, **process**, **action**, permission for a suit.

ACTION (AT LAW) a **judicial** proceeding whereby one party **prosecutes** another for a wrong done, or for protection of a right or prevention of a wrong.

ACTIONABLE giving rise to a **cause of action**; thus, it refers to wrongful conduct which may form the basis of a civil **action**, as in ACTIONABLE NEGLIGENCE which is the **breach** or nonperformance of a **legal duty** through neglect or carelessness, resulting in damage or injury to another. See 49 A. 673.

ACTION EX DELICTO *(ĕx dĕl-ĭk'-tō)*—Lat: **cause of action** which arises out of fault, misconduct, or **malfeasance**. 100 S.W. 2d 687, 689. "If the cause of action given expression in the **complaint** arises from a **breach of promise**, the action is 'ex contractu' [but] if that cause of action arises from a breach of duty growing out of the **contract**, it is in form 'ex delicto'." 120 So. 153, 154.

ACTIO NON *(äk′-tē-ō nŏn)* in **pleading**, a nonperformance, nonfeasance; also, a **nonsuit**.

ACTIONS IN PERSONAM see **jurisdiction**.

ACTIONS IN REM see **jurisdiction**.

ACTIONS QUASI IN REM see **jurisdiction**.

ACT OF GOD [PROVIDENCE] manifestation of the forces of nature which are unpredictable and difficult to anticipate; "the result of the direct, immediate and exclusive operation of the forces of nature, uncontrolled or uninfluenced by the power of man and without human intervention, [which]is of such character that it could not have been prevented or avoided by foresight or prudence. Examples are tempests, lightning, earthquakes, and a sudden illness or death of a person." 226 A. 2d 160, 162. In law of torts, proof that an Act of God was the sole or proximate cause of injury is an **affirmative defense** to an action for **negligence**. An intervening Act of God generally will not excuse an absolute contractual duty in the absence of statutory or contractual language to the contrary. 244 F. 2d 565. The law here is generally governed by the law of **impossibility**.

ACTUAL DAMAGES see **damages**.

ACTUAL NOTICE see **notice**.

ACTUAL POSSESSION see **possession**.

ACTUAL VALUE see **market value**.

ACTUARY one who computes various insurance and property costs; especially, one who calculates the cost of life insurance risks and insurance premiums.

ACTUS REUS *(äkt′-ŭs rā′-ŭs)*-Lat: loosely, the criminal act; but the term more properly refers to the "guilty act" or the "deed of crime." Every criminal offense has two components: "One of these is objective, the other is subjective; one is physical, the other is psy-

chical; one is the actus reus, the other is the **mens rea**. The actus reus generally differs from crime to crime. In **murder** it is **homicide**; in **burglary** it is the nocturnal breaking into the dwelling of another; in uttering a forged **instrument** it is the act of offering as good an instrument which is actually false. In like manner the mens rea differs from crime to crime. In murder it is **malice aforethought**; in burglary it is the intent to commit a **felony**; in uttering a forged instrument it is 'knowledge' that the instrument is false plus an intent to defraud." Perkins, Criminal Law 743 (2d ed. 1969). The actus reus must be causally related to the mens rea for a crime to occur: "An evil intention and an unlawful action must concur in order to constitute a crime." 93 N.E. 249. Although it is frequently said that no mens rea is required for a **strict liability** offense, the actus reus alone being sufficient (see e.g., 361 U.S. 147, 150 and 342 U.S. 246, 256), it is more useful to identify a special mens rea for the civil offense that recognizes the low level of **culpability** connected with a strict or civil offense. As to the act being sufficient even in the **strict liability** setting, a "guilty act" (as opposed to a coerced act for example) would seem required. Hall, General Principles of Criminal Law 222-27 (2d ed. 1960). See **corpus delicti**.

AD DAMNUM *(äd däm′-nŭm)*—Lat: the amount of **damages** demanded. 7 A. 391, 392. In a **pleading** it fixes the amount beyond which a party may not recover on the **trial** of his **action**. 68 N.W. 2d 500, 506. In a **complaint** it is the claim for damages. 55 A. 177, 179.

ADDITUR *(ăd′-dĭ-tûr)*—Lat: it is increased. An increase by the court in the amount of **damages** awarded by the **jury**. This is a power vested in a **trial court** to assess damages and to increase an inadequate award as a condition of the denial of a **motion** by the **plaintiff** for a new trial. It cannot be done without the **defendant's** consent as this would impair his right to a jury trial on the question of damages. See 226 P. 2d 677. Compare **remittitur**; **set-off**.

ADEMPTION removal or extinction; a

taking away; one of the ways in which a **devise** or **bequest** lapses is the extinction or withdrawal of the disposition by some act of the **testator** clearly indicating an intent to revoke such. Ademption may be effected by the testator's **inter vivos gift** of the property devised or bequeathed and/or the existence of attendant circumstances which render it impossible to effect the transfer or payment as directed by the **will.** See 167 S.W. 2d 345, 348.

ADHESION CONTRACT a contract so heavily restrictive of one party, while so non-restrictive of another, that doubts arise as to its representation as a voluntary and uncoerced agreement; implies a grave inequality of bargaining power. The concept often arises in the context of "standard-form printed contracts prepared by one party and submitted to the other on a 'take it or leave it' basis. The law has recognized there is often no true equality of bargaining power in such contracts and has accommodated that reality in construing them." 347 F. 2d 379, 383.

AD HOC *(ăd hŏk)*—Lat: for this; for this particular purpose. An "ad hoc" committee is one commissioned for a special purpose and likewise an "ad hoc" attorney is one designated for a particular client in a special situation.

ADJUDICATION the determination of a controversy and a pronouncement of a **judgment** based on **evidence** presented; implies a final judgment of the court or other body deciding the matter. Compare **disposition.**

ADJUSTER one who adjusts or settles an insurance claim; one who makes a determination of the amount of a claim and then makes an agreement with the insured as to a settlement.

ADMINISTRATIVE HEARING see **hearing.**

ADMINISTRATOR one who is appointed to handle the affairs of a person who has died **intestate**; one who manages the **estate** of a deceased person who left no **executor**; "an instrumentality established by law 'for performing the acts necessary for the transfer of the effects left by the deceased to those who succeed to their ownership'." 169 F. Supp. 647, 650. If decedent died with a will, an executor carries it out.

ADMIRALTY AND MARITIME JURISDICTION expansive jurisdiction over all actions related to events occurring at sea; "extends to all things done upon and relating to the sea, to transactions relating to commerce and navigation, to damages and injuries upon the sea, and all maritime contracts, torts, and injuries." 15 A. 49, 50.

ADMISSIBLE EVIDENCE evidence which may be received by a trial court to aid the **trier of fact** (judge or jury) in deciding the merits of a controversy. Each jurisdiction has established rules of evidence to determine questions of admissibility. The judge may properly receive only admissible evidence but he need not permit a party to introduce all admissible evidence. Cumulative evidence, for example, may be excluded. Moreover, under the Uniform Rules of Evidence a judge may within his discretion exclude otherwise admissible evidence when the court determines that its **probative** value is outweighed by countervailing factors such as undue consumption of time, prejudice, confusion of the issues, or misleading of the jury. Uniform Rule of Evidence 4. A lurid, gory photograph, for example, depicting the scene of the crime, the weapon used, or the injury to the victim may have very high probative value as to several issues in a criminal trial for atrocious assault and battery but is so highly inflammatory as to cause undue prejudice in the minds of the jurors, and it will be excluded if there is any other way to prove the necessary facts.

ADMISSIONS in criminal law, the voluntary acknowledgment that certain facts do exist or are true; but, of themselves, admissions are insufficient to be considered a **confession** of guilt. It is a statement by the **accused** which tends to support the **charge,** but which is not sufficient to determine guilt. In civil procedure, a pretrial **discovery** device by which one party asks another for a positive affirmation or denial of a material fact or **allegation** at issue.

AD TESTIFICANDUM *(äd tĕs'-tĭ-fĭ-cän'-dŭm)*—Lat: for testifying. Any person sought "ad testificandum" is sought to appear as a **witness**. See **subpoena ad testificandum**.

AD VALOREM *(äd vä-lô'-rĕm)*—Lat: according to value; "used in taxation to designate an assessment of taxes against property at a certain rate upon its value." 74 P. 2d 47, 50. An AD VALOREM TAX is thus a tax assessed according to the value of the property.

AD VALOREM TAX see **tax**.

ADVERSARY Opponent or litigant in a legal controversy or litigation. See **adverse party**.

ADVERSARY PROCEEDING a **proceeding** involving a real controversy contested by two opposing **parties**. Contrast **ex parte**. See also **case** or **controversy**.

ADVERSE INTEREST against the interest of some other person, usually so as to benefit one's own interest.

ADVERSE PARTY the party on the opposite side of the **litigation**. See **adversary**.

ADVERSE POSSESSION a method of acquiring complete **title** to land as against all others, including the **record owner**, through certain acts over an uninterrupted period of time, as prescribed by statute. 13 So. 2d 649, 650; 502 P. 2d 672, 682; 226 S.W. 2d 484, 486. It is usually prescribed that such **possession** be actual, visible, open, notorious, hostile, under claim of right, definite, continuous, exclusive, etc. 138 So. 2d 696, 699; 71 A. 2d 318, 320. The purpose of such requirements is to give **notice** that such possession is not subordinate to the claims of others. 244 P. 2d 582, 584. Possession by a **mortgagor** is not generally considered to ripen into title through adverse possession because it is not notorious or hostile. 9 N.W. 2d 421, 426. See **hostile possession; notorious possession**.

ADVISORY OPINION a formal opinion by judge, court, or law officer upon a question of law submitted by a legislative body or a governmental official, but not actually presented in a concrete case at law. Such opinion has no binding force as law. Compare **declaratory judgment**. See also **case or controversy**.

ADVOCACY in practice, the active espousal of a legal cause, see 268 U.S. 652; the art of persuasion. "The duty of a lawyer, both to his client and to the legal system, is to represent his client zealously within the bounds of the law...." A.B.A. Code of Professional Responsibility, Canon 7.

AFFIANT the person who makes and subscribes to a statement made under oath [**affidavit**].

AFFIDAVIT a written statement made or taken under oath before an officer of the court or a **notary public** or other person who has been duly authorized to so act.

AFFIRM the assertion of an **appellate court** that the **judgment** of the court below is correct and should stand; to approve, confirm, ratify. Compare **reverse**.

Also, to attest to as in an affirmation of faith or fidelity.

AFFIRMATIVE DEFENSE see **defense**.

AFFIRMATIVE RELIEF that **relief** granted a **defendant** in a situation in which "the defendant might maintain an **action** entirely independent of **plaintiff**'s **claim**, and which [claim] he might proceed to establish and recover even if plaintiff abandoned his **cause of action**, or failed to establish it. In other words, [defendant's] answer must be in the nature of a [cross-claim], thereby rendering the action defendant's as well as plaintiff's." 41 N.W. 656.

AFFIX to attach to or add to; to annex, as to affix a **chattel** to **realty**; e.g., to attach a chandelier to the ceiling is to affix it to the **real property**. A tree is also "affixed" to the land.

A FORTIORI *(ä fôr'shē-ô'rē)*—Lat: from the most powerful reasoning; to draw inference that because a certain conclusion or fact is true, then a second conclusion must also be true because it is "lesser-included;" e.g., if a person is not guilty of **larceny**, then "a fortiori" he is not guilty of **robbery**.

AGAINST THE [MANIFEST] [WEIGHT OF THE] EVIDENCE an evidentiary standard permitting the **trial court** after **verdict** to order a new trial where the verdict, though based on legally sufficient evidence, appears in the view of the trial court judge to be unsupported by the substantial credible evidence. "On such a motion it is the duty of the trial judge to set aside the verdict and grant a new trial, if he is of the opinion that the verdict is against the clear weight of the evidence, or is based upon evidence which is false, or will result in a **miscarriage of justice**, even though there may be substantial evidence which would prevent the direction of a verdict," (see **directed verdict**), 122 F. 2d 350, 352-53. It is not proper for the trial judge to substitute his judgment for that of the jury on matters of credibility or weight of the evidence, even if the judge disagrees with the jury, "unless the verdict is clearly against the undoubted general current of the evidence, so that the court can clearly see that they have acted under some mistake, or from some improper motive, bias, or feeling." 6 F. 128, 129-30. See also **judgment** (JUDGMENT N.O.V.).

AGENCY relation in which one person acts on behalf of another with the authority of the latter; "a **fiduciary** relation which results from the manifestation of consent by one person, the principal, that another, the agent, shall act on the former's behalf and subject to his control, and consent by the other so to act." 122 N.W. 2d 290, 294. The acts of an agent will be binding on his principal. See also **apparent authority; respondeat superior; scope of employment**. Compare **partnership**.

AGENT one who, by mutual consent, acts for the benefit of another; one authorized by a party to act in that party's behalf. Compare **servant**.

AGGRAVATED ASSAULT see **assault**.

AGGREGATE a total of all the parts; the whole, the complete amount; also, to combine, as to aggregate several **causes of action** in a single **suit**. See **joinder**.

AGGRIEVED PARTY one who has been injured, who has suffered a loss; "a

party or person is aggrieved by a **judgment, order**, or **decree** whenever it operates prejudicially and directly upon his property, pecuniary, or personal rights." 223 S.W. 2d 841, 845.

AID AND ABET to actively, knowingly, intentionally, or purposefully facilitate or assist another individual in the commission or attempted commission of a crime. Aiding and abetting is characterized by affirmative criminal conduct and is not established as a result of omissions or negative acquiescence. 24 A. 2d 85, 87. Compare **accessory; accomplice; conspiracy**.

ALEATORY uncertain; risky, involving an element of chance.
   ALEATORY CONTRACT an agreement the performance of which by one party depends upon the occurrence of a contingent event. "An ALEATORY PROMISE is one the performance of which is by its own terms subject to the happening of an uncertain and fortuitous event or upon some fact the existence or past occurrence of which is also uncertain and undetermined." Corbin, Contracts 684 (One vol ed. 1952). Examples of such contracts include life and fire insurance contracts. Such agreements are enforceable notwithstanding an uncertainty of terms at the time of the making so long as the risk undertaken clearly appears. A contract where performance is contingent upon the outcome of a bet, however, is a gambling contract and is generally unenforceable by statute or as matter of public policy in most jurisdictions. See generally Id. §§ 728-732.

ALIAS an indication that a person is known by more than one name; "means 'or' or 'otherwise called' or 'otherwise known as'." 234 S.W. 2d 535, 539. "AKA" and "a / k / a" mean "also known as" and are used in **indictments** to introduce the listing of an alias.

ALIBI a provable account of an individual's whereabouts at the time of the commission of a crime which would make it impossible or impracticable to place him at the scene of the crime. An alibi negates the physical possibility that the suspected individual could have committed the crime. See 220 N.W. 328, 330. Compare **justification**.

ALIEN a person born in a foreign country, who owes his allegiance to that country; one not a citizen of the country in which he is living. A RESIDENT ALIEN is a person admitted to permanent resident status in the country by the immigration authorities but who has not been granted citizenship.

ALIENATION in the law of real property, the voluntary and absolute transfer of **title** and **possession** of **real property** from one person to another. The law recognizes the power to alienate property as one of the essential ingredients of fee simple **ownership** and therefore unreasonable restraints on alienation are generally prohibited as contrary to public policy. See 169 U.S. 353. See **restrictive covenant**. See also **rule against perpetuities**.

ALIENATION OF AFFECTIONS "a **tort** based upon willful and malicious interference with the marriage relation by a third party, without justification or excuse. . . . By definition, it includes and embraces mental anguish, loss of social position, disgrace, humiliation and embarrassment, as well as actual pecuniary loss due to destruction or disruption of the marriage relationship and the loss of financial support, if any." 415 S.W. 2d 127, 132. The interference may be in the nature of adultery (a tort called then CRIMINAL CONVERSATION) or may result from lesser acts which deprive the other spouse of affection from his or her marital partner. "More actions of this kind have been brought against parents than anyone else and the meddling mother-in-law is more frequently a defendant than the wicked lover." Prosser, Torts 876 (4th ed. 1971). Statutes in several states have abolished this **cause of action** because of the potential for abuse through **blackmail** and **extortion**. See Id. at 887. See **consortium**.

ALIMONY the allowance which one pays for the support of his estranged spouse by order of the court. Generally it has been the husband who has been ordered to support his wife but under some modern statutes the wife could be ordered to support a husband if he were in "actual need." See, e.g., N.J. Laws of 1971, c. 212 (N.J.S.A. 2A: 34-23). The award of alimony is separate from the divorce in that the court may reserve the power to modify or set aside the award of alimony. See 155 F. 2d 737, 738. CHILD SUPPORT is a distinct obligation which may be imposed by the court upon the spouse with or without an award of alimony.

ALIQUOT *(ä'-lē-kwō)*—Lat: an even part of the whole; one part contained in a whole which is evenly divisible, i.e., divisible without leaving a remainder. In the case of a resulting **trust**, it is a particular fraction of the whole property involved, as distinguished from a general interest. 68 N.E. 37.

ALIUNDE *(äl'-ē-ûn'-dā)*—Lat: from another source; from elsewhere; from outside. ALIUNDE RULE refers to the doctrine that a **verdict** may not be **impeached** by the **evidence** of a juror unless the foundation for introduction of the evidence is made first by competent evidence from another source. See 141 Ohio St. 423. EVIDENCE ALIUNDE refers to evidence from an outside source.

ALLEGATION in **pleading**, an assertion of fact; the statement of the issue which the contributing party is prepared to prove.

ALLEN CHARGE an instruction given by the **court** to a **jury** which is experiencing difficulty reaching a **verdict** in a criminal case, in an attempt to encourage such jury to make a renewed effort to arrive at a decision. Such a supplementary **charge** was approved by the United States Supreme Court in *Allen* v. *United States*, where the trial court in effect told the jury "that in a large proportion of cases absolute certainty could not be expected; that although the verdict must be the verdict of each individual juror, and not a mere acquiescence in the conclusion of his fellows, yet they should examine the question submitted with candor and with a proper regard [for] and deference to the opinions of each other; that it was their duty to decide the case if they could conscientiously do so; that they should listen, with a disposition to be convinced, to each other's arguments; that, if much the larger number were for **conviction**, a dissenting juror should consider whether his doubt was a reasonable one which made no impression upon the minds of so many men, equally honest, equally intelligent with himself. If, upon the other hand, the majority was for **acquittal**, the minority ought to ask themselves whether they might not reasonably doubt the correctness of a judgment which was not concurred in by the majority." 164 U.S. 492, 501. This sort of instruction has been the target of complaints that it is coercive or constitutes a mandatory charge in terms of its likely effect on a jury. See, e.g., 309 F. 2d 852. Although use of such a charge had not yet been declared unconstitutional by any federal court, modifications of the Allen charge to ensure non-coerciveness have been insisted upon in many jurisdictions, see, e.g., 411 F.2d 930; and its use has been banned outright by some state courts, see, e.g., 342 P.2d. 197.

ALLOCUTION the requirement at **common law** that the trial judge address the **defendant** asking him to show any legal cause why the sentence of conviction should not be pronounced upon the **verdict** of conviction. Modern **appellate procedures** have eliminated the original purposes for this formal address but it continues to be a part of the **sentencing** procedure in a majority of the states and is a mandatory part of a valid sentencing in the federal system. See Fed. R. Crim. Proc. 32(a); 365 U.S. 301 and 368 U.S. 424. The modern allocution does not ask the defendant why sentence ought not be imposed but rather for any statement that he would like to make on his own behalf in **mitigation** of punishment. It may be held to include the right of the defendant to offer evidence in mitigation beyond his own statement. 464 F. 2d 215.

ALLODIAL owned freely without obligation to one with superior right; not subject to the restriction on **alienation** which existed with feudal tenures; free of any superior rights vested in another, such as a lord. Compare **tenurial**.

ALLUVION deposits of sedimentary material (earth, sand, gravel, etc.) which have accumulated gradually and imperceptibly along the bank of a river, 47 A. 745; the term may also apply to such accumulations along the bank of the sea, 134 U.S. 178, 189; alluvion is the result of the process of **accretion**, and any alluvion is considered "an inherent and essential attribute of the original property," Id., i.e., a part of the property to which it has become attached, 192 S.W. 2d 338; whether the effect of natural or artificial causes, alluvion must accumulate so gradually that the change from moment to moment cannot be visibly perceived. 55 P. 2d. 90. See also **reliction; avulsion**.

ALTERNATIVE PLEADING at common law a pleading which alleged facts so entirely separate that it was difficult to determine upon which set of facts the person pleading intended to rely as the basis of recovery; e.g., pleading a case of personal injury alleging facts constituting negligence by the defendant, or, "in the alternative," evidence of intentional conduct by the defendant. "[W]hen a plaintiff pleads his case in the alternative, one version of which is good and the other not, his petition will, on **demurrer**, be treated as pleading no more than the latter, since it will be construed most strongly against him." 93 S.E. 2d. 3, 5. See **election of remedies**. Today alternative pleading is generally permitted under modern procedure.

AMELIORATING WASTE see **waste**.

AMEND to alter; to improve upon. Thus, one amends a bill by altering or changing an established law—the law is continued in changed form. One amends a **pleading** by making an addition to or a subtraction from an already existing pleading.

AMICUS CURIAE (*ă-mē′-kŭs kyŭ′-rē-ī*) —Lat: friend of the court; one who gives information to the court on some matter of law which is in doubt. See 264 F. 276, 279. The function of an amicus curiae is to call the court's attention to some matter which might otherwise escape its attention. See 64 N.Y. S.2d 510, 512. An AMICUS CURIAE BRIEF (or AMICUS BRIEF) is one submitted by one who is not a party to the **lawsuit** to aid the court in gaining information which it needs to make a proper decision or to urge a particular result on behalf of the public or a private interest of third parties who will be indirectly affected by the resolution of the dispute.

AMORTIZATION a gradual **extinguishment** of a **debt**, as the term is used for accounting purposes; "the provision for the gradual extinction of [a future obligation] in advance of maturity, either by an annual charge against capital account, or, more specifically, by periodic contributions to a **sinking fund** which will be adequate to discharge a debt or make a replacement when it becomes necessary." 78 F. Supp. 111, 122, n. 1. Compare **depreciation.**

ANCILLARY JURISDICTION the jurisdiction assumed by federal courts, largely as a matter of convenience to the parties, which extends beyond that conferred upon them expressly by the Constitution or by enabling statutes. Under the doctrine of ancillary jurisdiction, it is recognized "that a district court acquires jurisdiction of a case or controversy in its entirety and may as an incident to disposition of a matter properly before it, possess jurisdiction to decide other matters raised by the case of which it could not take cognizance were they independently presented. Thus when the court has jurisdiction of the principal action, it may hear also any ancillary proceeding therein, regardless of the citizenship of the parties, the amount in controversy, or any other factor that would normally determine jurisdiction." Wright, Federal Courts § 9 (2d ed. 1970). The most common example of ancillary jurisdiction is represented by **compulsory counterclaims**, which the Federal Rules of Civil Procedure expressly require the defendant to bring and which accordingly have been held cognizable without regard to an independent federal jurisdictional basis. See, e.g., 286 F.2d 631. **Permissive counterclaims** are probably not within the federal courts ancillary jurisdiction and independent jurisdictional bases must be established. 29 F.R.D. 348. **Cross-claims, impleader** of third parties, **interpleader,** and

intervention as of right are further examples of ancillary jurisdiction. Wright, supra. § 9. **Joinder** of **claims** (federal and non-federal grounds) is not within ancillary jurisdiction unless the claims are so closely related as to fall within the concept of **pendent jurisdiction.**

It is generally held that where ancillary jurisdiction suffices to allow a particular claim or party to be joined in the lawsuit without an independent jurisdictional basis, it is not necessary to satisfy the **venue** requirements with respect to such a claim or party. See, e.g., 174 F. Supp. 587; but see 73 Harv. L. Rev. 1164.

AND HIS HEIRS see **heirs.**

ANIMO *(än'-ĭ-mō)* —Lat: purposefully; intentionally.
ANIMO TESTANDI *(tĕs-tän'-dē)* with the intention to make a **will.**
ANIMO REVOCANDI *(rĕ-vō-kän'-dē)* with the intention to revoke.
ANIMO REVERTENDI *(rĕ-vĕr-tĕn'-dē)* with the intention to return.

ANNUITANT one who receives the benefits of an **annuity.**

ANNUITY a fixed sum payable periodically, subject to the limitations imposed by the **grantor.** "Generally speaking, it designates a right—bequeathed, donated or purchased—to receive fixed, periodical payments, either for life or a number of years. Its determining characteristic is that the **annuitant** has an interest only in the payments themselves and not in any principal fund or source from which they may be derived." 13 A. 2d 419, 421.

ANNUL to make void; to dissolve that which once existed, as to "annul" the bonds of matrimony. A marriage which is annulled [by an "action for annulment"] is void **ab initio** as compared with a marriage which is dissolved by a decree of divorce; divorce operates only to terminate the marriage from that point forward and does not affect the former validity of the marriage.

ANSWER the principle **pleading** on the part of the **defendant** in response to **plaintiff's complaint**; it must contain a denial of all of the **allegations** of plaintiff's complaint which the defendant wishes to controvert; it may also contain any **affirmative defenses** which the defendant may have, which should be stated separately; it may contain a statement of any **permissive counterclaim** which the defendant has against the plaintiff and which is legally available to him in the action; **compulsory counterclaims** arising out of the same transaction must generally be pleaded in the answer or they will be barred in any subsequent separate suit. See, e.g., Fed. R. Civ. Proc. 13.

ANTICIPATORY BREACH (OF CONTRACT) a breach committed before the arrival of the actual time of required performance. It occurs when one party by declaration repudiates his contractual obligation before it is due. The repudiation required is "a positive statement indicating that the promisor will not or cannot substantially perform his contractual duties." Restatement of Contracts § 318 (a); UCC § 2-610. In the case of a **bilateral contract,** the **aggrieved party** may urge the repudiating party to perform without giving up the right to claim a present breach. Restatement of Contracts § 320; UCC § 2-610(b). If, however, the repudiating party withdraws his repudiation before there has been a material change in position, the repudiation will be nullified. Restatement of Contracts § 319; UCC § 2-611(3). A repudiation will justify a demand by the aggrieved party for an "assurance of performance" under UCC § 2-609. Where the anticipatory repudiation is by the party's conduct rather than by declaration it is called VOLUNTARY DISABLEMENT. Thus, in a contract for the sale of land the seller breaches through voluntary disablement if he transfers land to a third party during the executory interval before performance is due on the first contract. In some jurisdictions no distinction is drawn between the two forms of preliminary breach.

ANTILAPSE STATUTE statutes enacted to allow the **heirs** of a **devisee** (or **legatee**) who predeceases the **testator** [the party making the devise or legacy] to be substituted as the takers of what the testator has attempted to give the deceased devisee (or legatee). Such laws abrogate the **common law** rule that such testamentary gifts "lapsed" upon the death of the specified recipient. Most American jurisdictions have adopted such laws; and in view of the fact that the common law doctrine operated most harshly on grandchildren, who became disinherited when a parent predeceased the testator/grandparent, many of these statutes apply only to relatives of the testator. See Powell, Real Property § 367 (1973).

ANTI-TRUST LAWS statutes such as the Sherman Anti-Trust Act, directed against unlawful restraints of trade and monopolies.

A POSTERIORI *(ä pŏs'-tĕr-ē-ô'-rē)*—Lat: from the most recent aspect or point of view. This concept is akin to factual knowledge which relates to those things which can only be known from experience. The term relates to the means by which a concept or proposition is known or validated. It is distinguished from **a priori** reasoning, in which a proposition is known or validated solely through logical necessity; a posteriori reasoning achieves its goal of ascertaining truth by means of actual experience or observation.

APPARENT AUTHORITY refers to a doctrine involving the accountability of a **principal** for the acts of his **agent** "which operates to make a principal liable for operative words spoken by an agent in the course of a transaction with another to whom the principal has represented that the agent has authority . . ." Seavey, Handbook of the Law of Agency §106C (1964). It refers to that situation created when a principal such as a **corporation** "manifests to a third person that an 'officer' or 'agent' may act in its behalf, and such third person in good faith believes that such 'authority' exists. In such a case, lack of actual authority, express or implied, is no **defense**. In certain cases the corporation [or other principal] may be estopped from denying the 'authority' of the 'officer' or 'agent'." Henn, Handbook of the Law of Corporations §226 (1970). The concept is also sometimes termed OSTENSIBLE AUTHORITY.

APPEARANCE the coming into court by a **party summoned** in an **action**; to come into court, upon being summoned, either by one's self or through one's attorney; to voluntarily submit one's self to the **jurisdiction** of the court.

GENERAL APPEARANCE where a party appears and participates in a **proceeding** for any reason other than for the purpose of attacking the court's jurisdiction. See 32 S.E. 2d 742, 745.

SPECIAL APPEARANCE one made for the sole purpose of attacking the **jurisdiction** of the court over the defendant's person. See 173 N.W. 468. "Whether an appearance is general or special is determined by the relief sought and if a defendant, by his appearance, insists only upon the objection that he is not in court for want of jurisdiction over his person, and confines his appearance for that purpose only, then he has made a special appearance, but if he raises any other question or asks any relief which can only be granted upon the hypothesis that the court has jurisdiction of his person, then he has made a general appearance." 209 P. 2d 843, 845.

COMPULSORY APPEARANCE where one has been validly served **process**, and so is compelled to appear in court.

VOLUNTARY APPEARANCE where one appears in court without having had process served on him.

APPEARANCE DE BENE ESSE see **de bene esse.**

APPELLANT the party who appeals a decision; the party who brings the proceeding to a reviewing court; at common law, the "plaintiff in error." See also **appellee.**

APPELLATE COURT a court having jurisdiction to review the law as applied to a prior determination of the same case; "not a forum in which to make a new case. It is merely a court of review to determine whether or not the rulings and judgment of the court below upon the case as made were correct." 24 S.E. 913. A trial court first decides a law suit in most instances, with review then available in one or more appellate courts. Compare **trial de novo.**

APPELLATE JURISDICTION see **jurisdiction.**

APPELLEE the **party** who argues, on **appeal**, against the setting aside of the **judgment**; the party prevailing in the court below; the party at whom the attack on appeal is aimed; at **common law**, the "defendant in error." See also **appellant.**

APPOINTMENT, POWER OF see **power of appointment.**

APPORTION to divide fairly or according to the parties' respective interests; proportionately, but not necessarily equally.

APPRAISAL RIGHTS a statutory remedy available in many states to corporate minority **stockholders** who object to certain extraordinary actions taken by the **corporation** (such as **mergers**). This remedy allows dissenting stockholders to require the corporation to repurchase their stock at a price equivalent to its value immediately prior to the extraordinary corporate action.

This remedy is a statutory exception to the principle of corporate democracy. It allows minority stockholders the opportunity to withdraw from the corporation when the corporation takes an extraordinary action which they feel is harmful to their interests. The nature of the extraordinary corporate action which triggers this right differs in every state, but almost all include corporate consolidations and mergers.

APPRAISE to estimate the value; to put in writing the worth of property.

APPRECIATE to incrementally increase in value. See 300 N.W. 241, 243. Compare **depreciation.**

To be aware of the value or worth of a thing or person. See 18 N.Y.S. 2d 662, 664. In criminal law, as part of the insanity test, the word is used in some statutes to signify the defendant's subjective understanding of the wrongfulness of his conduct. See Model Penal Code §4.01(1) (Approved Draft 1962).

APPROPRIATE "to set apart for, or assign to, a particular purpose or use, in exclusion of all others." 137 P. 2d 233, 237. To wrongfully and unlawfully appropriate the property of another to one's own use constitutes theft [**larceny**]. 158 S.W. 2d 796. See **misapplication of property**; compare **conversion**.

APPROPRIATION as generally used in a legislative context, refers to the designation of funds for a specific governmental expenditure. A governmental program needs "enabling legislation" creating the program and usually annual appropriations to fund it.

APPURTENANT attached to something else; in the law of property, it refers especially to a burden (e.g., an easement or covenant) which is attached to a piece of land and benefits or restricts the owner of such land in his use and enjoyment thereof, e.g., where A allows B the right of way over his land so that B has access to the highway, such is an EASEMENT APPURTENANT to B's land. 155 S.W. 928, 930.

A PRIORI (*ä prē-ô'-rē*)—Lat: from the preceding, from the first. To reason "a priori" is to reason with the factual and historical knowledge that certain facts are proven to be true, so that certain factual situations which follow in time must follow the reasoning of those truths; i.e., if X is true then it may be deduced that certain subsequent facts will necessarily follow.

ARBITER (*är'-bĭt-ér*)—Lat: referee, umpire; one appointed to decide a controversy, according to the law, although the decision-maker is not a judicial officer.

ARBITRATOR an impartial person chosen by the parties to solve a dispute between them, who is vested with the power to make a final determination concerning the issue(s) in controversy, bound only by his own discretion, and not by rules of law or equity.

ARGUENDO (*är-gyū-ĕn'-dō*)—Lat: to put in clear light; for the sake of argument, e.g., "let us assume arguendo that X is true." A person arguing in this fashion is not being inconsistent if he later argues that X is not true.

ARGUMENT "a connected discourse based upon reason; a course of reasoning tending and intended to establish a position and to induce belief." 119 N.W. 289, 290. Often refers specially to an oral argument in appellate advocacy.

ARRAIGN to accuse of a wrong, see 116 N.W. 2d 68, 71; to call a person in custody to answer the charge under which an **indictment** has been handed down. See 138 N.W. 2d 173.

ARRAIGNMENT an initial step in the criminal process wherein the defendant is formally charged with an offense, i.e., given a copy of the **complaint** or other accusatory instrument, and informed of his constitutional rights (e.g., to plead not guilty, be indicted, have a jury trial, appointed counsel if indigent, etc.). Where the appearance is shortly after the arrest it may properly be called a **presentment** since no plea is taken, at least not if it is a **felony** charge. If it is called an arraignment, it is termed an ARRAIGNMENT ON THE WARRANT [or on the complaint].

"After the **indictment** or **information** is filed, the defendant is arraigned—i.e., he is brought before the trial court, and informed of the charges against him and the pleas he might enter (usually guilty, not guilty, or **nolo contendere**). A substantial percentage of all felony defendants, usually between 70-85%, will plead guilty at this point or some later point in the proceedings." Kamisar, LaFave, and Israel, Modern Criminal Procedure 11 (4th ed. 1974).

ARREARS that which is unpaid although due to be paid; a person "in arrears" is behind in payment.

ARREST "to deprive a person of his liberty by legal authority," 249 N.E. 2d 553, 557; in the technical criminal law sense, seizure of an alleged or suspected offender to answer for crime. See 214 N.E. 2d 114, 119. To be **actionable** in the event that such seizure is improper or unlawful, there must be an intent on the part of the arresting officer or agent to bring the suspect into custody. See 266 F. Supp. 718, 724. The seizure or detention must be understood by the arrested person to be an arrest. 94 Ohio App. 313. The elements are: (1) purpose or intention to effect the arrest under real or pretended authority; (2) actual or constructive seizure or detention of the person to be arrested by the person having present power to control him; (3) communication by the arresting officer of intention or purpose then and there to make the arrest; and (4) understanding by the person to be arrested that such is the intention of the arrestor. See 250 F. Supp. 278, 280.

ARREST OF JUDGMENT the withholding of **judgment** because of some error apparent from the face of the **record**; "the method by which a court refuses to give judgment in a case, though it be regularly decided, where it appears on the face of the record, not including the **evidence,** either that intrinsically no **cause of action** exists, or that if judgment were rendered for the prevailing party it would be erroneous." 73 N.E. 2d 75, 79. Compare **abstention**.

ARSON at common law, "the willful and malicious burning of the dwelling house of another." 152 A. 2d 50, 70. In some states, the burning of a house by its owner under specific circumstances, or the burning of a house by a part-owner. See 221 S.W. 2d 285, 286. Several jurisdictions divide arson into degrees. STATUTORY ARSON refers to analogous offenses involving destruction of property other than dwellings by methods other than burning, e.g., exploding. See Perkins Criminal Law 230 (2d ed. 1969).

ART, WORDS OF see **words of art**.

ARTICLES OF IMPEACHMENT analogous to an **indictment** in an ordinary criminal proceeding, it is the formal statement of the grounds upon which the removal of a public official is sought. A federal judge holding life tenure may be removed from office only through the **impeachment** process but he may be prosecuted for a crime while still holding office. See 493 F. 2d 1124, 1142.

ARTICLES OF INCORPORATION the **instrument** which creates a private **corporation**, pursuant to the general corporation laws of the state.

ARTIFICE a fraud or a cunning device used to accomplish some evil; usually implies craftiness or deceitfulness.

ARTIFICIAL PERSON see **corporation**.

ASSAULT an attempt, with unlawful force, to inflict bodily injury upon another, accompanied by the apparent present ability to give effect to the attempt if not prevented. 125 P. 2d 681, 690. As a tort, an assault may be found even where no actual intent to make one exists (as where a "joke" is intended) if the actor places the victim in reasonable fear. Because an assault need not result in a touching so as to constitute a **battery**, no physical injury need be proved to establish an assault. An assault is both a personal **tort** and a criminal offense and thus may be a basis for a civil **action** and/or a criminal **prosecution**. Some jurisdictions have by statute defined the criminal assault to include what at common law was the battery—the actual physical injury. In those jurisdictions an offense of "menacing" often replaces the common law assault. See e.g., N.Y. Penal Law Art. 120.

AGGRAVATED ASSAULT an assault where "serious bodily injury" is inflicted on the person assaulted, 282 P. 2d 772; a particularly fierce or reprehensible assault; an assault exhibiting peculiar depravity or atrocity—including assaults committed with dangerous or **deadly weapons**; an assault committed intentionally concomitant with further crime.

ASSESS to determine the value of something; to fix the value of property upon which a tax rate will be imposed.

ASSETS anything of value; any interest in **real** or **personal property** which can be **appropriated** for the payment of **debts**.

ASSIGN to transfer one's interest in property, contract, or other rights to another. 19 S.E. 601. See **assignment**. Compare **delegate**.

ASSIGNMENT act whereby one transfers to another his **interest** in a right or property. Compare **subrogation**.

ASSIGNMENT FOR BENEFIT OF CREDITORS a transfer by a **debtor** of his property to an assignee in **trust** to apply that which is transferred to the debts of the assignor (debtor).

ASSIGNMENT OF A LEASE transfer of the lessee's entire interest in the **lease**.

When there exists an express covenant in the original lease to pay rent, the assignor (original **tenant**) remains secondarily liable to the **landlord** after an assignment; i.e., the assignee is primarily liable and if he does not pay then the assignor must. Compare **sublease, subtenant.**

ASSIGNMENT OF ERROR "the **appellant**'s declaration or complaint against the trial judge charging **error** in the acts of the lower court, which assignments are the basic grounds for **reversal.**" 177 So. 2d 833, 835.

ASSIGNS all those who take from or under the assignor, whether by **conveyance, devise, descent** or **operation of law.** 26 N.W. 907.

ASSIZE ancient writ issued from a **court of assize** to the sheriff for the recovery of property, Littleton §234; actions of the special court which issues the writ. See **Court of Assize and Nisi Prius.** "A real action which proves the title of the demandant merely by showing his or his ancestor's possession," 3 Bl. Comm. *185; jury summoned to decide upon the writ of assize, 3 Bl. Comm. *185; the verdict of that jury, 3 Bl. Comm. *57, *59.

ASSUMPSIT (*à-sŭmp'-sĭt*) — Lat: he promised; he undertook. In the law of contracts, "a promise or undertaking, either express or implied, made either orally or in writing not under seal." The term refers especially to one of the old **forms of action** at common law, and as such was an equitable action "applicable to almost every case where money has been received which in equity and good conscience ought to be refunded. An express promise is not necessary to sustain it, but it may be maintained wherever anything is received or done from the circumstances of which the law implies a promise of compensation." 178 S.E. 889, 892. Compare **trespass; trespass on the case.**

ASSUMPTION OF THE RISK in torts, an **affirmative defense** used by the **defendant** to a **negligence** suit in which it is claimed that **plaintiff** had knowledge of a condition or situation obviously dangerous to himself and yet voluntarily exposed himself to the hazard created by defendant, who is thereby relieved of legal responsibility for any resulting injury; see 70 N.E. 2d 898, 903; in contract, it is the express agreement by employee to assume the risks of ordinary hazards arising out of his occupation, see 225 P. 501, 505; **contributory negligence** arises when plaintiff fails to exercise due care, while assumption of risk arises regardless of the care used and is based fundamentally on consent. 79 Cal. Rptr. 426, 430.

A minority of jurisdictions have abolished the distinct defense of assumption of risk and treat it instead either as an aspect of whether the situation is one in which defendant owes plaintiff a duty of care, or as a question of plaintiff's contributory negligence in undertaking the risk. See 196 A. 2d 238; Prosser, Torts 454-57 (4th ed. 1971).

ASSURED see **insured.**

ASYLUM a shelter for the unfortunate or afflicted, e.g., for the insane, the crippled, the poor, etc.; a POLITICAL ASYLUM is a state which accepts a citizen of another state as a shelter from prosecution by that other state.

AT BAR see **bar.**

AT EQUITY see **equity.**

AT ISSUE see **issue.**

AT LAW see **law.**

ATROCIOUS outrageously wicked and vile. See 283 So. 2d 1, 10. An atrocious act is one that demonstrates depraved and insensitive brutality on the part of the perpetrator. An atrocious act is conduct which exhibits a senselessly immoderate application of extreme violence for a criminal purpose.

ATTACHMENT a **proceeding** in law by which one's property is seized; "a proceeding to take a defendant's property into legal custody to satisfy plaintiff's demand. The object of the proceeding is to hold property so taken for the payment of a **judgment** in the event plaintiff's demand is established and judgment rendered therefor in his favor." 55 N.W. 2d 589, 592. **Due process** requires a hearing before property is taken from an owner. See 407 U.S.

67. See **in rem**. See also **garnishment**. Compare **replevin**.

ATTAINDER at common law a mark of infamy caused by one's conviction for a **felony** or capital crime, which results in the elimination of all civil rights or liberties. See 55 N.W. 774, 781. See **bill of attainder**.

ATTAINDER, BILL OF see **bill of attainder**.

ATTEMPT an overt act, beyond mere preparation, moving directly toward the actual commission of a substantive offense. See 263 A. 2d 266, 271. It is an offense, separate and distinct from the object crime. See 438 S.W. 441, 446. "The overt act, sufficient to establish an 'attempt,' must extend far enough toward accomplishment of the object crime to amount to the commencement of the consummation." 500 P. 2d 1276, 1282. Various legal tests used to determine if enough has been done to cross the line between innocent preparation (mere planning of the crime) and a criminal attempt include "dangerous proximity," "indispensable element," "last act," "probable desistance," "substantial step." Acts of **solicitation** alone generally do not establish the elements of an attempt. See 252 A. 2d 321, 324.

ATTEST to affirm as true; to sign one's name as a **witness** to the **execution** of a document; to bear witness to.

ATTORNEY, POWER OF see **power of attorney**.

ATTORNEY GENERAL the chief law officer of the federal government or of each state government.

ATTORNEY'S FEES in general, the charge made by the attorney for his services in representing a client; also the charge made by other professionals for services they have rendered in the course of preparing and trying a case. A CONTINGENT FEE is a charge made by an attorney dependent upon a successful outcome in the case and is often agreed to be a percentage of the party's **recovery**. Such fee arrangements are often used in **negligence** cases and other **civil** actions but it is unethical for an attorney to charge a criminal defendant

a fee substantially contingent upon the result. ABA DR 2-106 (C).

ATTRACTIVE NUISANCE the doctrine in tort law which holds that one who maintains a dangerous instrumentality on his **premises** which is likely to attract children, is under a duty to reasonably protect those children against the dangers of that attraction. See 299 S.W. 2d 198, 199, 200. Under this doctrine the fact that the child may be a **trespasser** is merely one fact to be taken into account, with others, in determining the defendant's **duty**, and the care required of him. The basis of this liability is generally held to be nothing more than the **foreseeability** of harm to the child, and the considerations of common humanity and social policy which, in other **negligence** cases, operate to bring about a balancing of the conflicting interests, and to curtail to some reasonable extent the defendant's privilege to act as he sees fit without taking care for the protection of others. Therefore, one has a duty to fence swimming pools, to remove doors from discarded refrigerators, to enclose partially constructed buildings, and to be sensitive to other potentially dangerous conditions which attract curious children. See Prosser, Torts §59 (4th ed. 1971).

AUDITOR a public officer charged by law with the duty of examining and approving the payment of public funds; may also refer more generally to any accountant who performs a similar function for private parties.

AUTOMOBILE GUEST STATUTE see **guest statute**.

AVERMENT a positive statement or **allegation** of facts in a pleading as opposed to an **argumentative** one or one based on inference.

AVOIDANCE see **confession and avoidance**.

AVULSION an abrupt change in the course or channel of a stream which forms the boundary between two parcels of land, resulting in the loss of part of the land of one **riparian** landowner and a consequent increase in the land of the other. 341 S.W. 2d 18, 21. The sudden and perceptible nature of this change distinguishes avulsion from **accretion**. This distinction is important, for when the change is abrupt, the boundary between the two properties remains unaltered. 143 U.S. 359.

B

BAD DEBT   a **debt** which is not collectible, and which is therefore worthless to the **creditor**. See 232 F. 2d 621.

BAD FAITH   "breach of faith, willful failure to respond to plain, well-understood statutory or contractual obligations." 124 F. 2d 875, 883. "Good faith means being faithful to one's duty or obligation; bad faith means being recreant thereto." 235 N.W. 413, 414. It is thus the absence of "honesty in fact in the conduct or transaction concerned." U.C.C. §1-201 (19).

BADGES OF FRAUD   facts or circumstances surrounding a transaction which indicate that it may be fraudulent, especially that it may be in **fraud** of **creditors**. These "badges" include fictitious consideration, false statements as to consideration, transactions different from the usual method of doing business, transfer of all of a debtor's property, insolvency, confidential relationship of the parties, and transfers in anticipation of suit or execution. 92 S.W. 2d 733, 736.

BAD TITLE   one which is legally insufficient to **convey** property to the purchaser, 36 N.Y.S. 668; a title which is not a **marketable title** is not necessarily a bad title, 4 App. D.C. 283, but a title which is bad is not marketable and is one that a purchaser may not be compelled to accept.

BAIL   a monetary or other security given to insure the **appearance** of the **defendant** at every stage of the **proceedings**. See 120 P. 2d 980. Those posting bail are in the position of **surety** and the money is the **security** for the ac-

cused's appearance. It is thus used as a means "to procure release of a **prisoner** by securing his future attendance." 42 F. 2d 26, 28; object is to relieve the **accused** of imprisonment, and the state of the burden of keeping him pending **trial** or **hearing**, and at the same time to secure the appearance of the accused at the trial or hearing. 190 F. 2d 16, 19. Compare **release on recognizance**.

BAIL BOND   the document executed in order to secure the release of an individual in **custody** of the law. The surety forfeits his security in the event the defendant fails to appear as required for court dates, subject to the right of the surety to petition to set aside all or part of the forfeiture. The **surety**'s obligation is satisfied by the **appearance** of the accused in court on the day or days required.

BAILEE   "one to whom the property involved in the **bailment** is delivered," 55 A. 346, 348; "species of **agent** to whom something movable is committed in **trust** . . . for another." 75 So. 711, 713; party who holds the goods of another for a specific purpose pursuant to an agreement between the parties.

BAILIFF   a court attendant; "a person to whom some authority, care, **guardianship** or **jurisdiction** is delivered, committed or entrusted." 92 S.E. 2d 89, 95. "A servant who has the administration and charge of lands, goods and chattels to get the best benefit for the owner . . . and also a person appointed by private persons to collect their rents and manage their estate." 202 Ill. App. 387, 391. "Signifies a keeper or protector," 20 So. 818, 819, especially one appointed as such by the court, as in the case of a court-appointed guardian of a feeble-minded person. 189 A. 753, 755.

BAILMENT   "delivery of **personal property** in **trust**," 277 S.W. 2d 695, 698; "delivery of a thing in trust for some special object or purpose and upon a **contract**, express or implied, to conform with the object or purpose of the trust," 75 S.W. 2d 761, 764; also, that relationship which arises where one delivers property to another to keep for hire, and control and **possession** of the property passes to the keeper or **bailee.** 108 A. 2d 168, 170. "An express agreement between the parties is not always necessary. The element of lawful **possession,** however created, and the duty to account for the article as the property of another is sufficient," 351 P. 2d 840, 842; e.g., the finder of **mislaid property** becomes a bailee thereof.

ACTUAL BAILMENT one established by an actual or constructive delivery of the property to the bailee or his **agents.**

CONSTRUCTIVE BAILMENT one which arises when the person having possession holds it under such circumstances that the law imposes an obligation to deliver to another, even where such person did not come into possession voluntarily, and where therefore no bailment was voluntarily established. See 140 N.Y.S. 955, 956.

GRATUITOUS BAILMENT "results when care and custody of **bailor's** property is accepted by **bailee** without charge and without any expectation of benefit or **consideration.** In a gratuitous bailment, the bailee is liable to bailor for the loss of bailed property only if the loss is proximately caused by bailee's **gross negligence.**" 197 P. 2d 1008, 1014. It "consists of gratuitous loaning of **personal property** to be used by bailee and returned **in specie.**" 120 A. 2d 552.

INVOLUNTARY BAILMENT "arises by the accidental leaving of **personal property** in the **possession** of any person without **negligence** on the part of its owner." 152 P. 816, 817. Such a bailment arises whenever the goods of one person have by an unavoidable casualty or accident been lodged upon another's land or person. If the person upon whose land the personal property is located should refuse to deliver the goods to their owner upon demand or to permit him to remove them, he might be liable for **conversion** of said property. 67 S.E. 722, 724. Compare **lost property; mislaid property.**

BAILOR "person who delivers **personal property** to another to be held in **bailment**—the one who places the thing in **trust,**" 27 S.E. 487, 488. The bailor need not be the owner of the property involved.

BAIT AND SWITCH a method of consumer deception practiced by retailers which "involves advertising in such an attractive way as to bring the customer in, followed by disparagement of the advertised product so as to cause the customer to switch to a more expensive product." 50 A.L.R. 3d 1008. It "consists of an attractive but insincere offer to sell a product or service which the seller in truth does not intend or desire to sell." 493 P. 2d 660, 665. This device is also frequently termed DISPARAGEMENT. Id. at 666. Statutes in many states prohibit this sort of advertising.

BANKRUPTCY popularly defined as **insolvency,** i.e., an inability of a **debtor** to pay his **debts** as they become due; technically, however, it is the legal process under the federal Bankruptcy Act (11 U.S.C. 1 et seq.) by which assets of the debtor are **liquidated** as quickly as possible to pay off his creditors and to free the bankrupt to start anew. See 356 F. Supp 567, 568. In **reorganization,** on the other hand, liquidation may be avoided and the debtor may continue to function, pay his **creditors** and carry on business. 174 F.2d 783, 786. At the state level, INSOLVENCY PROCEEDINGS are brought to obtain more limited relief.

BAR in procedure, a barrier to the relitigating of an **issue;** "where **causes of action** are the same, final **judgment on the merits** in the first action is a complete bar to the second action." 179 S.W. 2d 441, 444. Issues which have been decided by a court become bars in further **litigation** as between the **parties** to the decision. A bar operates to deny a party the right or privilege of rechallenging issues in subsequent litigation. The prevailing party in a lawsuit can use his favorable decision to bar retrial of the cause of action.

A particular position in the courtroom is also termed a "bar;" hence, the defendant standing before the judge is sometimes called the "prisoner AT BAR." The complete body of attorneys is called "the bar" because they are the persons privileged to enter beyond the bar that separates the general courtroom audience from the bench of the judge. The

"CASE AT BAR" refers to the particular action before the court. See **collateral estoppel; double jeopardy; estoppel; merger; res judicata.**

BARGAIN a bargain is a mutual voluntary **agreement** between two parties for the **exchange** or **purchase** of some specified goods. "An agreement of two or more persons to exchange promises or to exchange a promise for a performance." Restatement, Contracts, §4. The term also "implies negotiation over the terms of an agreement." 118 P. 77, 78.

BARGAIN AND SALE a **contract,** or **deed** in the form of a contract, which conveys **property** and raises a **use** in the buyer thereof; by operation of the **Statute of Uses,** such contract or deed is also effective to transfer **title** to the buyer. See 137 S.E. 744, 745. Absent the inclusion of a "**covenant** against the grantor's acts" this deed lacks any guarantee from the seller as to the validity of the title. Compare **warranty deed; quitclaim deed.**

BARRISTER in England one of two classes of legal practitioners, whose function is "the advocacy of causes in open court" and related duties. 29 A. 559. His function is somewhat similar to that of the American trial lawyer, but the barrister, unlike the American trial lawyer, does not prepare the case from the start. His SOLICITER assembles the materials necessary for presentation to the court and settles cases out of court.

BASTARD "an illegitimate child," 281 So. 2d 587, 588; "children who are not born either in lawful wedlock or within a competent time after its termination," 93 P. 2d 825; also, a child of a married woman conceived with one who is not the husband of the mother. See 17 N.W. 2d 546. "A child born out of lawful matrimony or born to a married woman under conditions where the presumption of legitimacy is not conclusive and has been rebutted." 30 N.E. 2d 587, 589.

BATTERY "the unlawful application of force to the person of another," Perkins, Criminal Law 107 (2d ed. 1969); the least touching of another's person **willfully,** or in anger, 3 Bl. Comm. *120; the actual touching involved in an "**assault** and battery.**" In **tort** law the legal protection from battery extends to any part of one's body or to "anything so closely attached thereto that it is customarily regarded as a part thereof." Restatement, Torts §18. "Thus, contact with the plaintiff's clothing, or with a cane, . . . the car which he is riding [sic] or driving" will be sufficient to create civil tort **liability.** Prosser, Torts 34 (4th ed. 1971). If the contact is offensive, even though harmless, it entitles the plaintiff to an award of **nominal damages.** In the criminal law, every punishable application of force to the person of another is a criminal battery (a **misdemeanor** at common law). Conviction of battery may be based upon **criminal negligence** but not ordinary civil negligence. See Perkins, supra at 111-12.

BEARER PAPER commercial **paper** which is negotiable upon delivery by any party, or which does not purport to designate a specific party by whom it is negotiable. U.C.C. 3-202 (1), 3-111. Such commercial paper is said to be PAYABLE TO BEARER.

BELIEF see **information and belief.**

BENCH the court; the judges composing the court collectively. The place where the trial judge sits (as "approach the bench").

BENCH WARRANT an order from the court empowering the proper legal authorities to seize a person; most commonly used to compel one's attendance before the court to **answer** a **charge** of **contempt** or for failure of a **witness** to attend in response to a **subpoena** which has been duly served. See 321 P. 2d 15, 17.

BENEFICIAL INTEREST the interest of the beneficiary as opposed to the interest of the trustee who holds legal **title;** the **equitable** interest in property held in **trust** which the **beneficiary** may enforce against the **trustee** according to the terms of the trust. "[A]ny person who under the terms of a trust instrument has the right to income or principle of the trust fund has a beneficial interest in the trust." 27 N.Y.S. 2d 648, 652. It "is such a right to its enjoyment as exists where the legal title is in one person, and the right to such beneficial use or interest is in another, and where such right is recognized by law, and can be enforced by the courts." 200 U.S. 118, 128.

In a trust the beneficial equitable interest must be distinct from the legal interest or a **merger** will occur and the effort by the creator of the trust [**settlor**] to create separate legal and equitable interests in particular property will be ineffective. "Where a single individual has the whole legal interest and the whole beneficial interest, there is no trust. Where the sole trustee has also the whole beneficial interest, he simply holds the property free of trust. He cannot maintain a **bill** in equity against himself to compel himself to carry out the terms of the trust; and since there is no one else who has any interest in the property, there is no one who can prevent him from dealing with the property as he likes. Where the intended trustee and the intended beneficiary are the same, no trust is created. Where at the outset a trust existed, but a single individual subsequently holds the whole legal interest and the whole beneficial interest, the trust terminates." Scott, Abridgement of the Law of Trusts § 99 (1960). A valid trust can be created even though a trustee holds a part of the beneficial interest and even where a group of beneficiaries holds the whole beneficial interest and the identical persons hold the whole legal title, although some courts have found ineffective any attempts to create trusts in such circumstances. See Id, at §§ 99.1-99.5.

BENEFICIAL USE with respect to property, such right to its enjoyment as exists where legal **title** is in one person while right to such use or interest is in another. 131 P. 2d 189, 191. A person who has beneficial use does not hold legal title of property. Legal title is held in **trust** by another. See **beneficial interest; mortgage; trusts; use.**

BENEFICIARY "one receiving [or designated to receive] benefit or advantage, or one who is in receipt of benefits, profits, or advantage." 244 F. 902, 908; "person for whose benefit property is held in **trust**," Restatement, Trusts, §6 (4); "person to whom another is in a **fiduciary** relation, whether the relation is one of **agency**, trust, **guardianship, partnership,** or otherwise," Restatement, Restitution §190; "one for whose benefit a trust is created," 180 S.W. 2d 268,

271; "the person named in an **insurance** policy as the one to receive proceeds or benefits accruing thereunder," 155 P. 2d 772, 774. The person named in a will to receive certain property is a beneficiary under the **will.**

INCIDENTAL BENEFICIARY a person who may incidentally benefit from the creation of a trust. Such a person has no actual interest in the trust and cannot enforce any right to incidental benefit. "The beneficiaries of a trust include only those persons upon whom the **settlor** intended to confer a **beneficial interest** under the trust, or persons who have succeeded to their interests." Scott, Abridgement of the Law of Trusts §126 (1960).

BEQUEATH the appropriate term for making a **gift** of **personalty** by means of a **will.** 134 N.W. 498, 500. Strictly, it signifies a gift of **personal property,** which distinguishes it from a **devise,** which is a gift of **real property.** A **disposition** is the generic name encompassing both a bequest of personalty and a devise of realty.

BEQUEST a **gift** of **personal property** contained in a **will,** see 133 P. 2d 626, 634; "a **disposition** of personal property by will," 9 P. 2d 1065, 1067. "A **devise** ordinarily passes **real estate** and a 'bequest' personal property." 103 N.Y.S. 36, 44. Compare **devise; legacy.**

CONDITIONAL BEQUEST a bequest, "the taking effect or continuing of which depends upon the happening or non-occurrence of a particular event." See 42 N.E. 465, 467.

EXECUTORY BEQUEST a bequest of **personalty** or money which does not take effect until the happening of a possible or certain future event, upon which it is thus said to be contingent. See 36 S.E. 404, 408.

RESIDUARY BEQUEST bequest consisting of that which is left in an **estate** after the payment of **debts** and general legacies and other specific gifts. See 155 P. 353, 355.

SPECIFIC BEQUEST a bequest of "particular items or a part of a testator's estate which is capable of identification from all others of the same kind and which may be satisfied only by delivery of the particular thing (given by the will), not merely a corresponding amount in value or like property." 477 S.W. 2d 771, 773.

BEST EVIDENCE RULE a rule of evidence law requiring that the most persuasive evidence available be used to prove the terms of a writing. "Where the terms are material, the original writing must be produced unless it is shown to be unavailable for some reason other than the serious fault of the proponent." McCormick, Evidence 229 (2d ed. 1972).

BESTIALITY sexual intercourse with an animal; constitutes a **crime against nature**. 122 P. 2d 415, 416. See also **sodomy**.

BEYOND A REASONABLE DOUBT see **reasonable doubt**.

B.F.P. see **bona fide purchaser**.

BID an offer by an intending purchaser to buy goods or services at a stated price, or an offer by an intended seller to sell his goods or services for a stated price; in a construction of buildings context, general **contractors** usually solicit bids based on building specifications from several subcontractors in order to complete the project. Governmental units are often required by law to construct highways and buildings, and to buy goods and services, only in accordance with a procedure wherein competitive bids are solicited by advertisement from the public, with the lowest competent bid winning the contract.

BID SHOPPING "the practice of a **general contractor** who, before the award of the prime contract, discloses to interested **subcontractors** the current low subbids on certain subcontracts in an effort to obtain lower subbids." 482 P. 2d 226, 228.

BIGAMY the criminal offense of "the having of two or more wives or husbands at the same time." 194 P. 877. "The state of a man who has two wives, or of a woman who has two husbands, living at the same time." 189 S.E. 321, 323. A bigamous marriage is **void**.

BILATERAL CONTRACT see **contract**.

BILATERAL MISTAKE see **mistake**.

BILL a proposition or statement reduced to writing. In commercial law, an "account for goods sold, services rendered and work done," 11 Cal. Rptr., 893, 897; in the law of negotiable instruments, bills are "all forms of paper money," 127 S.W. 961, 962; a single **bond** without condition, 36 U.S. 257, 328; an order drawn by one person on another to pay a certain sum of money absolutely and at all events. 61 N.Y. 251, 255.

In legislation, a bill is a draft of a proposed statute submitted to the legislature for enactment. 226 F. 135, 137.

In **equity pleadings** a bill is the name of pleadings by which the complainant sets out his cause of action.

BILL FOR A NEW TRIAL one submitted to a **court of equity** stating equitable grounds for enjoining the execution of a judgment rendered in a **court of law** and proposing a new suit in **equity**.

BILL OF ATTAINDER see **bill of attainder**.

BILL OF CERTIORARI see **certiorari**.

BILL OF DISCOVERY see **discovery**.

BILL OF EXCEPTIONS a writing submitted to a trial court stating for the **record** objections to rulings made and instructions given by the trial judge.

BILL OF EXCHANGE an order written from one party to another directing him to pay a certain sum to a third party.

BILL OF INTERPLEADER see **interpleader**.

BILL OF LADING see **bill of lading**.

BILL OF PARTICULARS see **bill of particulars**.

BILL OF REVIEW see **bill of review**.

BILL OF RIGHTS the first eight amendments to the United States Constitution creating individual rights. Because they were adopted at the same time, Amendments 9 and 10 are referred to by many as part of the Bill of Rights.

BILL OF SALE a written agreement under which **title** to personal **chattels** is transferred. See 172 S.E. 672.

CROSS BILL brought in a court of equity by defendant against plaintiff or against another defendant in the suit;

similar to **cross-claim** and **counter-claim** at law.

BILL OF ATTAINDER a legislative act, in any form, that applies "either to named individuals or to easily ascertainable members of a group in such a way as to inflict punishment on them without a judicial trial," 381 U.S. 437, 448; such enactments are prohibited in the United States Constitution, Art. 1, §9, Cl. 3. At the time of the adoption of the federal constitution it "was a legislative judgment of conviction, an exercise of judicial power by parliament without a hearing, and in disregard of the first principles of natural justice." 35 N.E. 951. It should be noted, however, that a "legislature, like a court, must of necessity, possess the power to act immediately and instantly to quell disorder in the chamber," and therefore a legislature may punish and impose a jail sentence for **contempt** of the legislature as long as its procedures conform with **due process** requirements, i.e., the **accused** must have some opportunity to appear and to respond to the charges against him. 404 U.S. 496, 503, 504. An example of a bill of attainder was Section 304 of the Urgent Deficiency Appropriation Act of 1943 which forbade the paying of salaries to certain named government employees because Congress objected to their political views. See 328 U.S. 303.

BILL OF EXCHANGE see **draft**.

BILL OF LADING "a written acknowledgement of the receipt of goods and the **contract** in which is contained the agreement for their carriage and delivery at a specified time to a specified person or his order; . . . one of its most important functions is 'to give formal expression to the stipulations and conditions under which the carrier seeks to obtain a modification or limitation of the **liability** that otherwise would be imposed upon it under common law.' " 31 So. 2d 180, 182.

BILL OF PARTICULARS the criminal law **procedural** equivalent of a **civil action** request for a "more definite statement." 1 F.R.D. 229, 231. Its function "is to inform the defense of the specific occurrences intended to be investigated on the trial and to limit the course of the **evidence** to the particular scope of the inquiry." 155 S.E. 2d 802, 810. It is "in the nature of an amplification of the **pleading** to which it relates, and it is to be construed as part of it for certain purposes." 216 P. 2d 151, 155. "In legal effect, [it] is a more specific statement of details of offenses charged and is designed to advise the court, and more particularly, the **defendant**, of what facts he will be required to meet." 10 F.R.D. 191, 192.

BILL OF REVIEW form of **equitable proceedings** brought to secure an explanation, alteration, or **reversal** of a final **decree** by the court which rendered it. 192 N.E. 229, 234. Most commonly, only errors of law appearing on the face of the **record**, new evidence not susceptible to use at the trial and coming to light after the decree is issued, and **new matter** arising after entry of the decree, could have been the basis for a successful bill of review. 84 N.E. 2d 318, 322. It is also appropriate where there is evidence of **fraud** impeaching the original transaction. 114 N.E. 592, 593.

BIND something which obligates or constrains the bound individual. A bind places one under legal duties and obligations. One can "bind" himself as in a **contract** or one can be "bound" by a **judgment**. "To **guaranty**, to promise, to secure, to warrant, and to defend." 1 Ark. 325, 333.

BINDER a "contract for temporary insurance," 120 A. 2d 501, 502; "merely a written memorandum of the most important items of a preliminary contract," 155 S.E. 2d 246, 251; "insurer's bare acknowledgment of its contract to protect insured against casualty of a specified kind until a formal policy can be issued or until insurer gives notice of its election to terminate," 142 S.E. 2d 659; "a cover note." 185 P. 2d 832, 836.

BINDER RECEIPT evidence of an application for insurance previously accepted; "a contract of insurance in praesenti, temporary in nature, intended to take the place of an ordinary policy until it can be issued." 104 S.E. 2d 633, 637.

BINDING "as used in statute, commonly means obligatory," 172 N.E. 2d 703, 705.

BINDING AGREEMENT a conclusive agreement, see 148 S.W. 290, 291.

BINDING INSTRUCTION an instruction "which directs jury how to determine a case only if the conditions stated in that one instruction are shown to exist." 207 S.W. 2d 304, 307.

BIND OVER to order that a defendant be placed in custody pending the outcome of a proceeding (usually criminal) against him. He may be released on bail or other conditions of release thereafter. See 124 N.W. 492, 493. When **probable cause** is found to exist at a **preliminary hearing**, the court will direct that the defendant be "bound over" for action by the **grand jury** [or for trial on a prosecutor's information].

BLACKMAIL extortion, 68 N.E. 2d 464, 465; "the exaction of money either for the performance of a duty, the prevention of an injury, or the exercise of an influence," 24 P. 979, 980; "malicious threatening to do injury to person of another or to accuse one of crime or offense, to compel him to do an act against his will," 258 N.W. 62; "extortion of things of value from a person by menaces of personal injury, or by threating to accuse him of crime or any immoral conduct, which, if true, tends to degrade or disgrace him." 82 N.E. 1039.

BLANK INDORSEMENT see **indorsement.**

BLASPHEMY at **common law**, the **misdemeanor** of reviling or ridiculing the established religion (Christianity) and the existence of God, see 168 Eng. Rep. 1140, 1149. Blasphemy statutes exist in the United States in many jurisdictions, but are rarely, if ever, enforced, and hence have not been the subject of major constitutional attack even though there appears to be a basis for such attack. Perkins, Criminal Law 397 (2d ed. 1969). See **establishment clause.**

BLOOD, CORRUPTION OF THE see **corruption of the blood.**

BLUE SKY LAWS popular name given to state statutes regulating the sales of **corporate securities** through investment companies, imposed to prevent the sale of securities of **fraudulent** enterprises. See 242 U.S. 539.

BONA *(bō'-nà)*—Lat: good, virtuous; also, goods and chattels, property.

BONA FIDE PURCHASER "one who pays a valuable **consideration**, has no notice of outstanding rights of others and who acts in **good faith**" concerning the purchase, 303 S.W. 2d 110, 117; "one who acquires the apparent legal **title** to **property** in good faith for a valuable consideration and without notice of a claim or interest of a third person under the common source of title," 294 S.W. 2d 308, 311; innocent purchaser for value. 498 S.W. 2d 73, 75. The Uniform Commercial Code defines "bona fide purchaser" as a "purchaser for value in good faith and without notice of any adverse claim who takes delivery of a security in bearer form or of one in registered form issued to him or indorsed to him or in blank." U.C.C. §8-302.

BONA FIDE PURCHASE "one made in good faith for valuable consideration and without notice of an inconsistent third-party claim." 69 S.W. 2d 603, 609.

BONA FIDE "in or with **good faith**; without fraud or deceit; genuine." 173 P. 2d 545, 550.

BOND "written **instrument** with **sureties**, guaranteeing faithful **performance** of acts or duties contemplated," 71 N.E. 2d 742, 749; evidence of a debt; a binding agreement, a **covenant** between two or more persons, [or] an instrument under **seal** by which the **maker** binds himself, and usually also his **heirs**, **executors** and **administrators** or, if a **corporation**, their **successors**, to do or not to do a specified act." 166 N.Y.S. 2d 679, 680.

A bond may thus be the "obligation of a state, its subdivision, or a private corporation, represented by certificate for principal, and by detachable coupons for current interest; includes all interest-bearing obligations of persons, firms, and corporations," 95 S.W. 2d 39, 40; "certificate of indebtedness," 52 S.W. 2d 650; "security." 74 F. Supp. 133, 134.

BONDED DEBT that "part of the entire indebtedness of a **corporation** or state which is represented by **bonds** it has issued; . . . A debt contracted under the obligation of a bond." 40 S.E. 523, 527.

BOND FOR DEED [TITLE] "an instrument given by the owner of **real estate** to **convey** the same upon being paid money," 6 Minn. 38; "an agreement to make **title** in the future, and so long as it remains **executory** [not yet performed] the title is **vested** in the original owner." 41 N.E. 177.

BOND FOR GENERAL PURPOSES "bonds which are a charge against the taxpayers generally as distinguishable from those for improvements the cost of which is charged to the property specially benefited." 251 P. 413.

BOND DISCOUNT occurs where bonds are sold on the market for cash at a price less than the face amount of the bonds. 469 F. 2d 340, 345. Since bonds may **mature** [become due] many years hence, they are "discounted" to reflect present value, i.e., $20 due in 5 years may be worth only $10 today. The exact discount will depend upon the interest rate, inflation, and economic market conditions.

BOND ISSUE the offering of bonds for sale to investors; "commonly intended to distribute **indebtedness** among many investors over a period of years." 137 So. 665. The distribution of a bond or bonds. 138 S.W. 381, 383.

BOND PREMIUM amount that purchaser pays in buying a bond that exceeds face or call value of the bond.

BONDSMAN a **surety**; one who is bound or gives surety for another, 59 N.E. 557, 558; a person who obtains surety bonds for others for a fee; also, the individual who arranges for the defendant in a criminal case to be released from jail by posting a **bail bond**.

BOYCOTT to refrain from commercial dealing with by concerted effort; "[r]efusal to work for, purchase from or handle the products of an employer," 292 N.E. 2d 647, 655; "within the meaning of the 'Sherman Act,' [it] includes even the peaceful persuasion of a person to refrain from doing business with another." 344 F. Supp. 118, 141. Boycotting is not necessarily illegal. 284 N.W. 126, 130.

BREACH the failure of **performance** by a **party** of some contracted-for or agreed-upon act; "the act or omission on the part of the defendant without which there would be no cause of action or right of recovery." 134 S.W. 2d 760.

ANTICIPATORY BREACH see **anticipatory breach**.

MATERIAL BREACH see **material breach**.

PARTIAL BREACH see **partial breach**.

BREACH OF CONTRACT "a wrongful non-performance of any contractual duty of immediate performance, which may take place by failure to perform acts promised, by prevention or hindrance, or by repudiation," Restatement, Contracts §312; "a failure to perform for which legal excuse is lacking." 100 N.E. 2d 28, 30.

ANTICIPATORY BREACH see **anticipatory breach**.

MATERIAL BREACH see **material breach**.

PARTIAL BREACH see **partial breach**.

BREACH OF DUTY any failure to perform a duty owed to another or to society, "a violation by the **trustee** of any duty which, as trustee, he owes to the **beneficiary**," Restatement, Trusts, §201.

BREACH OF PROMISE failure to do what one promises in order to induce action in another, see 3 So. 2d 236, 239; often used as a shorthand for "breach of the promise of marriage."

BREACH OF THE COVENANT OF WARRANTY a failure of the seller's guarantee of **good title** which occurs when the buyer [**covenantee**] is evicted by a person claiming under a **paramount title**; since it is a future covenant it is not breached until that eviction occurs; see Cribbit, Principles of the Law of Property 207 (1962). See **breach of contract**.

BREACH OF THE PEACE the offense known as breach of the peace embraces a great variety of conduct destroying or menacing public order and tranquility. It includes not only violent acts but acts and words likely to produce violence in others. 310 U.S. 296, 308. In its broadest sense the term refers to any criminal offense (or at least any **indictable offense**, 207 U.S. 425). Today the term is generally used to describe conduct which unreasonably threatens the public peace and which lacks a specific criminal label;

by statute such conduct is often called "disorderly conduct" as the specific criminal offense. See, e.g., New York Penal Law §240.20. The term has been defined by state courts as "disturbances of the public peace violative of order and decency or decorum," 147 N.W. 2d 886, 892; "any violation of any law enacted to preserve peace and good order." 236 P. 57, 59. It "signifies disorderly, dangerous conduct disruptive of public peace." 261 A. 2d 731, 739. See also **fighting words; slander.**

BREACH OF TRUST "violation by a **trustee** of a **duty** which **equity** lays upon him, whether willful and **fraudulent,** or done through **negligence,** or arising through mere oversight and forgetfulness." 150 P. 2d 604, 648.

BREACH OF TRUST WITH FRAUDULENT INTENT "a **larceny** after **trust,** which includes all of the elements of larceny except the unlawful taking in the beginning."31 S.E. 2d 906, 907.

BREACH OF WARRANTY "infraction of an express or implied agreement as to the title, quality, content or condition of a thing sold or **bailed.**" 151 N.W. 2d 477, 482. A **warranty** is a **guarantee** and is breached when the thing so guaranteed is deficient according to the terms of the warranty.

BREAKING A CLOSE the **common law trespass** of unlawful entering upon the land of another. 187 S.E. 349, 350.

BRIBERY "voluntary giving of something of value to influence performance of official duty." 237 F. Supp. 638, 641. The "essential elements are offer of gift, purpose to corruptly influence, and official status of offeree." 103 S.E. 2d 666, 670. "At common law the voluntary giving or receiving of anything of value in unlawful payment of an official act done or to be done." 119 P. 901, 907. COMMERCIAL BRIBERY is a statutory expansion of the crime to include the breach of duty by an employee in accepting secret compensation from another in exchange for the exercise of some discretion conferred upon the employee by his employer. See, e.g., New York Penal Law Art. 180.

BRIEF a written argument concentrating upon legal points and authorities, which is used by the lawyer to convey to the court (trial or appellate) the essential facts of his client's case, a statement of the questions of law involved, the law that he would have applied, and the application that he desires made of it by the court; it is submitted in connection with an application, motion, trial, or appeal. See 107 P. 630, 631. Compare **memorandum.**

BROKER "one who for commission or fee, brings parties together and assists in negotiating contracts between them." 170 P. 2d 727. "Persons whose business it is to bring buyer and seller together." 110 S.W. 206, 208. Compare **jobber.**

BRUTUM FULMEN *(brū'-tŭm fŭl'-mĕn)* Lat: inert thunder. It refers to an empty threat or charge, or a void **judgment** which is in legal effect no judgment at all. See 179 S.W. 2d 346, 348. Brutum fulmen are any potentially powerful and effective orders, documents, **decrees,** or judgments that are powerless due to some imperfection causing them to be unenforceable. The following statement is exemplary: "Any decree by this court directed against the legislature would be unenforceable and no basis for a charge of contempt, if ignored. It would be a classic example of what the law describes as brutum fulmen." 153 A. 2d 888, 892.

BULK SALE ACTS "a class of statutes designed to prevent the defrauding of **creditors** by the secret sale in bulk of substantially all of the merchant's stock of goods." 125 S.E. 870. These laws generally require that notice be given to creditors before any sale of debtor's goods. See generally U.C.C. Art. 6.

BURDEN OF PROOF the duty of a party to substantiate an **allegation** or **issue** either to avoid the **dismissal** of that issue early in the trial or in order to convince the "trier of facts" as to the truth of that claim and hence to prevail in a civil or criminal **suit.** Thus defined, the burden of proof embodies at least two distinct concepts:

The burden of proof may refer to the RISK OF NONPERSUASION, 9 Wigmore, Evidence §2485 (3d ed. 1940), [also called simply PERSUASION BURDEN]. This kind of burden of proof means essentially that the party carrying it will lose if the trier of fact in deliberating the final outcome of the case, remains in doubt or is not convinced to the degree required. "If at the close of the evidence the [trier of fact] finds itself in doubt as to the facts, the decision must go against the party who has the burden of persuasion on the particular issue in question." 251 F. Supp. 474, 476. In civil cases this burden is met by proving a case by a **preponderence** of the evidence, while in criminal cases the state's persuasion burden is met only by proof beyond a **reasonable doubt.** 397 U.S. 358. In some **equity** matters the burden of persuasion is met by **clear and convincing** evidence (e.g., to **reform** a **contract** the party seeking reformation must present clear and convincing evidence that the writing does not accurately reflect the agreement of the parties).

The burden of proof may also refer to the DUTY OF PRODUCING EVIDENCE [also called BURDEN OF EVIDENCE or simply PRODUCTION BURDEN]. This is the duty that the **plaintiff** has at the beginning of the trial to produce evidence sufficient to avoid a preemptory finding at the close of his case [such as a **nonsuit, directed verdict; dismissal**], 54 Cal. Rptr. 528, 530; the duty of producing evidence is the "burden of making a **prima facie** [sufficient on its face] showing as to each fact necessary to establish a prima facie case." 126 S.W. 2d 915, 918. This burden is met if the court determines that there are enough facts on an issue sufficient to support a decision by the trier of fact favorable to the party who has the production burden [in a jury trial, sufficient to "permit the case to go to jury"]; if the burden is not met, that party loses on that issue. This burden, once allocated, often is shifted in the course of the trial to the opposing side. See generally, James, Civil Procedure §7.5 (1965).

A third distinct burden which may be included within the phrase "burden of proof" is the PLEADING BURDEN. This burden refers to the obligation to plead each element of a **cause of action** or **affirmative defense** on pain of suffering a dismissal.

See also **moral certainty; presumption; res ipsa loquitur.**

BURGLARY at common law, an actual breaking of a dwelling, in the nighttime,

with intent to commit a **felony.** See 90 P. 2d 520, 521. The common law offense has been expanded by statutes so that today burglary "connotes the entering of a building [not necessarily a dwelling] in the night season with intent to commit a felony or with intent to steal property of value." 116 N.E. 2d 311, 312. Some modern statutes have expanded the crime even further so that any unlawful entry into or remaining in any building, with intent to commit any crime, constitutes burglary. See, e.g., N.Y. Penal Law Art. 140.

BUSINESS RECORDS EXCEPTION see **hearsay rule.**

BY OPERATION OF LAW see **operation of law.**

BY THE ENTIRETY see **tenancy** (TENANCY BY THE ENTIRETY).

CALL in corporation law, a demand by a **corporation** on a **shareholder** to pay an additional sum to the corporation proportionate to his share of **stock,** if provided for by contract or by corporation law, see 101 U.S. 205; also, an obligation of a corporation to issue stock at a certain price on demand; the privilege of "calling" for stock belongs in this context to the buyer. See 79 Ill. 351.

In property law, a call is an identifiable natural object designated in an **instrument** of **conveyance** as a landmark, which serves to mark the boundary of the land conveyed. 98 F. 913, 922.

CALUMNY **slander, defamation;** false prosecution or accusation; a word once used in **civil law** "which signified an unjust prosecution or defense of a suit, and the phrase is still said to be used in the courts of Scotland and the **ecclesiastical** and **admiralty** courts of England." 30 Ohio St. 115, 117.

CANON a rule of **ecclesiastical law,** primarily concerning the clergy, but also at times, embracing lay members of a congregation. A rule of **construction**; one of an aggregate of rules indicating the proper way to construe statutes, ordinances, etc. See 161 N.Y.S. 484, 487.

A professional canon is a rule or standard of conduct adopted by a professional group to guide or discipline the professional conduct of its members. The Canons of Professional Ethics were originally 32 in number and were adopted by the American Bar Association in 1908. Today a new Code of Professional Responsibility containing seven broad canons and a large number of "ethical considerations" and "disciplinary rules" have replaced the original Canons. A familiar Canon, Number Seven, provides that "A Lawyer Should Represent a Client Zealously Within the Bounds of the Law." The new Code has been adopted by most of the states' highest courts.

CAPITAL broadly, all the money and other property of a corporation or other enterprise used in transacting its business, 61 N.W. 851, 852; each investment. A corporation's legal **liability** is ordinarily limited by its capital.

CAPITAL ASSETS property with a relatively long life or fixed **assets** in a trade or business; in taxation, property held for investment by the taxpayer which when sold is subject to special tax treatment ("**capital gains**" and losses); property which is part of one's stock in trade does not qualify as a capital asset.

CAPITAL EXPENDITURE expenditure made for the improvement or betterment of a capital asset, or expenditure made in the purchase or sale of a capital asset or the collection of capital records. See 388 F. 2d 184, 187.

CAPITAL GAIN income realized from the appreciation in value of **property** in which one has invested money. See 326 F. 2d 287. If the property qualifies under the federal income tax law as a "capital asset," special tax treatment will be available to reflect the fact that the property appreciated over time and to encourage **investment** in capital assets. A SHORT-TERM CAPITAL GAIN involves the sale or exchange of a capital asset which the taxpayer has held not more than six months; a LONG-TERM CAPITAL GAIN results from

a sale or exchange of a capital asset held for more than six months.

CAPITAL INVESTMENT money paid out for acquisition of something for permanent use or value in a business or home, see 205 F. 2d 538, 542; also monies paid out for an interest in a business as in the purchase of **stock**.

CAPITAL STOCK the amount of money or property contributed by **shareholders** to be used as the financial foundation from which the business of **incorporation** is to be carried on. See 74 Cal. Rptr. 920, 925. The **charter** of the corporation limits the total capital stock to be offered to the public, which is divided into **shares**.

CAPITAL OFFENSE a criminal offense punishable by death. **Bail** is generally unavailable to **defendants charged** with a capital offense. Where the death penalty is no longer in force, offenses heretofore "capital" have been held to be bailable by most courts. See, e.g., 60 N.J. 60 (1972).

CAPTION the heading of a legal document containing the names of the **parties**, the court, index or docket, number of case, etc.

It also refers to one element of common law, **larceny**, together with asportation. Caption is the seizing, asportation the carrying away.

CARTEL a group of independent industrial **corporations**, usually on an international scale, which agree to restrict trade to their mutual benefit. See **monopoly**; **oligopoly**.

CASE an **action**, cause, **suit**, or controversy, **at law** or in **equity**, see 220 S.W. 2d 45, 51; also, abbreviation for **trespass on the case**.

CASE, ON THE see **trespass on the case**.

CASE AT BAR see **bar**.

CASE LAW see **common law**.

CASE OF FIRST IMPRESSION see **first impression**.

CASE OR CONTROVERSY see **controversy**.

CASHIER'S CHECK see **check**.

CASH VALUE see **market value.**

CAUSA (käw'-zȧ)—Lat: lawsuit, case; grounds, cause, motive, purpose, reason; good reason; pretext, pretense; inducement, occasion.

CAUSA MORTIS (käw'-zȧ mōr'-tǐs)-Lat: in anticipation of approaching death. A gift causa mortis will be void if the donor survives the contemplated death.

CAUSA PROXIMA (käw'-zȧ prŏk'-sǐ-mȧ)— Lat: **proximate cause,** most closely related cause. It is used to indicate legal cause. That which is sufficiently related to the result as to justify imposing liability on the actor who produces the cause, or likewise, to relieve the actor who produces a less closely related cause from liability.

CAUSA SINE QUA NON (käw'-zȧ sē'-nȧ kwä nŏn)—Lat: a cause without which it would not have occurred; used most often in connection with the "but for" test of causation. See **cause.**

CAUSE that which effects a result. 169 F. 2d 203, 206. In law "cause" is not a constant and agreed-upon term. The following is a list of some of the attempts to conceptualize "that which effects a result":

DIRECT CAUSE the active, efficient cause that sets in motion a train of events which brings about a result without the intervention of any other independent source, see 6 N.E. 2d 879, 881; often used interchangeably with "proximate cause," 199 F. Supp. 951, 954.

IMMEDIATE CAUSE the nearest cause in point of time and space.

INTERVENING CAUSE [SUPERVENING] "one which comes into active operation in producing the result after the negligence of the defendant. 'Intervening' is used in a time sense; it refers to later events. If the defendant sets a fire with a strong wind blowing at the time, which carries the fire to the plaintiff's property, the wind does not intervene, since it was already in operation; but if the fire is set first, and the wind springs up later, it is then an intervening cause." Prosser, Torts 271 (4th ed. 1971).

PROXIMATE CAUSE that which in natural and continuous sequence unbroken by any new independent cause, produces an event, and without which the injury would not have occurred, see 323 P. 2d 108, 114. In criminal and tort law, one's **liability** is generally limited to results "proximately caused" by his conduct or omission.

SUPERSEDING CAUSE an intervening cause which is so substantially responsible for the ultimate injury that it acts to cut off the liability of preceding actors regardless of whether their prior negligence was or was not a substantial factor in bringing about the injury complained of. Courts sometimes use "superseding" interchangeably with "intervening" in which case it does not have this meaning. But properly the term "superseding" is limited to an intervening cause which "by its intervention prevents the actor from being liable for harm to another which his antecedent negligence is a substantial factor in bringing about." Restatement, 2d, Torts § 440.

SUPERVENING CAUSE see INTERVENING CAUSE, above.

CAUSE OF ACTION a claim in law and fact sufficient to demand judicial attention; the composite of facts necessary to give rise to the enforcement of a right. 254 A. 2d 824, 825. A RIGHT OF ACTION is the legal right to sue; a **cause of action** is the facts which give rise to a right of action. If the **complaint** fails to state a proper cause of action, it will be **dismissed.**

CAVEAT (kä'-vē-ät)—Lat: let him beware. In general, a warning or emphasis for caution; "an intimation given to some judge or officer notifying him that he ought to beware how he acts in some particular affair, and suspend the **proceedings** until the merits of the caveat are determined," 38 N.J. Eq. 485, 488; also, "an **in rem** proceeding attacking the validity of an **instrument** purporting to be a **will,**" 118 S.E. 2d 17, 18; also, "a remedy given to prevent a **patent** from issuing in certain cases where the directions of the law have been violated." 5 U.S. 45, 101.

CAVEAT EMPTOR (kä'-vē-ät ĕmp'-tôr)— Lat: let the buyer beware. Expresses the rule of law that the purchaser buys at his own risk. 26 S.W. 148, 149. This harsh principle has been modified substantially by statutes and court decisions that have given consumers certain rights respecting the purchase of goods, e.g., **warranties** of fitness and merchantibility (except where the goods are bought expressly as is) and in landlord tenant law, e.g., the implied **covenant of habitability**.

CENTER OF GRAVITY see **conflict of laws**.

CERTIFICATE OF DEPOSIT "an acknowledgment by a bank of receipt of money with an engagement to repay it." U.C.C. §3-104(2) (c). The writing may or may not be a **negotiable instrument** depending on whether it meets the requirements for negotiability. See id. at §3-104(3).

CERTIFICATION see **certiorari**.

CERTIFIED CHECK see **check**.

CERTIORARI a means of gaining **appellate** review; a **common law writ**, issued from a superior court to one of inferior jurisdiction, commanding the latter to certify and return to the former the record in the particular case. 6 Cyc. 737. The writ is issued in order that the court issuing the writ may inspect the proceedings and determine whether there have been any irregularities. In the United States Supreme Court the writ is discretionary with the Court and will be issued to any court in the land to review a **federal question** if at least 4 of the 9 justices vote to hear the case. A similar writ used by some state courts is called CERTIFICATION.

CHAIN OF TITLE the successive **conveyances** of a certain property, "commencing with the patent from the government [or other original source], each being a perfect conveyance of the **title** down to and including the conveyance to the present holder." 46 S.W. 2d 329, 332.

The recorded chain of title consists only of the documents affecting title which are recorded in a manner that makes the fact of their existence readily available to a **bona fide purchaser**. See Cribbet, Property 224 (1962). Of the two systems in general use for recording such documents, the TRACT INDEX is the one best-equipped to insure accessibility of title-affecting documents, since it records in the same place all **instruments** relating to a particular piece of property. Id. The GRANTOR-GRANTEE INDEXING systems, on the other hand, index all such instruments under the names of the various grantors or grantees of the property. See **abstract of record**; **clear title**; **title search**; **Recording Acts**; **warranty deed**.

CHANCELLOR in early English law, the name of the King's minister who would dispense justice in the King's name by extraordinary **equitable relief** where the remedy **at law** was inadequate to do substantial justice. Later, the name given to the chief judge of the court of **chancery**. In American law it is the name used in some states to signify any judge sitting in a court of **chancery**.

CHANCERY that jurisprudence which is exercised in a **court of equity**, originally by the **chancellor**; synonymous with **equity** or equitable jurisdiction.

CHARGE in criminal law, the underlying substantive offense contained in an **accusation** or indictment. In trial practice, an address delivered by the **court** to the **jury** at the close of the **case**, instructing the jury as to what principles of law they are to apply in reaching a decision, 168 N.E. 2d 285, 287-8; the charge may also, in some jurisdictions, comprehend any instructions given for the jury's guidance at any time during the trial, 15 S.E. 758; the charge to the jury need not originate with the court, but may be, and often are, requested by the **parties**. 168 N.E. 2d 285, 287. In its broader signification, the term means simply to entrust with, by way of responsibility, duty, etc. Compare **complaint**.

CHARTER a document issued by the government [sovereign] establishing a corporate entity. See **certificate of incorporation**.

In earlier law, the term referred to a grant from the sovereign guaranteeing to the person or persons therein named certain rights, privileges, and powers. Thus, the earlier American colonies were recognized by charters granted by the King of England.

The Magna Charta or the GREAT CHARTER, granted by King John to the barons of England in 1215, established the basis for English constitutional government.

CHATTEL any tangible, movable thing; personal, as opposed to real property, 170 S.E. 660, 662; goods. See **personalty**.

CHATTEL PAPER "a writing or writings which evidence both a monetary obligation and a **security interest** in or a **lease** of specific goods." U.C.C. §9-105 (1)(b). Chattel paper and other non-negotiable instruments creating a security interest are subject to special rules as to priority over other security interests in the same collateral. See id. at §9-308.

CHECK a "**draft** drawn upon a bank and payable on **demand**, signed by the **maker** or **drawer**, containing an unconditional promise to pay a **sum certain** in money to the order of the **payee**," 503 P. 2d 1063, 1066.

CASHIER'S CHECK one "issued by the authorized officer of a bank directed to another person, evidencing the fact that the **payee** is authorized to demand and receive upon presentation from the bank the amount of money represented by the check." 277 S.W. 625, 627. The cashier's check is drawn upon the bank's own account and not that of a private person and as such has a higher guarantee that it will be honored and is accepted for many transactions where a personal check would not be.

CERTIFIED CHECK check containing a "certification that the drawer of the check has sufficient funds to cover payment of the check." 286 N.E. 2d 80, 82. It indicates that the bank will retain a sufficient amount of the drawer's funds to cover the payment of the check on demand; it makes the bank liable to a **bona fide holder** of the check for value. See 85 P. 81, 82.

MEMORANDUM CHECK it "is in the ordinary form of a bank check, with the word 'memorandum' written across its face, and is not intended for immediate presentation, but simply as evidence of an indebtedness by the **drawer** to the **holder**." 84 U.S. 496, 502.

CHILD SUPPORT see **alimony**.

CHILL [CHILLING EFFECTS] self-imposed limitations on the exercise of First Amendment rights by citizens who, fearful of the possible application of laws and sanctions, choose to circumscribe their legitimate rights rather than risk prosecution. The effect may be present even if the prosecution is not successful. In recognition of the chilling effect of statutes that may be constitutionally overbroad, a facial attack on such statutes is permitted by any person properly before the court even if he lacks personal **standing** to assert the facial invalidity of the statute because his own conduct falls squarely within some hardcore valid application of the statute. See 380 U.S. 479; 94 S. Ct. 1209.

CHOSE *(shōz)*—Fr: thing; A thing, either presently possessed [chose in possession] or claimed [chose in action].

CHOSE IN ACTION a **claim** or **debt** upon which a recovery may be made in a **lawsuit**. It is not a present possession, but merely a right to sue; it becomes a "possessary thing" only upon successful completion of a lawsuit.

CHOSE IN POSSESSION as opposed to **chose in action**, a thing actually possessed or possessable. 372 P. 2d 470, 476.

C.I.F. cost, insurance, and freight, see 264 F. 2d 405, 408; also written c.f.i. See 182 N.Y.S. 30, 33. In a **contract** of sale it means the cost of the goods, insurance thereon, and freight to the destination is included in the contract price, and "[u]nless there is something in a c.i.f. contract to indicate to the contrary, the seller completes his contract when he delivers the merchandise called for to the shipper, pays the freight thereon to point of destination, and forwards to the buyer **bill of lading**, invoice, insurance policy and receipt showing payment of freight." 135 N.E. 329, 330.

CIRCUIT COURT one of several courts in a given jurisdiction; a part of a system of courts extending over one or more counties or districts; formerly applied to United States Courts of Appeal. See **federal courts**. Compare **district court**.

CIRCUMSTANTIAL EVIDENCE indirect evidence; secondary facts by which a principal fact may be rationally inferred.

CITATION a reference to a source of legal authority, e.g., a citation to a statute or case. It is analogous to a **sum-**

mons at law, in that it commands the appearance of a party in a proceeding; "a writ issued out of a court of competent **jurisdiction**, commanding the person named therein to appear on the day named, and do something therein mentioned, or show cause why he should not." 56 P. 725, 726. Compare **subpoena**.

CIVIL that branch of law that pertains to suits outside of criminal practice, pertaining to the rights and duties of persons in **contract**, **tort**, etc.; also refers to **civil law** as opposed to **common law**.

CIVIL ACTION action maintained to protect a private, **civil** right, or to compel a civil remedy, as distinguished from a criminal **prosecution**.

CIVIL CONTEMPT see **contempt of court**.

CIVIL LAW Roman law embodied in the Justinian Code (Codex Justinianeus) and presently prevailing in most Western European States. It is also the foundation of the law of Louisiana. The term may also be used to distinguish that part of the law concerned with non-criminal matters, or may refer to the body of laws prescribed by the supreme power of the state, as opposed to **natural law**. See 244 P. 323, 325.

CIVIL LIABILITY amenability to **civil action**, as opposed to criminal action, 50 A. 2d 39, 43; liability to actions seeking private remedies or the enforcement of personal rights, based on contract, tort, etc.

CIVIL LIBERTIES see **civil rights**.

CIVIL RIGHTS rights given, defined, and circumscribed by positive laws enacted by civilized communities. 252 N.E. 2d 463, 474. Civil rights differ from CIVIL LIBERTIES in that civil rights are positive in nature, and civil liberties are negative in nature; that is, civil liberties are immunities from governmental interference or limitations on governmental action (such as those embodied in the First Amendment) which have the effect of reserving rights to individuals.

CIVITAS *(sĭ'-vĭ-täs)*—Lat: in the Roman Law, any body of people living under the same laws; citizenship, state, commonwealth, community.

CLAIM the assertion of a right to money or **property**; the aggregate of operative facts giving rise to a right enforceable in the courts. 309 F. Supp. 1178, 1181. A claim must show the existence of a right, an injury, and a **prayer** for **damages**. See 149 F. Supp. 615, 618. One who makes a claim is the **claimant**.

CLASS ACTION a **lawsuit** brought by representative member(s) of a large group of persons on behalf of all the members of the group. See Fed. R. Civ. Proc. 23. The class must be ascertainable, the members must share a common interest in the issues of law and fact raised by the plaintiff(s), and the action must satisfy a variety of other special requirements applicable to class actions before the **trial court** will specifically certify the **action** to be one maintainable as a class action. If so certified, all members of the class must receive **notice** of the pendency of the action and an opportunity to exclude themselves from the class if they so desire. Members not so excluding themselves are bound by the **judgment**. Subclasses may be formed to reach an identifiable and manageable class size for purposes of litigation. See 94 S. Ct. 2140.

CLEAN HANDS the concept in **equity** that **claimants** who seek **equitable relief** must not themselves have indulged in any impropriety in relation to the transaction upon which relief is sought; freedom from participation in unfair conduct. A party with "unclean hands" cannot ask a court of conscience [the equity court] to come to his aid.

CLEAR AND CONVINCING as a standard of proof, it is that quantum of evidence beyond a mere **preponderance**, but below that of "beyond a **reasonable doubt**," 464 F. 2d 471, 474; and such that it will produce in the mind of the **trier of fact** a firm belief as to the facts sought to be established. 220 N.E. 2d 547, 574. It "indicates a degree of proof required in [some] civil cases [e.g., **reformation** of a contract] . . . less than the degree required in criminal cases but more than required in the ordinary civil action." 110 N.E. 493. In the ordinary civil cases the degree of proof is characterized as a preponderance; in the exceptional civil case (e.g., a contract to pay for services between persons in a family relation), it should be clear and convincing. See 110 N.E. 493.

CLEAR AND PRESENT DANGER in constitutional law, a standard used to determine if one's First Amendment right to speak may be curtailed or punished. "[T]he character of every act depends upon the circumstances in which it is done. . . . The most stringent protection of free speech would not protect a man in falsely shouting fire in a theatre and causing a panic. It does not even protect a man from an injunction against uttering words that may have all the effect of force [**fighting words**]. The question in every case is whether the words used, are used in such circumstances and are of such a nature as to create a clear and present danger that they will bring about the substantive evils that [the government] has a right to prevent." 249 U.S. 47, 52.

CLEAR TITLE title free from any encumbrance, obstruction, burden or limitation that presents a doubtful or even a reasonable question of law or fact. See 29 N.E. 2d 41, 43. See **good title; marketable title**.

CLEMENCY see **executive clemency**.

CLERICAL ERROR immediately correctable mistake resulting from the copying or transmission of legal documents. As opposed to a **judicial error**, a clerical error is not made in the exercise of judgment or discretion, but is made by a mechanical or other inadvertence. A clerical error is known by the character of the error, and is not dependent on who makes the error, be it clerk or judge.

CLOSE an ancient term referring to an enclosure, whether surrounded by a visible or an invisible boundary; land rightfully owned by a party, the **trespass** upon which is **actionable** at law. See 4 Ill. 258, 259. See **breaking a close**.

CLOSE CORPORATION see **corporation**.

CO-CONSPIRATOR EXCEPTION see **hearsay rule**.

CODE a systematic compilation of laws. The criminal code refers to the penal laws of the jurisdiction, the motor vehicle code to the laws relating to automobiles, etc. Today most jurisdictions have codified a substantial part of their laws.

All jurisdictions record each new law in a volume of session laws or Statutes at Large; e.g., Public Law No. 91-112 (i.e. the 112th law passed by the 91st Congress of the United States, etc.). If the laws are not codified they will appear only in these volumes.

CODE PLEADING "the term applied to the system of **pleading** developed in this country through practice codes enacted in the majority of the states, beginning with the New York Code of 1848, as a consolidation and improvement of the **common law** and **equity** systems of pleading previously in vogue. Since the union of law and equity procedures is basic in present-day procedural reform, it has now become appropriate to regard modern English and American pleading as advanced systems of code pleading." Clark, Code Pleading, 1-26 (1947).

CODICIL a supplement to a **will**; "an instrument of a **testamentary** nature, the purpose of which is to change or alter an already executed will by adding to and enlarging, subtracting from and restricting, or qualifying, modifying, or revoking the provisions of a prior existing will." 176 P. 2d 281, 288. Compare **testamentary disposition**.

COGENT appealing forcibly to the mind or reason; compelling; convincing. The word cogent is frequently used to describe the quality of a particular legal argument. It is derived from the Latin "cogo", "cogere", which means "to bind, drive or compress into a mass." See Oxford Latin Dictionary, Fascicle 11, p. 347. "A forcible argument tells strongly, but may not convince; cogent reasoning is more apt to be conclusive or to compel assent." 22 N.W. 2d 218, 219.

COGNIZABLE within the **jurisdiction** of the court. An interest is "cognizable" in a court of law when that court has power to **adjudicate** the interest in controversy. See 113 F. 2d 703, 707. See **jurisdiction**.

COHABITATION literally, the act of living together. Often statutorily expanded to include living together publicly, as husband and wife; indulgence in sexual intercourse. Cohabitation among unmarried persons of the opposite sex is often proscribed by local laws. Such cohabitation will produce an **inference** of criminal **fornication**.

CO-HEIR one who inherits the same property together with another. The co-heirs will be deemed **joint-tenants** or **tenants in common** according to the language employed in the **conveyance** and the controlling law of the jurisdiction, the latter being the preferred designation in most jurisdictions. Moynihan, Introduction to the Law of Real Property, 216-17 (1962). The term "co-heir" grew out of the concept of **coparceners**.

COIF headress formerly worn by English sergeants at law. "Order of the Coif" is an honorary legal fraternity in the United States.

COINSURANCE a scheme of **insurance** wherein the **insurer** provides **indemnity** for only a certain percentage of the insured's loss. The scheme reflects "a relative division of the risk between the insurer and the **insured**, dependent upon the relative amount of the policy and the actual value of the property insured thereby." 160 N.Y.S. 566, 569. A typical coinsurance clause, commonly called the New York Standard Coinsurance Clause, is as follows: "This company shall not be liable for a greater proportion of any loss or damage to the property described herein than the sum hereby insured bears to the percentage specified on the first page of the policy of the actual cash value of said property at the time such loss shall happen, nor for more than the portion which this policy bears to the total insurance thereon." See Keeton, Insurance Law §3.7(b) (1971).

COLLATERAL secondary; not of the essence of the principal thing; on the side, divergent or auxiliary. See 57 S.W. 2d 222, 223. In commercial transac-

tions, "collateral means the property subject to a **security interest**, and includes accounts, contract rights, and **chattel paper** which have been sold." U.C.C. §9-105(c). To obtain credit it is sometimes necessary to offer some collateral, i.e., to place within the legal control of the lender some property which may be sold in the event of a default and applied to the amount owing.

In contracts, a COLLATERAL PROMISE is one ancillary to an integrated contractual relationship; its enforcement is not precluded by the **parol evidence rule**. The term may also refer to a promise ancillary to a principal transaction; its **breach** does not entitle the other party to rescind [see **rescission**].

COLLATERAL ATTACK a challenge to the integrity of a **judgment**, brought in a special **proceeding** intended for that express purpose. A **direct attack,** on the other hand, is an attempt to impeach a judgment within the same **action** in which the judgment was obtained, through an appeal, request for a new trial, etc. Lack of proper jurisdiction is often grounds for collateral attack. See 145 P. 2d 402, 405. **Habeas corpus** is a "collateral attack" remedy.

COLLATERAL ESTOPPEL the doctrine which recognizes that the determination of facts **litigated** between two **parties** in a **proceeding** is binding on those parties in all future proceedings against each other. "In a subsequent **action** between the parties on a different **claim,** the judgment is conclusive as to the **issues** raised in the subsequent action, if these issues were actually litigated and determined in the prior action." Restatement, Judgments §45. The constitutional prohibition against **double jeopardy** includes within it the right of the **defendant** (but not the state) to **plead** "collateral estoppel" and thereby preclude proof of some essential element of the state's case found in the defendant's favor at an earlier trial. 397 U.S. 436. Thus, if D is charged with robbing six persons at a poker game and his defense in the first trial involving the alleged robbery of only one of the victims is that he wasn't there [**alibi**], and if he is **acquitted** at that trial, the state will be **estopped** to relitigate the alibi question with respect to the other related robberies. See id.

See **estoppel**. See also **bar; merger; res judicata**.

COLLATERAL FRAUD   see **fraud**.

COLLATION "the bringing into the **estate** of an **intestate** [person who dies without a **will**] an estimate of the value of advancements made by the intestate to his or her children, in order that the whole may be divided in accordance with the **Statute of Descents**." 267 N.W. 743, 744.

COLLECTIVE BARGAINING mechanism for settling labor disputes by negotiation between employer and representatives of employees, see 223 F. 2d 872, 877; an agreement resulting from collective bargaining between an employee and a **labor union** is one which regulates the terms and conditions of employment with reference to hours of labor and wages, and deals also with strikes, lockouts, **arbitration,** etc., the enforceability and interpretation of such agreement and of numerous other relations existing between employer and employee." 44 N.Y.S. 2d 601, 605, 606.

COLLOQUIUM words in a **declaration** or **complaint** of **libel** under **common law pleadings**, which purport to connect the libelous words with the **plaintiff** by setting forth extrinsic facts, showing that they applied to him and were so intended by defendant. See 69 N.E. 288, 289.

COLLUSION the making of an agreement with another for the purposes of perpetrating a **fraud**, or engaging in illegal activity, or in legal activity while having an illegal end in mind. In divorce law, the term refers to an agreement by husband and wife to suppress facts or fabricate **evidence** material to the existence of lawful grounds for divorce. 5 N.W. 2d 133, 137.

COLLUSIVE ACTION an impermissible **action** maintained by non-**adversary parties** to determine a hypothetical point of law, or to produce a desired legal precedent. Because such suits do not contain an actual **controversy**, they will not be entertained. See 140 P. 2d 666, 669, 670. Compare **advisory opinions; declaratory judgments**.

COLOR semblance; disguise. Color is often used to designate the hiding of a set of facts behind a sham, but technically proper, legal theory.

COLORABLE that which presents an appearance which does not correspond with the reality, or an appearance intended to conceal or to deceive. See 172 P. 23, 24.

COLOR OF LAW "mere semblance of legal right." 202 N.W. 144, 148. An action done under color of law is one done with the apparent authority of law but actually in contravention of law. A federal **cause of action** may be maintained against a state officer who deprives a person of his **civil rights** under "color of law." 42 U.S.C. § 1983.

COLOR OF TITLE lending the appearance of **title**, when in reality there is no title at all; an **instrument** which appears to pass title, and which one relies on as passing title, but which fails to do so; an instrument which, on its face, professes to pass title, but which fails to do so either because title is lacking in the person conveying or because the **conveyance** itself is defective. Thus, one possessing a forged or false **deed** has mere color of title. Color of title is sometimes an element of **adverse possession**.

COMITAS   see **comity**.

COMITY a rule of courtesy by which one court defers to the concomitant **jurisdiction** of another. "Judicial comity is not a rule of law, but one of practical convenience and expediency based on the theory that a court which first asserts jurisdiction will not be interfered with in the continuance of its assertion by another court...unless it is desirable that one give way to the other." 177 U.S. 485, 488. Comity will ordinarily prevent a federal court from interfering with a pending state criminal prosecution. 401 U.S. 37. The doctrine of comity, rather than **full faith and credit**, is applicable when a state is asked to honor a judgment (e.g., a **divorce** decree) of a foreign country.

COMMENT refers to the statements made by a judge or counsel concerning the defendant, such statements not being based on fact, but rather on alleged facts. A judge may comment "on the weight of the evidence and indicate his own opinion concerning the credibility of witnesses and the relative strength of competing permissible inferences, provided always that he makes it clear to the jury that it is their province to decide such questions of weight and credibility." James, Civil Procedure §7.14 (1965). However, a prosecutor may not "comment" on the refusal of a defendant in a criminal proceeding to testify, and the court may not instruct a jury that such silence is evidence of guilt. See 380 U.S. 609.

COMMERCIAL BRIBERY see **bribery.**

COMMERCIAL FRUSTRATION s e e **frustration.**

COMMERCIAL PAPER a **negotiable instrument,** i.e., a writing **indorsed** by the **maker** or **drawee,** containing an unconditional promise or order to pay a certain sum on demand or at a specified time, made **payable to order** or to bearer. U.C.C. §3-104(1). The term comprehends **bills of exchange, checks, notes,** and **certificates of deposit.** U.C.C. §3-104(2).

COMMERCIAL PREFERENCE see **preference.**

COMMODITY any tangible **good;** commercially, commodities refer to products that are the subject of **sale** or barter. See also **futures.**

COMMON LAW the system of jurisprudence, which originated in England and was later applied in the United States, which is based on judicial **precedent** rather than legislative enactments; it is to be contrasted with **civil law** (the descendant of Roman Law prevalent in other western countries). Originally based on the unwritten laws of England, the common law is "generally derived from principles rather than rules; it does not consist of absolute, fixed, and inflexible rules, but rather of broad and comprehensive principles based on justice, reason, and common sense. It is of judicial origin and promulgation. Its principles have been determined by the social needs of the community and have changed with changes in such needs. These principles are susceptible of adaptation to new conditions, interests, relations, and usages as the progress of society may require." 37 N.W. 2d 543, 547.

COMMON LAW COPYRIGHT see **copyright.**

COMMON NUISANCE see **nuisance.**

COMMON PROPERTY see **property.**

COMMONS land set aside for public use, e.g., public parks; also, the untitled class of Great Britain, represented in Parliament by the House of Commons.

COMMUTATION substitution, change; the substitution of a lesser penalty or punishment for a greater one, such as from death to life imprisonment, or from a longer term to a shorter one. The chief executive officer (President, governor) has the constitutional power of **executive clemency** which includes the broad power in his discretion to commute a sentence. Compare with **pardon** and **reprieve.**

COMPANY broadly, any group of people voluntarily united for performing jointly any activity, business, or commercial enterprise. See 23 Tex. 295, 303.

In reference to trades, "company" applies to the combination of individuals' capital, skill and labor for the purpose of business carried on for such individuals' common benefits. 6 So. 362, 364.

The term also applies to a wide range of activities, and under statutory construction has been held to include private **corporations,** joint stock companies (see below), all **partnerships,** etc. See 222 S.W. 736, 739. "Company" has also been considered synonymous with "firm".

HOLDING COMPANY see **holding company.**

JOINT STOCK COMPANY a company or association, usually unincorporated, which has the capital of its members pooled in a common fund; the capital **stock** is divided into **shares** and distributed to represent ownership **interest** in the company, see Henn, Law of Corporations §50 (1961); a form of partnership, but one which is distinguished from a "partner-ship" in the ordinary sense of that term in that the membership of a joint stock company is changeable, its shares are transferable, its mem-bers can be many and not necessar-ily known to each other, and its members cannot act or speak for the company. See 154 S.E. 357, 361. There is an important distinction be-tween joint stock companies at com-mon law, and those under statutory authority in certain states; in certain jurisdictions, "joint stock companies" are regulated more like corporations than partnerships, and thus have ex-tensive power unknown at common law. See 279 F. 2d 785.

COMPARATIVE NEGLIGENCE see neg-ligence.

COMPELLING INTEREST see equal protection of the laws.

COMPENSATION "remuneration for work done; indemnification for injury sustained," 245 P. 2d 352, 355; recom-pense, remuneration, equivalence; pay for injury done or service performed; "that which constitutes, or is regarded as, an equivalent or recompense; that which compensates for loss or privation; amends." 112 A. 2d 716, 719. As used in constitutional law, with reference to the taking of property for public use, the word means "a compensation which is just and fair both to the owner of the property being taken and to the public represented by the **condemning** author-ity." 131 A. 2d 180, 182.

COMPETENT capable of doing a cer-tain thing; capacity to understand, and act reasonably. Competent **evidence** is evidence relevant to the issues being **liti-gated**; a competent court is one having proper **jurisdiction** over the person or property at issue. An individual is com-petent to make a **will** if he understands the extent of his **property**, the identity of the natural objects of his bounty, and the consequences of the act of making a will. 26 N.Y.S. 2d 96. An individual declared incompetent to attend to his daily affairs may nevertheless be com-petent to make a will. See 63 N.Y.S. 2d 572. A criminal defendant is competent to stand trial if he "has sufficient present ability to consult with his lawyer with a

reasonable degree of rational under-standing and . . . has a rational as well as a factual understanding of the **pro-ceedings** against him." 362 U.S. 402. Compare **insanity**. See **compos mentis**.

COMPLAINANT the party who initiates the **complaint** in an **action** or **proceed-ing**. "[F]or all practical purposes it is synonymous with **petitioner** and **plain-tiff**. The nature of the proceeding and the court in which it is instituted deter-mines which term is the more appropri-ate under the circumstances." 62 S.E. 2d 80, 81.

COMPOS MENTIS ($k\breve{o}m'$-$p\bar{o}s$ $m\breve{e}n'$-$t\breve{i}s$) mentally competent. See **non-compos mentis**.

COMPOUNDING A FELONY the offense of refusing to **prosecute** a **felon**, by one who was injured by the felony, in ex-change for which the party injured re-ceives a bribe or reparation for his **for-bearance**; "[t]he offense consists of per-verting public justice in some way by making a bargain to allow the criminal to escape conviction or showing some favor to him for that purpose." 106 N.E. 215, 217. Compare **accessory**.

COMPULSORY APPEARANCE see ap-pearance.

COMPULSORY COUNTERCLAIM see counterclaim.

COMPULSORY JOINDER see joinder.

COMPULSORY PROCESS the right of a **defendant** to have the resources of the court (i.e., the **subpoena** power) utilized on his behalf to compel the **appearance** of **witnesses** before such court. See 44 A. 2d 520. See **process**. In civil actions, the right to compulsory process is often secured through state constitutional or statutory provisions. 97 C.J.S. Wit-nesses §3. State constitutions and stat-utes may also provide this right to legis-lative or administrative bodies conduct-ing **hearings** or investigations. 133 N.E. 2d 104; 118 F. 2d 8. In any criminal proceeding, this right is guaranteed the defendant by the 6th Amendment to the United States Constitution. See 388 U.S. 14. Defendant must exercise this right, i.e., request the attendance of witnesses, reasonably and diligently, especially where their attendance is sought to be secured at government expense. See 224 F. 2d 801; the constitutional right extends, however, as reasonably necessary throughout the trial. 257 P. 385. It may be asserted only with respect to competent, **material witnesses** subject to the court's process whose expected testimony will be admissible. 97 C.J.S. Witnesses §9.

CONCERTED ACTION [CONCERT OF ACTION] "action which has been planned, arranged, adjusted, agreed upon, and settled between parties acting together, in pursuance of some design or in accordance with some scheme." 416 F. 2d 857, 860. Thus, in the criminal law, concerted action is found only where there has been a **conspiracy** to commit an illegal act, i.e., all must share the criminal intent of the actual perpetrator. 6 S.E. 2d 647, 649. The term also applies to joint **tort-feasors** where there is tort liability for conspiracy. See Prosser, Torts §46 (4th ed. 1971).

CONCLUSION OF FACT conclusion reached solely through use of facts and natural reasoning, without resort to rules of law; inferences from evidentiary facts. 22 P. 2d 819, 822.

CONCLUSION OF LAW conclusion reached through application of rules of law. "Where the ultimate conclusion can be arrived at only by applying a rule of law, the result so reached embodies a conclusion of law, and is not a finding of fact." 229 N.W. 194, 197.

CONCLUSIVE PRESUMPTION see **presumption**.

CONCUR to agree. A concurring opinion states agreement with the conclusion of the **majority**, but may state different reasons why such conclusion is reached. An opinion "concurring in the result only" is one which implies no agreement with the reasoning of the prevailing opinion, but which fails to state reasons of its own. Compare **dissent**.

CONCURRENT to run together, in conjunction with; to exist together. "The words, 'concurrent' [or] 'consecutive' . . . are generally used to indicate the intention of the Court. . . . When used in ordinary legal parlance and especially

as adapted to **judgments** in criminal cases, the opposite of concurrent is consecutive and accumulative. If the sentences are not concurrent they are consecutive, and accumulative, and they are to be served in their numerical order." 122 F. 2d 85, 87. In many jurisdictions the presumption is that multiple sentences imposed at the same time upon the same defendant by a court are concurrent unless the court otherwise directs. See 100 F. 2d 280. See **sentence** (CONCURRENT SENTENCE).

CONCURRENT CONDITION see **condition**.

CONCURRENT COVENANTS see **covenant**.

CONCURRENT JURISDICTION see **jurisdiction**.

CONCURRENT NEGLIGENCE see **negligence**.

CONCURRING OPINION see **opinion**.

CONDEMN to declare as legally useless or unfit for habitation as when an unsafe building is condemned and demolished; as to land, a taking of private property for public use such as building a highway which raises a duty of **just compensation** under the laws governing **eminent domain**. Also to sentence one to death upon conviction of a **capital offense**.

CONDITION "the equivalent of 'requisite' or 'requirement.' In legal signification, the term 'condition' denotes something attached to and made a part of a grant or privilege." 67 N.E. 2d 439, 442. A condition is a possible future event, the occurrence of which will trigger the **performance** of a legal obligation.

In the law of contracts, conditions may be precedent, subsequent, or concurrent. A CONDITION PRECEDENT is a fact (act or event) which must exist or occur before a duty of immediate performance of a promise arises. Restatement, Contracts §250(a). A CONDITION SUBSEQUENT is a fact which will extinguish a duty to make compensation for **breach of contract** after the breach has occurred. Id. at §250(b). A CON-CURRENT CONDITION is a condition precedent which exists only when parties to a contract are found to render performance at the same time. Id. at §251. Real property interests can be affected by like conditions. See **determinable fee**; **estate**; **fee simple conditional**.

CONDITIONAL dependent upon the happening or non-happening of the **condition**; implies a type of **encumbrance**.

CONDITIONAL BEQUEST see **bequest**.

CONDITIONAL CONTRACT see **contract**.

CONDITIONAL FEE [ESTATE] a fee simple [complete ownership of **real property**] which is limited in that it must eventually pass from the **donee** to certain **heirs** or the **issue** [children] of the donee [**heirs of the body**]. 194 S.E. 817. Should the designated heir fail to be in existence at the time of the death of the donee, the property **reverts** [goes back] to the donor or his **estate**. However, the entire estate rests with the donee until his death, the donor having the mere **possibility of reverter**. Such a reverter may be released to the donee, thereby converting his estate from a fee simple conditional to a fee simple absolute. 275 P. 45, 52. See also **determinable fee**; **defeasible fee**; **life estate**.

CONDITION PRECEDENT see **condition**.

CONDITION SUBSEQUENT see **condition**.

CONDOMINIUM "a system of separate ownership of individual units in multi-unit projects. . . . In addition to the interest acquired in a particular unit, each unit owner is also a **tenant in common** in the underlying **fee** and in the spaces and building parts used in common by all the unit owners," such as elevators. Rohan & Reskin, 1 Condominium Law and Practice §1.01(1). A condominium is distinguished from a COOPERATIVE, which consists of "a **corporate** or business **trust** entity holding **title** to the **premises** and granting rights of occupancy to particular apartments by

means of proprietary **leases** or similar arrangements." Id. at §1.01(2).

CONFESSION an admission of guilt or other incriminating statement made by the **accused**; not admissible against the **defendant** at his **trial** unless the state demonstrates that it was voluntarily made and, if applicable, consistent with the **Miranda** doctrine. The voluntariness of the confession must be established at least by a **preponderance of the evidence**, 404 U.S. 477, 489; and in some jurisdictions must be **beyond a reasonable doubt**. Id. at n. 1.

CONFESSION AND AVOIDANCE pleading by which a **party** admits the **allegations** against him, either expressly or by implication, but which presents **new matter** which **avoids** the effect of the failure to deny those allegations. Thus, a litigant "confesses," rather than denies, the allegation, but his presentation of new matter acts to "avoid" a **judgment** against him. See Stephen, Pleading 230, 233 (Williston ed. 1895).

CONFESSION OF JUDGMENT entry of a judgment upon a written **admission** or **confession** of the **debtor** without the formality, time or expense of an ordinary legal **proceeding**. 105 N.W. 698, 701. It is accomplished through an advance, voluntary submission to the **jurisdiction** of the court as when a buyer of goods on **credit** agrees in his purchase **contract** that if he fails to pay the amounts due timely that he will consent to the entry of a judgment against him for the amount outstanding (and often reasonable **attorney's fees** not exceeding a fixed percentage [commonly 20%]). A judgment entered upon an attorney's **affidavit** that his client owes the **plaintiff** the sum **pleaded** in the lawsuit and consents to the entry of a judgment for that amount. These procedures are now regulated and often prohibited by statute because of their coercive effect on debtors and because of the potential for abuses. The confession of judgment procedures may also offend **due process**. See 407 U.S. 67, 94.

CONFIDENCE GAME "[a]ny scheme whereby a swindler wins the confidence of his victim and then cheats him out of his money by taking advantage of the confidence reposed in him." 95 N.E. 2d

80, 83. The elements of the crime of the confidence game are "(1) an intentional false representation to the victim as to some present fact . . . (2) knowing it to be false . . . (3) with the intent that the victim rely on the representation . . . (4) the representation being made to obtain the victim's confidence . . . and thereafter his money and property." 304 A. 2d 260, 275.

CONFISCATE to take private property without **just compensation**; to transfer property from a private use to a public use. See also **condemn.**

CONFLICT OF LAWS [CHOICE OF LAW] that body of law by which the court in which the **action** is maintained determines or chooses which law to apply where a diversity exists between the applicable law of that court's state [the forum state] and the applicable law of another jurisdiction interested in the controversy. The considerations comprising that decison formerly rested on simple and traditional rules such as LEX LOCI CONTRACTUS or place of making a contract, and LEX LOCI DELICTI or place of the wrong in tort. More modern doctrine focuses on an interest analysis which very often arrives at the same choice but includes, along with the traditional considerations of place of contracting and place of the wrong, the public policy of the forum and in general which jurisdiction maintains the most significant relationship or contacts with the subject matter of the controversy. The "interest analysis" is referred to as CENTER OF GRAVITY or CONTACTS APPROACH. As a general rule the forum state will apply its own law on questions of **procedure** regardless of a "conflict."

A federal court must follow the choice of laws principles of the forum state. See 313 U.S. 487. Where a controversy has been reduced to a judgment in the courts of one of the United States, the choice of laws principles employed cannot be challenged in another state of the United States unless the **full faith and credit** doctrine would permit a challenge. See also **comity; forum non conveniens.**

CONFUSION OF GOODS "results when **personal property** belonging to two or more owners becomes intermixed to the point when the property of any of them no longer can be identified except as part of a mass of like goods." 264 P. 2d 283.

CONGLOMERATE a group of **corporations** engaged in unrelated businesses which are controlled by a single corporate entity. "The term conglomerate . . . describes a company that controls a group of other companies engaged in unrelated businesses. . . ." 339 N.Y.S. 2d 347, 348.

A **merger** of corporations into a single conglomerate, standing alone, does not violate the antimonopoly sections of the federal **antitrust** laws. The reason for this is that there were no economic relationships between the acquiring and acquired corporations and hence there is no lessening of competition in any relevant market. See 386 U.S. 568, 577; and 258 F. Supp. 36, 56.

CONJUGAL RIGHTS the rights of married persons which include "the enjoyment of association, sympathy, confidence, domestic happiness, the comforts of dwelling together in the same habitation, eating meals at the same table, and profiting by the joint property rights, as well as the intimacies of domestic relations." 286 P. 747. In the prison setting, a CONJUGAL VISITATION permits sexual intercourse between the inmate and his spouse. See Hopper, Sex in Prison (1969). See also **consortium.**

CONJUNCTIVE DENIAL see **denial.**

CONSCIOUS PARALLELISM knowledge that a particular course of conduct has been followed by a competitor combined with an independent decision by another party to follow the same course of conduct; it is distinguished from **conspiracy,** which requires an agreement, either tacit or express, between the parties engaged in the parallel conduct. See 346 U.S. 537, 540-41.

Conscious parallelism alone is not a violation of the **anti-trust statutes.** See 75 Harv. L. Rev. 655 (1962). Evidence of such consciously parallel conduct, however, is highly probative on the issue of whether an actual conspiracy did exist. See 306 U.S. 208.

CONSENT DECREE see **decree.**

CONSENT, INFORMED see **informed consent.**

CONSEQUENTIAL DAMAGES see **damages**.

CONSERVATOR temporary court-appointed guardian or custodian of **property**. 223 P. 2d 1039, 1041.

CONSIDERATION something of value given in return for a performance or a promise of performance by another, for the purpose of forming a **contract**; one element of a contract that is generally required to make a promise binding and to make the agreement of the parties enforceable as a contract. To find consideration there must be a performance or a return promise which has been bargained for by the parties. Restatement, Contracts 2d §75 (Tent. Draft No. 2 1965). Consideration represents the element of bargaining to indicate that each party agrees to surrender something in return for what it is to receive. It is consideration which distinguishes a contract from a mere **gift**.

Courts have used the word "consideration" with many different meanings. "It is often used merely to express the legal conclusion that a promise is enforceable. Historically, its primary meaning may have been that the conditions were met under which an action of **assumpsit** [an early form of contract action] would lie. It was also used as the equivalent of the **quid pro quo** required in an action of **debt**. A **seal**, it has been said, 'imports a consideration,' although the law was clear that no element of bargain was necessary to enforcement of a promise under seal. On the other hand, consideration has sometimes been used to refer to almost any reason asserted for enforcing a promise, even though the reason was insufficient [as in] promises 'in consideration of love and affection,' 'illegal consideration,' 'past consideration,' and consideration furnished by reliance on a gratuitous promise" where in fact there has been no consideration at all. Id. at Comment A.

The phrase SUFFICIENT CONSIDERATION is used by some courts to express the legal conclusion that one requirement for an enforceable bargain has been met. This is redundant and misleading, however, since any performance or return promise which has been bargained for and received is legally sufficient to satisfy the consideration element of a contract. Other unneces-

sary qualifications to the word consideration include LEGAL CONSIDERATION and VALUABLE CONSIDERATION. The law will not in general inquire into the adequacy of "consideration" and hence these terms do not add anything of substance to the phrase consideration. So long as the bargained for promise is not **illusory** or the performance a sham pretext, a sufficient exchange will have taken place to justify the enforcement of the agreement so far as consideration is at issue.

The performance may be any lawful act done for the benefit of the other contracting party or a third person and may include an act of forebearance. A MORAL CONSIDERATION will not generally qualify as consideration so as to render the promise enforceable unless the promise is "made in recognition of a benefit previously received by the promisor from the promisee" in which instances it is "binding to the extent necessary to prevent injustice." Id. §89A(1).

FAILURE OF CONSIDERATION refers to the circumstance in which consideration was bargained for but has either become worthless, has ceased to exist, or has not been performed as promised. Failure of Consideration may be partial or total. The Term is often used interchangeably with WANT OF CONSIDERATION.

CONSIDERED DICTUM see **dictum**.

CONSOLIDATION see **merger**.

CONSORTIUM "the conjugal fellowship of husband and wife, and the right of each to the company, cooperation and aid of the other in every conjugal relation." 134 Mass. 123. Where a person willfully interferes with this relation, he deprives one spouse of the consortium of the other, and is liable in damages. 119 S.E. 222. Purposeful interference with consortium may give rise to an action for **alienation of affection**, more generally, loss of consortium often figures in the award of damages in a **tort** action for injury or **wrongful death** of a spouse.

CONSPIRACY "a combination of two or more persons to commit a criminal or unlawful act, or to commit a lawful act by criminal or unlawful means; or a combination of two or more persons by concerted action to accomplish an unlawful purpose, or some purpose not in itself unlawful by unlawful means. It is essential that there be two or more conspirators; one cannot conspire with himself.' 314 P. 2d 625, 631. A conspiracy to injure another is an actionable **tort**; it may also be a criminal offense if the object of the conspiracy is within the reach of the definition of criminal conspiracy in the particular jurisdiction. Compare **accessory; accomplice; aid and abet.**

CONSPIRATOR one involved in a **conspiracy**; one who acts with another, or others, in furtherance of an unlawful transaction. "It is not necessary that all of the conspirators either meet together or agree simultaneously. . . . It is not necessary that each member of a conspiracy know the exact part which every other participant is playing; nor is it necessary in order to be bound by the acts of his associates that each member of a conspiracy shall know all the other participants therein; nor is it requisite that simultaneous action be had for those who come on later, and cooperate in the common effort to obtain the unlawful results, to become parties thereto and assume responsibility for all that has been done before." 47 F. Supp. 395, 400-01. According to the Model Penal Code, a conspirator is one who, with another person or persons with the purpose of promoting or facilitating the commission of a crime "a) agrees with such other person or persons that they or one or more of them will engage in conduct which constitutes such crime or an **attempt** or **solicitation** to commit such crime; or b) agrees to **aid** such other person or persons in the planning or commission of such crime or an attempt or solicitation to commit such crime." Model Penal Code 5.03 (Approved Draft 1962).

CONSTRUCTION the giving of an interpretation to something, which thing is less than totally clear, e.g., to determine the construction of a statute or **constitution** is to determine the meaning of an ambiguous part of it; to give a coherent meaning to; the act of CONSTRUING.

STRICT CONSTRUCTION conservative interpretation of statutes stressing rigid adherence to the terms specified. A conservative or literal interpretation of a constitution is referred to as "strict construction." See also **strict construction.**

CONSTRUCTIVE not actual, but accepted in law as a substitute for whatever is otherwise required. Thus, anything which the law finds to exist "constructively" will be treated by the law as thought it were actually so. If an object is not in one's actual possession but he intentionally and knowingly has dominion and control over it, the law will treat it as though it were in his actual possession by finding a constructive possession. The same is true in many other contexts.
[For the meaning of "constructive" as applied to various legal concepts, refer to specific entries.]

CONSTRUCTIVE CONTEMPT see **contempt of court.**

CONSTRUCTIVE DELIVERY see **delivery.**

CONSTRUCTIVE EVICTION see **eviction.**

CONSTRUCTIVE FRAUD see **fraud.**

CONTACTS APPROACH see **conflict of laws.**

CONTEMPT OF COURT an act or omission tending to obstruct or interfere with the orderly administration of justice, or to impair the dignity of the court or respect for its authority. There are two kinds, direct and constructive. 249 S. 2d 127, 128. DIRECT CONTEMPT openly and in the presence of the court, resists the power of the court, 102 A. 400, 406; and consequential, or CONSTRUCTIVE CONTEMPT results from matters outside the court, such as failure to comply with orders. 114 P. 257, 258.
Another classification differentiates between civil and criminal contempt. CIVIL CONTEMPT consists of failure to do something which is ordered by the court for the benefit of another party to the proceedings (sometimes called RELIEF TO LITIGANTS), while CRIMINAL CONTEMPTS are acts in disrespect of the courts or its processes which obstruct the administration of justice. 199 S.W. 2d 613, 614.

The penalty for civil contempt is usually payment of a fine, or imprisonment for an indefinite period of time until the party in contempt agrees to perform his legal obligation, unless the imprisonment clearly fails to act as coercion and acts merely to punish; 65 N.J. 257. The penalty for criminal contempt is a fine or imprisonment for a specific period of time, intended as punishment which must be tried by a jury if post-conviction contempt proceedings impose sentences exceeding an aggregate of six months. 94 S. Ct. 2687.

CONTIGUOUS near to or in close proximity to. 78 N.W. 2d 86, 91.

CONTINGENT ESTATE an **interest** in land which may begin at some point in the future, but which may never begin, depending upon the occurrence of a specific but uncertain event or depending on the determination or existence of the person(s) to whom the estate is limited, see 260 S.W. 357, 359; e.g., if property is granted "to A for life and then to the heirs of B," there is a contingent estate (a "contingent **remainder**") in the heirs of B, which will **vest** [become certain] at the death of A unless B is without heirs. If B is without heirs, the estate **reverts** [goes back] to the original **grantor**. Because a contingent estate was regarded as a mere possibility or expectancy it was not **alienable inter vivos** [transferable during one's lifetime] at common law. Contingent remainders were made alienable in England in 1845 and are freely alienable today in the majority of American jurisdictions. Moynihan, Introduction to the Law of Real Property 135-137 (1962). Compare **conditional fee; defeasible fee; determinable fee**. See also **condition; future interest**.

CONTINGENT FEE see **attorney's fee**.

CONTINUANCE the adjournment or postponement to a subsequent date of an **action** pending in a court. 257 A. 2d 705, 709.

CONTRA *(kôn'-trà)*—Lat: against; in opposition to; in answer to, in reply to; contrary to; in violation of; the reverse of; in defiance of. Thus, "the Court's most recent decision is contra an established line of **precedent**."

CONTRA BONOS MORES *(kôn'-trà bō'-nōs mô'rāz)*—Lat: against good morals; "conduct of such character as to offend the average conscience, as involving injustice according to commonly accepted standards." 231 F. 950, 969.

CONTRACT a promise, or set of promises, for **breach** of which the law gives a **remedy**, or the performance of which the law in some way recognizes as a **duty**. 1 Williston, Contracts §1. The essentials of a valid contract are "parties **competent** to contract, a proper subject-matter, **consideration**, **mutuality** of agreement, and mutuality of obligation," 286 N.W. 844, 846; "a transaction involving two or more individuals whereby each becomes obligated to the other, with reciprocal rights to demand performance of what is promised by each respectively." 282 P. 2d 1084, 1088. "The total legal obligation which results from the parties' agreement as affected by law." U.C.C. §1-201 (11). Types of contracts include:

BILATERAL CONTRACT one in which there are mutual promises between two parties to the contract, each party being both a **promisor** and a **promisee**. Restatement, Contracts §12.

COST-PLUS CONTRACT "one where the total cost to the contractor represents the whole payment to be made to him, plus a stated percentage of profit," 59 N.W. 2d 368, 370; frequently used in government contracts. See, e.g., 139 F. 2d 661, 667; 144 F. 2d 207, 208.

ORAL CONTRACT one which is not in writing or which is not signed by the parties; "within the **statute of frauds** [it] is a real existing contract which lacks only the formal requirement of a memorandum [signed by the party to be charged] to render it enforceable in **litigation**." 84 N.E. 2d 466, 467.

OUTPUT CONTRACT where one promises to deliver his entire output to another and the other promises to accept the entire output supplied.

REQUIREMENTS CONTRACT where one party agrees to purchase all his requirements of a particular product from another. See 276 F. 2d 1; U.C.C. §2-306.

UNILATERAL CONTRACT one in which

no promisor receives a promise as consideration for his promise, Restatement, Contracts §12; one-sided agreement whereby one makes a promise to do, or refrain from doing something in return for a performance not a promise.

See also **adhesion contract; breach of contract.**

CONTRACT OF ADHESION see **adhesion contract.**

CONTRACTOR one who is a party to a contract; also one who contracts to do the work for another. An INDEPENDENT CONTRACTOR is "one who makes an agreement with another to do a piece of work, retaining in himself control of the means, method and manner of producing the result to be accomplished, neither party having the right to terminate the contract at will." 45 N.E. 2d 342, 345. A GENERAL CONTRACTOR in a building contract context is one who contracts directly with the owner of the property upon which the construction occurs, as distinguished from a **subcontractor** who would only deal with one of the general contractors. It is not necessary that the individual perform the entire construction involved. See 66 Va. 509, 511.

CONTRACTUAL BREACH see **breach of contract.**

CONTRACT UNDER SEAL see **sealed instrument.**

CONTRA PACEM *(kôn'-trà pä'-kĕm)*— Lat: against the peace. This phrase was used in the Latin forms of **indictments,** and also in **actions** for **trespass** as a signification that the offense alleged was committed against the public peace. Modern **pleading** uses the phrase "against the peace of the commonwealth," "of the people," etc.

CONTRIBUTION a right to demand another person jointly responsible for an injury to another to contribute to the one required to compensate the victim. Equal sharing of a common burden. In the law of torts, a right of contribution exists, if at all, generally by statutes although some courts have upheld the right of contribution upon "the broad equitable principal that persons who are equals in the duty of bearing a common burden may be compelled by their associates to bear their share of that burden." 34 F. Supp. 77, 80. The duty generally involves an equal sharing of the loss but in some jurisdictions it may be apportioned among the **joint tortfeasors** according to their degrees of relative fault. See, e.g., 114 N.W. 2d 105. Compare **indemnity.**

CONTRIBUTORY NEGLIGENCE see **negligence.**

CONTROVERSY a dispute; occurs when there are adversaries on a particular **issue;** an **allegation** on one side and a **denial** on the other. In constitutional law, in order to constitute a CASE OR CONTROVERSY sufficient to permit a constitutional **adjudication** within the limits of Article III of the United States Constitution, a controversy "must be definite and concrete, touching the legal relations of parties having adverse legal interests. . . . It must be a real and substantial controversy admitting of **specific relief** through a decree of a conclusive character, as distinguished from an option advising what the law would be upon a hypothetical state of facts." 300 U.S. 227, 240-41. Compare **advisory opinion.** See also **justiciable.**

CONTUMACY willful disobedience to the **summons** or orders of a court; signifies overt defiance of authority. 133 N.E. 2d 796, 800. Contumacious conduct may result in a finding of contempt of court.

CONVERSION the **tortious** deprivation of another's property without his authorization or **justification.** "To constitute a 'conversion' there must be a wrongful taking, or a wrongful detention, or an illegal assumption of ownership, or an illegal [use or misuse]. . . . A 'conversion' in the sense of the law of **trover** consists either in **appropriation** of a thing to the party's own use and beneficial enjoyment, or in destruction, or in exercising dominion over it, in exclusion or defiance of plaintiff's right, or in withholding **possession** from plaintiff under **claim of title** inconsistent with his own." 339 F. Supp. 506, 511.

CONVEY in the law of **real property,** to transfer property from one to another; in its widest sense, it means the "transfer of property or the **title** to property from one person to another by means of a written **instrument** and other formalities." 47 S.E. 784, 787. Compare **alienation**. See also **grant**.

CONVICT one who has been determined by the court to be guilty of the crime charged; also, so to determine such guilt. "As ordinarily used, [the term] carries with it the idea that the person of whom it is spoken is **guilty** of a crime of such infamous character as to be punishable by imprisonment . . . and therefore is to be taken **prima facie** as importing guilt of such crime and imprisonment in consequence." 32 A. 19. One is convicted upon a valid plea of guilty or a verdict of guilty and judgment of conviction entered thereupon.

COOPERATIVE see **condominium**.

COOPERATIVE ASSOCIATION a "union of individuals, commonly laborers, farmers, or small capitalists, formed for the prosecution in common of some productive enterprise, the profits being shared in accordance with the capital or labor contributed by each." 164 N.W. 804, 805.

CO-ORDINATE JURISDICTION see **jurisdiction** [CONCURRENT JURISDICTION].

COPARCENERS persons who, by virtue of **descent**, have become concurrent owners. 3 Holdsworth, History of English Law 126-8. See **parcener**. See also **co-heir; joint tenancy; tenancy in common**.

COPARTNER see **partner**.

COPYRIGHT the protection by **statute** or by the **common law** of the works of artists and authors giving them exclusive right to publish their works or to determine who may so publish; when by statute, it is exclusively a matter of federal law, and exists for a limited period of time, presently 28 years, with a renewal available for an additional 28 years. 17 U.S.C. §24.

As to written work, copyright is said to extend "only to the arrangement of words. A copyright does not give a monopoly in any incident in a play. Other authors have a right to exploit the facts, experiences, and field of thought and general ideas, provided they do not substantially copy a concrete form, in which the circumstances and ideas have been developed, arranged, and put into shape." 133 F. 2d 889, 891.

COMMON LAW COPYRIGHT exists before a work is published or otherwise placed in the public domain and protects against unauthorized publication of the unpublished work. This is also called the RIGHT OF FIRST PUBLICATION. 39 N.E. 2d 249.

COPYRIGHT INFRINGEMENT action seeking **damages** and other relief against an unauthorized use of the work.

CORAM NOBIS, WRIT OF see **writ of coram nobis.**

CORONER a public official who investigates the causes and circumstances of deaths that occur within his jurisdiction and makes a finding in a CORONER'S INQUEST. See also **post mortem.**

CORPORAL PUNISHMENT p u n i s h-ment inflicted upon the body, such as whipping. 69 F. 2d 905. The term may or may not include imprisonment. Id. Thus it often serves simply to distinguish physical punishment from non-physical punishment, such as a fine. See 43 P. 1026. Whipping has been found to violate contemporary standards of civilized conduct, and thus to be prohibited by the 8th Amendment's ban on "cruel and unusual punishment," whether administered pursuant to a **sentence** or in the course of prison discipline. 404 F. 2d 571.

CORPORATION an association of **shareholders** (or even a single shareholder) created under law and regarded as an ARTIFICIAL PERSON by courts, "having a legal entity entirely separate and distinct from the individuals who compose it, with the capacity of continuous existence or **succession**, and having the capacity as such legal entity, of taking, holding and conveying **property**, suing and being sued, and exercising such other powers as may be conferred on it by law, just as a **natural person** may." 200 N.W. 76, 87.

A corporation's **liability** is normally limited to its **assets** and the **stockholders** are thus protected against personal liability in connection with the affairs of the corporation. [But see **piercing the corporate veil**.] The corporation is taxed at special corporate tax rates and the stockholders must pay an additional tax upon **dividends** or other profits obtained from the corporation. Corporations are subject to regulation by the state of incorporation and by the jurisdictions in which they carry on their business. State laws in some jurisdictions give the corporate board of directors and officers more freedom from stockholder consent and scrutiny than other states and thereby induced many corporations to form within their jurisdictions. Delaware is the leading example. Special statutes have been enacted in many jurisdictions to permit single individuals or closely-knit groups of individuals to form corporations to limit their personal liability but to carry on business without all of the formality of annual meetings, action by boards of directors, etc. These corporations are called CLOSE CORPORATIONS. They generally have only a single or a very small number of stockholders. See, Henn, Law of Corporations 401 (1961).

A small corporation earning limited amounts of money may elect to be taxed as an ordinary **partnership** and its individual stockholders thus enjoy limited personal liability and only individual (and not also corporate) taxation. A corporation electing to be so treated for federal income taxation purposes is called a SUB-CHAPTER S CORPORATION. Id., at 39.

DE FACTO CORPORATION one existing **de facto**, i.e., without actual authority of law. Three elements of de facto corporations are: the existence of a statute under which the corporation might have been validly incorporated; a **colorable** attempt to comply with such statute; and some use or exercise of corporate privileges. Henn, Law of Corporations 240 (1961).

PUBLIC CORPORATIONS [POLITICAL CORPORATIONS] those created by the state to fulfill certain purposes, such as lesser governmental bodies (towns, cities), school districts, water districts. The United States Post Office is now a public corporation (called United States Postal Service). 39 U.S.C. §201 (1974).

PRIVATE CORPORATIONS the common corporation, created by and for private individuals for non-governmental purposes.

QUASI CORPORATION a body which exercises certain functions of a corporate character, but which has not been established as a corporation by any statute, general or special. 103 U.S. 707, 708. See **quasi**.

CORPOREAL HEREDITAMENT see **hereditament**.

CORPUS DELICTI *(kôr'-pŭs dĕ-lĭk'-tī)*— Lat: body of the crime. It is the objective proof that a crime has been committed. It is sometimes thought of mistakenly as the body of the victim of a **homicide**, but correctly understood, a corpus delicti in a **murder prosecution** is a "**prima facie** showing that the alleged victim met death by a criminal agency." 323 P. 2d 117, 123. The body of the victim is often helpful in this regard, and in the absence of the victim's body, it is frequently very difficult to establish either that the victim is dead or that he died by a criminal agency. In such instances the corpus delicti must be established to a **moral certainty**. See [1955] 1 Q.B. 388.

Corpus delicti applies to every crime. In order for the state to introduce a **confession** or convict the **accused** it must prove a corpus delicti, the elements of which are "first, the occurrence of the specific kind of injury or loss (as, in homicide, a person deceased); [and] secondly, somebody's criminality (in contrast, e.g., to mere accident) as the source of the loss. These two together [involve] the commission of a crime by somebody." 7 Wigmore, Evidence §2072 (3rd ed. 1940). Only a prima facie showing of the corpus delicti is necessary to admit a confession. 323 P. 2d 117, 123. **Proof beyond a reasonable doubt** is necessary if the corpus delicti is used to refer to all of the elements of the crime charged. 247 P. 2d 665.

CORPUS JURIS *(kôr'-pŭs jûr'-ĭs)*–Lat: body of law. Refers to a series of texts which contained much of the **civil,** as well as **canon [ecclesiastical]** law.

CORRUPTION OF BLOOD incapacity to **inherit** or pass **property**, usually because of **attainder**, such as for treason; "the doctrine of corruption of blood was of feudal origin ... the blood of the attainted person was deemed to be corrupt, so that neither could he transmit his **estate** to his **heirs**, nor could they take by **descent** from the ancestor." 18 N.E. 148, 150.

COST-PLUS CONTRACT see **contract**.

COST OF COMPLETION in a **breach of contract** situation, a measure of damages representing the total amount of additional expense, over and above the **contract** price, that the injured party would have to incur in order to obtain a substituted **performance** that would place him in the same position he would have been in if the contract had not been breached. See 212 N.Y.S. 222, 226; and 187 N.Y.S. 807, 813; often used as a measure of damages for breaches of construction contracts. Compare **diminution in value; expectation damages; specific performance**.

COSTS TO ABIDE THE EVENT court order requiring the losing party to pay for legal expenses of the prevailing party "up to and including the decision of the **court of appeals**," 200 N.Y.S. 796, 797, and sometimes on retrial.

COTENANCY possession of a unit of property by two or more persons; does not refer to an **estate**, but rather a relationship between persons as to their **holding** of property; encompasses both **tenancy in common** and **joint tenancy** [and thus, **tenancy by the entirety** as well].

COUNT a distinct statement of **plaintiff's cause of action**. See 126 F. Supp. 395, 397. In **indictments**, a count, like a **charge**, is an **allegation** of a distinct offense. See 167 S.W. 2d 192, 193. A complaint or indictment may contain one or more counts.

COUNTERCLAIM a counter-demand made by **defendant** in his favor against the **plaintiff**. It is not a mere **answer** or **denial** of plaintiff's allegations, but rather asserts an independent **cause of action**, 275 N.E. 2d 688, 690, the purpose of which is to oppose or deduct from plaintiff's claim. 16 F.R.D. 225, 228.

In federal practice, counterclaim may be either: "compulsory"—"those arising out of the transaction or occurrence that is the subject matter of the opposing party's claim," Green, Civil Procedure 71 (1972); or "permissive"—any other, i.e., those not arising out of the present claim. See **set-off**. Compare **cross-claim**.

COUNTERFEIT "[f]orged; false, fabricated without right; made in imitation of something else with a view to defraud by passing the false copy for genuine or original," 197 F. Supp. 264, 265; e.g., counterfeit coins, paper money, bonds, deeds, stocks, etc.

COURT-MARTIAL "a military or naval tribunal which has jurisdiction of offenses against the law of the service, military or naval, in which the offender is engaged." 6 C.J.S. Army and Navy §51.

In order for a crime to be subject to court-martial rather than civilian criminal proceedings, it is not enough that the accused has military "status;" the crime itself must be "service - connected;" thus, a soldier on an evening pass is not subject to discipline by a court-martial for attempted rape or burglary while away from his base, but must be prosecuted under civilian authority. 395 U.S. 258.

The Uniform Code for Military Justice, Chapter 47 (see 10 U.S.C. §816-820) establishes three kinds of court-martial in each of the armed forces:

GENERAL COURT-MARTIAL presided over by a law officer and not less than five members, has jurisdiction over all members of the armed services of which it is a part, and is authorized to try defendants for all military offenses, and to prescribe any permitted sanctions.

SPECIAL COURT-MARTIAL presided over by three members, may try all non-capital offenses, but is limited in its authority to prescribe sanctions as dismissal, hard labor, and extended confinement, and may not authorize execution.

SUMMARY COURT-MARTIAL presided over by a single commissioned officer, and is limited in respect to the military personnel over whom it has jurisdiction and the sanctions it may prescribe. The accused may refuse trial by a summary court-martial, but the charges may then be referred to a higher level court-martial.

COURT OF APPEALS see **appellate court.**

COURT OF ASSIZE AND NISI PRIUS in English law courts, "composed of two or more commissioners, who [were] twice in every year sent by the king's special commission all around the kingdom to try by jury cases under their jurisdiction." See 3 Bl. Comm.*58,*59.

COURT OF CLAIMS refers to the court of the United States created in 1855, by an act of Congress, to "bear and determine all claims founded upon any law of Congress, or upon any regulation of an executive department, or upon any contract, express or implied, with the government of the United States, which may be suggested to it by a petition filed therein; and also all claims which may be referred to said court by either House of Congress." 10 Stat. 612. It has no power over matters in **equity.** 33rd Congress, Session II, Ch. 122 (1855).

COURT OF CUSTOMS AND PATENT APPEALS see **federal courts.**

COURT OF EQUITY "a court having jurisdiction in cases where a plain, adequate and complete remedy cannot be had at **law.**" 3 N.Y. 498, 499. Courts of equity were common law courts but had their own principles (e.g., **clean hands doctrine**) and their own unique remedies (e.g., **injunction, specific performance**). Actions were brought either equitably "in **chancery**" or legally "at law." Courts which are guided primarily by equitable doctrine are said to be courts of equity. Thus, a **bankruptcy** court is a court of equity. "A court of equity is a court of conscience, and whatever, therefore, is unconscionable is odious in its sight." 47 A. 693, 695. Courts of equity, which arose independently of courts of law in England, have merged with the latter in most jurisdictions of the United States. See **equity.**

COURT OF KING'S [QUEEN'S] BENCH see **King's Bench.**

COURT OF STAR CHAMBER see **Star Chamber.**

COVENANT an agreement or promise to do or not to do a particular thing; to enter into a formal agreement; to **bind** oneself in **contract**; to make a stipulation; a promise incidental to a **deed** or contract, which is either express or implied; "an agreement, convention or promise of two or more parties, by deed in writing signed, and delivered, by whichever of the parties pledges himself to the order that something is either done or shall be done or stipulates for the truth of certain facts." 279 P. 2d 276, 278.

DEPENDENT COVENANTS those in which the obligation to perform one covenant arises only upon the prior **performance** of another and therefore, until the prior **condition** of performance has been met, the other party is not liable to an **action** on his covenant.

CONCURRENT COVENANTS those which require the performance by one party of his obligation when the other party is ready and offers his performance.

INDEPENDENT [MUTUAL] COVENANTS those which must be performed by one party without reference to the obligations of the other party. See 125 F. 536, 541.

In deeds, the usual covenants for **title** include:

COVENANTS OF SEISIN AND RIGHT TO CONVEY covenant that the **grantor** has an **estate,** or the right to **convey** an estate, of the quality and quantity which he purports to convey.

COVENANT AGAINST ENCUMBRANCES a guarantee given to the **grantee** of an estate that such estate is without **encumbrances.**

COVENANT OF WARRANTY AND QUIET ENJOYMENT obligates the **covenantor** to protect the estate against the existence of lawful claims of ownership. A cause of action arises only when there is an actual or constructive **eviction.**

COVENANT OF FURTHER ASSURANCE obligates the covenantor to perform whatever acts are reasonably demanded by the covenantee for the purpose of perfecting or "assuring" the title which is conveyed. See Burby, Real Property §125 (3rd ed. 1965). This type of covenant 'is no longer in general use.

COVENANT AGAINST THE ACTS OF THE GRANTOR often inserted into a **bar-**

gain and sale deed and assures that the grantor has not done, nor caused to be done, any act by means of which the premises or any part thereof may be impeached or encumbered in any way. See 8 N.J.L. 90.

COVENANT OF QUIET ENJOYMENT see **quiet enjoyment**.

"Covenants such as **warranty,** quiet enjoyment, and further assurance are continuous in nature and may be enforced by a remote party. Other covenants, such as **seisin,** right to convey, and against encumbrances, are not continuous in nature and do not 'run with the land.'" Burby, Real Property 126 (3rd ed. 1965). See **warranty** (WARRANTY OF HABITABILITY, WARRANTY OF MERCHANTABILITY).

RESTRICTIVE COVENANT see **restrictive covenant**.

COVENANTEE one who receives the **covenant,** or for whom it is made.

COVENANTOR one who makes a **covenant**.

COVERTURE at common law, a married woman's legal condition; "a term used to describe the condition or state of a married woman whereby the civil existence of the wife was for many purposes merged with that of her husband." 327 S.W. 808, 811. "In England, and in all of the United States except the **community property** jurisdictions, statutes have been enacted which give a wife almost unlimited control over her **real** and **personal property**. Known as "Married Woman's Property Acts," these statutes generally provide that her property shall be wholly free from the husband's claims or control. Accordingly, they have the practical efect of abolishing the husband's estate by the marital right." 1 American Law of Property §5.56 (1952).

CREDIT that which is extended to a buyer or borrower on the seller or lender's belief that that which is given will be repaid. The term can be applied to unlimited types of transactions. Under the Uniform Commercial Code, any credit transaction creating a **security** interest in property is called a "secured transaction." U.C.C. Art. 9. In accounting, a credit is money owing and due

to one, and is considered an **asset**. The word is also used with respect to one's reputation or business standing in a given community. For example, a person with a healthy, profitable business who has always repaid debts in the past, will be considered a good "credit risk" by a prospective lender.

CREDITOR one to whom money is owed by the **debtor**; one to whom an obligation exists. "In its strict legal sense, [a creditor] is one who voluntarily trusts or gives credit to another for money or other property, but in its more general and extensive sense it is one who has a right by law to demand and recover of another a sum of money on any account whatever. 38 S.W. 13, 14.

CREDITOR'S BILL [OR SUIT] a **proceeding** in **equity** in which a **judgment creditor** [a creditor who has secured **judgment** against a **debtor** and whose **claim** has not been satisfied] attempts to gain a discovery, accounting, and deliverance of **property** owed to him by the **judgment debtor**, which property cannot be reached by execution [seizure and forced sale] at law. See 42 A. 2d 872, 875.

CRIME any act which the sovereign has deemed contrary to the public good; a wrong which the government has determined is injurious to the public and, hence, prosecutable in a **criminal proceeding**. Crimes include **felonies** and **misdemeanors**. A "common law crime" was one declared to be an offense by the developed case law method of the **common law** courts. Today, nearly all criminal offenses are statutory, as most jurisdictions either do not recognize common law crimes at all, or at least refuse to develop "new" offenses not punishable under the early common law. See 427 P. 2d 928; 1 Wheat. 415.

CRIME AGAINST NATURE associated with sexual deviations which were considered crimes at common law and have been carried over by statute; includes **sodomy** as well as **bestiality**.

CRIMEN FALSI (krĭ'-mĕn fäl'-sē)–Lat: literally, a **crime** of **deceit**. At **common law** a crimen falsi was a crime containing the elements of falsehood and **fraud**. See 141 N.E. 2d 202, 206. A person who had committed such a crime, which was described as one which "injuriously affects the administration of justice by the introduction of falsehood and fraud," was generally disqualified from appearing as a **witness** in any judicial **proceeding**. See 1 F. 784, 787 and 207 F. 327, 331. Examples of crimen falsi include **forgery; perjury; subornation of perjury;** suppression of testimony by, or **conspiracy** to procure the absence of, a **witness;** and the fraudulent making or alteration of a writing. See 5 A. 2d 804, 805.

CRIMINAL one who has been convicted of a violation of the criminal laws; also, an adjective which denotes "an act done with **malicious intent,** from an evil nature, or with a wrongful disposition to harm or injure other persons or property." 96 P. 2d 588, 591. After the criminal has satisfied whatever sanction has been imposed upon him, he is called today an EX-OFFENDER. An HABITUAL OFFENDER (or HABITUAL CRIMINAL) is a person convicted on numerous occasions of crime and who for that reason is subject to an extended term of imprisonment under the habitual offender laws of many jurisdictions. See **recidivist.**

CRIMINAL CODE see **code.**

CRIMINAL CONTEMPTS see **contempt of court.**

CRIMINAL CONVERSATION see **alienation of affections.**

CRIMINAL NEGLIGENCE see **negligence.**

CROSS-CLAIM claim **litigated** by co-**defendants** or co-**plaintiffs** against each other, and not against a party on the opposite side of the litigation. See 424 F. 2d 52, 55. Compare **counterclaim.**

CRUEL AND UNUSUAL PUNISHMENT such punishment as is found to be offensive to the ordinary person; Amendment VIII to the United States Constitution provides: "Excessive bail shall not be required, nor excessive fines imposed, nor cruel and unusual punishment inflicted." "The term cannot be defined with specificity. It is flexible and tends to broaden as society tends to pay more regard to human decency and dig-

nity and becomes . . . more humane. Generally speaking, a punishment that amounts to torture, or that is grossly excessive in proportion to the offense for which it is imposed, or that is inherently unfair, or that is shocking or disgusting to people of reasonable sensitivity is a 'cruel and unusual punishment.' And a punishment that is not inherently cruel and unusual may become so by reason of the manner in which it is inflicted," 309 F. Supp. 362, 380; ". . . [t]he beatings, physical abuse, torture, running of gauntlets, and similar cruelty—was wholly beyond any force needed to maintain order [in a prison]" and thus constituted cruel and unusual punishment. 453 F. 2d 12, 22. "Although lawful incarceration . . . deprives the prisoners of many rights enjoyed by others . . . they are still entitled to protection against cruel and unusual punishment by the Eighth Amendment." Id. at 22-23.

The death penalty administered by juries exercising wide **discretion** to impose it or not has been held violative of this provision due to the resulting arbitrariness of its implementation. 408 U.S. 238 (1972). On this issue see 86 Harv. Law Review 76-85 (1972).

CULPABLE deserving of moral blame; implies fault rather than guilt; "criminal, reckless, gross . . . it means disregard of the consequence which may ensue from the act, and indifference to the rights of others," 183 N.E. 273, 275; as well as intentional wrong-doing.

CUMULATIVE DIVIDEND see **dividend.**

CURIA REGIS *(kyū'-rē-à rā'-gĭs)*—Lat: the King's Court.

CURTESY the husband's right, at common law, upon the death of his wife, to a **life estate** in all the **estates** of **inheritance** in land which his wife possessed during their marriage; "a life estate to which the husband was entitled in all lands of which his wife was **seised** in **fee simple** or in **fee tail** at any time during the marriage, provided that there was **issue** born alive capable of inheriting the estate. On the birth of such qualified issue the husband's **tenancy** by the marital right was enlarged to an estate for his own life. . . . Although . . . the husband's estate for his life was called 'curtesy initiate' prior to his wife's death and 'curtesy consummate' after her death, he had a present life estate in both situations and there was no substantial difference between the two types of curtesy." Moynihan, Property 54 (1972). Compare **dower.**

CURTILAGE   at common law the land around the dwelling house; "a piece of ground within the common enclosure belonging to a dwelling-house, and enjoyed with it, for its more convenient occupation." 29 N.J.L. 468, 474.

CUSTODY   as applied to property, not **ownership,** but "a keeping, guarding, care, watch, inspection, preservation, or security of a thing, [which] carries with it the idea of the thing being within the immediate personal care and control of the person to whose 'custody' it is subjected." 74 P. 962, 968. As applied to persons, it is such restraint and physical control over persons as to insure his presence at any **hearing,** or the actual imprisonment resulting from a criminal **conviction.** See 193 N.W. 789, 790. Custody of children is legal **guardianship,** often an **issue** between parents in a **divorce** action. Compare **possession.**

CUSTOMS COURT   see **federal courts.**

CY-PRÈS (sē'-prĕ)—Fr: so near, as near; in the law of trusts and wills the principle that "**equity** will, when a charity is illegal or later becomes impossible or impracticable of fulfillment, substitute another charitable object which is believed to approach the original purpose as closely as possible." 93 So. 2d 483, 486. "The courts will exercise this power, however, only when the purpose for which the fund was established cannot be carried out, and diversion of the income to some other purpose can be found to fall within the general intent of the donor expressed in the instrument establishing the trust." 133 A. 2d 792, 794.

D

DAMAGES   monetary compensation which the law awards to one who has been injured by the action of another; recompense for a legal wrong such as a **breach of contract** or a **tortious** act. There are various measures used for calculating damages, including **diminution in value** and **cost of completion.** Compare **specific performance.**

ACTUAL DAMAGES   those losses which can readily be proven to have been sustained, and for which the injured party should be compensated as a matter of right.

CONSEQUENTIAL [SPECIAL] DAMAGES   loss or injury that is indirect or mediate. In contract law, under the doctrine of *Hadley* v. *Baxendale,* one's "consequential damages" are recoverable if they "were reasonably foreseeable at the time the contract was entered into as [being] probable if the contract were broken." 161 N.E. 240, 242. They are damages "which follow an account of knowledge of special conditions imputed to the defaulting party and increasing the standard of **liability.** Thus they are synonymous with special damages." 328 F. Supp. 190, 193.

DOUBLE [TREBLE] DAMAGES   twice [or three times] the amount of damages that a court or jury would normally find a party entitled to, which is recoverable by an injured party for certain kinds of injuries pursuant to a statute authorizing the double [or treble] recovery. See 6 Fed. Cas. 892, 893. They are intended in certain instances, as a kind of punishment for improper behavior.

EXEMPLARY [PUNITIVE] DAMAGES   compensation in excess of actual damages; a form of punishment to the wrongdoer and excess enhancement to the injured; nominal or actual damages must exist before exemplary damages will be found and then they will be awarded only in rare instances of **malicious** and **willful** misconduct.

INCIDENTAL DAMAGES   includes losses reasonably incident to, or conduct giving rise to, a claim for actual damages. A buyer's incidental damages would include "expenses reasonably incurred in inspection, receipt, transportation, and care and custody of goods rightfully rejected . . .," U.C.C. §2-715; while the seller's incidental damages would include "any commercially reasonable charges, expenses or commissions incurred in stopping delivery, in the transportation, care and custody of goods after the buyer's breach, in connection with return or resale of the goods. . . ." U.C.C. § 2-710.

LIQUIDATED DAMAGES see **liquidated damages**.

NOMINAL DAMAGES a trivial sum awarded, frequently $1.00, as recognition that a legal injury was sustained, though slight; in actuality the amount is usually so small as to not really constitute damages. Nominal damages will be awarded for a breach of contract or for an intentional tort to vindicate the plaintiff's claim where no recoverable loss can be established.

DAMNUM ABSQUE INJURIA *(däm'-nŭm äb'-skwā ĭn-jû'-rē-à).*—Lat: harm without **injury**. The gist of this maxim is that there is harm or damage without a legally recognized injury, which means that the law provides no **cause of action** to recover for one's loss. See 330 P. 2d 459, 462. These situations arise where a lawful act causes injury, where there is damage without any violation of a legal right, where there is damage for which the law provides no remedy, and where damage is caused by nature (such as damage from running water). Thus, "loss to a party . . . not caused by any breach of legal or equitable duty is damnum absque injuria." See 29 A. 2d 823. Where the loss cannot be attributed to the defendant in terms of legal **fault** there can be no **recovery** against him. For example, if the operation of a hospital causes **depreciation** of neighborhood property values and discomfort and inconvenience to the residents, it is "damnum absque injuria." See 46 N.E. 2d 823, 824.

DANGEROUS WEAPON [INSTRUMENTALITY] almost any instrumentality which is used, or attempted to be used, which has the potentiality to cause serious bodily injury or endanger a life; not synonymous with **deadly weapon**. "A dangerous weapon may possibly not be deadly; but a deadly weapon, one which is capable of causing death, must be dangerous." 33 A. 978, 979.

DAY IN COURT a time when a person who is a party to a lawsuit "has been duly cited to appear [before the court] and has been afforded an opportunity to be heard [by the court]." 45 A. 1035, 1036. See **appearance**.

DEADLY WEAPON any instrumentality that is capable of producing death or serious bodily injury; an instrument may be intrinsically deadly, e.g., knife, pistol, rifle, or deadly because of the way it is used or the force with which it is used, e.g., a wrench, hammer, stick.

DEBAUCHERY over-indulgence in sensual pleasures; sexual immorality; as used in the Mann Act [prohibiting travel across state lines for immoral purposes], it is "a broad term and includes all sexual immoralities, whether for hire or not for hire, or for **cohabitation**." 274 F. 2d 15, 18.

DE BENE ESSE *(dā bā'-nā ĕs'-sĕ)*–Lat: conditionally; provisionally.

APPEARANCE DE BENE ESSE a conditional **appearance**.

DEPOSITIONS DE BENE ESSE conditional **depositions** which are non-usable if the **witness** is available at the trial.

EVIDENCE DE BENE ESSE refers to the doctrine of conditional relevancy, and stands for the situation where the admission of **evidence** is conditioned upon a subsequent showing of facts necessary to demonstrate valid admissibility. See 100 A. 2d 246, 252.

DEBENTURE a written acknowledgment of a **debt** with a promise to pay, see 16 N.E. 2d 352; unsecured **bonds**; financial obligation of **corporations** often bought and sold as **investments**. Compare **certificate of deposit; note**.

DEBT money, goods, or services owing from one person to another. See 238 P. 316, 323. An absolute promise to pay a certain sum on a certain date, see 281 S.W. 968, 972; or any obligation of one person to pay or compensate another. See **bankruptcy; creditor; insolvency**.

DEBTOR one who has the obligation of paying a **debt**; one who owes a debt; "one who owes another anything, or is under any obligation, arising from express agreement, implication of law, or from the principles of natural justice, to render and pay a sum of money." 38 S.W. 13, 14.

DECEASED one who has ceased to live; in property, the alternate term DE-CEDENT is generally used. In criminal law, "the deceased" refers to the victim of a **homicide**.

DECEDENT see **deceased**.

DECEIT the **tort** of **fraudulent** representation. "The elements of actionable deceit are: a false representation of a material fact made with knowledge of its falsity, or recklessly, or without reasonable grounds for believing its truth, and with intent to induce **reliance** thereon, on which **plaintiff** justifiably relies to his **injury**." 300 P. 2d 14, 16.

DECISION ON THE MERITS see **judgment on the merits**.

DECLARATION at common law, the formal document setting forth plaintiff's **cause of action**, which includes those facts necessary to sustain a proper cause at action and to advise defendant of the grounds upon which he is being sued. See 103 A. 228. A declaration may contain one or more **counts**. See 82 S.W. 115, 117-18.

DECLARATORY JUDGMENT a **judgment** of the court the purpose of which is "to establish the rights of the parties or express the opinion of the court on a question of law without ordering anything to be done. The distinctive characteristic of a declaratory judgment is that it stands by itself, and no executory process follows as a matter of course. A declaratory judgment is distinguished from a direct judgment in that the former does not seek execution or performance from the defendant or the opposing litigants." 258 So. 2d 555, 558-59. If it becomes necessary, a more coercive remedy such as an **injunction** may be sought by the **aggrieved party**. Compare **advisory opinion**. See also **controversy**; **justiciability**.

DECLARATORY STATUTES those which merely declare the existing law without proposing any additions or changes, for the purpose of resolving conflicts or doubts which have arisen concerning the meaning of a previous statute or portion of the **common law**. 34 N.W. 2d 640, 642.

DECREE "the judicial decision of a litigated cause by a **court of equity**. It is also applied to the determination of a cause in courts of **admiralty** and **probate**. It is accurate to use the word **judgment** as applied to **courts of law**, and 'decree' to courts of equity, although the former term is now used in a larger sense to include both." 146 A. 372, 375.

Historically, "[a] judgment at law was either simply for the **plaintiff** or for the **defendant**. There could be no qualifications or modifications of the judgment. But such a judgment does not always touch the true justice of the cause or put the parties in the position they ought to occupy. While the plantiff may be entitled, in a given case, to general **relief**, there may be some duty connected with the subject of litigation which he owes to the defendant, the performance of which, equally with the fulfillment of his duty by the defendant, ought, in a perfect system of remedial law, to be exacted. This result was attained by the decree of a court of equity which could be so molded, or the execution of which could be so controlled and suspended, that the relative duties and rights of the parties could be secured and enforced." Bisph. Eq. §7 (10th ed. 1925).

CONSENT DECREE an agreement of the parties made under the sanction of the court; not the result of a judicial determination, but merely their agreement to be bound by certain stipulated facts. A consent decree is not appealable in the sense that no errors will be considered which were in law waived by the consent given. 104 U.S. 767, 768.

DECREE NISI in English Law, a provisional decree of divorce, which becomes absolute only upon the passage of a specified interval of time, usually six months, during which time parties have the opportunity of showing cause why the decree should not become absolute. 2 Steph. Com. 281.

FINAL DECREE those which ultimately dispose of every matter of contention between the parties and constitute a bar to another **bill of equity** filed between the same parties for the same subject matter. 2 Del. Ch. 27.

INTERLOCUTORY DECREES those made upon some point arising during the progress of the suit which does not determine finally the **merits** of the questions involved.

DEDICATION a **conveyance** of land by a private owner in the nature of a gift or grant and an acceptance of that land by or on behalf of the public. 143 P. 941, 943. Streets in a development are usually acquired by the town through a dedication to the public of the property comprising the streets.

DEED an **instrument** in writing which **conveys** an **interest** in land from the **grantor** to the **grantee**; instrument used to effect a transfer of **realty**; main function is to pass a **title** to land. Deeds are generally classified as **bargain and sale**, general **warranty deeds**, or **quitclaim deeds**. See **speciality**.

DEED OF TRUST a transfer of legal **title** to property from the **trustor** [settlor] to the **trustee**, for the purpose of placing the legal **title** with the **trustee** as security for the **performance** of certain obligations, monetary or otherwise.

DEED POLL a **deed** made by and obligatory to one **party** alone. See 120 U.S. 464.

DE FACTO (dā fäk'-tō)—Lat: in fact; by virtue of the deed or accomplishment; in reality; actually. Compare **de jure**. Used to qualify many legal terms:

DE FACTO AUTHORITY authority exercised in fact. See 139 P. 1057, 1059.

DE FACTO BOARD OF DIRECTORS the board which in fact is in charge of the affairs of a company and is recognized as such and is performing the legitimate functions and duties of a board. See 71 N.W. 2d 652, 658.

DE FACTO CORPORATIONS those which have inadvertently failed to comply with the provisions of the laws relating to the creation of a **corporation** but have made a good faith effort to do so and have in **good faith** exercised the **franchise** of a corporation. See 261 S.W. 2d 127, 131.

DE FACTO COURT one established and exercising judicial functions under the authority of an apparently valid statute. If the statute is subsequently declared invalid, the court exists in fact though not in law [de jure].

DE FACTO INCUMBENT one who was elected in an election which is later declared void. See 370 S.W. 2d 829, 839.

DE FACTO JUDGE one acting under **color** of right, and who exercises the judicial functions he assumed while the appointment is contested. See 77 P. 2d 114, 115.

DE FACTO JURY a jury selected in pursuance of a void law. See 97 P. 96, 98.

DE FACTO OFFICER one whose title is not good in law, but who in fact possesses an office and discharges his duties. See 197 A. 667, 669.

DE FACTO SEGREGATION segregation which results without purposeful action by government officials; real or actual segregation which occurs concomitant to social and psychological conditions as they exist. See 269 F. Supp. 401, 445.

DE FACTO TRUSTEE one who assumes an office or position under color of right or title and who exercises the duties of the office. See 403 F. 2d 16, 20, 21. Compare **de jure**.

DEFALCATION failure of one entrusted with money to pay over when it is due to another. The term is like misappropriation and **embezzlement**, but is wider in scope because it does not imply any criminal **fraud**. See 123 N.Y.S. 403, 410. See also **misapplication**.

DEFAMATION the publication of anything injurious to the good name or reputation of another, or which tends to bring him into disrepute. A defamation designed to be read is a **libel**; an oral defamation is a **slander**. 207 N.E. 2d 482,484. There is no legal cause of action called defamation; "libel and slander may be founded on defamation, but the right of action itself is libel or slander." 221 So. 2d 772, 775.

DEFAULT a failure to discharge a duty, to one's own disadvantage; default means anything wrongful—some omission to do that which ought to have been done by one of the parties. 90 N.Y.S. 589, 590.

The term is most often used to describe the occurrence of an event which cuts short the rights or **remedies** of one of the parties to an agreement or a legal dispute. It is often used in the context of **mortgages** to describe the failure of the mortgagor to pay mortgage **installments** when due, and in the context of judicial **proceedings** to describe the failure of one of the parties to take the **procedural** steps necessary to prevent the entry of a **judgment** against him (called a JUDGMENT BY DEFAULT).

DEFAULT JUDGMENT a **judgment** entered against **defendant** due to defendant's failure to respond to **plaintiff's action** or to appear at the **trial**; "one taken against a defendant who, having been summoned in an action, fails to enter an appearance," 80 N.W. 2d 548, 553; judgment which is given without the defendant being heard in his own defense. 303 A. 2d 139, 140.

DEFEASANCE an **instrument** which, in effect, negates the effectiveness of a **deed** or of a **will**; a **collateral** deed which defeats the force of another deed upon the performance of certain conditions. See 82 N.E. 1064.

DEFEASIBLE subject to revocaton if certain conditions are not met; capable of being avoided or annulled or liable to such avoidance or annulment. See **condition** (CONDITION PRECEDENT, CONDITION SUBSEQUENT).

DEFECTIVE something that is wanting as to an essential; incomplete, deficient, faulty, 331 S.W. 2d 140, 143; also, not reasonably safe for a use which can be reasonably anticipated. 148 A. 2d 261, 265. See **warranty** (WARRANTY OF FITNESS, WARRANTY OF MERCHANTIBILITY). See also **products liability**; **strict liability**.

DEFECTIVE TITLE one which is unmarketable. With reference to **title** in land, it means that the person making the **conveyance,** claiming to own **good title**, is actually subject to the partial or complete **ownership** of the title by someone else. As to **negotiable instruments**, the term denotes title obtained through illegal means or means that amount to **fraud**. See 23 N.E. 2d 431. A defective title is unmarketable.

DEFENDANT in **civil proceedings**, the **party** responding to the **complaint**; "one who is sued and called upon to make satisfaction for a wrong complained of by another, [the **plaintiff**]." 203 S.W. 2d 548, 552. In criminal proceedings, also called the **accused**.

DEFENDANT IN ERROR the prevailing party in the lower court who is the adverse party in the **appellate proceeding** wherein review has been sought on a **writ of error**. The person who brings the **action** at the appellate level is called the PLAINTIFF IN ERROR. See also **appellee**.

DEFENSE a denial, answer, or plea opposing truth or validity of plaintiff's case. This may be accomplished by cross-examination or by **demurrer**. It is more often done by introduction of defense testimony or other evidence designed to refute all or part of the allegations of the plaintiff's case.

AFFIRMATIVE DEFENSE one which serves as a basis for proving some new fact; in such a defense, defendant does not simply **deny** a **charge**, but offers new **evidence** to avoid **judgment** against him; defendant has the **burden of proof** on an affirmative defense.

EQUITABLE DEFENSE a defense which is recognized by **courts of equity** acting solely upon inherent rules and principles of **equity**. 78 A. 2d 572, 576. Examples of such defenses include **fraud, duress,** illegality. Such defenses can now be asserted in **courts of law** as well. James, Civil Procedure §8.2 n. 5 (1965). The term also refers to equitable doctrines such as **unclean hands** that may operate to **bar** a plaintiff from pursuing an equity action and thus constitute equitable defenses to such an action.

DEFERRED PAYMENTS payments extended over a period of time or put off to a future date. **Installment** payments are usually a series of equal deferred payments made over a course of time.

DEFINITE FAILURE OF ISSUE see **failure of issue**.

DEFRAUD to deprive a person of **property** or **interest**, **estate** or right by **fraud, deceit** or **artifice**. 438 P. 2d 250, 252.

DE JURE *(dā jû'-rā)*—Lat: by right; by justice; lawful; legitimate. Generally used in contrast to **de facto** in that de jure connotes "as a matter of law" while de facto connotes "as a matter of conduct or practice not founded upon law." For example, "de jure segregation" refers to segregation directly intended and sanctioned by law or otherwise issuing from an official racial classification. See 269 F. Supp. 401, 443.

DELINQUENT in a monetary context, something which has been made payable and is overdue and unpaid; implies a previous opportunity to make payment; with reference to persons, implies carelessness, recklessness. See also **juvenile delinquent.**

DELIVERY a voluntary transfer of **title** or **possession** from one **party** to another; a legally recognized handing over of one's possessory rights to another. Actual delivery is sometimes very cumbersome or impossible and in those instances the courts will find a CONSTRUCTIVE DELIVERY sufficient where there is no actual delivery provided that the intention is clearly to transfer title. Thus, one may deliver the contents of a safety deposit box by handing over to another the key thereto together with any necessary authorization. Such an action is also called a "symbolic delivery". See **gift; livery of seisin.** Compare **bailment; conveyance; grant.**

DEMAND NOTE an **instrument** which by its express terms is payable immediately on an agreed-upon date of **maturation** without requiring any further demand; the **maker** of the **note** acknowledges his **liability** as of the due date; also includes those instruments payable at sight, or upon presentation, or those in which no time for payment is stated. See 448 S.W. 2d 495, 497.

DE MINIMIS (dā mĭ'-nĭ-mĭs)—Lat: insignificant; minute, frivolous. Something or some act which is "de minimis" in interest is one which does not rise to a level of sufficient importance to be dealt with judicially. "Trifles, or matters of a few dollars or less." 121 F. 2d 829, 832. A crime which is "de minimis" may be dismissed under the Model Penal Code and similar statutes. M.P.C. §2.12.

DE MINIMIS NON CURAT LEX (nŏn kyū'-rät lĕx)—Lat: the law does not care for small things; the law does not bother with trifles.

DEMISE term used to describe a **conveyance** of an **estate** in **real property.** Most commonly used as a synonym for "let" in a **lease.** "The word 'demise' used as a noun, means a lease for a term of years; a conveyance **in fee,** or for life, or for years, most commonly the latter. As a verb, it means to lease for a term of years. In its primitive meaning, it was always used in reference to a lease, and while it has been held that, where the context clearly justified such construction, it meant a conveyance or transfer. This is not its usual signification." 142 P. 131, 133.

DEMURRER formal **allegation** that facts as stated in the **pleadings,** even if admitted, are not legally sufficient for the case to proceed any further. It does not admit anything, in reality, but for purposes of testing the sufficiency of the **complaint,** a demurrer declares that even if everything stated in the complaint were true, it does not state facts sufficient to constitute a **cause of action.** 145 P. 2d 784. At **common law** a demurrer was either **sustained** or **overruled,** which in either event ended the case with **judgment** for the prevailing **party.** James, Civil Procedure §4.1 n. 10 (1965). In modern **procedure** a **motion** to **dismiss** replaces the demurrer, but if denied the **case** simply proceeds to **trial** on the **merits.** Fed. R. Civ. Proc. 12(b)(6). See Id. §§4.1-2. Compare **summary judgment.**

DENIAL a contradiction or **traverse;** in practice, a controverting of affirmative **allegations** in a **pleading** by an adversary. A defendant in his **answer** must admit, deny, or state he has insufficient information upon which to admit or deny the allegations. The latter amounts to a denial. See Fed. R. Civ. Proc. 8(b). Any allegations in a complaint not denied (or given an insufficient information response) is taken as true. See Fed. R. Civ. Proc. 8(d). See also **confession and avoidance.**

DE NOVO (dā nō'-vō)—Lat: new, young, fresh; renewed, revived. A second time. See 47 N.W. 2d 126, 128. See also **appeal** (APPEAL DE NOVO); **trial** (TRIAL DE NOVO).

DE NOVO HEARING a new hearing. "In a 'de novo hearing,' the judgment of the trial court is suspended and [the reviewing court] determine[s] the case as though it originated in [the reviewing court] and give[s] no attention to the findings and **judgment** of the **trial court** except as they may be helpful . . . in the reasoning." 46 N.E. 2d 429, 430.

DEPENDENT COVENANTS see **covenant.**

DEPONENT a **witness**; one who gives information, concerning some fact or facts known to him, under oath in a **deposition.**

DEPOSITION a method of pre-trial **discovery** which consists of "a statement of a **witness** under oath, taken in question and answer form as it would be in court, with opportunity given to the **adversary** to be present and cross-examine, with all this reported and transcribed stenographically." James, Civil Procedure 184-85 (1965). Such statements are the most common form of discovery, and may be taken of any witness (whether or not a **party** to the **action**). When taken in the form described it is called an 'oral deposition.' Depositions may also be taken upon written **interrogatories** where the questions are propounded to the witness by the officer who is taking the deposition [called in that case "depositions on written interrogatories."] See Id. 184-189. Compare **affidavit.**

DEPOSITIONS DE BENE ESSE see **de bene esse.**

DERELICTION "a recession of the waters of the sea, a navigable river, or other stream, by which land that was before covered with water is left dry." 260 S.W. 2d 257, 259. "In such case, if the alteration takes place suddenly and sensibly, the ownership remains according to former bounds; but if it is made gradually and imperceptibly, the derelict or dry land belongs to the **riparian** owner from whose shore or bank the water has so receded." Id. The term may also refer to the land itself which is thus left uncovered. 188 S.W. 2d 550. In order for **contiguous** landowners to gain ownership of the newly uncovered land, the withdrawal of the water must appear permanent, and not merely seasonal. 156 N.W. 591. Compare **accretion; avulsion.**

DERIVATIVE ACTION an action based upon a primary right of a **corporation,** but asserted on its behalf by the **stockholder** because of the corporation's failure, deliberate or otherwise, to act upon the primary right, see 138 N.Y.S. 2d 163, 166; shareholder's action on behalf of corporation. Also used to describe a **cause of action** that is founded upon an injury to another as when a husband sues for loss of **consortium** or services of his wife on account of an injury to her by the defendant, or when a father sues for loss of services of children. See 36 N.Y.S. 2d 465, 467. See **stockholder's derivative action.**

DERIVATIVE TORT an action in **tort** based on the **criminal** conduct of **defendant** which resulted in **injury** to **plaintiff,** and for which injury plaintiff seeks **compensation.** The action is distinct from any criminal prosecution which may result from the same conduct by defendant.

DEROGATION partial taking away of the effectiveness of a law; to partially repeal or abolish a law. A rule (or canon) of statutory **construction** is that "statutes derogating from the **common law** are to be strictly construed." Cardozo, The Paradoxes of the Legal Science 9, 10 (1928).

DESCENT a method of acquiring **property,** usually **real property,** from a decedent without the use of **wills;** "generally used and applied to **inheritance** only by **operation of law** rather than by provision by will; that is, it is applied only to **intestate succession.**" 129 F. Supp. 609, 614. Compare **devise.** See **Doctrine of Worthier Title.**

DESTRUCTIBILITY a **common law** rule "that a **freehold contingent remainder** which does not **vest** at or before the termination of the preceding freehold estate is destroyed. Such termination of the preceding estate might result from the natural expiration of that estate, or from forfeiture, or from **merger.**" Moynihan, Introduction to the Law of Real Property 129 (1962).

DETAINER keeping a person from goods or land to which he has a legal right; "a **writ** or **instrument**, issued or made by a competent officer, authorizing the keeper of a prison to keep in his **custody** a person therein named." 131 S.E. 2d 382, 388.

UNLAWFUL DETAINER refusal to deliver on demand, as in a **lease** situation where the **tenant** remains after his lease has ended or has been terminated; actual repudiation of owner's rights must exist. Compare **tenancy—at sufferance; trespass.**

DETERMINABLE FEE [FEE SIMPLE DETERMINABLE] an **interest** in **property** which may last forever, but which will automatically terminate upon the happening or non-happening of a specified event, e.g., "A, owner of Blackacre in **fee simple absolute,** conveys it 'to B and his heirs so long as Brookline remains a town [and no longer] and if Brookline becomes a city then the said premises shall **revert** to A and his heirs.' B has a fee simple determinable.... If the town becomes a city [or ceases to exist as a town] B's estate expires automatically and A becomes the owner in fee simple." Moynihan, Introduction to the Law of Real Property 95-96 (1962).

DETINUE at **common law,** an **action** for the wrongful detention of **personal property;** "a mode of action given for the recovery of a specific thing, and **damages** for its detention, though judgment is also rendered in favor of the **plaintiff** for the alternate value, provided the thing [itself] cannot be had; yet the recovery of the thing itself is the main object and inducement to the allowance of the action.... The action is not adopted to the recovery alone of the value of a thing detained, nor can it be maintained therefore." 59 N.E. 265, 267. See **detainer, unlawful; replevin; trover.**

DEVEST see **divest.**

DEVISE traditionally a gift of real property made by will. As defined by Restatement, Property §12 (1), "A testamentary act by which a now-deceased person manifested his intent to create one or more interests in land or in a thing other than land, irrespective of whether such act is effective to create such interest." "Simplicity of statement requires that a single word be available to describe a testamentary act intended to dispose of interests in land, interests in things other than land or both these types of interests. The employment of two words, such as 'devise' and 'bequeath,' is awkward...."Id., Comment (a). Compare **bequest; legacy.**

DEVOLVE "when by **operation of law,** and without any voluntary act of the previous owner, [an **estate**] passes from one person to another; it does not devolve from one person to another as the result of some positive act or agreement between them.... [the word] implies a result without the intervention of any voluntary actor." 29 P. 495.

DICTUM a statement, remark, or observation in a judicial **opinion** not necessary for the decision of the case. Dictum differs from the **holding** in that it is not binding on the courts in subsequent cases. See 14 Ohio N.P., N.S. 97. Holdings are guides to future conduct, whereas dicta [plural] are not. CONSIDERED DICTUM is a phrase used to refer to a discussion of a point of law that, though it is dictum, is nevertheless so well developed that it is later adopted or incorporated into an opinion of a court as though it were authority.

DIE WITHOUT ISSUE see **failure of issue.**

DILATORY PLEA [PLEA IN ABATEMENT] at **common law,** a **plea** not going to the **merits,** but constituting rather a **defense** which simply delays or defeats the present **action,** leaving the **cause of action** unsettled, 32 S.W. 2d 674, 675; such as a challenge to **jurisdiction** or other plea in abatement on the grounds of disability of the **plaintiff** or the **defendant,** etc. If a defendant can defeat the plaintiff's cause of action in whole or in part, upon establishing the facts, or can obtain any substantial relief against the plaintiff, the plea is not dilatory, but rather **on the merits.** 68 S.E. 1086. This kind of plea has largely disappeared under modern practice, James, Civil Procedure, §4.1 n. 3 (1965). Instead these defenses are now raised by **motion** or in an **answer.** Id. nn. 6-7.

DIMINUTION IN VALUE a measure of damages for breach of contract which reflects a decrease, occasioned by the breach, in the value of property with which the contract was concerned. In a building contract it "is the difference between the value of the building as constructed and its value had it been constructed conformably to the contract." 143 N.E. 2d 802, 803. "There are two general rules with variations where there are damages to realty and, in some cases, personalty attached to realty. There is the before and after value of realty rule, sometimes referred to as the diminution rule. There is also the restoration or replacement rule which will generally be applied by the court if the injury is temporary and replacement is possible, or if it involves an amount less than that derived from application of the diminution rule." 388 F. 2d 165, 168. Compare cost to complete; expectation damages; specific performance.

DIRECT ATTACK as applied to a judicial proceeding, an attempt by appellants to avoid or correct a judgment in some manner provided by law, 191 S.E. 779, 782; an attempt to amend, correct, reform, vacate or enjoin execution of a judgment in a proceeding instituted for that purpose, 441 S.W. 2d 653, 655; generally an attack is "direct" where it constitutes a resort to the primary appellate review procedure. Compare collateral attack.

DIRECT CAUSE see cause.

DIRECT CONTEMPT see contempt of court.

DIRECTED VERDICT that verdict returned by the jury at the direction of the trial judge, by whose instruction the jury is bound. In civil proceedings either party may receive a directed verdict in its favor if the opposing party fails to present a prima facie case, or fails to present a necessary defense. In criminal proceedings, while there may be a directed verdict of acquittal (sometimes called a "judgment of acquittal"), there may be no directed verdict of conviction as such a procedure would violate the defendant's constitutional right to a jury determination of his guilt or innocence.

DIRECT ESTOPPEL see estoppel.

DIRECTOR one who sits on a board of directors of a company or corporation, and who has the legal responsibility of exercising control over the officers and affairs of the company or corporation.

A director has a fiduciary duty, to the corporation and to its stockholders to manage the affairs of the corporation in a manner which is consistent with their interests. Any breach of his fiduciary duty may subject him to personal liability to both the shareholders and the corporation.

DISABILITY state of not being fully capable of performing all functions, whether mental or physical. Any want of legal capacity such as infancy, insanity, or past criminal conviction which renders a person legally incompetent. In property, one person's inability to alter a given legal relation with another person. Restatement, Property, §4a. See also non compos mentis; minority; Durham Rule.

DISBAR to deprive an attorney of the right to practice law by rescinding his license to so practice, as a result of illegal or unethical conduct by the attorney.

DISCHARGE general word covering methods by which a legal duty is extinguished, 375 S.W. 2d 85, 92; to release, annul or dismiss the obligations of contract or debt. See 41 N.E. 2d 979, 981. See also satisfaction.

"When it is said that a contract is discharged, it is always meant that one or more of the legal relations of the parties have been terminated. The meaning that is most commonly intended is that the legal duty of one of the parties has been terminated. A party who is asserted to be under a legal duty by virtue of his contract may reply that the duty has been discharged by some factor that has occurred since the making of the contract." Corbin, Contracts §1228 (one-vol. ed. 1952). The factors bringing about discharge of contractual obligation include full performance, rescission, release, informal written renunciation, contract not to sue.

DISCHARGED IN BANKRUPTCY the release of the bankrupt from all his debts which are provable, including a fixed liability, whether then payable or not, and debts founded on a contract, express or implied, but not a release against such debts as are specifically excepted from discharge by the bankruptcy statute. See 293 N.W. 346, 348.

Discharge also refers to the termination of one's employment by his employer.

DISCHARGE A DEBT settlement of a **debt**; [A] debt is discharged and the **debtor** is released when the **creditor** has received something from the debtor which satisfies him. It may be money or its equivalent. It may consist of **offsetting** mutual demands, or wiping out mutual disputed **claims** by mutual concessions, in which event no money is required to pass from one to the other. See 79 Mich. 484.

DISCLAIMER a denial or repudiation of a person's **claim** or right to a thing, though previously that person insisted on such a claim or right; complete renunciation of right to **possess** and claim of **title**. Denial of a right of another, e.g., where an **insurer** disclaims an allegation of **liability** against its **insured** and thereby refuses to defend the insured in a **lawsuit**. In such instances the insured can sue the insurance company to challenge the DISCLAIMER OF LIABILITY.

DISCONTINUANCE in practice, the cessation of the **proceedings** in an **action** where the **plaintiff** voluntarily puts an end to it, with or without judicial approval; judicial approval may be required, depending upon each jurisdiction's rules of practice. See also **dismissal; non-suit.**

DISCOUNT a deduction from a specified sum. Often used in connection with transactions in negotiable **commercial paper** in which the buyer purchases the instrument at a price below its face amount with the intention of ultimately collecting the face amount. "To discount" in finance is to purchase or pay an amount in cash less a certain per cent, as on a promissory note which is to be collected by discounter or purchasor at maturity. 117 So. 124, 126.

Discount is the difference between the price and the amount of the debt, the evidence of which is transferred. 14 Ill. App. 566, 570.

DISCOVERY modern pre-trial procedure by which one **party** gains vital information concerning the case held by the adverse party; the disclosure by the adverse party of facts, deeds, documents and other such things which are within his possession or knowledge exclusively, and which are necessary to the other party's defense. 73 N.W. 2d 103, 106. See **depositions; interrogatories; work-product.**

DISCRETION the reasonable exercise of a power or right to act in an official capacity; involves the idea of choice, of an exercise of the will, so that **abuse of discretion** involves more than a difference in judicial opinion between the **trial** and **appellate** courts, and in order to constitute an "abuse" of discretion, the **judgment** must demonstrate a perversity of will, a defiance of good judgment, or bias. 94 N.W. 2d 810, 811.

JUDICIAL DISCRETION the reasonable use of judicial power, i.e., freedom to decide within the bounds of law and fact. See 5 F. 2d 188.

LEGAL DISCRETION the use of one of several equally satisfactory provisions of law. 32 N.E. 2d 431, 432.

PROSECUTORIAL DISCRETION the wide range of alternatives available to a prosecutor in criminal cases, including the decision to prosecute, the particular charges to be brought, plus bargaining, mode of trial conduct, and recommendations for sentencing, parole, etc. See La Fave, Arrest 72 (1969).

A public officer has discretion whenever the effective limits on his power leave him free to make a choice among possible courses of action or inaction. Davis, Administrative Law §4.02 (3rd ed. 1972).

DISHONOR to refuse to make payment on a **negotiable instrument** when such an instrument is duly presented for payment. A negotiable instrument may be either rightfully or wrongly dishonored. See U.C.C. §§3-507, 4-402. When a bank, for example, refuses to pay a check which has been presented to it for payment, it may do so because there are not adequate funds in the **drawer**'s account to "cover" the check, or it may do so for other reasons. When such an instrument is dishonored, for whatever reason, the holder may pursue his **remedies** against either the principal party [**drawer** or **maker**] or any subsequent **indorser**. U.C.C. §3-507 (2).

DISINHERIT (DISINHERITANCE) the act by the **donor** which dissolves the right of a person to **inherit** that **property** to which he previously had such right; the act of terminating another's right to inherit.

DISJUNCTIVE ALLEGATIONS "those which **charge** that the **defendant** did one thing *or* another. The rule is that, whenever the word 'or' would leave the **averment** uncertain as to which of two or more things is meant, it is inadmissible." 419 P. 2d 569, 574. An **allegation** that charges the commission of a **crime** by one act 'or' another is defective if it is not sufficiently clear to enable the defendant to be properly informed of what he is charged with so that he can prepare a **defense**. See 419 P. 2d 569, 574. The same standard is applied to **pleadings** in **civil** cases, where both disjunctive allegations and DISJUNCTIVE DENIALS generally constitute **defective pleadings** and are therefore inadmissible. See 41 A. 2d 270, 271. Compare **alternative pleading**; **denial** [LITERAL DENIAL, CONJUNCTIVE DENIAL]. See also **negative pregnant**.

DISMISS in a legal context, to remove a **case** out of the court; to terminate a case without a complete **trial**. See **demurrer**. Compare **summary judgment**.

DISMISSAL equivalent of a cancellation, 91 N.E. 748, 749; dismissal of a **motion** is a denial of the motion, 57 P. 684, 685; a dismissal of an **appeal** places the parties in the same condition as if no appeal had been taken or allowed, and is thus a confirmation of the judgment below. Compare **summary judgment**.

DISMISSAL WITH PREJUDICE usually considered an **adjudication** upon the **merits** and will operate as a **bar** to future action. 135 P. 2d 71, 74. See **res judicata**.

DISMISSAL WITHOUT PREJUDICE usually an indication that the dismissal affects no right or **remedy** of the parties, i.e., is not **on the merits** and does not bar a subsequent **suit** on the same **cause of action**. See **estoppel—collateral**; **res judicata**.

DISPARAGEMENT see **bait and switch**.

DISPOSITION the giving up of, or the relinquishment of, anything, 13 F. 2d 756, 758; often used in reference to a testamentary **proceeding**, e.g., "the disposition of the estate;" **satisfaction** of a debt. Courts are also said to "dispose of" **cases**, i.e., finally determine the rights of the parties or otherwise terminate the proceedings. In criminal law, the **sentence** the **defendant** receives is the disposition; i.e., the post-adjudicative phase of the criminal proceeding is called the disposition or the dispositionary stage (process). See also **bequeath**.

DISPUTABLE PRESUMPTION see **rebuttable presumption**.

DISSEISIN the act of wrongfully depriving a person of the **seisin** of land, see 49 A. 1043, 1044; to take **possession** of land under claim or **color of title**, see 5 Conn. 255, 257; the dispossession of the **freeholder**, and the substitution of the disseisor as **tenant**, see 3 Watts 69, 71; an **estate** gained by wrong and injury. See 5 Conn. 371, 374. Mere entry on another's land is no disseisin unless accompanied by expulsion or refusal to allow one claiming paramount title to enter, see 163 S.W. 984, 988; but it is any act the necessary effect of which is to **divest** the estate of the former owner. See 74 Ala. 122, 130. There are two self-explanatory categories of disseisin: (1) at the election of the owner of the land; (2) in spite of the true owner. See 3 Me. (3 Greenl.) 174, 175.

DISSENT to differ in opinion; to disagree; to be of contrary sentiment. See 201 F. 2d 607, 609. The most common usage is in a situation where a judge's **opinion** of the **case** differs from that of the majority of the court and the "dissenting judge" writes a contrary opinion explicating the deficiencies of the majority opinion, and his reasons for arriving at a contrary conclusion. If the court decides a matter 5-4 this means that four judges dissented in one or more DISSENTING OPINIONS. Compare **concur**.

DISSENTING OPINION see **opinion**.

DISTRICT COURT with respect to the judicial system of the United States, constitutional courts each having territorial **jurisdiction** over a district which may include a whole state or only a part of it. Thus the designation "S.D.-N.Y." refers to District Court for the Southern District of New York. They have **original jurisdiction**, exclusive of courts of the individual states, of all offenses against laws of the United States, 255 F. 2d 9, 13; and are courts of general jurisdiction for **suits** between **litigants** of different states [see **diversity of citizenship**]. Also refers to inferior courts in several states having limited jurisdictions to try certain minor cases. See also **federal question jurisdiction.**

DISTURBANCE OF THE PEACE "to agitate, to arouse from a state of repose, to molest, to interrupt, to hinder and to disquiet." 156 So. 2d 448, 449. "Any act which molests inhabitants in enjoyment of peace and quiet or which excites disquietude or fear among normal persons." 138 So. 851. See **breach of the peace.**

DIVERS many, several, sundry; a grouping of unspecified persons, things, acts, etc.

DIVERSITY JURISDICTION see **diversity of citizenship.**

DIVERSITY OF CITIZENSHIP that basis of federal **jurisdiction** first promulgated in the First Judiciary Act which grants to federal courts **original jurisdiction** over **cases and controversies** between citizens of different states or between a citizen of a state and an alien, subject to a **jurisdictional amount** of $10,000. See Wright, Federal Courts §23-31 (2d ed 1970); 28 U.S.C.A. § 1332. The constitutional grant of **diversity jurisdiction** extends "to Controversies . . . between Citizens of different states . . . and between a State, or the Citizens thereof, and foreign States, Citizens or Subjects." United States Constitution Art. III Sec. 2.

DIVESTITURE a remedy, by virtue of which the court orders the offending party to rid itself of property or assets before the party would normally have done so. Divestiture, like **restitution**, has the purpose of depriving a defendant of the gains of his wrongful conduct. 91 F. Supp. 333. It is a remedy commonly used in the enforcement of the **antitrust laws**. It is an extreme remedy and before it is invoked the court must find

it both necessary and practicable in preventing a monopolization or restraint of trade.

DIVIDEND profits appropriated for division among **stockholders**. See 378 S.W. 2d 161, 167, 169. A distribution of profits or earnings to shareholders See 224 N.Y.S. 2d 985, 988.

CUMULATIVE DIVIDEND a dividend with regard to which it is agreed that, if at any time it is not paid in full, the difference shall be added to the following payment.

DIVIDEND ADDITION as used in a life-insurance policy, it means **insurance** purchased with dividends in addition to the face [value] of the policy. See 19 N.E. 2d 854, 857.

EXTRAORDINARY DIVIDENDS " 'ordinary dividends' are usual or customary dividends [such] as 6 percent, or sum per share, paid at regular periods, while 'extraordinary dividends' may assume unusual form and amount, paid at irregular intervals from accumulated surplus or earnings, and require investigation into their source and apportionment according to equitable principles rather than application of common law rule that a dividend belongs to the party entitled to it at the date of its declaration." 193 A. 33, 37.

LIQUIDATION DIVIDEND act or operation in **winding up** affairs of firm or **corporation**, a settling with its **debtors** and **creditors**, and an appropriation and distribution to its stockholders proportionately of the amount of profit and loss. See 68 F. 2d 763, 765.

PREFERRED DIVIDEND fund paid to one class of stockholders in priority to that to be paid to another class. 55 Utah 129.

SCRIP DIVIDEND a dividend not payable in cash, but in certificates of indebtedness which give the holder certain rights against the corporation. See 142 N.Y.S. 847, 849.

STOCK DIVIDEND a dividend paid not in cash, but in **stock** so that each stockholder obtains a greater absolute number of shares but the same relative number of shares.

DIVISIBLE CONTRACT see **severable contract.**

DOCKET a list of cases on a court's calendar. In **procedure**, a formal record, included in a **brief**, of the proceedings in the court below.

DOCTRINE OF WORTHIER TITLE see **worthier title, doctrine of.**

DOMAIN "ownership of **land**; immediate or absolute ownership; paramount or ultimate ownership, an estate or patrimony which one has in his own right; land of which one is absolute owner," 30 Cal. 645, 648; territory.

DOMESDAY BOOK a record made in the time of William the Conqueror (1081-1086) consisting of accurate and detailed surveys of the lands in England and the means by which the alleged owners obtained title. See 2 Bl. Comm. *49.

DOMICILE the place where an individual has his permanent home or principal establishment, to where, whenever he is absent, he has the intention of returning, 168 So. 2d 873, 877; "the one technical pre-eminent headquarters, which as a result either of fact or of fiction, every person is compelled to have in order that by aid of it certain rights and duties which have been attached to it by the law may be determined." 51 N.E. 531, 532. "Every person has at all times one domicile, and no person has more than one domicile at a time." Restatement of Conflict of Law, §11 (1934). Residence is not equal to domicile since a person can have many transient residences where he may temporarily be found but only one legal domicile which is the residence to which he always intends to return and to remain indefinitely.

A business or corporation may have a domicile which refers to the place where the establishment is maintained or where the governing power of the corporation is exercised. For purposes of taxation, it is often a principal place of business. 123 S.W. 353, 359.

DOMINANT ESTATE [TENEMENT] an estate whose owners are entitled to the **beneficial use** of another's property; **property** retained by an original grantor when a particular tract is subdivided and a portion is conveyed, and to which certain rights or benefits are legally owed by the conveyed or **servient estate.** 116 S.W. 668. These rights and benefits may be in the nature of an **easement,** so that the owner of the retained land [dominant estate] is said to have a right of easement in the servient estate.

DONATIO (*dō-nä'-shē-ō*)—Lat: a **gift.** A donation.

DONATIVE INTENT see **gift.**

DONEE the recipient of a **gift** or **trust;** one who takes without first giving **consideration.** See 76 N.C. 82, 83. One who is given a power, see 70 S.W. 742, 743, e.g., one who exercises a **power of appointment.** 274 S.W. 2d 431, 439. Compare **bailee; trustee.**

DONOR one who gives or makes a **gift;** creator of a **trust,** 195 N.E. 557, 564; the party conferring a power, e.g., the grantor of a **power of appointment.** 274 S.W. 2d 431, 439.

DOUBLE DAMAGES see **damages.**

DOUBLE JEOPARDY provision in the Fifth Amendment to the Constitution of the United States which provides that "No person . . . shall . . . be subject for the same offense to be twice put in jeopardy of life or limb." This provision has been fundamental to the common law and finds expression in state constitutions. See 18 Wall. 163, 168. It has now been held applicable to the states through the due process clause of the Fourteenth Amendment. See 395 U.S. 784. The clause operates only in criminal settings and prevents a second prosecution, regardless of the outcome of the first trial (acquittal, conviction, or mistrial) unless there has been an appeal from a conviction, see 163 U.S. 662, or a **mistrial** granted upon manifest necessity. See 410 U.S. 458; 400 U.S. 470.

The bar against double jeopardy applies only after "jeopardy has attached," i.e., after the jury has been sworn or after a judge in a non-jury trial receives the first piece of evidence at the trial. A dismissal prior to jeopardy attaching does not preclude a second or renewed prosecution under the double jeopardy clause.

Double jeopardy bars double punishment as well as double prosecution. While a higher penalty upon a retrial following a successful appeal does not itself violate the double jeopardy guarantee, there must generally appear independent justification for the increased penalty in order to insure that the higher penalty is not vindictive. See 395 U.S. 711. See also **collateral estoppel.**

DOWER a **life estate** to which a wife is entitled upon the death of her husband. 290 S.W. 244, 250. At **common law,** the widow was entitled to one-third of all the property in which her husband was **seized in fee** at any time during the marriage [coverture]. See 278 Ill. App. 564; 261 N.Y.S. 400; 131 S.E. 585, 586. Her dower is a **freehold** estate, and cannot derive from an **estate for years.** 42 So. 290, 298. Compare **homestead rights.** See **curtesy.**

Dower rights have been abrogated in many jurisdictions or limited to interests which the husband holds at his death. American Law of Property §§ 5.31-5.32. Where they still exist, a wife can join in a **conveyance** and thereby give up her dower rights. Id. at § 18.95.

DOWRY money and personalty which the wife brings to the husband to support the expenses of marriage; a donation to the maintenance and support of the marriage. See 22 Mo. 206, 254.

DRAFT an order in writing directing a person other than the **maker** to pay a specified sum of money to a named person; automobiles are often purchased by used car dealers through "dealer's drafts," i.e., by a document setting forth a bank's promise to pay on the dealer's behalf for the automobile once it has been properly **indorsed** by the dealer. Drafts may or may not be **negotiable instruments** depending upon whether the elements of negotiability are satisfied. See U.C.C. §3-104(3). Draft is synonymous with BILL OF EXCHANGE although "draft" is the preferred term. See id. at §3-104(2)(a).

In a military context, the term connotes the compulsory conscription of citizens into the military service.

More generally, it refers to the preliminary form of a legal document (e.g., the draft of a contract—often called "rough draft"). It also refers to the process of preparing or DRAWING a legal document (e.g., drafting a will) or piece of proposed legislation.

DRAW see **draft.**

DRAWEE one to whom a **bill of ex-**change or a **check** directs a request to pay a certain sum of money specified therein. In the typical checking account situation, the bank is the drawee, the person writing the check is the **maker** or **drawer,** and the person to whom the check is written is the **payee.**

DRAWER person by whom a **check** or **bill of exchange** is drawn.

DROIT *(drwäh)*—Fr: a right; law; the whole body of the law.

DUCES TECUM see **subpoena** (SUBPOENA DUCES TECUM).

DUE CARE a concept used in **tort** law to indicate the standard of care or the **legal duty** one owes to others. **Negligence** is the failure to use due care, [which is] that degree of care which a person of ordinary prudence and reason [the **reasonable man**] would exercise under the same circumstances. See 198 S.E. 2d 526, 529. "Failure to exercise due care is the failure to perform some specific duty required by law." 153 S.E. 2d 356, 359. It "means care which is reasonably commensurate with a known danger and the seriousness of the consequences which are liable to follow its omission . . . . Due care may be either ordinary care or a high degree of care, according to the circumstances of the particular care." 438 P. 2d 477, 482.

DUE DATE time fixed for payment of debt, tax, etc.

DUE PROCESS OF LAW a phrase which was first expressly introduced into American jurisprudence in the Fifth Amendment to the Constitution which provides that "nor [shall any person] be deprived of life, liberty, or property, without due process of law;" This provision is applicable only to the actions of the federal government. 7 Pet. 243 (1833). The phrase was made applicable to the states with the adoption of the Fourteenth Amendment, Section 1, which states that "Nor shall any State deprive any person of life, liberty or property, without due process of law"; The phrase does not have a fixed meaning, but expands with jurisprudential attitudes of fundamental fairness. 302 U.S. 319. The legal substance of the phrase is divided into the areas of substantive due process, and procedural due process. The constitutional safe-guard of SUBSTANTIVE DUE PROCESS requires that all legislation, state or federal, must be reasonably related for the furtherance of a legitimate governmental objective. 123 U.S. 623. Not only must the legislation be rationally related, but it must utilize that method of promoting the governmental interest which is least burdensome of other rights. See 80 Harv. L. Rev. 1463 (1967). The use of the substantive due process approach to invalidate legislation is no longer widely accepted but the clause has been used recently in a substantive sense to declare legislation unconstitutional which invaded marital privacy, see 381 U.S. 479; and infringed women's right to have an **abortion**. See 410 U.S. 113.

The original content of the phrase was a PROCEDURAL DUE PROCESS protection, i.e., in guaranteeing procedural fairness where the government would deprive one of his property or liberty. This requires that notice and the right to a fair hearing be accorded prior to a deprivation. 237 U.S. 309. The enumeration of those procedures required by due process varies according to the factual context. The extent to which procedural due process must be afforded a person is influenced by the extent to which he may be "condemned to suffer grievous loss . . . and depends upon whether the [person's] interest in avoiding that loss outweighs the governmental interest in summary adjudication. Accordingly . . . 'considerations of what procedures due process may require under any given set of circumstances must begin with a determination of the precise nature of the government function involved as well as the private interest that has been affected by governmental action'." 397 U.S. 254, 262-263. Recently the due process clause of the Fourteenth Amendment has been used as the vehicle for the application of most of the substantive and procedural rights in the Bill of Rights to state action.

Due process of law does not have a fixed meaning. As the constitution itself it adjusts with changing jurisprudential values. Said Justice Frankfurter: "The requirement of 'due process' is not a fair weather or timid assurance. It must be respected in periods of calm and in times of trouble; it protects aliens as well as citizens. But 'due process,' unlike some legal rules, is not a technical conception with a fixed content unrelated to time, place and circumstances. Expressing as it does in its ultimate analysis respect enforced by law for that feeling of just treatment which has been evolved through centuries of Anglo-American constitutional history and civilization, 'due process' cannot be imprisoned within the treacherous limits of any formula. Representing a profound attitude of fairness between man and man, and more particularly between the individual and government, 'due process' is compounded of history, reason, the past course of decisions, and stout confidence in the strength of the democratic faith which we profess. Due process is not a mechanical instrument. It is not a yardstick. It is a delicate process of adjustment inescapably involving the exercise of judgment by those whom the Constitution entrusted with the unfolding of the process." 341 U.S. 123, 162-163.

DUPLICITOUS refers to a **pleading** which joins in the same **count** two or more distinct grounds of **action** to enforce a single right; to allege more than one distinct claim in the same **indictment** is 'duplicitous.'

DUPLICITY in practice, the technical invalidity resulting from uniting two or more **causes of action** in one **count** of a **pleading**, or multiple defenses in one plea, or multiple **crimes** in one count of an **indictment**, or two or more incongruous subjects in one legislative act, all contrary to proper **procedural** or constitutional requirements, see, e.g., 47 F. Supp. 524, 529, 530 (pleadings); 173 N.E. 2d 474, 475 (indictments); 273 P. 928, 930 (legislation). See also **joinder; misjoinder.**

DURESS action by a person which compels another to do what he need not otherwise do. It is a recognized **defense** to any act, such as a **crime**, contractual **breach** or **tort**, which must be voluntary in order to create **liability** in the actor. Restatement, Contracts §492 defines duress as "a) any wrongful act of one person that compels a manifestation of apparent assent by another to a transaction without his volition, or b) any wrongful threat of one person by words or conduct that induces another to enter into a transaction under the influence of such fear as precludes him from exercising free will and judgment, if the threat was intended or should reasonably have been expected to operate as an inducement." Duress negates the free assent necessary to create a binding **contract**, and may be accomplished by force or threat of force to a person or his property. Neither the threats alone nor the fear alone is sufficient to prove duress, and the test of fear is the actual state of mind of the victim, without resort to an objective standard of reasonableness. See 50 N.E. 555. To qualify as duress, threats must be unlawful. Dobbs, Remedies, see 10.2. Thus, the "threat" to pursue a legal remedy (such as a lawsuit) will not qualify as duress, as long as the "threat" is made in good faith. See 274 F. Supp. 1003, 1005.

In tort law, duress is most often used to invalidate the consent which will otherwise exclude the defendant's liability. Prosser, Torts 106 (4th ed. 1971).

In criminal law, duress is an **affirmative defense** which will excuse the action under some circumstances, if a person of reasonable firmness could not have resisted the fear induced by another. 180 N.W. 418, 422.

At common law, duress was not recognized as a defense to felonious **homicides**. 12 So. 301, 303.

DURHAM RULE a test of criminal responsibility, adopted by the District of Columbia Court of Appeals in 1954, which states that "an accused is not criminally responsible if his unlawful act was the product of mental disease or defect." 214 F. 2d 862, 874-75. The Durham Rule was the first major modification of the **common law M'Naghten Rule** but is no longer in force in the District of Columbia, having been negated by the American Law Institute's Model Penal Code test, §4.01(1), now used by a number of jurisdictions. 471 F. 2d 969, 971. See **insanity**.

DUTY obligatory conduct owed by a person to another person. In **tort** law, duty is a legally sanctioned obligation the **breach** of which results in the **liability** of the actor. See 247 F. Supp. 188, 191. Thus, under the law of **negligence**, an individual owes to others a

DUTY OF CARE in that he must conduct himself so as to avoid negligent injury to them.

In tax law, a duty is a levy [tax] on **imports** and **exports**. See 119 F. Supp. 352, 354.

DUTY, LEGAL see **legal duty**.

DUTY OF PRODUCING EVIDENCE see **burden of proof**.

DWELLING HOUSE one's residence or abode; a structure or apartment used as a home for a family unit. As used in a **restrictive covenant** the term PRIVATE DWELLING may be limited to single-family occupation even though two-family use does not change the outward character of the house. 198 N.Y.S. 311, 312. In the law of real property, it "includes everything pertinent and accessory to the main building and may consist of a cluster of buildings." 121 Ga. App. 240.

In criminal law, a house in which the occupier and his family usually reside, temporary absence being insufficient to destroy the status of the structure as a dwelling. 4 Blackstone's Comm. *225. For the purpose of the crime of **burglary** the dwelling house includes mobile homes, 46 A. 2d 35, 36; apartment units, 26 N.Y. 200; even a hotel room if one is living therein and thus is not a mere transient. Compare 99 N.E. 357, 359 with 86 N.Y. 360. See generally, Perkins, Criminal Law 200-05 (2d ed. 1969).

DYING DECLARATIONS see **hearsay rule**.

EASEMENT a right of one owner of land to make lawful and **beneficial use** of the land of another, created by an express or implied agreement. 46 Cal. Rptr. 25, 33; 62 Cal Rptr. 113; 172, S.W. 2d 885, 887. Such use must not be

inconsistent with any other uses which are already being made of the land. See 45 N.W. 2d 895. An easement is an **inchoate** privilege connected with the land, and is therefore not an **estate** or **fee.** 91 P. 2d 428. See also **public easement.**

EASEMENT APPURTENANT a "pure" easement, or "easement proper," i.e., one that requires a **dominant estate** to which the benefit of the easement attaches, or "appertains." In contrast to an **easement in gross,** an "easement appurtenant" "passes with the dominant estate to all subsequent **grantees** and is **inheritable.**" 206 N.Y.S. 42, 44. See 258 N.Y.S. 695.

EASEMENT IN GROSS a personal privilege to make use of another's land. It is not **appurtenant** to a **dominant estate** and is therefore not **assignable** or **inheritable,** but "dies" with the person who acquired it. See 156 A. 121, 122; 210 P. 2d 593, 596.

EASEMENT OF NECESSITY an **easement** necessary for the continued use of the land when a larger tract of land has been subdivided. The existence of such an easement is determined by assessing the facts surrounding the original **conveyance** severing the **dominant estate** from the **servient estate.** If without the easement either the **grantee** or **grantor** cannot make use of his property, then the existence of an "easement of necessity" is implied by **operation of law.** See 146 N.E. 2d 171, 175, 137 A. 2d 92, 98, 99, 139 A. 2d 318, 322.

PUBLIC EASEMENT see **public easement.**

EGRESS see **ingress and egress.**

EJECTMENT a legal action brought by one claiming a right to possess **real property** against another who possesses the premises adversely or who is a **holdover** [**tenant** who remains beyond that termination of a **lease**]. See 469 F. 2d 211, 214. At **common law,** the action was originally commenced by a copyholder or **lessee** against an intruder. Later it became a possessory action brought by a fictitious lessee to **try the title** of the possessor or **real party in interest.** See 51 A. 509, 510. Under modern statutory law the action is generally between real parties in interest, and the holder of legal title is entitled to recover possession from one holding under an invalid title. See 244 N.W. 160. See also **adverse possession; trespass.**

EJUSDEM GENERIS *(ā-yūs'-děm jěn'-ěr-ĭs)*—Lat: a rule of statutory **construction,** generally accepted by both state and federal courts, that where general words follow enumerations of particular classes or persons or things, the general words shall be construed as applicable only to persons or things of the same general nature or kind as those enumerated. 49 F. Supp. 846. Thus, in a statute forbidding the concealment on one's person of "pistols, revolvers, derringers, or other dangerous weapons," the term "dangerous weapons" may be construed to comprehend only dangerous weapons of the kind enumerated, i.e., firearms, or perhaps more narrowly still, handguns.

ELECTION OF REMEDIES a choice of possible **remedies** permitted by law for an **injury** suffered. A rule of **procedure** which requires that the party make a choice between two or more alternative and inconsistent remedies both (all) of which are allowed by law on the same facts. See 112 F. Supp. 365, 367; 85 A. 2d 493, 496; 231 P. 2d 39, 47. Once the choice is made, the alternatives not chosen are waived. See 194 P. 721, 722. Thus, while the plaintiff may seek the alternative remedies of **specific performance** or **damages** for a **breach of contract** he may not ask for alternative inconsistent remedies such as **recission** and damages, since the recission elects to treat the **contract** as **void** and the request for damages seeks to enforce a valid contract. See **alternative pleading.**

ELECTION UNDER THE WILL the principle that to take under a will is to adopt and require conformity to all its provisions. See 191 S.E. 14, 16. More specifically, it consists of the choice of accepting the benefit given under the will and relinquishing a claim to some property which the will disposes of to another; or retaining that claim and rejecting the benefit. See 136 N.E. 695, 696, 284 P. 411, 414. See also **widow's election.**

ELECTIVE FRANCHISE see **franchise.**

EMANCIPATION the freeing of some-one from the control of another. The express or implied relinquishing by a parent of rights in, or authority and control over, a **minor** child. While eman-cipation frees the child of parental con-trol, and gives him the right to his own earnings and the right to purchase prop-erty free from his parent's claims, the child surrenders his right to maintenance and support from the parents. See 269 N.Y.S. 667; 118 S.W. 956, 958. It is sometimes said that the acts of a child alone are not enough to establish eman-cipation; that some act or omission by the parent is necessary, see 117 N.E. 2d 42, 43; but it may be sufficient for a child merely to enter into a relation, such as marriage, which is inconsistent with his subjection to control by the parent. 37 Vt. 528, 529; 63 A. 2d 586, 587-8.

EMBEZZLEMENT the **fradulent** appro-priation to one's own use of property lawfully in his **possession.** It is a type of **larceny** which did not exist at **common law** because it does not involve a **tres-passory** or wrongful taking; thus it is a crime created by statute. Embezzlement is often associated with bank employees, public officials, or officers of organiza-tions, who may in the course of their lawful activities come into possession of property, such as money, actually owned by others. Compare **misapplication.**

EMBRACERY the **common law mis-demeanor** of attempting to bribe or cor-ruptly influence a juror. 4 Blackstone's Comm. *140. It is immaterial that the influence might be in the direction of a just or proper **verdict** since the **crime** is the impermissible interference with the jury function. The crime is complete when the **attempt** is made, "and there can be no such crime as an attempt to commit embracery." 130 S.E. 249, 251. It has been held that embracery may also be committed by corruptly attempt-ing to influence members of the **grand jury** as well as the **petit** [trial] **jury.** 115 S.E. 2d 576, 579.

The crime need not involve bribery as such but where it does it is often assumed today under modern statutes broadly defining the bribery offenses. Modern statutes have also treated the remaining aspects of embracery under the general offense of **obstructing justice** and the offense of embracery itself is tending to disappear as a distinct offense. Perkins, Criminal Law 494 (2d ed. 1969).

EMINENT DOMAIN the right of the state or **sovereign** to take private prop-erty for **public use;** since "eminent do-main" is an inherent attribute of sover-eignty, 15 A. 2d 647; the individual property owner's consent to the taking is immaterial. 29 N.E. 1062. The Fifth Amendment to the United States Consti-tution requires that **just compensation** be made whenever private property is tak-en for public use by the Congress. See **condemn.**

EMOLUMENT profit derived from of-fice, employment, or labor, including salary, wages, fees, rank, and other compensation. "Emoluments" are not generally considered to include travel or other business expenses, vacation or compensatory time, or other items not thought of as strictly profit. See 508 P. 2d 1151, 1156; 360 S.W. 2d 307, 311; 122 A. 2d 800, 801.

EMPLOYER'S LIABILITY ACTS statutes specifying the extent to which employ-ers shall be **liable** to make **compensation** for **injuries** sustained by their employees in the course of employment. 53 Am. Jur. 2d, Master and Servant §341, 353. Unlike **workmen's compensation** laws, which have replaced these acts in many states, the employer is made liable only for injuries resulting from his **breach** of a **duty** owed the employee—i.e., his negligence—and is not **strictly liable.** 52 So. 878. Like workmen's compensation, however, many of these acts do abolish the use by the employer of the common law defenses of **contributory negligence, assumption of the risk,** and the **fellow-servant rule.** See 53 Am. Jur. 2d, Master and Servant §341.

ENACTING CLAUSE generally, the pre-amble of a **statute,** or that part which identifies the statute as a legislative act and authorizes it as law. See 61 N.E. 1116, 1117; 139 F. Supp. 922. Thus,

"Be it enacted by the Senate and House of Representatives of the United States in Congress assembled," etc. is the enacting clause used in Congressional legislation.

EN BANC *(ähn bähnk)*—Fr: by the full court. Many **appellate courts** sit in parts or divisions of three or more judges from among a larger number on the full court. These parts will generally decide a particular case but sometimes either on the court's **motion** or at the request of one of the **litigants** the court will consider the matter by the full court rather than by only a part thereof; a matter may also be reconsidered by the whole court after a part thereof has rendered its decision. This is called a REHEARING EN BANC. The phrase is sometimes spelled "en bank." Courts which generally hear matters by the full court may nevertheless indicate this usual fact by an "en banc" notation at the head of the opinion.

ENCLOSURE see **inclosure**.

ENCROACH to gain unlawfully upon the lands, property, or authority of another; to intrude slowly or gradually upon the rights or property of another. 82 N.Y.S. 961, 964. An "encroachment" is any infringement on the property or authority of another. Id.

ENCUMBRANCE see **incumbrance**

ENDORSEMENT see **indorsement**.

ENDOWMENT a permanent fund of **property** or money bestowed upon an institution or a person, the income from which is used to serve the specific purpose for which the "endowment" was intended. See 45 F. 2d 345, 346, 187 A. 632, 636. For example, an endowment may be bestowed on a college or hospital for the support of the institution.

ENFEOFF to create a **feoffment** [early common law means of conveying **freehold** estates]. "Enfeoff" has been used as a word granting **title** in some modern **deeds**. See 31 N.J.L. 143, 151.

EN GROS *(ähn grō)* — Fr: in gross (large) amount; total; by wholesale.

ENJOIN to command or instruct with authority; to abate, suspend, or restrain. See 138 F. 2d 320, 326; 32 Hun. 126, 129. For example, one may be "en-

joined" or commanded by a court with **equitable** powers, either to do a specific act or to refrain from doing a certain act. See **injunction**.

ENTAIL to create a **fee tail**; to create a fee tail from a **fee simple**.

ENTIRETY see **tenancy** (TENANCY BY THE ENTIRETY).

ENTRAPMENT in criminal law, an **affirmative defense** created either by statute or by court decision in the given jurisdiction which excuses a **defendant** from criminal liability for **crimes** induced by certain governmental persuasion or trickery. The prevailing "subjective" view of entrapment requires that the particular defendant demonstrate that but for the objectionable police conduct, he would not have committed the crime. This means that the predisposition of the defendant to commit the offense must be balanced against the police conduct to determine whether the police can be said to have caused the crime. The "objective" test favored by a minority of United States Supreme Court justices in 1932 and again in 1973 (but recommended by the Model Penal Code § 2.13(2)(b)) looks solely to the police conduct to determine if an ordinary, law-abiding citizen would have been persuaded to commit the crime. "Under the objective test the prosecution is not permitted to introduce evidence of the defendant's character, past criminal convictions, rumored criminal activities, or reaction to the Government's offer since such evidence relates only to the defendant's predisposition to commit the crime. Because the subjective test focuses on such evidence, it is open to substantial abuse." 87 Harv. L. Rev. 243, 244 n. 5; 287 U.S. 435. Merely presenting the opportunity is not entrapment under either test. Entrapment as such is not a **due process** guarantee applicable to the states, but "outrageous" governmental conduct may violate due process of law and condemn a **prosecution** which is the fruit thereof. 411 U.S. 423, 431-32.

ENTRY, FORCIBLE see **forcible entry**.

ENURE see **inure**.

EQUAL PROTECTION OF THE LAWS constitutional guarantee embodied in the Fourteenth Amendment to the U.S. Constitution, which states in relevant part that "No State shall . . . deny to any person within its jurisdiction the equal protection of the laws." This has not been interpreted to imply that all persons in the state must be equally affected by each statute that the legislature enacts. "The equal protection clause of the Fourteenth Amendment does not take from the State the power to classify in the adoption of police laws, but admits of the exercise of a wide scope of discretion in that regard, and avoids what is done only when it is without any reasonable basis and therefore is purely arbitrary." 220 U.S. 61, 78. Thus, in the general case, courts presume the validity of a state statute if there is any rational basis for it. However, in certain special instances, the court will subject the law to "strict scrutiny." This test requires that the law be held to violate the equal protection clause unless the state can show a COMPELLING INTEREST which can only be furthered by enactment of the statute in question. 394 U.S. 618, 634. One situation which will trigger the "strict scrutiny" test occurs where the statute singles out for special treatment a class of persons that the court finds to be a SUSPECT CLASSIFICATION. The criteria for suspectness are that the class must be "saddled with such disabilities, or subjected to such a history of purposeful unequal treatment, or relegated to such a position of political powerlessness as to command extraordinary protection from the majoritarian process." 411 U.S. 1, 28. Classifications based upon the following have been held to be suspect: alienage, 403 U.S. 365, 372; nationality, 332 U.S. 633, 644-646; race, 379 U.S. 184, 191-192. In some instances the courts have required the statute to pass the stricter test where the law infringed upon the exercise of a "fundamental right," such as those embodied in the First Amendment. 394 U.S. 618, 634 (right to travel). Although wealth classifications have not been held to be inherently suspect the courts have struck down legislation which denied indigents free trial transcripts and hence in effect access to appellate review of their criminal convictions. "There can be no equal justice where the kind of trial a man gets depends on the amount of money he has."

351 U.S. 12, 19. Under the equal protection guarantee indigents have also won the right to appointed counsel, first in felony cases, 372 U.S. 335; and today in any instance where they are actually subjected to any period of imprisonment. 407 U.S. 25.

EQUITABLE DEFENSE see **defense**.

EQUITABLE ESTATE see **estate**.

EQUITABLE ESTOPPEL see **estoppel**.

EQUITABLE RELIEF see **relief**.

EQUITABLE SEISIN see **seisin**.

EQUITABLE TITLE see **title**.

EQUITY most generally, "justice." Historically, "equity" developed as a separate body of law in England in reaction to the inability of the **common law** courts, in their strict adherence to rigid **writs** and **forms of action**, to entertain or provide a **remedy** for every injury. The King therefore established the high **court of chancery**, the purpose of which was to do justice between **parties** in those cases where the common law would give no or inadequate redress. Equity law to a large extent was formulated in maxims, such as "equity suffers not a right without a remedy," or "equity follows the law," meaning that equity will derive a means to achieve a lawful result when legal procedure is inadequate. Equity and **law** are no longer bifurcated but are now merged in most jurisdictions, though equity jurisprudence and equitable doctrines are still independently viable. See 29 N.Y.S. 342, 343, 6 N.Y.S. 2d 720, 721, 293 F. 633, 637.

"Equity" also refers to the value of **property** minus **liens** or other **incumbrances**. See 67 Cal. Rptr. 104, 107. For example, one's "equity" in a home he has **mortgaged** is the value of the property beyond the amount of the mortgage to be paid. See **equity of redemption**.

EQUITY OF REDEMPTION right of **mortgagor** to redeem his property after defaulting in the payment of the **mortgage debt**, by the subsequent payment of all costs and interest, in addition to the mortgage debt to the **mortgagee**. See 95 F. 2d 487, 489. It is a right available to mortgagors prior to actual **fore-closure**. The concept is more applicable in **title jurisdictions** than in **lien jurisdictions**, because in the former, redemption actually brings title to the mortgaged property back to the mortgagor. 230 P. 724. Equity of redemption has been held to be an interest in **real property** and, as such, subject to the ordinary rules of **conveyancing**. 272 P. 1063, 1064.

ERGO (ĕr′-gō) Lat: therefore; consequently; hence; because.

ERRONEOUS involving a mistake. It signifies a deviation from the requirements of the law. 15 F. 2d 285. It does not connote a lack of legal authority, and is thus distinguished from "illegal." See 23 P. 508. "It means having the power to act, but [committing] error in its exercise." 15 F. 2d 285, 286.

ERRONEOUS JUDGMENT "one rendered according to course and practice of court, but contrary to law, upon mistaken view of law, or upon erroneous application of legal principles." 157 S.E. 434. An erroneous judgment is not **void**, and is not subject to **collateral attack**, but remains in effect until **reversed** or modified on **appeal**. 81 S.E. 2d 409.

ESCALATOR CLAUSE that part of a **lease** or **contract** which provides for an increase in the contract price upon the determination of certain acts or other factors beyond the parties' control, such as an increase in the cost of labor or of a necessary commodity, or the fixing of maximum prices by a governmental agency. See 176 F. 2d 675, 212 S.E. 2d 293. For example, an escalator clause in a lease may permit an increase in rent whenever the rent control laws are relaxed so that the landlord can charge more; or a wife's **alimony** may have an escalator clause so that as the cost of living increases or as her husband's income increases so will her alimony.

ESCHEAT the reversion of **property** to the state or **sovereign**, as the ultimate proprietor of **realty**, by reason of the lack of anyone to **inherit** it, or by reason of a breach of **condition**, etc. See 252 N.W. 826, 104 N.W. 2d 338, 340. Compare **forfeiture**.

ESCROW a written **instrument**, such as a **deed**, temporarily deposited with a neutral third party (called the ESCROW AGENT), by the agreement of two parties who have entered into a valid **contract**. The escrow agent will hold the document until the conditions of the contract are met, at which time he will deliver it to the **grantee** or **obligee**. The depositor has no control over the instrument after it is in "escrow." At **common law**, "escrow" applied to the deposits only of instruments for the **conveyance** of land, but it now applies to all instruments so deposited. Money so deposited is also loosely referred to as "escrow." See generally 74 N.E. 2d 619, 622.

ESQUIRE term originally used to designate a rank of English landed gentry, and afterward used to designate English barristers, sergeants and judges. See 1 Bl. Comm.*406. Used now as an appendage to the name of a person admitted to practice law in the United States.

ESTABLISHMENT CLAUSE that provision in the First Amendment of the Federal Constitution, which has been applied to the states by the Fourteenth Amendment, prohibiting the enactment of laws respecting "the establishment of religion." The Supreme Court has stated that the establishment clause "means at least this: Neither a state nor the Federal government can set up a church. Neither can pass laws which aid one religion, aid all religions, or prefer one religion over another. Neither can force a person to go to or to remain away from a church against his will or force him to profess a belief or disbelief in any religion. . . . No tax in any amount, large or small, can be levied to support any religious activities or institutions, whatever they may be called, or whatever form they may adopt to teach or practice religion. . . . In the words of Jefferson, the clause against establishment of religion was intended to erect a 'wall of separation between Church and State'." 330 U.S. 1, 15.

If either the purpose or primary effect of public aid to parochial schools is to advance or inhibit religion, it violates the establishment clause, 392 U.S. 236 (upholding a school textbook program). Traditional local tax-exemptions for church-owned property have been upheld, 397 U.S. 664; but various forms of financial aid to nonpublic schools have been condemned under this clause on the grounds of "excessive entanglement between government and religion" in the implementation of the programs. See, e.g. 403 U.S. 602.

Non-denominational prayers to be said aloud daily by public school students violate this clause. 370 U.S. 421. School busing programs financed by the public treasury but applicable to both public and nonpublic schools have been upheld. 330 U.S. 1.

ESTATE interest, right, or **ownership** in land; technically, the degree, quantity, nature, and extent of a person's interest or ownership of land. In its broad sense, "estate" applies to all that a person owns, whether **real** or **personal property.** See 205 P. 2d 1127, 1130. 175 S.E. 2d 351, 353.

CONTINGENT ESTATE   see **contingent estate.**

DOMINANT ESTATE   see **dominant estate.**

EQUITABLE ESTATE   an estate or interest which can only be enforced in **equity;** especially applies to every **trust,** express or implied, which is not converted to a legal estate by the **statute of uses.** "In law, the legal estate is the whole estate, and the holder of the legal title is the sole owner. But this title may be held for the beneficial interest of another, which interest has come to be called an 'equitable estate.' It is not, however, strictly speaking, an interest in the land itself, but a right which can be enforced in equity." 35 A. 213.

ESTATE IN FEE SIMPLE   see **fee simple.**

ESTATE IN FEE TAIL   see **fee tail.**

FUTURE ESTATE   an estate in land which is not **possessory** but which will or may become so at some time in the future. "Future estates" are either **vested** or **contingent,** and include **remainders** and **reversions.** See 112 N.Y.S. 310, 311. See also **future interest.**

LEGAL ESTATE   originally, an interest in land that was enforced by courts of **common law,** as opposed to an equitable estate, enforced by **courts of equity.** Prior to the fifteenth century, the law conceived of only one type of ownership in the same property, which was the "legal estate." The development of **uses** and **trusts,** how-

ever, led to the present dual system of ownership whereby a **title** to property does not necessarily imply the right to **beneficial use and enjoyment.** For example, in a trust relationship the **trustee** possesses legal title to the trust **property;** however, the **beneficiary** of the trust has the equitable estate and is entitled to the exclusive benefit of the trust. Similarly, one who purchases property under an installment land contract has an "equitable estate" and is entitled to possession. However, the seller holds the "legal estate" or "title" to the property, until the property is paid in full. See Restatement of Property §6. See **Statute of Uses; lien (title) jurisdiction.**

PRECEDING ESTATE   see **preceding estate.**

SERVIENT ESTATE   see **servient estate.**

VESTED ESTATE   one either presently in **possession,** or one owned by a presently existing person to whom the property interest will automatically accrue upon the termination of a **preceding estate.** See 68 N.E. 1057. Such an estate thus represents a present interest and as such is neither subject to any contingency nor otherwise capable of being defeated. Compare **contingent estate.** See **vested.**

ESTATE AT SUFFERANCE   see **tenancy** (TENANCY AT SUFFERANCE).

ESTATE AT WILL   see **tenancy** (TENANCY AT WILL).

ESTATE BY THE ENTIRETY   see **tenancy** (TENANCY BY THE ENTIRETY).

ESTATE FOR LIFE   see **life estate.**

ESTATE FOR YEARS   see **tenancy** (TENANCY FOR YEARS).

ESTATE FROM YEAR TO YEAR [PERIOD TO PERIOD] see **tenancy** (TENANCY FROM YEAR TO YEAR).

ESTATE IN COMMON   see **tenancy** (TENANCY IN COMMON).

ESTATE PER AUTRE VIE [PUR AUTRE VIE]   see **per autre vie.**

ESTATE TAX   see **tax.**

ESTOPPEL   a bar; preclusion. "A bar which precludes a person from denying the truth of a fact which has, in contemplation of law, become settled by the facts and **proceedings** of judicial or legislative officers, or by the act of the **party** himself, either by conventional writing, or by representations, express or implied. An estoppel arises where man has done some act which the policy of the law will not permit him to gainsay or deny." 51 S.E. 514, 521. It is an **equitable** doctrine, and as such, is used when good conscience requires it. Thus, some injury to a party invoking the doctrine of estoppel is generally required, and the elements of the claim, then, consist of ignorance on the part of the person invoking estoppel, representation by party estopped which misleads, and an innocent and detrimental change of position in reliance on the representation. See 159 A. 2d 345, 351. Estoppel is distinguished from **waiver** in that a waiver generally refers to a voluntary surrender or relinquishment of some known right, benefit, or advantage; estoppel creates an inhibition or inability to assert it. 106 F. 2d 687, 691.

COLLATERAL ESTOPPEL see **collateral estoppel**.

ESTOPPEL BY DEED a bar which precludes a party from denying the truth of his deed. It may be invoked only in a suit on the deed or concerning a right arising out of it. See 170 S.W. 2d 240, 243.

ESTOPPEL BY JUDGMENT see **judgment**.

ESTOPPEL BY LACHES. see **laches**.

ESTOPPEL IN PAIS strictly, an **estoppel** which arises out of a person's statement of fact, or out of his silence, acts, or omissions, rather than from a **deed** or record or written **contract**. 35 P. 512. Also called an EQUITABLE ESTOPPEL. 136 N.J. Eq. 430. See generally **estoppel**.

ESTOVERS the right of the **tenant** to use during the period of his **lease** whatever timber there may be on the leased **premises** to the extent necessary to promote good husbandry. . . . "The right includes, when necessary for that purpose, timber for fencing, bridges, corn cribs; cotton houses, fire wood, repairs and other necessary purposes." 13 So. 2d 652, 653.

ET AL. *(ĕt äl)*—Lat: the abbreviated form of "et alii," which means "and others."

ET NON *(ĕt nŏn)*—Lat: and not. This phrase is used primarily in introducing a special **traverse** in **pleading** and thus is called the "inducement to the traverse." Synonymous in use with **absque hoc** which means "without this." 18 N.J.L. 339, 352.

ET SEQ. *(ĕt sĕk)*—Lat: the abbreviated form of "et sequentes" or "et sequentia" which means "and the following." It is most commonly used in denominating page reference numbers.

ET UX. *(ĕt ŭx)*—Lat: the abbreviated form of "et uxor" which means "and wife" for the purpose of **wills** and other **instruments** which purport to **grant** or **convey**.

EVICTION originally, the physical expulsion of someone from land by the assertion of **paramount title** or through legal **proceedings**. See 173 S.E. 812. Also, in reference to modern landlord-tenant law, "eviction" is sometimes used to refer to what is actually a "constructive eviction."

CONSTRUCTIVE EVICTION refers to circumstances existing under the control of the **landlord** which compel the **tenant** to leave the **premises** though he is not asked to do so by the landlord. The tenant may be deemed constructively evicted if the premises are rendered unfit for occupancy in whole or in substantial part, or if the use and enjoyment has been substantially impaired. No physical expulsion or legal **process** is necessary, see 95 N.Y.S. 2d 883, 886; and the tenant is not responsible for further rent, 263 N.Y.S. 695; but the tenant must actually vacate the premises. Compare **eject-ment; ouster; warranty** (WARRANTY OF HABITABILITY).

PARTIAL ACTUAL EVICTION occurs when part of the leased premises has been rendered unusable through the fault of the landlord. If the lease rental is not apportioned by room, nor the premises partitioned in the **lease** agreement, the tenant is not responsible for any part of the lease rental while actually evicted from a part of the leased premises, and he need not vacate the habitable part of the premises. 48 N.E. 781; 117 N.E. 579.

EVIDENCE all the means by which any alleged matter of fact, the truth of which is submitted to investigation at judicial **trial**, is established or disproved. See 16 A.2d 80, 89. Evidence includes the **testimony** of **witnesses**, introduction of records, documents, exhibits, objects or any other probitive matter offered for the purpose of inducing belief in the **party**'s contention by the **trier of fact**. An **allegation** is not itself evidence but rather is something to be proved or disproved through the introduction of **competent** admissable evidence. See **circumstantial evidence; hearsay; presumptive evidence**.

EVIDENCE ALIUNDE see **aliunde**.

EVIDENCE DE BENE ESSE see **de bene esse**.

EXCISE broadly, "any kind of tax which is not directly on property or the rents or incomes of real estate." 4 A. 2d 861, 862. "An inland impost upon articles of manufacture or sale and also upon licenses to pursue certain trades, or to deal in certain commodities." 184 U.S. 608. It is imposed directly and without assessment and is measured by amount of business done, income received, etc. 161 So. 735, 738.

EXCLUSIONARY RULE a constitutional rule of law which provides that otherwise admissible evidence may not be used in a criminal trial if it was the product of illegal police conduct. The rule does not apply in civil proceedings although statutes sometimes specifically provide for exclusion of such evidence. See **fruit of the poisonous tree doctrine**.

EXCLUSIVE USE see **use**.

EXCULPATORY refers to **evidence** and/or statements which tend to clear, justify, or excuse a **defendant** from alleged fault or **guilt**. See 501 S.W. 2d 101, 103. Contrast **incriminate**.

EXECUTE "to complete, as a legal instrument; to perform what is required to give validity to, as by signing and perhaps **sealing** and **delivering**; as to execute a **deed**, **will**, etc." 171 N.E. 2d 553, 563. For example, a **contract** is "executed" when all acts necessary to

complete it and to give it validity as an **instrument** are carried out, including signing and delivery. See 3 S.W. 2d 185. It is synonymous with "make."

The term also refers to the killing of a person by the authority of the State, as a criminal sanction pursuant to his **conviction** of a **capital offense**.

EXECUTED fully accomplished or performed; leaving nothing unfulfilled; opposite of **executory**.

EXECUTED INTEREST see **interest**.

EXECUTIVE AGREEMENT see **treaty**.

EXECUTOR (EXECUTRESS OR EXECUTRIX) "a person who either expressly or by implication is appointed by a **testator** [one who dies leaving a **will**] to carry out the testator's directions concerning the dispositions he makes under his will." 285 N.E. 2d 548, 550. Compare **administrator**.

EXECUTORY not fully accomplished or completed, but contingent upon the occurrence of some event or the performance of some act in the future; not **vested**; opposite of **executed**. An executory **contract** is one in which some performance remains to be accomplished. See **executory interest**.

EXECUTORY BEQUEST see **bequest**.

EXECUTORY INTEREST see **interest**.

EXEMPLARY DAMAGES see **damages**.

EX GRATIA (*ĕx grä'-shē-à*)—Lat: out of grace; out of favor. That which is done as a favor rather than as a required task or as of right.

EX-OFFENDER see **criminal**.

EX OFFICIO (*ĕx ō-fē'-shē-ō*) from the office, by virtue of his office, see 44 S.E. 2d 88, 95; officially. See 90 So. 423, 424.

EX OFFICIO MEMBER one who is the member of a board, committee or other body by virtue of his title to a certain office, and who does not require warrant or further appointment. See 31 N.W. 2d 5, 9.

EX OFFICIO SERVICES services which are imposed by law on a public officer by virtue of his office. See 251 N.W. 395.

EX PARTE *(ĕx pär'-tā)*-Lat: in behalf of on the application of one party, by or for one party. An ex parte judicial **proceeding** is one brought for the benefit of one party only, without notice to or challenge by an **adverse party**. It refers to an application made by one party to a proceeding in the absence of the other. Thus, an ex parte **injunction** is one having been granted without the adverse party having had **notice** of its application. An uncontested application where notice was given is not ex parte.

EXPECTANCY contingency as to **possession** or enjoyment. In the law of **property, estates** may be either in possession or in expectancy; if an expectancy is created by the parties it is a **remainder**; if by **operation of law** it is a **reversion**. 2 Bl. Comm.*163. See also **future interest; vested**.

EXPECTATION DAMAGES a measure of the money **damages** available to **plaintiff** in an action for **breach of contract**, based on the value of the benefit he would have received from the contract if the **defendant** had not breached, but had completed **performance** as agreed. The amount is generally computed on the basis of the monetary value of the contract to the plaintiff, based on full performance thereof minus whatever costs plaintiff was able to avoid by not performing his own part of the contract. When the buyer breaches, the expectation damages will ordinarily be the contract price, less costs saved; when the seller breaches, the buyer's expectation damages will be measured by the fair **market value** of the promised performance at the time and place of promised **tender** [delivery]. Compare **cost of completion; diminution in value; specific performance**.

EXPERT TESTIMONY [EVIDENCE] see **expert witness**.

EXPERT WITNESS a **witness** having "special knowledge of the subject about which he is to **testify**," 26 A. 2d 770, 773; that knowledge must generally be such as is not normally possessed by the average person. 22 A. 2d 28. The expert witness is thus "able to afford the tribunal having the matter under consideration a special assistance." 139 P. 2d 239, 242. This expertise may de-

rive from either study and education, or from experience and observation. 43 P. 2d 716. An expert witness need not have formal training but before one can qualify as an expert witness, the court must be satisfied that the testimony presented is of a kind which in fact requires special knowledge, skill or experience. 83 F. Supp. 722. Such testimony, given by an expert witness, constitutes EXPERT EVIDENCE or EXPERT TESTIMONY. 168 Ill. App. 419. Hypothetical questions [asking the witness to assume certain stated facts] may be asked of an expert witness as a way of educating the **trier of fact** in the area of the expert's knowledge or experience. See generally McCormick, Evidence, 29-41 (2d ed. 1972).

EX POST FACTO *(ĕx pōst fäk'-tō)*—Lat: after the fact; "every law that makes an action done before the passing of the law and which was innocent when done to be criminal and punishable as [a crime]; every law that aggravates a **crime** or makes it greater than when it was committed; every law that changes and inflicts a greater punishment; and every law that alters the legal rules of **evidence**, and requires less, or different, testimony than the law required at the time of the commission of the offense, in order to convict the offender." 171 S.W. 2d 880. Such a law violates Art. 1, §§9 (cl. 3) & 10 of the Constitution of the United States which provide that neither Congress nor any state shall pass an ex post facto law; these provisions have been held applicable only to criminal statutes. 3 U.S. (3 Dall.) 386. Compare **bill of attainder**.

EXPRESSIO UNIUS EST EXCLUSIO ALTERIUS *(ĕx-prĕ'-shē-ō ū-nē'-ŭs ĕst ĕx-klū' -shē-ō äl-tĕr'-ē-ŭs)*-Lat: The expression of one thing is the exclusion of another. In construing statutes under this maxim the mention of one thing within the statute implies the exclusion of another thing not so mentioned. See 95 P. 2d 1007, 1012. "The maxim . . . though not a rule of law, is an aid to construction, and is applicable where, in the natural association of ideas, that which is expressed is so set over by way of contrast to that which is omitted that the contrast enforces the affirmative inference that that which is omitted must be intended to have opposite and contrary treatment." See 34 So. 2d 132. Thus a statute granting certain rights to "police, fire, and sanitation employees" would be interpreted to exclude other public employees not enumerated from the legislation. This is based on presumed legislative intent and where for some reason this intent cannot be reasonably inferred the court is free to draw a different conclusion. See 16 N.E. 2d 459.

EX REL. *(ĕx rĕl)*—Lat: the abbreviated form of "ex relatione" which means "upon relation or report." Legal **proceedings** which are initiated "ex rel." are brought in the name of the state but on the information and at the instigation of a private individual with a private interest in the outcome. The **real party in interest** is called the "relator." The action will be captioned "State of X [or United States] ex rel. Y v. Z."

EXTENUATING CIRCUMSTANCES unusual factors related to and tending to contribute to the consummation of an illegal act, but over which the actor had little or no control. These factors therefore reduce the responsibility of the actor and serve to mitigate his punishment or his payment of **damages**. See **mitigating circumstances**. Compare **justification**.

EXTINGUISHMENT a discharge of an obligation or contract by **operation of law** or by express agreement.

EXTORTION at common law, the corrupt collection by a public official under **color of office** of an excessive or unauthorized fee. It was punishable as a **misdemeanor**. Under modern statutes the offense is broadened to include the illegal taking of money by anyone who employs threats, or other illegal use of fear or coercion in order to obtain the money, and whose conduct falls short of the threat to personal safety required for **robbery**. See 148 A. 2d 848, 850; 2 Mass. 522, 523; 160 F. 2d 754, 756. Extortion is used interchangeably with **blackmail** and is commonly punished as a felony. See generally Perkins, Criminal Law 367-375 (2d ed. 1969). Compare **bribery**.

EXTRAORDINARY DIVIDEND see **dividend**.

EXTRAORDINARY REMEDY see **remedy**.

EXTREMIS see **in extremis**.

EXTRINSIC FRAUD see **fraud**.

EX TURPI CAUSA NON ORITUR ACTIO *(ĕx tûr′-pē käw′-zȧ nŏn ôr′-ē-tûr äk′-shē-ō̇)*—Lat: no disgraceful, [foul, immoral, obscene] matter can give rise to an **action**. 24 S.E. 2d 895, 897.

F

FACILITATION in criminal law, a new statutory offense rendering one guilty of criminal facilitation when, believing it probable that he is aiding a person who intends to commit a **crime**, he engages in conduct which assists that person in obtaining the means or opportunity to commit it and in fact his conduct does aid the person to commit the crime. See N. Y. Penal Law §115. For example, if a store owner sells a gun to someone who is enraged and uttering threats about killing a third party, the store owner may be guilty of criminal facilitation. At common law, knowing facilitation may give rise to **liability** for **aiding and abetting** if the requisite **mens rea** can be established for the **accessorial** liability; but there was no distinct offense of criminal facilitation as such at common law. Compare **accomplice**; **conspiracy**.

FACINUS QUOS INQUINAT AEQUAT *(fä′-sĭ-nŭs kwōs ĭn′-kwĭ-nät ī′-kwät)* — Lat: villany and guilt make all those whom it contaminates equal in character.

FACTA SUNT POTENTIORI VERBIS *(fäk′-tȧ sŭnt pō-tĕn′-tē-ô̇′-rē vĕr′-bēs)*—Lat: the facts, deeds or accomplishments are more powerful than words.

FACT-FINDER in a judicial or administrative **proceeding**, the person or group of persons that has the responsibility of determining the facts relevant to decide a controversy. It is the role of a **jury** in a jury trial; in a non-jury trial the judge sits both as a fact-finder and as the trier of law; in administrative proceedings it may be a hearing officer or a hearing body. The term TRIER OF FACT generally denotes the same function.

FACTO *(fäk'-tō)*–Lat: in fact; by a deed, accomplishment or exploit. See also **de facto.**

FACTOR a person who receives and sells goods for a commission (which is called FACTORAGE); he is entrusted with the **possession** of the goods he sells and generally sells them in his own name. 209 N.W. 660, 661. For example, a used car dealer is a "factor" when the owner puts it in the dealer's possession so that the dealer can sell it. See 285 P. 2d 632, 634. Consignee. A financier who lends money and takes in return an **assignment** of accounts receivable or some other security. 294 F. 2d 126, 129. The **garnishee** in states where "factorizing" is the name for **garnishment.** 33 A. 147, 157. See **factor's acts.** Compare **jobber.**

FACTOR'S ACTS the name of certain English statutes, which have also been enacted in a number of states, whose "general effect is to make a **factor's** [agent's] possession** of property or documents of **title** such evidence of ownership as to enable him to do all acts which the true owner might, thus making the owner responsible for the factor's acts and protecting **bona fide purchasers** in any transaction fairly effected with the apparent owner [factor]." 32 Am. Jur. 2d Factors §53. The purpose of such statutes is to protect the purchaser where the agent has exceeded his authority. See 30 N.E. 2d 876, 880.

FACTUAL IMPOSSIBILITY see **impossibility.**

FACTUM *(fäk'-tūm)*–Lat: literally, a deed, act, exploit or accomplishment. When used with respect to a change in a person's domicile, the "factum" is the person's physical presence in the new domicile. See 169 Va. 548. In the civil law the word "factum" is used to distinguish a matter of **fact** from a matter of **law.** See **fraud—in the factum.**

FACTUM PROBANDUM *(fäk'-tūm prō-bän'-dūm)*–Lat. in the law of **evidence,** the **fact** to be proved.

FAILURE OF CONSIDERATION see **consideration.**

FAILURE OF ISSUE words used in a **will** or **deed** to refer to a **condition** which operates in the event either no children be born or no children survive the decedant. Often the words "die without issue" are employed. The words may fix a condition, whereby an estate, instead of being alienable and therefore capable of being conveyed to a third person will in the event of "failure of issue," pass automatically to an alternative designated in the original instrument. Unless the instrument indicated to the contrary, the common law read the condition as operating ad infinitum. This construction is termed INDEFINITE FAILURE OF ISSUE. Thus, if children of the first taker themselves fail to leave children, the estate will still go to the alternative. The first taker is regarded as possessing a **fee tail,** and his descendants continue as **tenants in tail.** 9 Watts 447, 450; 20 A. 560. A majority of American jurisdictions by statute have reversed this presumption and construe "die without issue" as a DEFINITE FAILURE OF ISSUE; i.e., the condition is satisfied fully if the first taker has issue surviving at the time of his death. 5 Amer. Law of Property §21.50 (1952). Alternative expressions include "if he dies before he has any issue;" "for want of issue;" "without leaving issue."

FAIR COMMENT a **plea** by one involved in a **libel** suit that the statements made, even if untrue, were not intended to create ill will or malice but rather were intended to state the facts as the writer honestly intended them to be. "**Defendant** is not entitled to publish defamatory misstatements of fact without reasonable grounds for a belief of truth, with conscious indifference to truth, or without ascertaining reasonably available facts. Only honest and unintentional mistake of facts are protected." 139 F. Supp. 35, 38.

FAIR HEARING a statutorily authorized extra-judicial hearing which is granted primarily in situations where the normal judicial processes would be inadequate to secure **due process**, either because a judicial remedy does not exist, or because one would suffer grievous harm or substantial prejudice to his rights before a judicial remedy became available. Thus, fair hearings have been authorized as forums for the administrative determination of a citizen's rights in the event of termination of welfare benefits (42 U.S.C.A. §602(a)(4)), before deportation of an alien (8 U.S.C.A. §1252(b)), where the granting or revocation of a broadcasting license is at issue (47 U.S.C.A. §409(b)), etc; and it has been determined judicially that due process requires in some situations the opportunity for a fair hearing. See, e.g., 294 F. 2d 150. The fair hearing must be conducted in a manner consistent with the requirements of due process, including the opportunity of one whom the decision will affect to present evidence in his favor, as well as to be apprised of the evidence against him in the matter so that he will be fully aware of the basis for the judgment. See 212 F. 275.

FAIR MARKET VALUE see **market value.**

FAIR TRADE LAWS state statutes which permit a manufacturer to establish minimum resale prices which cannot be varied by the wholesaler or distributor.

Almost all vertical minimum pricing agreements are **per se** violations of the **conspiracy** sections of the Federal **Anti-Trust** Acts. Under the provisions of the McGuire Act, 15 U.S.C. §45 (1952), however, such agreements do not violate the antitrust laws when they are entered into under the provisions of state Fair Trade Statutes. See also 283 F. 2d 90.

FAIR USE in federal **copyright** law refers to an insubstantial permitted use by copying and acknowledgment. Whether a particular use will be considered insubstantial and hence a fair use will turn on the reasonableness of the copying under the circumstances. Important factors will be whether the copied material was creative or research-oriented; the status of the user (reviewer, scholar, compiler, parodist); extent of use (both qualitatively and quantitatively); whether the use will diminish the value of the

copyright; the absence of an intent to plagiarize as evidenced by proper acknowledgement; the original contribution of the user. See Kaplan and Brown, Copyright 309-351 (1960).

The doctrine is not a part of the statutory law itself but is case developed. "It is certainly not necessary, to constitute an invasion of copyright, that the whole of a work should be copied, or even a large portion of it, in form or in substance. If so much is taken, that the value of the original is sensibly diminished, or the labors of the original author are substantially to an injurious extent appropriated by another, that is sufficient, in point of law, to constitute a piracy 'pro tanto' and hence to amount to an unjustified use." 9 Fed. Cas. 342, 348. See also 366 F. 2d 303.

Photocopying of single copies of research articles for one's own use also constitutes a fair use and is not an infringement of the copyright.

FALSE ARREST unlawful **arrest;** unlawful restraint of another's personal liberty or freedom of locomotion. 193 N.E. 2d 485, 489. It may be a criminal offense and/or the basis of a **civil action** for **damages.** See **false imprisonment.**

FALSE IMPRISONMENT as a **tort,** the unjustified detention of a person. The restraint must be total so that it amounts to an imprisonment; mere obstruction, stopping, locking one out of his room, etc. is not enough. 219 F. 2d 622. The total restraint may, however, be of any appreciable duration. 70 So. 734. No physical force need be used so long as the victim reasonably believes that he is being restrained against his will. 195 S.W. 2d 312 (woman remained in a store when her purse was wrongfully taken from her). The tort must be intentional, Restatement Torts §35; but no actual **damages** need be proved. 109 A. 2d 128.

Where the restraint is imposed by virtue of purported legal authority and an arrest occurs, it will be a **false arrest** and hence a false imprisonment; the defendant need not be a police officer but must merely assert improper legal authority to detain. 116 P. 234 (railroad conductor).

As a **common law misdemeanor** it is the unlawful confinement of a person. This need not consist of wrongfully locking him in a jail, but comprehends "any unlawful exercise or show of force by which a person is compelled to remain where he does not wish to remain or to go where he does not wish to go." 172 N.E. 2d 380, 381-82.

FALSE RETURN a **return** (statement) to a **writ** made by a ministerial officer in which there is a false statement that is injurious to a party having an interest in such writ. 266 S.W. 723, 726. For example, if a sheriff is supposed to serve a **summons** and claims on his return that he did serve it, when he actually did not serve the summons, this would constitute a false return.

In tax situations, an incorrect return in which there appears either an intent to mislead or deceive on the part of the taxpayer, or at least **negligence** that is sufficiently gross to warrant holding the taxpayer liable for his error. See 52 N.E. 635, 638.

FALSE SWEARING a **common law misdemeanor** which would amount to **perjury** except that it is not committed in a judicial **proceeding**; the giving of a false oath in connection with some proceeding or matter in which an oath is required by law. "A FALSE OATH is a wilful and corrupt sworn statement made without sincere belief in its truthfulness." Perkins, Criminal Law 454 (2d ed. 1969). Thus, the giving of a false oath in an **affidavit** used to obtain a marriage license will not support a charge of perjury because it is extrajudicial but it will support a charge of false swearing which is a separate offense. 3 S.W. 662. Statutes sometimes group perjury, false swearing, and "making false written statements" together as different degrees of the same crime, often called loosely "perjury." See, e.g., N.Y. Penal Law Art. 210.

FALSE VERDICT a manifestly unjust **verdict**; one not true to the **evidence.** When such a verdict is rendered, the court can enter a **judgment n.o.v.** ("notwithstanding the verdict").

FALSI CRIMEN see **crimen falsi.**

FAMILY PURPOSE DOCTRINE doctrine establishing **tort liability** of the owner of a "family car" when that car is used by another member of the fam-

ily. The rule thus imputes a relationship of **principal** and **agent** where one maintains an automobile for pleasure or other use of members of his family. See 180 S.W. 2d 102, 104.

FAMOSUS LIBELLUS *(fä-mō'-sŭs lē'-bĕl-ŭs)*—Lat: literally, a **slanderous** or **libelous** letter, handbill, advertisement, petition, written **accusation** or **indictment.** Its legal usage is that of a libelous writing.

FATAL VARIANCE see **variance.**

FAVORED BENEFICIARY "[o]ne who, in the circumstances of the particular case, has been favored over others having equal claim to the **testator**'s bounty." 1 So. 2d 890, 892. "Confidential relations, accompanied with activity of a favored beneficiary in the preparation and execution of a will, raises a presumption of **undue influence.**" 112 So. 313, 316.

FEALTY in feudal times, "the oath sworn by the **tenant** to be faithful to his lord." Moynihan, Introduction to the Law of Real Property 18 (1962). It was one of the **incidents** of free **tenures.** See also **homage.**

FEDERAL COMMON LAW the body of decisional law developed by the federal courts, not resting on state court decisions. Before the decision in *Erie Railroad* v. *Tompkins*, 304 U.S. 64, it referred primarily to the decisional law that federal courts developed in **diversity of citizenship** cases. After *Erie*, federal courts sitting in diversity cases have been bound to follow the general (substantive) **common law** of the state from which, respectively, each case arose. It has been argued that *Erie* strengthened federal common law in those areas where a federal standard is intended and necessary, such as in interstate commerce, federal labor statutes, unfair competition, and defamation by multi-state media. See 39 N.Y.U.L. Rev. 383, 408-418 (1964). See **pre-emption.**

FEDERAL COURTS the courts of the United States, as distinguished from the courts of the individual states. These courts derive their legitimacy from the Constitution, Art. III, Sec. I. Clause 1: "The judicial Power of the United

States, shall be vested in one supreme court, and in such inferior courts as the Congress may from time to time ordain and establish." Presently, the principle federal courts are the **district courts** (general courts of **original jurisdiction**; federal **trial courts**), the **courts of appeal** (formerly circuit courts of appeals; principally **appellate** review courts), and the **Supreme Court** (only court created directly by the Constitution; court of last resort in federal system; having final appellate review of lower federal courts, and of state court decisions involving questions of federal law). All of these courts are limited in their power to hear cases by the grant of **jurisdiction** in the Constitution (Art. III, Sec. 2). The principal instances of federal jurisdiction are those cases "arising under [the] Constitution, [and] the laws of the United States," those "to which the United States shall be a Party" and those either between two states, a state and the citizen of another state or between the citizen of two different states [**diversity of citizenship**].

There are a few other specialized courts within the federal system: COURT OF CLAIMS (hears suits involving such claims against the United States government as are allowed by federal law); COURT OF CUSTOMS AND PATENT APPEALS (review of Customs Court decisions); CUSTOMS COURT (review decision of the several collectors of customs). See Wright, Federal Courts §§1-5 (2d ed. 1970).

FEDERALISM a system of government wherein power is divided by a constitution between a central government and local governments, the local governments maintaining control over local affairs and the central government being accorded sufficient authority to deal with national needs and affairs. The power of local governments can be revoked, expanded or contracted at the will of the central government without the concurrence of the local governments. Since the United States is a federal "republic," considerations of federalism play a major role in the interpretation of the Constitution.

FEDERAL QUESTION JURISDICTION one kind of **original jurisdiction** given to federal courts by virtue of Article III

of the Constitution and enabling legislation, it allows federal courts to hear **cases** wherein the meaning or application of something in the Constitution, laws, or treaties of the United States is being disputed. For example, if the meaning of a federal law or the application of a provision of the federal Constitution were raised in a case, then the case would present a federal question, and if federal law granted federal courts jurisdiction to hear that specific federal question, then there would be federal question jurisdiction. See also **diversity of citizenship**.

FEDERAL TORT CLAIMS ACT an act passed in 1946, which confers exclusive **jurisdiction** on United States **District Courts** to hear claims against the United States, "for money **damages**, accruing on and after January 1, 1945, for **injury** or loss of **property**, or personal injury or death, caused by the **negligent** or **wrongful act** or omission of any employee of the government while acting within the scope of his office or employment, under circumstances where the United States, if a private person, would be liable to the claimant in accordance with the law of the place where the act or omission occurred." 28 U.S.C. 1346 (b). The act is, in substance, a broad waiver of **sovereign immunity** although there are a number of qualifications and conditions on the waiver, principally as to intentional torts (e.g. **assault, battery**, etc.) and acts within the "discretionary function or duty" of any federal agency or employee. See 28 U.S.C. 2671-2680. Some state governments have enacted similar legislation.

FEE in **real property**, an **estate** of complete **ownership** which can be sold by the owner or **devised** to his **heirs**. 106 F. 2d 217, 224; 7 A. 2d 696, 698-99. "Fee" derives from "feudal," or "feodor," meaning "land," importing that such land is held by some superior to whom certain **services** are due. "Fee," "fee simple," and "fee simple absolute," are often used as equivalents. The word "fee" indicates that it is an estate of **inheritance**; the word "simple" signifies that there are no restrictions on the inheritable characteristics of the estate. See **fee simple**. But a fee may be qualified, such as a **conditional** or **determi-**

nable fee which could continue forever but would be discontinued upon the happening of a certain event.

FEE SIMPLE a **freehold estate** of virtually infinite duration and of absolute **inheritance** free of any condition, limitations, or restriction to particular **heirs.** 78 P. 2d 905, 907, 908. Also called FEE SIMPLE ABSOLUTE. At **common law,** it was mandatory that the words "to B and his heirs" be used to create a fee simple; a transfer "to B in fee simple" gave B only a **life estate** under the common law. Today, the presumption is in favor of fee simple estates unless an intention to create a more limited estate clearly appears. Compare **fee tail.** See also **words of limitation.**

FEE SIMPLE CONDITIONAL see **conditional fee.**

FEE SIMPLE DEFEASIBLE see **defeasible fee.**

FEE SIMPLE DETERMINABLE see **determinable fee.**

FEE TAIL a conveyance by **deed** or **will** to a person "and the **heirs of his body**" creates a "fee tail." A fee tail establishes a fixed line of inheritable **succession** and cuts off the regular succession of **heirs** at law. 243 P. 2d 1030. It is a limited estate in that **inheritance** is through lineal descent only, which, if exclusively through males, is called FEE TAIL MALE, while exclusively through females, is called FEE TAIL FEMALE. If the family line runs out **(failure of issue)** the fee **reverts** to the **grantor** or his successors in interest. See **words of limitation.**

FELLOW SERVANT a co-worker, defined for the purpose of the FELLOW SERVANT RULE which absolves an employer of **liability** for **injury** to a worker resulting from the **negligence** of a coworker. Fellow servants, who were said to **assume the risk** of each other's negligence, are employees engaged in the same common pursuits under the same general control, serving the same master, engaged in the same general business and deriving authority and compensation from a common source. See 16 F. 2d 517, 519. **Employer's Liability Acts** and **Workmen's Compensation statutes** have abrogated the fellow servant doctrine.

FELONY generic term employed to distinguish certain high crimes from minor offenses known as **misdemeanors;** crimes declared to be such by statute or as "true crimes" by the **common law.** Statutes often define felony in terms of an offense punishable (or punished in fact) by death or imprisonment generally, (180 So. 717; 126 P 2d 406, 408), or by death or imprisonment for more than one year (18 U.S.C. §1). The original common law felonies were felonious **homicide,** mayhem, **arson, rape, robbery, burglary, larceny,** prison breach [escape], and rescue of a felon. Perkins, Criminal Law 9-11 (2d ed. 1969).

Conviction for felony meant at common law that the felon "forfeited life and member and all that he had." 2 Pollock & Maitland, History of English Law 462 (2d ed. 1899). Originally all felonies were punishable by death except for mayhem which was punished by mutilation (as were the other felonies very early [pre-13th century]); "the fiction of benefit of clergy was extended ultimately to the point where the death penalty was not applied to one convicted of felony unless by statute that offense had been declared to be without benefit of clergy. Hence, . . . it is better to define felony . . . in terms of an offense punishable by forfeiture." Perkins, supra at 10. See also **misprision of felony.**

FELONY, MISPRISION OF see **misprision of felony.**

FELONY MURDER an unlawful **homicide** that occurs in the commission or **attempted** commission of a **felony,** which is considered first degree **murder** by operation of this doctrine. In many modern statutes, only homicides that occur in the course of certain specified felonies are "felony murders." See 64 Cal. Rptr. 669, 675. The evil mind or **malice** that is necessary to find someone **guilty** of murder is implied or imputed from the actor's intent to commit a felony. See 383 F. 2d 421, 426. For example, if someone burned down a warehouse and thereby committed **arson,** which resulted in the death of a person in the building, the arsonist is guilty of first degree murder ("felony murder") even if he did not know of the presence of the person and he had taken special precautions to try to avoid any loss of life.

FEOFFMENT the name given at common law to the means of conveying title to freehold estates, which required the **livery of seisin**. At the site of the land and in the presence of neighboring **tenants**, the **vendor** would point out the boundaries to the purchase and hand over to the vendee the appropriate symbol of seisen. 3 N.H. 234, 260. The method was used until the use of the written deed came to be prescribed by statute. See **enfeoff**.

FERAE NATURAE *(fĕr'-ī nä-tûr'-ī)*–Lat: wild beasts of nature. "Ferae naturae" are wild animals, that is to say, animals of natural disposition and character in that their nature, unlike that of domestic animals, is untamed.

FERTILE OCTOGENARIAN a legal fiction which means that, for the purposes of the **Rule Against Perpetuities**, a woman in her eighties can conceive and give birth. "For the purpose of the rule against perpetuities every living person is conclusively presumed capable of having children as long as he lives." Smith, and Boyer, Survey to the Law of Real Property 119 (2d ed. 1971). Thus, even though it may be biologically impossible for one to reproduce, for the purposes of the rule this is not so. The impact of this fiction under the rule against perpetuities has been modified by statute in many jurisdictions today.

FEUDALISM a system of government and a means of holding property in England and Western Europe that grew out of the chaos of the dark ages (the fifth to tenth centuries). Through a ceremony, called **homage**, in which mutual duties of support and protection were promised, the "vassal" in effect gave his land to the "lord" and the lord then had a duty to protect it and the vassal. Though the vassal thenceforth owned no land, he held the land of the lord as a **tenant** and retained a **use** in that land. This method of holding land was very different from the modern landlord-tenant situation. The land which the vassal held was called his feud, fief or feudum. The relationship between the lord and his vassals could become more indirect by the process of **subinfeudation**, so that theoretically there could be placed between the lord and his vassal any number of persons at different levels, each serving as a link in the chain of relations between the lord at the top and the least of the vassals. Eventually, the king became the ultimate lord over all, and all land in England was held of him. Only in England was feudalism the sole method of holding land, although it was the general method elsewhere in Western Europe. See Cribbet, Principles of the Law of Property, 27-29 (1962).

The feudal land holding system influenced all of the early common law concerning real property, and despite the fact that the feudal system never existed in the United States, it has played a vital role in shaping modern land law. Id. at 37.

FIAT JUSTITIA *(fē'-ät jūs-tĭ'-shē-ä)* — Lat: let justice be done.

FIDUCIARY a person having a duty, created by his undertaking, to act primarily for the benefit of another in matters connected with his undertaking, 34 N.E. 2d 68, 70; in the nature of a position of trust or holding confidence. For example, a **trustee** has fiduciary obligations to the beneficiary of the **trust** and acts as a fiduciary in his management of the trust property. An attorney has a fiduciary relationship with a client, etc.

FIGHTING WORDS "those which by their very utterance inflict injury or tend to incite an immediate **breach** of the peace." 315 U.S. 568, 572. The utterance of fighting words is not protected by the First Amendment guarantee of free speech. Id. Later cases support the view that it is not merely the words themselves, but the context in which they are uttered that qualify them as "fighting words," and there is often a further requirement that the words be spoken with intent to have the effect of inciting the hearer to an immediate breach of the peace. 266 A. 2d 579, 584.

In tort law one who uses fighting words towards another, and who thereby creates reasonable apprehension in that person, may be guilty of an **assault** despite the doctrine that words alone do not constitute an assault. See generally Prosser, Torts 40 (4th ed. 1971). See also **defamation; slander**.

FINAL DECISION decision that settles the rights of **parties** respecting the subject-matter of the **suit** and which concludes them until it is **reversed** or set aside. 291 N.W. 118, 121. It ends the **litigation** on the **merits** and leaves nothing for the court to do but execute the **judgment**. 183 F. 2d 29, 31. 403 F. 2d 674, 678. The expression is equivalent to **final decree** or **final judgment**. 150 F. 32, 34. Contrast **interlocutory**.

FINAL DECREE see **decree**.

FINAL HEARING see **hearing**.

FINAL ORDER see **order**.

FINDER OF FACT see **fact-finder**.

FINDING decision of a court on **issues** of fact. The purpose of it is to answer questions raised by the **pleadings** or charges. It is designed to facilitate review by disclosing the grounds on which the **judgment** rests. See 2 Cal. Rptr. 719, 721. Findings of fact are made by a **jury** in an **action at law**, if there is a jury. If there is no jury then the judge makes the findings of fact. When there is a general **verdict** ("we find for the plaintiff" or "not guilty") the factual basis of the jury's verdict will not be known and may not easily be ascertained unless there was only one issue of fact in the case. In "special verdicts" specific findings of fact are made by the jury.

FIRST DEVISEE the first person who is to receive an **estate devised** by **will**. "Next devisee" refers to those who will receive the **remainder** in **tail**. 5 N.J.L. 689, 709-10. See **fee tail**.

FIRST IMPRESSION first discussion or consideration; refers to the first time a question of law is considered for determination by a court. A case is one of "first impression" when it presents a **question of law** that was never before considered by any court, and thus is not influenced by the doctrine of **stare decisis**.

FISCAL of or pertaining to the public finance and financial transactions. See 14 So. 2d 19, 26. Belonging to the public treasury (called the FISC).

FIXTURE something which was once a chattel but has become physically attached to **real property** such that its removal would damage the property; it is thus considered a part of the realty. 35 Am. Jur. 2d Fixtures §§1-2. A lighting fixture will not be a fixture in the legal sense if it can easily be removed; area carpets are not fixtures but wall to wall carpeting may be. A built-in bookcase will almost always be considered a fixture.

TRADE FIXTURE an article which a tenant has annexed to the leased premises to aid him in a business conducted thereon. Leases often expressly permit (or require) removal at the end of the term with a payment for any damage sustained, or make other provision for restoring the premises to their original condition.

FLIGHT any leaving or self-concealment to avoid **arrest** or **prosecution** after arrest. 184 A. 2d 321, 324. The act of leaving the scene of the crime, done by one who feels **guilt**, in order to avoid arrest. See also **abscond**.

FORCIBLE DETAINER see **detainer** [UNLAWFUL DETAINER].

FORCIBLE ENTRY entry on **real property** in the **possession** of another, against his will and without authority of law, by actual force, or with such an array of force and apparent intent to employ it for the purpose of overcoming resistance that occupant, in yielding and permitting possession to be taken from him, must be regarded as acting from a well-founded fear that resistance would be perilous or unavailing. 193 S.W. 2d 643, 644. In many states a mere **trespass** without any force will be considered "forcible" and a simple refusal to surrender possession after a lawful demand will constitute a "forcible **detainer**." See 198 P. 646.

FORCIBLE ENTRY AND DETAINER the "violent taking and keeping possession by one of any lands and tenements occupied by another, by means of threats, force, or arms, and without authority of law." 17 N.Y.S. 522, 523. After a forcible entry and detainer the aggrieved party is entitled to bring "a **summary** statutory **proceeding** for restoring to the **possession** of land one who is wrongfully kept out or has been wrongfully deprived of the possession, in the particular cases mentioned in the statute. It is a possessory action only and it usually arises where one's possession has been forcibly invaded between **landlord** and **lessee**, **vendor** and **vendee**, or the purchaser at a **judicial sale** and a party to the judicial proceeding. The question of **title** cannot be tried, but only the right to possession." 100 N.E. 520, 521. Its purpose is "to protect the actual possession of **real estate** against unlawful and forcible invasion, to remove occasion for actual violence in defending such possession, and to punish **breaches of the peace** committed in the entry upon the detainer of **real property**." 17 N.Y.S. 522, 523. Compare **try title**.

FORECLOSURE generally, the cutting off or termination of a right to **property**; specifically, an **equitable** action to compel payment of a **mortgage** or other **debt** secured by a **lien**. As to real **property**, it is precipitated by non-payment of the debt, and leads to the selling of the property to which the mortgage or lien is attached in order to satisfy that debt. As a consequence, the mortgagor's **equity of redemption** is irrevocably destroyed subject to any statutory redemption rights which may survive for a limited time in some jurisdictions. A **security interest** in **personal property** can also be foreclosed by a **judicial sale** of the **collateral**. See U.C.C. §9-501.

FORESEEABILITY a concept used in various areas of the law to limit **liability** of a party for the consequences of his acts to consequences that are within the scope of a "FORESEEABLE RISK," i.e., risks whose consequences a person of ordinary prudence would reasonably expect might occur.

In a contract setting, a party's liability for consequential or special **damages** is limited, under the *Hadley* v. *Baxendale* rule, to damages arising from the foreseeable consequences of his breach. See Calamari and Perillo, Contracts, §206 (1970).

In tort law, in most cases, a party's actions may be deemed **negligent** only where the injurious consequences of those actions were "foreseeable." See 73 S.W. 2d 626, 628.

FORGERY **fraudulent** making or alter-ing of a writing with the intent to prejudice the rights of another, 167 N.E. 101, 104; making of a false **instrument** or the passing of an instrument known to be false, 72 P. 2d 656, 660; the false making or material altering, with intent to defraud, of any writing which, if genuine, might apparently be of legal efficacy or the foundation of a legal liability. 97 P. 2d 779, 785.

The fabrication or **counterfeiting** of **evidence**; the artful and fraudulent manipulation of physical objects, or the deceitful arrangement of genuine facts or things, in such a manner as to create an erroneous impression or a false inference in the minds of those who may observe them. 466 F. 2d 748, 752.

FORM model of a document containing the phrases and **words of art** that are needed to make the document technically correct for **procedural** purposes. They are used by lawyers in drafting legal documents.

FORMAL CONTRACT see **sealed instrument**.

FORMS OF ACTION technical categories of personal actions developed at common law, containing the entire course of legal proceedings particular to those actions. The forms of actions are no longer required, but they continue to effect modern civil procedure and tort law.

Forms of action consisted of proceedings for recovery of debts, and recovery of money damages resulting from breach of contract, or injury to one's person, property or relations. The forms can be classified as a) actions in form ex contracto, including assumpsit, covenant, debt and account; and b) actions in form ex delicto (i.e. those not based on contracts) including trespass, trover, case, detinue and replevin. See Shipman, Handbook of Common-Law Pleading, Chap. 2 (3rd ed. 1923).

"In the early English law, remedies for wrongs were dependent upon the issuance of **writs** to bring the defendant into court. . . . The number of such writs available was very limited and their forms were strictly prescribed; and unless the plaintiff's cause of action could be fitted into the form of some recognized writs he was without a remedy. The result was a highly formal and artificial system of procedure." Prosser, Torts 28 (4th ed. 1971).

FORNICATION   generally, sexual intercourse of two unmarried persons of different sexes, which is punished as a **misdemeanor** by statute in some states. 10 A. 727, 731. In some states, it refers to illicit sexual intercourse between a man, whether married or single, and an unmarried woman. See 425 S.W. 2d 183, 188. 175 N.E. 661, 662. In some states, illicit intercourse can be fornication for the party who is not married, and **adultery** for the party who is married. See 23 N.E. 747, 748. It is not a **common law** crime and is not part of modern penal codes. See Model Penal Code Art. 213. Compare **cohabitation**.

FORUM   a court; a place where disputes are heard and decided according to law and justice; a tribunal; a place of jurisdiction; place where **remedies** afforded by the law are pursued. See 292 N.W. 584, 586.

FORUM NON CONVENIENS *(fôr'-ŭm nōn kôn-vē'-nē-ĕns)*—Lat: an inconvenient court. Under this doctrine a court, though it has **jurisdiction** of a case, may decline to exercise it where there is no legitimate reason for the case to be brought there, or where presentation of the case in that court will create a hardship on the **defendants** or on relevant **witnesses** because of its distance from them. The court will not **dismiss** the case under the doctrine unless the **plaintiff** has another **forum** open to him. Green, Civil Procedures 54 (1972).

FOUR UNITIES   see **unities**.

FRANCHISE   special privilege which is "conferred by the government upon individuals and which do[es] not belong to the citizens of the country generally, of common right." 93 P. 2d 872, 879. For example, a municipality may grant a "franchise" to a local bus company that will give them the sole authority to operate buses in the municipality for a certain number of years.

ELECTIVE FRANCHISE (sometimes called simply "the franchise") refers to the right of citizens to vote in public elections.

"Franchise" also refers to the right

given to a private person or **corporation** to market another's product within a certain area. Thus, gas stations that sell brand-name gasoline often operate the station through a franchise granted by the oil company.

FRAUD   intentional deception resulting in **injury** to another. Elements of fraud are: a false and material misrepresentation made by one who either knows it is falsity or is ignorant of its truth; the maker's intent that the representation be relied on by the person and in a manner reasonably contemplated; the person's ignorance of the falsity of the representation; the person's rightful or justified reliance; and proximate injury to the person. See 310 F. 2d 262, 267.

It usually consists of a misrepresentation, concealment or nondisclosure of a material fact, or at least misleading conduct, devices, or contrivance. 234 F. Supp. 201, 203. It embraces all the **multifarious** means which human ingenuity can devise to get an advantage over another. It includes all surprise, trick, cunning, dissembling and unfair ways by which another is cheated. At **law**, fraud must be proved, in **equity** it suffices to show facts and circumstances from which it may be presumed. 425 P. 2d 974, 978. See also **deceit**.

CONSTRUCTIVE FRAUD (LEGAL FRAUD) comprises all acts, omissions, and concealments involving **breach** of **equitable** or **legal duty**, trust or confidence and resulting in damage to another, 38 Cal. Rptr. 148, 157; i.e., no **scienter** is required. It consists of a material misrepresentation, though innocently made, that is relied upon and acted upon by the party to whom it is made, and which causes him an injury. Thus, the party who makes the misrepresentation need not know that it is false. See 437 S.W. 2d 20, 27.

EXTRINSIC FRAUD (COLLATERAL FRAUD) fraud that prevents a party from knowing about his rights or **defenses** or from having a fair opportunity of presenting them at a trial, or from fully **litigating** at the trial all the rights or defenses that he was entitled to assert. 468 S.W. 2d 160, 163. It is a ground for **equitable relief** from a **judgment**. See 247 P. 2d 801, 803.

FRAUD IN FACT (POSITIVE FRAUD) actual fraud. Deceit. Concealing something or making a false representation with an evil intent [scienter] when it causes injury to another. It is used in contrast to **constructive fraud** which does not require evil intent. See 144 A. 2d 836, 838.

FRAUD IN LAW fraud that is presumed from circumstances, where the one who commits it need not have any evil intent to commit a fraud; it is a **constructive fraud**. See 225 N.E. 2d 813, 814 and 109 N.W. 136, 138. For example, if a **debtor's transfer** of **assets** impairs the rights of his **creditors**, then the transfer might be a fraud in law and the **conveyance** could be set aside although the debtor had no intention of prejudicing the creditors' rights.

FRAUD IN THE FACTUM generally arises from a lack of identity or disparity between the **instrument** executed and the one intended to be executed, or from circumstances which go to the question as to whether the instrument ever had any legal existence; as for example, when a blind or illiterate person executes a deed when it has been read falsely to him after he asked to have it read. 5 S.E. 2d 138, 141.

FRAUD IN THE INDUCEMENT fraud which is intended to and which does cause one to execute an **instrument**, or make an agreement, or render a **judgment**. The misrepresentation involved does not mislead one as to the paper he signs but rather misleads as to the true facts of a situation, and the false impression it causes is a basis of a decision to sign or render a judgment. See 255 N.Y.S. 2d 608, 610. It renders an agreement **voidable**. See 174 N.E. 2d 304, 308.

INTRINSIC FRAUD fraudulent representation that is presented and considered in rendering a **judgment**. 208 S.W. 2d 111, 112. Generally, "intrinsic fraud" is not a sufficient ground for granting **equitable relief** from a judgment. For example, **perjury** is only intrinsic fraud because it does not prevent a completely **adversary proceeding**. It only influences the judgment, so it will not be a ground

for equitable relief from a judgment resulting from it. 299 N.W. 108, 109.

FREE AND CLEAR unincumbered. In property law, a **title** is "free and clear" if it is not incumbered by any **liens**; one conveys land "free and clear" if he transfers a **good** or **marketable title** (i.e. unincumbered by any interest in the land held by another). 53 A. 477, 480.

FREEDOM OF CONTRACT the liberty or ability to enter into agreements with others. "Freedom of contract" is "a basic and fundamental right reserved to the people" by the Fifth and Fourteenth Amendments to the Constitution which prohibit "the deprivation of liberty without due process of law." 32 F. Supp. 964, 987. "Freedom of contract" is subject to legislative regulation in the interests of public health, safety, morals or welfare; but such legislation must not be unreasonable, arbitrary, or capricious, and the means selected must have a real and substantial relation to the object sought to be obtained." 57 A. 2d 421, 423. See also **obligation of a contract**.

FREE EXERCISE CLAUSE provision in First Amendment to the United States Constitution providing that "Congress shall make no law . . . prohibiting the free exercise" of religion. It is applicable to both the federal and state governments through the due process clause of the fourteenth amendment. See 293 U.S. 245. The clause is distinguished from its counterpart, the "**establishment clause**," in that the free exercise clause guarantees against governmental compulsion in religious matters while the establishment clause insures that the government will maintain neutrality towards religion.

In the exercise of one's religion one cannot insist on conduct which threatents important interests of the society in an unreasonable manner. The courts must, therefore, balance the importance of a religious exercise claim against the state interest involved in a rule or practice which prevents or hinders the exercise. Thus, although the state can prescribe educational standards, it may not require public education (vs. private or sectarian education) of a religious group. See 268 U.S. 510. On the same reasoning, mandatory education beyond the eighth grade in violation of Amish history of informal education, has been held violative of the right to free exercise. See 406 U.S. 205. But the balance has been struck in favor of laws prohibiting polygamy and bigamy against the challenge that they offend the tenets of the Mormon church, see 136 U.S. 1; and compulsory vaccination or x-ray laws have been sustained against objections by Christian Scientists or others claiming an invasion of their religious principles. See 197 U.S. 11.

FREEHOLD an estate in **fee** or a **life estate.**

FREEHOLD ESTATE **estate** or **interest** in **real property** for life or of uncertain duration, lasting at least as long as the life of the present holder. 144 P. 457, 460. It is an "estate of inheritance or for life in either a corporeal or incorporeal **hereditament** existing in or arising from **real property** of free **tenure**." 33 P. 144, 147. Estates created under the common law could only be conveyed by engaging in the **livery of seisin**; upon assuming title by such livery, the **tenant** [or owner] became **seised** to the land and established ownership. Although a charter of enfeoffment may have recorded the ceremonious livery of seisin, under the common law, initially, no writing was required to transfer a freehold estate.

At **common law**, "freehold" referred to those interests in land which could be associated with one who was considered a free man. "In medieval times the only estates fully recognized by the law and given protection in the King's courts were the freehold estates: the **fee simple**, the **fee tail** and the **life estate**." Moynihan, Introduction to the Law of Real Property 28 (1967). In the later common law, non-freehold estates (**copyholds**) such as estates for a term of years were given protection through the development of the action for ejectment through which the **tenant for years** could recover **possession** of his property. Id. at 64.

FRESH PURSUIT in criminal law, "the **common law** right of a police officer to cross jurisdictional lines in order to arrest a **felon**." 112 N.W. 2d 693, 697. Also refers to the power of a police officer to make an arrest without a **warrant** when he is in immediate pursuit of a criminal. 11 So. 632.

FRIENDLY SUIT an action brought by agreement between the **parties** in order to obtain a **judgment** which will have a binding effect in circumstances where a mere agreement or settlement will not. For example, the friendly suit is employed when a **claim** in favor of an infant is settled because the infant cannot effectively **release** the claim by a release **contract**, though the entry of a judgment does bind him. The friendly suit is usually brought without formal **process** but the court will demand some kind of proof (often **affidavits** are sufficient) that the settlement is a just and fair one. Suits that are "**collusive**," that is, those wherein the parties purport to have a controversy but do not, or where they agree to certain facts in order to obtain a particular legal result (as in divorce cases), will be **dismissed**. Compare **adversary proceeding; controversy; declaratory judgment**.

FRIEND OF THE COURT see **amicus curiae**.

FRISK quick, superficial search. It is "a contact or patting of the outer clothing "to detect, by the sense of touch, if a concealed weapon is being carried." 235 A. 2d 235, 239. See **stop and frisk**.

FRIVOLOUS clearly lacking in substance; clearly insufficient as a matter of law, 185 N.E. 2d 583, 593; presenting no debatable question. 227 F. Supp. 735, 740. For example, a **claim** is "frivolous" if it clearly appears either that it is insufficient because it is not supported by the facts or that it is one for which the law recognizes no remedy.

FRUIT OF THE POISONOUS TREE DOCTRINE under this rule evidence which is the direct result or immediate product of illegal conduct on the part of an official is inadmissible in a criminal trial against the victim of the conduct (or other person with **standing**) under the **due process** clause of the fourteenth amendment. See 371 U.S. 471. An exception has been made in that such evidence may be used to impeach the **testimony** of a defendant who takes the stand in his own defense. See 401 U.S. 222. This rule does not apply to evidence resulting from illegal conduct by private persons unless there has been some complicity on the part of the state. See 256 U.S. 465. Also, if evidence is acquired in a way sufficiently distinct from the original illegal activity, it may be used if the **taint** has dissipated. Thus, where the defendant has been illegally arrested, then released, then sometime thereafter returns to confess, his confession has been held admissible. See 371 U.S. 971.

The doctrine draws its name from the idea that once the tree is poisoned (the primary evidence is illegally obtained) then the fruit of the tree (any secondary evidence) is likewise poisoned or tainted and may also not be used. "Evidence obtained by independent means, not search-connected to the poisonous tree, and otherwise admissible, may, however, still be used, although the burden of showing non-taint is upon the proponent [the government]." Forkosch, Constitutional Law 479 (1969).

FRUSTRATION (OF PURPOSE) occurs in contract law when an implied **condition** of an agreement does not occur or ceases to exist without fault of either party, and the absence of the implied condition "frustrates" one party's intentions in making the agreement. It may be a basis for terminating or **rescinding** an agreement if there has been no previous **breach** of the agreement and if there has been no specific **warranty** that the condition would continue to exist or would occur. 127 P. 2d 1027, 1028. The concept is also termed COMMERCIAL FRUSTRATION. See also U.C.C. §2-615. Compare **impossibility**.

FUGITIVE FROM JUSTICE "one who commits a **crime** within a state, and then withdraws himself from that state without waiting to abide the consequences of the crime he there committed," 270 S.W. 2d 39, 42; also one who conceals himself within the state in order to avoid its **process**; is applicable even to those who leave the state for another purpose. 255 U.S. 52. The fugitive status will toll the **statute of limitations**. See also **long-arm statute**.

FULL FAITH AND CREDIT federal constitutional requirement that the "public Acts, Records, and judicial Proceedings" of one state be respected by each of the sister states. Art. 4, §1. Thus it has been said that "if a **judgment** is conclusive in the state where it was pronounced, it is equally conclusive everywhere in the courts of the United States." 72 U.S. 290, 302. Not even a claim of fraud will be a sufficient basis to challenge the judgment of a sister state—at least not beyond that permitted by the original **forum** itself. Id.; 356 U.S. 604. The sister state's judgment may be challenged in the second state, however, if proper **jurisdiction** was lacking in the sister state which rendered the judgment. 325 U.S. 226. But the "judgment is entitled to full faith and credit—even as to questions of jurisdiction—when the second court's inquiry discloses that those questions have been fully and fairly **litigated** and finally decided in the court which rendered the original judgment." 375 U.S. 106, 111.

Full faith and credit does not apply to foreign judgments where principles of **comity** operate instead.

FUTURE ESTATE see **estate**.

FUTURE INTEREST an **interest** in presently existing **real** or **personal property**, or in a **gift** or **trust**, which will commence in **use**, **possession**, and/or enjoyment at a time in the future. 213 F. 2d 520, 521, 145 So. 2d 455, 462. A **legatee** to receive an annual income upon reaching the age of twenty-one has a "future interest" which, when that age is reached, will ripen into a "present interest." Future interests may constitute either a **vested** or a **contingent estate**. 138 F. 2d 254, 257. Compare **remainder**.

FUTURES agreements where one person says that he will sell a commodity at a certain time in the future for a certain price. The buyer agrees to pay that price, knowing that the person has nothing to deliver at the time, but with the understanding that when the time arrives for delivery the buyer is to pay him the difference between the market value of that commodity and the price agreed upon if the commodity's value declines; and if it advances, the seller is to pay to the buyer the difference between the agreed-upon price and the market price. See 58 S.E. 401, 410; 14 R.I. 131, 138. So if the price of the commodity rises, the buyer makes a profit, and if the price declines, the buyer suffers a loss.

Formerly, such speculative agreements were generally unenforceable in courts of law as being against public policy because they were a form of gambling. See 26 N.E. 568, 569. Today, futures are traded on commodity futures exchanges. In order to make the transactions legal, the parties must intend to deliver or receive delivery of the commodity, each party being obligated to make delivery or accept delivery of the commodity unless the contract has been **liquidated** by offset on the exchange. If a "trader insists on literal satisfaction of his contract rights, it must be fulfilled by conveyance of the physical commodity." 73 Yale L. J. 174 (1963). "Thus, the fundamental principle underlying all commodity exchanges is that a person who buys or sells a futures contract and does not offset it by a contra-transaction on the exchange must receive the commodity or be called upon to deliver it. The fact that most persons who trade on a commodity exchange expect to offset their contracts before the date of delivery or receipt is not a denial of this principle." 311 F. 2d 52, 56.

G

GAINFUL EMPLOYMENT [OCCUPATION] generally, any employment that is suited to the ability and potentiality of the one employed. For purposes of disability covered by insurance, it may mean "the ordinary employment of the particular person insured, or such other employment, if any, approximating the same livelihood, as the insured might fairly be expected to follow, in view of his station, circumstances, and physical and mental capabilities." 30 S.E. 2d 879, 883.

GAOL the British and early-American spelling of "jail."

GARAGEMAN'S LIEN see **lien.**

GARNISH to bring a **garnishment** proceeding or to **attach** wages or other property pursuant to such a proceeding.

GARNISHEE a person who receives notice to retain **custody** of **assets** in his control that are owed to or belong to another person until he receives further notice from the court; the garnishee merely holds the assets until legal **proceedings** determine who is entitled to the property. The term thus signifies one on whom process of **garnishment** is served. In a statutory garnishment proceeding the garnishee may be directed to pay over to the **creditor** a portion of the **debtor's** property (often employee's wages).

GARNISHMENT process in which money or **goods** in the hands of a third person which are due a **defendant**, are attached by the **plaintiff**; e.g., **property** controlled by a third person which is owed to or belongs to a **debtor** is used to repay a debt of the debtor.

It is a statutory remedy that consists of notifying a third party to retain something he has belonging to the defendant (debtor), to make disclosure to the court concerning it, and to dispose of it as the court shall direct. 267 So. 2d 18, 20. Compare **attachment.**

GENERAL APPEARANCE see **appearance.**

GENERAL CONTRACTOR see **contractor.**

GENERAL INTENT see **intent.**

GENERIC general, relating to a group or class of related things; something not specific, not referring to a particular thing. "The term 'generic' has reference to a class of related things. . . . While the term 'specific' is limited to a particular, definite, or precise thing." 2 F. 2d 113, 114.

GERRYMANDER to create a civil division of an unusual shape within a particular locale for improper purpose, as for example, to redistrict a state with unnatural boundaries, isolating members of a particular political party, so that a maximum number of the elected representatives will be of that political party.

GIFT a voluntary transfer of any thing made without **consideration**, i.e. without any compensation received in return. The essential components of a valid completed gift of personal property are: **competency** of the donor to **contract**; voluntary intent on the part of the donor to make a gift (called DONA‐TIVE INTENT); **delivery**, either **actual or symbolic**; acceptance, actual or imputed; complete divestment of all control by the **donor**; and a lack of consideration for the gift. 201 Cal. App. 2d 361, 363. See **causa mortis; inter vivos.**

GIFT OVER an estate created upon the expiration of a **preceding estate**, e.g., a gift over to C is established when in default of the exercise of a **power of appointment** by B, the donee of the power, the donor A, has provided that C take in default, rather than that the property which is the subject matter of the power **revert** to A's estate.

GOOD CAUSE substantial or legally sufficient reason for doing something. For example, if a statute provides for granting a new **trial** upon a showing of "good cause," such "good cause" might include the existence of fraud, lack of **notice** to **parties**, or new **evidence.**

GOOD FAITH a total absence of any intention to seek an unfair advantage or to defraud another party; an honest and sincere intention to fulfill one's obligations. U.C.C. 2-103(1) defines "good faith" in the case of a merchant as honesty in fact and the observance of reasonable commercial standards of fair dealing in the trade. In property law, a "good faith" purchaser of land pays the value of the land and has no knowledge or notice of any facts that would cause an ordinary, prudent person to make inquiry concerning the validity of the conveyance. See 220 N.W. 795, 797. See also **bona fide; bona fide purchaser; notice-inquiry.**

GOOD TITLE a **title** free from present **litigation**, obvious defects and grave doubts concerning its validity or merchantability, 227 P. 476, 477; a title valid in fact which is marketable and which can be sold to a reasonable purchaser or **mortgaged** to a person of reasonable prudence as security for a loan of money. In a **contract** to **convey** "good title," the term also means there are no **encumbrances** on the land. 244 P. 424, 425. The term is often said to be synonymous with **marketable title** (174 S.W. 2d 830, 831) and **clear title** (96 S.W. 2d 808.) See **recording acts; warranty deed.**

GOVERNMENTAL IMMUNITY doctrine of implied limitation on the power of the federal government to tax a state or any of its instrumentalities, and of the power of any state to tax the federal government or any of its instrumentalities. The doctrine stems from *McCulloch* v. *Maryland*, 4 Wheat 316, and results from the dual governmental nature of our political system. The principle applies only to the taxing relationships between the federal and state governments. 21 A. 2d 228, 229. For instance, a state would not be permitted to tax a federal defense installation because of "governmental immunity." See also **sovereign immunity.**

GRACE PERIOD in **insurance** settings, a span of time after an insurance policy premium was due to be paid during which the insurance nevertheless remains in force. It is to be viewed as the **sale** of insurance on credit, and is not a **gift** of insurance but a grant of permission to defer payment for the insurance. 215 F. Supp. 586, 594. In general, any period specified in a **contract** during which payment is permitted beyond the due date of the debt without penalty.

GRADED OFFENSE one where an offender is subject to different penalties for various degrees of the offense, according to the terms of a statute. Modern criminal codes rely upon degrees of an offense to distribute sanction ranges according to the danger of harm caused or risked by the actor.

GRAFT the fraudulent obtaining of public money by the corruption of public officials, 199 F. 2d 44, 48; "a dishonest transaction in relation to public or official acts;" also commonly used to "designate an advantage which one person by reason of his peculiar position or superior influence or trust acquires from another." 104 P. 181, 183.

GRANDFATHER CLAUSE provisions permitting persons, engaged in a certain business before the passage of an act regulating that business, to receive a license or prerogative without meeting all the criteria that the new entrants into the field would have to fulfill. For example, The Interstate Commerce Act included a provision requiring the Interstate Commerce Commission to grant a permit to any carrier on its application for authorization to operate over any route on which it or its predecessor in interest were in **bona fide** operation on July 1, 1935. See 355 U.S. 554, 555.

GRAND JURY a body of people (generally 23 in number) drawn, selected, and summoned according to law to serve as a constituent part of a court of criminal **jurisdiction**. The purpose of the body is to investigate and inform on crimes committed within its jurisdiction and to accuse persons of (indict them for) crimes when it has discovered sufficient evidence to warrant holding a person for a trial. Compare **petit jury**. See **indictment**.

GRAND LARCENY see **larceny**.

GRANT to give, confer, consent, allow, surrender or transfer something to another with or without compensation; a gift or bestowal of land made by one having control or authority over it. 191 F. Supp. 495, 537. Any transfer of **real property**. 299 S.W. 2d 591, 594. Also, generally, to yield or concede, as to grant a request. Compare **convey**.

GRANTOR-GRANTEE INDEX see **chain of title**.

GRATIS free; given or performed without reward or **consideration**. 29 S.E. 2d 161.

GRATUITOUS BAILMENT see **bailment**.

GRATUITOUS PROMISE one by which a person promises to do, or refrain from doing, something without requiring any **consideration** in return. See Calamari & Perillo, Contracts, §§57, 102 (1970). Such a promise is generally not legally enforceable as a **contract**. Id. at §57. See **mutuality**. Compare **illusory promise**.

GRATUITY see **gift**.

GRAVAMEN the material part, substance, or essence of a **complaint, charge, grievance, cause of action,** etc. See 153 P. 2d 990, 991. For example, the gravamen of a **complaint** alleging that someone struck **plaintiff** and then went to Los Angeles would be the fact that he struck plaintiff.

GREAT CHARTER see **charter**.

GREAT WRIT see **habeas corpus**.

GRIEVANCE one's allegation that something imposes an illegal obligation or burden, or denies some equitable or legal right, or causes injustice. See 137 P. 400, 402. An employee may be entitled by a collective bargaining agreement to seek relief through a GRIEVANCE PROCEDURE.

GROSS NEGLIGENCE see **negligence**.

GROUND RENT an **estate of inheritance** in the **rent** of lands, i.e., an inheritable **interest** in and right to the rent collected through the **leasing** of certain lands, 48 A. 636, 637; it is a **freehold** estate, 69 N.E. 658; and as such is subject to **incumberance** by **mortgage** or **judgement** (**lein, attachment,** etc.). The ground rent is an incorporeal **hereditament** and is therefore an interest distinct from that held by the owner of the property, whose estate is in the land itself and is therefore corporeal. 163 A. 2d 297, 298; 48 A. 636, 637.

GUARANTEE one who receives a **guaranty,** see 168 S.E. 838, 839; also used, as in "guaranty," to mean a promise to answer for the **debt,** default or miscarriage of another; a **warranty** or promise to undertake an original obligation, see 292 S.W. 1079, 1083; something given as security for the performance of an act or the continued quality of a thing, see 109 N.E. 2d 795, 799; to assure the performance of an act or the continued quality of a thing.

GUARANTEE CLAUSE Art. IV, Sec. 4 of the United States Constitution, which states that "the United States shall **guarantee** to every state in this Union a Republican Form of Government." That section of the Constitution has been held to provide that the United

States "shall protect each of them [the states] against invasion; and on the application of the legislature or of the executive (when the legislature cannot be convened) against domestic violence." 48 U.S. 1, 42. The Court has declined to use the clause to identify a state's lawful government, 7 How. 1; or to enforce a representative form of government, *Baker* v. *Carr*, 369 U.S. 186; but has instead used the **equal protection clause** of the Constitution to achieve legislative apportionment of a representative character. Id.; *Reynolds* v. *Sims*, 377 U.S. 533.

GUARANTOR one who makes the **guaranty** for the benefit of the guarantee. See **guaranty**.

GUARANTY to agree or promise to answer for the **debt**, default or miscarriage of another; a promise or contract to answer for the debt, default or miscarriage of another; a **guarantor** will perform the act promised to be done or properly done by another person if that person does not fulfill his obligation.

GUEST a transient who rents a room at an inn or hotel. See 218 N.W. 510, 511. Someone to whom hospitality is extended; one entertained without being charged. See 185 P. 2d 784, 786. An AUTOMOBILE GUEST is one who rides in an automobile for his own benefit without giving the driver any compensation for the ride. See 219 A. 2d 374, 376. See **guest statute**.

For purposes of **tort** law, a SOCIAL GUEST is considered a "bare **licensee**" with respect to his entry upon the host's premises, so that, unlike an **invitee**, no duty of affirmative care or inspection is owed to him; he is thus entitled to no more than a warning as to dangers or defective conditions actually known to the occupier. Prosser, Torts §60 at 378-9 (4th ed. 1971). Some states have decided, however, that considering the social guest as an invitee is more in harmony with contemporary social realities. See, e.g., 98 So. 2d 730; 167 N.W. 2d 477.

GUEST STATUTE law which provides that a special standard of care is owed by an automobile owner or driver toward his gratuitous passenger; these statutes differ from state to state in their particulars, but all require more than just ordinary **negligence** on the part of an owner or driver in order for a "guest" to recover his **damages** in a **civil suit**. Some statutes require intentional misconduct, some require "heedlessness and reckless disregard" of others' rights, some require "**gross negligence**," and some require "intoxication or willful misconduct." See Harper and James, Law of Torts, §16.15 (1956).

GUILTY the condition of having been found by a **jury** to have committed the **crime charged**, or some **lesser-included** crime. The term may, though rarely does, refer to the commission of a **civil** wrong or **tort**.

In criminal cases, a judicial finding of guilt—i.e., a **verdict** of "guilty"—requires that the **evidence** indicate beyond a **reasonable doubt**, or to a **moral certainty**, that the **defendant** committed the crime. 397 U.S. 358. In civil cases involving an alleged tort, "guilt" indicates that the evidence shows by a **preponderance** that the defendant committed the wrongful act. Thus, the "standards of proof" of guilt are different in the two areas.

HABEAS CORPUS known as the "great writ" and means literally, "you have the body." The writ of habeas corpus has a varied use in criminal and civil contexts. It is basically a procedure for obtaining a judicial determination of the legality of an individual's custody. In the criminal context it is used to bring the petitioner before the court to inquire into the legality of his confinement. The writ of federal habeas corpus is used to test the constitutionality of a state criminal conviction. It pierces through the formalities of a state conviction to determine whether the conviction is consonant with **due process of law**. 261 U.S. 86. The writ is used in the civil context to challenge the validity of child custody and deportations. See **post conviction review proceedings**.

HABENDUM that clause of the deed which names the **grantee** and limits and defines the **estate** to be granted. Its function is to qualify the general language that appears in the granting clause, 213 N.W. 59, 60, 20 So. 877, 878; begins with the words "to have and to hold. . . ."

HABITUAL OFFENDER see **criminal**.

HARD CASES cases which, in order to meet the exigencies presented by the extreme hardship of one **party**, produce decisions which may deviate from the true principles of law.

It is sometimes said that "hard cases make bad law" because logic is often shortcut in a hard case, and later attempts to justify the new law thus created often compound the original inadequacy of reasoning.

HARDSHIP, UNNECESSARY see **unnecessary hardship**.

HARMLESS ERROR error which is not sufficiently prejudicial to an **appellant** or does not affect his substantial rights so as to warrant the reviewing court overturning or otherwise modifying the lower court decision. See 178 P. 2d 341.

Some violations of defendant's constitutional rights may be considered harmless error and thus permit a **conviction** to withstand constitutional challenge. Whether a particular error is harmless or not is a matter of federal and not state law as to federal constitutional questions. The prosecution has the burden of proving "beyond a reasonable doubt that the error . . . did not contribute to the verdict obtained." 386 U.S. 18, 24. Other properly received evidence may be considered in determining whether the valid proof was so overwhelming as to preclude the possibility that the constitutional violation contributed to the verdict. 395 U.S. 250. See also **error**.

HEAD NOTE summary of an issue covered in a reported case, summaries of all the points discussed and issues decided in a case, which are placed at the beginning of a case report, are referred to as the head-notes.

HEARING a **proceeding** wherein **evidence** is taken for the purpose of determining an issue of fact and reaching a decision on the basis of that evidence, 426 P. 2d 942, 951; describes "whatever takes place before magistrates clothed with judicial functions and sitting without jury at any stage of the proceeding subsequent to its inception." 15 N.E. 2d 1014, 1015. Thus a hearing, such as an ADMINISTRATIVE HEARING may take place outside the judicial process, before officials who have been granted judicial authority expressly for the purpose of conducting such hearings.

FINAL HEARING "is sometimes used to describe that stage of proceedings relating to the determination of a **suit** upon its **merits**, as distinguished from those of preliminary questions." 15 N.E. 2d 1014, 1015. See **preliminary hearing**. See also **due process**.

HEARING DE NOVO see **de novo** [DE NOVO HEARING].

HEARSAY RULE "evidence of a statement which is made other than by a witness while testifying at the hearing offered to prove the truth of the matter stated is hearsay evidence and inadmissible." Uniform Rule of Evidence 63. The statement may be oral or written and includes non-verbal conduct intended as a substitute for words. Id. at R. 62(1). A typical example of a hearsay statement involves the witness, W, being asked, "What did Y tell you or what did you hear Y say?" If Y's statement is elicited for the truth of the matter asserted, it is hearsay. If however, it is elicited to merely show that the words were spoken it is not hearsay. W's answer will be admissible only for the fact that Y may have made a statement and not for the truth of Y's statement.

The hearsay rule extends to virtually any in-court evidence which asserts for the truth therein an out-of-court statement. This includes a statement by W in court that on a previous instance W himself said X.

The basis of the hearsay rule is that the credibility of the assertor is the key ingredient in weighing the truth of the assertor's statement and thus when that statement is made out-of-court, without the benefit of cross-examination, and without the declarant's demeanor being exposed to the trier of fact, we are unwilling to permit the statement to be admitted. See Wigmore, Evidence § 1766 (3rd ed. 1940).

There are many exceptions to the hearsay rule of exclusion based on a combination of trustworthiness and necessity. Thus, official written statements, such as police reports, where the declarant's statements are based on firsthand knowledge and where the officer is under an official duty to make the report (and hence has no motive to falsify) are admissible under the BUSINESS RECORDS EXCEPTION. See, e.g., Uniform Rule 63(13). Another common exception is made for DYING DECLARATIONS, see, e.g., Uniform Rule 63(5). Under this rule a statement made by a person with knowledge or hopeless expectation of his impending death is admissible through another who overheard that statement where the declarant is unavailable because he died. Originally it was strongly believed that a dying person would tell the truth; thus W's testimony as to what the dying declarant said became admissible both on the grounds of trustworthiness and necessity. Today, with more skepticism about the effect of religiosity on truth-telling, necessity remains as a major factor in determining admissibility. The question of W's credibility is subject to demeanor examination and cross-examination for bias, memory, etc. Some jurisdictions permit any admission by a party to be offered by his adversary in a civil proceeding through any competent witness as another broad exception to the hearsay rule. See, Uniform Rule 63(7).

Hearsay exceptions may jeopardize the constitutional guarantee of confrontation and thus criminal exceptions may be more narrow (e.g., compare the "declaration against interest exception" with the "admissions exception." Id. RR. 63(10) and 63(7)). The confrontation clause has been held not identical with the general common law hearsay rule, see 399 U.S. 149; and state exceptions have been upheld where they have sufficient trustworthiness to satisfy the confrontation clause interests. See 400 U.S. 74 (permitting an unusually broad CO-CONSPIRATOR EXCEPTION which permits statements made by one conspirator to be admissible against the other conspirators even though the statement was made after the conspirators were in custody—contrary to the generally accepted rule that the exception does not extend to the post-custody stage, see 336 U.S. 440). See also 380 U.S. 400; 390 U.S. 719; 392 U.S. 293.

HEIR APPARENT one who has the rights to heirship (or **inheritance**) provided that he live longer than his ancestor; "before the death of the ancestor, persons who would become heirs on his death are only heirs apparent; and no inheritance which can descend to their children passes to heirs apparent who die before the ancestor." 42 S.E. 2d 215, 216. An **antilapse statute** may operate to save a **gift** to an heir apparent who predeceases the **testator**.

HEIRS strictly, those whom statutory law would appoint to inherit an **estate** should the ancestor die without a **will** [**intestate**]. 29 Cal. Rptr. 601, 605, 606, 332 P. 2d 773, 775. Synonyms: "heirs at law," "rightful heir," "legal heirs." The term is often applied indiscriminately to those who inherit by will or **deed** as well as by **operation of law**. Compare **devise**; **grant**; **inheritance**. See **intestate succession**.

AND HIS HEIRS at **common law** these words had to be included in order to convey a **fee simple**. See 112 S.W. 53, 55. The formal requirement has been abolished or modified by statute in most of the states, and now one may **convey** or devise **real property** without using these technical words. See 300 N.Y.S. 1279. These words are **"words of limitation** [describing the nature of the **estate** granted, a fee simple] not **words of purchase** [describing the persons to whom it is given]. . . . This construction prevails unless it plainly appears from the context of the will [or other instrument] that such was not the **testator's** [or grantor's] intention." 157 A. 328.

HEIRS OF THE BODY words that tend to create a fee simple conditional or a **fee tail**, after passage of the statute De Donis Conditionalibus rather than a **fee simple**; generally considered **words of limitation** and not **words of purchase**;

"issue of the body, offspring, progeny, natural children, physically born and begotten by the person named as parent. An adopted child is the issue of his natural parents and not of his adopted ones." 334 S.W. 2d 599, 606.

HEREDITAMENTS anything which can be inherited, including real, personal or mixed **property**. 160 N.W. 716, 719. There are two kinds of hereditaments: CORPOREAL and INCORPOREAL. The former generally refers to tangible things. 69 Cal. Rptr. 612, 625. The latter refers to rights growing out of or connected to land, such as an **easement** or **rent**. 286 S.W. 2d 380, 383. For example, the right to use water flowing across one's own land is not an easement and is therefore a "corporeal hereditament." The right to have the water flow to the land across the land of another, however, is an incorporeal hereditament. 46 Mass. 236, 238.

HEREDITARY SUCCESSION the passing of **title** according to the laws of **descent**; the title to an **estate** acquired by a person by **operation of law** upon the death of an ancestor without a valid **will** affecting the property inherited. 163 P. 118, 120. Synonymous with **inheritance**, **descent**. Compare **devise**.

HIT-AND-RUN STATUTES see **self-incrimination**.

HOLDER "a person who is in possession of a document of **title** or an **instrument** or an investment security **drawn**, issued or **indorsed** to him or to his order or to **bearer** or in blank." U.C.C. 1-201 (20) See **holder in due course**.

HOLDER IN DUE COURSE In commercial law, "nothing more than a highly refined species of **bona fide purchaser** who takes free of most defenses of prior parties to the [**negotiable**] **instrument** and free of conflicting title claims to the instrument itself." White and Summer, Uniform Commercial Code 456 (1972). A holder in due course generally takes free of "personal defenses" which the **maker** or any other prior party may have against the original **payee** or any subsequent **holder** but not free of "real defenses" such as **fraud** in the factum, **incapacity, duress, illegality**, etc. U.C.C. 3-305 (2). Thus, if S sells B a car, B

writes S a check in payment, S negotiates it to a holder in due course, B may not assert some fault with the car as a defense to the check when the HDC attempts to collect (a personal defense good only between S and B) but may defend if he was forced to sign the check against his will (duress—a real defense).

To qualify for this special status one must be a holder, who takes the negotiable instrument, for value, in **good faith**, without notice that it is overdue or has been dishonored or of any defense against or claim to it on the part of any person. U.C.C. 3-302 (1).

HOLDING in commercial and property law, **property** in which one has legal **title** and of which one is in **possession**, 246 S.W. 2d 990; the term may be used to refer specifically to ownership of **stocks**, or **shares**, of **corporations**. 36 S.E. 2d 5, 8.

In procedure, any ruling of the court, including rulings upon the admissibility of evidence or other questions presented during trial, may be termed a "holding." See 218 P. 2d 888, 893. Compare **dictum**.

HOLDING COMPANY "a supercorporation which owns or at least controls such a dominant **interest** in one or more other **corporations** that it is enabled to dictate their policies through voting power; . . . a corporation organized to hold the **stock** of other corporations; . . . [a]ny company, incorporated or unincorporated, which is in a position to control or materially to influence, the management of one or more other companies by virtue, in part at least, of its ownership of **securities** in the other company or companies." 20 P. 2d 460, 468.

HOLDOVER TENANCY see **tenancy** (TENANCY AT SUFFERANCE).

HOLOGRAPHIC WILL "a **will** that 'is entirely written, dated and signed by the hand of the **testator** himself.'" It is sometimes written "OLOGRAPHIC." In some states, under statute, such a will need not be witnessed and is valid under a statute of descents and distribution to pass **property**. 34 P. 614, 615.

HOMAGE during the **feudal** period, the ceremony "wherein the vassal knelt before the lord, acknowledged himself to be his man, and swore FEALTY [an oath of loyalty to the lord]. It was frequently accompanied by a grant of land from the lord to the vassal, the land to be held of the lord by the vassal as **tenant**." Moynihan, Real Property 4 (1962). As a consequence, any attempt by the vassal [or **tenant**] to convey more than the estate which had been granted him (e.g., an attempt by the vassal to convey a **fee simple** when his grant from the lord consisted only of a **life estate**), was not only **tortious** conduct with regard to the lord, but was also treasonous.

HOME RULE means of apportioning power between state and local governments by the granting of "power to the electorate of a local governmental unit to frame and adopt a charter of government." 48 Minn. L. Rev. 643, 645. The effect of this grant is to enable local government to legislate without first obtaining permission from state legislatures. Id. at 650. See also **preemption**.

HOMESTEAD see **life estate**.

HOMICIDE any killing of a human being by another human being; it does not necessarily constitute a **crime**; "the destruction of the life of one human being by the act, agency, procurement or **culpable** omission of another. The destruction of life must be complete by such act or agency; but although the injury which caused death might not, under other circumstances, have proved fatal, yet if such injury be the cause of death, without it appearing that there has been any gross neglect or improper treatment by some person other than the defendant . . . it would be homicide." 108 S.W. 699, 701. An unlawful homicide, or one resulting from an unlawful act, may constitute **murder** or **manslaughter**.

JUSTIFIABLE HOMICIDE "the killing of a human being by commandment of the law, in the execution of public justice, in **self-defense**, in [lawful] defense of habitation, property or person." etc. 45 S.E. 2d 798, 799.

HORNBOOK a book intended to aid one with the fundamentals of that being studied; a primer for the student studying in an area of knowledge.

HORNBOOK LAW those principles of law which are known generally to all and are free from doubt and ambiguity. They are therefore such as would probably be enunciated in a **hornbook**.

HORS *(ôr)*—Fr: outside of, besides, other than (sometimes: dehors *(dĕ-ôr')*).

HOSTILE POSSESSION actual occupation or **possession** of **real estate** without the permission of anyone claiming **paramount title**, coupled with a **claim**, express or implied, of **ownership**. Hostile possession is to be contrasted with **holding** in recognition of or in subordination to the true owner, as in the case of possession under a **lease**. 138 P. 2d 846, 851, 852, 350 S.W. 2d 729, 732. Hostile does not imply ill will or actual enmity but merely that the occupant claims ownership against all others, including the **record owner**. 468 P. 2d 702, 706. The term is usually used in connection with and as a condition for **adverse possession**. See also **notorious possession**.

HOSTILE WITNESS see **witness**.

HUNG JURY one whose members [jurors] cannot reconcile their differences of opinions and which therefore cannot reach a **verdict** by whatever degree of agreement is required (generally unanimity, but sometimes by a substantial majority, e.g., 10-2).

IBID. *(ĭb'-ĭd)*—Lat: in the same place, at the same time, in the same manner; abbreviated form of the word "ibidem." It is used to mean "in the same book" or "on the same page." It functions to avoid repetition of source data contained in the reference immediately preceding.

ID. *(ĭd)*—Lat: the same, the very same, exactly this, likewise; abbreviated form of the word "idem." This term is used in citations to avoid repetition of the author's name and title when a reference to an item immediately follows another to the same item.

IGNORANTIA LEGIS NON EXCUSAT *(ĭg-nō-rän'-shē-á lā'-gĭs nŏn ĕx-kū'-zät)-* Lat: ignorance of the law is no excuse; i.e., the fact that defendant did not think his act was against the law does not prevent the law from punishing the prohibited act.

ILLEGITIMATE illegal or improper; as applied to children, it means those born out of wedlock, i.e., **bastards.**

ILLUSORY PROMISE a promise which is so indefinite that it cannot be enforced or which, by virtue of provisions or conditions contained in the promise itself, is one whose fulfillment is optional or entirely discretionary on the part of the promisor. 287 P. 2d 735. Since such a promise does not constitute a legally binding obligation, it is not sufficient as **consideration** for a reciprocal promise and thus cannot create a valid **contract.** See 17 Am. Jur. 2d Contracts §§11-13, 1-5. See **mutuality.**

IMMEDIATE CAUSE see **cause.**

IMMIGRATION the movement of persons from one country into a country foreign to them for the purpose of permanently residing in that foreign country. See 128 F. 375, 380.

IMMORAL CONDUCT that "conduct which is willful, flagrant, or shameless, and which shows a moral indifference to the opinions of the good and respectable members of the community." 20 P. 2d 896, 897. It is sometimes the basis for suspension or revocation of authority to practice certain professions such as law and teaching. See id., 421 P. 2d 586, 589.

IMMUNITY a right of exemption from a duty or penalty; a favor or benefit granted to one and contrary to the general rule. Immunity from prosecution, such as that granted a **witness** to encourage answers to questions he might otherwise refuse to answer on fifth amendment grounds. See **self-incrimination.**

OFFICIAL IMMUNITY the personal im-

munity accorded to a public official from liability to anyone injured by any of his actions that are the consequence of the exercise of his official authority or duty. See 18 Ark. L. Rev. 82 (1964). This immunity is complete for judges, so long as they act within the jurisdiction of their respective courts; administrative officers, however, are generally immune only for **discretionary** as opposed to **ministerial acts** that are done honestly and in **good faith.** Prosser, Law of Torts § 132 (4th ed. 1971).

IMPANELLING the process by which jurors are selected and sworn in to their task, 119 N.E. 916; the listing of those selected to serve on a particular jury.

IMPEACH, IMPEACHMENT to charge a public official with a wrongdoing while in office. "The object of prosecutions of impeachment in England and the United States 'is to reach high and potent offenders, such as might be presumed to escape punishment in the ordinary tribunals, either from their own extraordinary influence, or from the imperfect organization and powers of those tribunals. These prosecutions are, therefore, conducted by the representatives of the nation, in their public capacity, in the face of the nation, and upon a responsibility which is at once felt and reverenced by the whole community.'" 188 P. 2d 592, 595, citing Story, Const., Sec. 688.

With reference to the testimony of a witness, to impeach "means to call into question the veracity of the witness by means of evidence offered for that purpose, or by showing that the witness is unworthy of belief." 190 P. 2d 193, 195.

IMPLEADER the procedure by which the **plaintiff's** primary **claim** against the original **defendant,** as well as any alleged **liability** of a third party, may be settled in one **action** by joining such third party in the original action. See 143 N.Y.S. 2d 327, 330. It is a **procedural** device available to any defendant where a third party is or may be liable to him for any liability which he [defendant] is found to have toward the plaintiff. This constitutes the defendant a "third-party plaintiff" with respect to the third party thus joined. Fed. Rule Civil Proc. 14. The device is also available to a plaintiff against whom a **counterclaim** has been made. Id. Compare **interpleader**; **joinder**. See also **crossclaim**.

IMPLICATION intention, meaning; that which is inferred; though not expressly stated, a state of mind or facts which is deduced.

> NECESSARY IMPLICATION "one which results from so strong a probability of intention that an intention contrary to that imputed to the testator cannot be supposed." 220 N.W. 25, 27.

IMPLIED not explicitly written or stated; referring, e.g., to a condition, consent, power, warranty, a state of mind, or a fact which is determined by deduction or inference from known facts and circumstances. Compare **express**.

IMPOSSIBILITY a **defense** to non-performance of a contract which arises when **performance** is impossible due to the destruction of the subject matter of the **contract** or the death of a person necessary for the performance of it; performance is then excused and the contract **duty** terminated. At common law, impossibility did not reach the cases where performance simply became very expensive or difficult. Thus, a builder was held not excused for his failure to perform even though the building collapsed in two attempts to build it due to unforeseen difficulties, 20 Minn. 494; and it has no application at all if the promise has been expressly made unconditional even as against unforeseen difficulties. But "the essence of the modern defense of 'impossibility' is that the promised performance was at the making of the contract, or thereafter became, impracticable owing to some extreme.or unreasonable difficulty, expense, injury or loss involved, rather than that it is scientifically or actually impossible." Williston on Contracts § 1931 (Rev. ed. 1938). The Uniform Commercial Code recognizes this broader "commercial impracticability" modification of the common law impossibility doctrine. Under the Code provision, if a contingency arises, the non-occurrence of which was an essential basis of the contract between the parties, then the seller is excused from performing and is required to follow certain procedures in allocating his available capacity to perform on like contracts. U.C.C. §§2-615, 2-616.

In the criminal law the term applies to situations in which an actor does an act which would be criminal but is not because the facts or circumstances render the crime impossible to commit. Thus, it is impossible to **murder** another if he is already dead. If the actor thought he was alive, however, in some jurisdictions he will be held for an **attempted** murder. The FACTUAL IMPOSSIBILITY prevents liability for the object crime of murder but in those jurisdictions it will not operate to prevent liability for an attempt to commit that crime. See New York Penal Law §110.10.

> LEGAL IMPOSSIBILITY the term in the criminal law context has sometimes been used to describe the failure to consummate a crime because of some legal bar. Thus, it has been said that one cannot legally receive stolen property that was never stolen in the first instance. 78 N.E. 169. Holdings of this kind have been much criticized and the recognized rule is that attempt liability will be attached for this conduct as well. If legal impossibility is limited to instances in which the actor lacks capacity to commit the crime in question, then legal impossibility is a complete defense. Perkins, Criminal Law 570-72 (2d ed. 1969). Compare **mistake**.

IMPROVEMENT any development of land or buildings through the expenditure of money or labor that is designed to do more than merely replace, repair, or restore to the original condition. 27 S.E. 2d 164, 172, 19 P. 2d 644, 49 S.E. 2d 779, 783. "Improvements" are generally thought of as permanent and fixed, and supposedly increase the value of the property. 203 N.Y.S. 2d 35, 38, 122 N.W. 2d 189, 190. See **ameliorating waste**.

IMPUTE to assign to a person or other entity the legal responsibility for the act of another, because of the relationship between the person so made liable and the actor, rather than because of actual participation in or knowledge of the act.

IN CAMERA *(ĭn kǎ'-mĕ-rà)*—Lat: in chambers. "The meaning of the word 'chambers' varies with the context in which it is used. It may mean a room adjacent to a courtroom in which a judge performs the duties of his office when his court is not in session. The word 'chambers' is also commonly used in a different sense. When a judge performs a judicial act while the court is not in session in the matter acted upon, it is said that he acted 'in chambers' whether the act was performed in the 'judge's chambers,' the library, at his home, or elsewhere." 66 Cal. Rptr. 825, 829.

INCAPACITY to lack the ability; the quality or state of being incapable; the lack of legal, physical, or intellectual power; inability. See **incompetence; minority; non compos mentis.**

IN CAPITE *(ĭn kǎ'-pēt)*—Lat: in chief; with reference to feudal tenures, an estate in land held by direct grant of the king.

INCARCERATION confinement in a jail, prison, or penitentiary.

INCENDIARY arsonist; one who maliciously and willfully sets another's property on fire; also, an object or thing capable of starting and sustaining a fire; e.g., "incendiary device."

INCEST a criminal offense which involves sexual intercourse between members of a family, or those among whom marriage would be illegal because of blood relations. 75 P. 166.

INCIDENTAL BENEFICIARY see **beneficiary.**

INCHOATE DOWER the **interest** which a wife has in her husband's lands prior to, and contingent upon, his death. The right of **dower** of a widow is considered "inchoate" until that death, at which time it becomes a **vested** right to a **life estate.** 1 S.E. 2d 853, 855, 258 P. 295, 297. An "inchoate dower" cannot be **alienated,** 32 N.E. 681, 683; and it cannot be reached by **creditors.**

INCIDENTAL DAMAGES see **damages.**

INCLOSURE any land enclosed by something other than an imaginary boundary line, i.e., some wall, hedge, fence, ditch or other actual obstruction. See 39 Vt. 326, 332, 113 N.W. 384, 388. The word "town" derives from the Anglo-Saxon word "tun," meaning "inclosure." See 23 P. 405, 406, 6 N.W. 607, 608. Compare **close.**

INCOMPETENCY inability; "a relative term which may be employed as meaning disqualification, inability or **incapacity.** It can refer to lack of legal qualifications or fitness to discharge the required duty. It may be employed to show want of physical or intellectual or moral fitness." 116 So. 2d 566, 567.

When a person is adjudicated an "incompetent," a **guardian** is appointed by the court in which the incompetency hearing was held, who will manage the incompetent's affairs until and unless the incompetent recovers his competency to the satisfaction of the court. In this event the guardian is discharged. An adjudicated incompetent lacks capacity to contract and his contracts are void. An incompetent who has not been so adjudged enters into contracts which are **voidable.** See **competency; minority; non compos mentis.**

INCOMPETENT EVIDENCE Inadmissible evidence. See **admissible evidence.**

INCORPORATE to combine together or unite so as to form one whole. To form a **corporation,** to organize and be granted status as a corporation by following procedures prescribed by law. See **articles of incorporation.**

When used in a document in reference to another writing, it means that the writing referred to is "incorporated" into or adopted and made part of the document. See 256 S.W. 2d 421, 422, 423.

INCORPOREAL HEREDITAMENT see **hereditament.**

INCORRIGIBLE uncorrectable; a person, usually a juvenile, whose behavior cannot be made to conform to the standards dictated by law.

INCREMENT an amount of increase or gain in number, amount or value; as to salaries, increments "are the periodic, consecutive additions or increases which do not become a part of the salary . . .

until they accrue under the rule making such provision. . . ." 29 A 2d 890, 891.

INCRIMINATE to hold another, or oneself, responsible for criminal misconduct; to involve someone, or oneself, in an accusation of a crime. See also **self-incrimination**.

INCULPATORY that which tends to incriminate or bring about a criminal conviction. Compare **exculpatory**.

INCUMBRANCE every right to, interest in, or legal **liability** upon **real property** which does not prohibit passing **title** to the land but which diminishes its value. See 113 F. 2d 748, 751. Incumbrances include **easements**, **licenses**, **leases**, timber privileges, **homestead** privileges, **mortgages**, judgment **liens**, etc.

INDEFEASIBLE cannot be defeated, or altered. An "indefeasible" estate is absolute and cannot be changed by any **condition**. 80 N.Y.S. 2d 380, 381. An "indefeasible" estate **in fee simple** implies a perfect **title**. 131 U.S. 75.

IN DELICTO *(ĭn dĕ-lĭk'-tō)*—Lat: in fault, though not in equal fault. See **in pari delicto**.

INDEMNIFY to secure against loss or damage which may occur in the future, or to provide compensation for loss or damage already suffered; to insure; to save harmless. See 235 App. Div. 382.

INDEMNITY broadly speaking, "the obligation [or duty] resting on one person to make good any loss or damage another has incurred or may incur by acting at his request or for his benefit," 92 S.E. 2d 54, 55; or, alternatively, the right which the person suffering the loss or damage is entitled to claim. 18 A. 2d 807. A party seeking indemnity from another acknowledges that a duty is (or was) in fact owed by him; but at the same time he asserts that for some specified reason(s), that duty should be (or should have been) performed by the other. "Indemnity" therefore comprehends his right to insist that that duty be performed by the other, or that he be compensated by the other if it has already been performed. "Indemnity refers to a total shifting of the economic loss to the party chiefly or primarily re-

sponsible for that loss." 124 N.Y.S. 2d 634, 636.

INDENTURE a **deed** between two parties conveying **real estate** by which both parties assume obligations. 94 N.Y. 86, 89, 10 N.Y.St. Rep. 357, 358. "Indenture" implies a **sealed instrument**. See 3 Ark. 565, 568. Historically, "indenture" referred to a crease or wavy cut that was made in duplicates of the deed so their authenticity could be verified later. 10 Serg. & R. 416, 417.

INDEPENDENT CONTRACTOR see **contractor**.

INDICIA indications; signs or circumstances which tend to support a belief in a proposition as being probable, but which do not prove to a certainty the truth of the proposition. It is often said to be synonymous with **circumstantial evidence**. 53 S.E. 2d 122, 125. Where one exercises dominion and control over **personal property** as if it were his own, such behavior is an indicium of ownership, see id.; a carbon copy of a bill of sale has also been held to be an indicia of title. 277 S.W. 2d 413, 416.

"Indicia" is important in many contexts. Thus, where the owner of property is responsible for giving another indicia of ownership, that other person may effectively transfer the owner's interest to a **bona fide purchaser**. See 34 N.Y.S. 2d 1008, 1009. An "indicia of reliability" is necessary for an informer's information to support a **search warrant**. 394 U.S. 410 (1969).

INDICTMENT a formal written accusation, drawn up and submitted to a **grand jury** by the public prosecuting attorney, charging one or more persons with a crime. The indictment is presented under oath by the prosecuting attorney to the grand jury for them to determine whether the accusation, if proved, would be sufficient to bring about a conviction of the accused, in which case the indictment is indorsed by the foreman as a TRUE BILL. See 137 A. 370, 372. Indictments also serve to inform an accused of the offense with which he is charged, and must do so with sufficient clarity to enable him to prepare his defense adequately. See 143 F. 2d 953, 955. Compare **charge**; **information**.

INDIGNITY in divorce law, an "affront to the personality of another, a lack of reverence for the personality of one's spouse." 176 A. 2d 919, 920. "Indignity" is a ground for divorce in some states; "the offense is not predicated upon a single act but consists of a persistent or continuous course of conduct which has the ultimate effect of rendering cohabitation intolerable." 363 P. 2d 86, 87, 88. Generally, indignities "consist of vulgarity, unmerited reproach, habitual contumely, studied neglect, intentional incivility, manifest disdain, abusive language, malignant ridicule, and any other plain manifestation of settled hate and estrangement." 180 A. 2d 82, 83. See **mental cruelty**.

INDISPENSABLE EVIDENCE that which is necessary to prove a submitted fact.

INDISPENSABLE PARTY a party who has such an interest that a final **decree** cannot be issued without either affecting that interest, or leaving the controversy in such a condition that its final determination may be wholly inconsistent with **equity** and good conscience. 254 U.S. 80. Therefore, an action may not proceed without an indispensable party, 316 P. 2d 296, 299; an indispensable party must be **joined** because his nonjoinder would result in prejudice to his rights and the rights of other parties to the **action**. See 50 F.R.D. 311, 314.

INDORSEMENT signature placed upon the back of an **instrument**, with or without other words, the effect of which is to transfer the instrument and to create "a new and substantive contract by which the indorser becomes a party to the instrument and liable, on certain conditions, for its payment." 370 S.W. 2d 811, 813 n. 4. The conditions which give rise to the indorser's liability generally comprehend the failure of the party primarily liable under the instrument to make payment in accordance with the terms thereof. 71 S.E. 148, 149. Indorsements are made primarily for the purpose of continuing the negotiability or enhancing the commercial value of the instrument. See 36 So. 668, 669. To constitute an indorsement, the writing must be effective to transfer the entire instrument to which it is af-

fixed; otherwise it operates as only a partial **assignment**, U.C.C. 3-202(3), which is merely a partial transfer of title. 182 N.W. 409, 413.

ACCOMMODATION INDORSEMENT one made in the absence of any **consideration** solely for the benefit of the holder. 34 A. 201. **Credit** is thereby extended to the holder by the indorser, 12 A. 566, generally for the purpose of enabling such holder to obtain credit or money from another on the basis of the indorsement. 97 N.W. 694.

BLANK INDORSEMENT one which specifies no particular party to whom the indorsed instrument is exclusively payable, and which therefore authorizes negotiation by the bearer upon **delivery** alone. U.C.C. 3-204(2).

SPECIAL INDORSEMENT one which specifies the party to whom or to whose order the instrument shall be payable; the instrument is then negotiable only by such person unless he makes a further indorsement. Id. at 3-204(1).

RESTRICTIVE INDORSEMENT one which is conditional, or which places restrictions on its transferability. Id. at 3-205.

IN EXTREMIS *(ĭn ĕx-trē'-mĭs)*—Lat: in extremity; at an end; especially, in anticipation of death. But "the term 'in extremis' is not exclusively applicable to an actor's anticipation of imminent death. It characterizes any situation in which the actor is 'in extremity' or in 'extreme circumstances.'" 67 Cal. Rptr. 297, 302. The fact that one has executed a document under such circumstances may affect its interpretation as his or her will. Id. Compare **causa mortis**.

INFANCY to have not yet reached the age of legal **majority**; minority; in some states it is terminated upon marriage.

An infant's contracts are generally **voidable**, except that by statute infants within certain age groups can validly contract for necessities and for business ventures on reasonable terms. Educational loans constitute another frequent exception to the ordinary contract defense of infancy. See 23 Vt. 378.

An infant will be liable for his own

torts although special rules relating to the capacity of very young actors to form necessary states of mind may apply and insulate them to some extent. See Prosser, Torts §134 (4th ed. 1971).

"At common law, children under the age of seven are conclusively presumed to be without criminal capacity, those who have reached the age of fourteen are treated as fully responsible, while as to those between the ages of seven and fourteen there is a rebuttable **presumption** of criminal incapacity. About one-third of the states have made some change by statute in the age of criminal responsibility for minors. In addition, all jurisdictions have adopted **juvenile court** legislation providing that some or all criminal conduct by those persons under a certain age (usually eighteen) must or may be adjudicated in the juvenile court rather than in a criminal proceeding." LaFave and Scott, Criminal Law 351 (1972). See **emancipation.** See also **incompetence.**

IN FEE [IN FEE SIMPLE] describes absolute ownership of an **estate** in land. It is not used to describe a quality of a title to an **easement,** or other appurtenance or incorporeal interest. 139 So. 2d 135, 138.

INFERENCE a deduction from the facts given, which is usually less than certainty but which may be sufficient to support a finding of fact; "a process of reasoning by which a fact or proposition sought to be established . . . is deducted as a logical consequence from other facts, or a state of facts, already proved or admitted. . . . It has also been defined as 'a deduction of an ultimate fact from other proved facts, which proved facts, by virtue of the common experience of man, will support but not compel such deductions.'" 186 A. 2d 632, 633. Compare **presumption.**

INFIRM sickly; a weak person. In particular circumstances the testimony of an "infirm" person may be obtained in a manner that differs from regular procedure to prevent its loss through the death of the witness. See **de bene esse.**

IN FORMA PAUPERIS (*ĭn fôr'-mà päw-pĕr'-ĭs*)—Lat: in the manner of a pauper. With regard to pleadings, oppor-tunity to sue in forma pauperis grants a party the right to proceed without assuming the burden of **costs** or formal niceties of pleading, such as page size and numbers of copies required.

INFORMATION AND BELIEF refers to a degree of certainty which falls short of actual knowledge, but which comprehends reasonable, **good faith** efforts to determine truth or falsity. See Fed. Rule Civ. Proc. 36. The term is used with reference to documents requiring verification, such as requests for **search warrants,** 122 P. 2d 815, 817; responses to **interrogatories, complaints, pleadings,** etc.; statements made "on information and belief" may or may not achieve the degree of certainty required for these various types of statements, depending on the jurisdiction, the circumstances, etc.

INFORMED CONSENT consent given only after full notice is given as to that which is being consented to; constitutionally required in certain areas where one may consent to what otherwise would be an unconstitutional violation of a right. See, e.g., **Miranda Rule.**

The phrase is also used in tort law with respect to the requirement that a patient be apprised of the nature and risks of a medical procedure before the physician can validly claim exemption from liability for **battery** or from responsibility for medical complications, etc. 104 N.W. 12; 159 So. 2d 888.

INFRA (*ĭn'-frà*)—Lat: below, beneath; when seen in text, refers to a discussion or a citation appearing subsequently in the text; opposite of **supra** (above or before).

INFRINGEMENT see **patent infringement;** see also **copyright; trademark.**

INFRINGEMENT OF COPYRIGHT see **plagiarism.**

INFRINGEMENT OF PATENT see **patent infringement.**

IN FUTURO (*ĭn fyū-tyū'-rō*)—Lat: in the future; at a later date. Contrast **in praesenti.**

IN GENERE (*ĭn jĕ'-nĕ-rā*)—Lat: in kind; in the same class or species. Articles or things in the same genus are "in genere;" expresses any class relationship. Laws on the same subject are likewise said to be "in genere." However, an in genere relationship between two statutes does not mean they are identical. Thus, laws in one area, though broadly designed to regulate one general field may be aimed at different portions of that field, and still be in genere. The term imports singleness in general purpose but permits diversity of individual purposes.

INGRESS AND EGRESS the entering upon and departure from, and the means of entering and leaving; the right of **lessee** to enter and leave leasehold. See **easement.**

INHERIT technically, to take as an **heir** at law solely by **descent**, rather than by **devise.** More commonly applies to taking either by devise, i.e., by **will**, or by descent, i.e., from one's ancestor as a matter of law. See 113 U.S. 340.

INHERITANCE real or personal **property** which is inherited by **heirs** according to the laws of **descent and distribution.** 216 P. 446, 449. 154 S.E. 2d 37, 39. **Real property vests** in the inheritor immediately on the death of the ancestor, subject to the rights of creditors. 70 P. 2d 1059, 1060. A nontechnical meaning of "inheritance" includes property passed by **will.** 277 S.W. 197, 198.

IN HOC *(ĭn hŏk)*—Lat: in this; respecting this.

INJUNCTION a judicial **remedy** awarded for the purpose of requiring a party to refrain from doing a particular act or activity. 104 A. 2d 884. Injunctions were first used by the **courts of equity** to restrain parties from conduct contrary to **equity** and good conscience. 344 S.W. 2d 257. Today, with the widespread merger of law and equity, injunctions are used as well in general **courts of law** whereas law courts were formerly constrained to use the writ of **mandamus.**

The injunction is a preventative measure which guards against future injuries rather than affording a remedy for past injuries.

Types of injunctions include:

MANDATORY INJUNCTIONS require positive action, rather than restraint.

TEMPORARY [or INTERLOCUTORY] INJUNCTIONS usually used to maintain the **status quo** or preserve the subject matter of the litigation during trial.

PERMANENT INJUNCTIONS issued upon completion of a trial wherein it has been actively sought by a party.

INJURIA ABSQUE DAMNO *(ĭn-jû'-rē-á äb'-skwä däm'-nō)* —Lat: wrong without damage; insult without damage. "Injuria" means a **tortious** act in legal terminology. See 7 Ill. App. 438, 446. Where a **cause of action** requires that damages be **pleaded** as an element, this maxim expresses the rule that a wrong which causes no damage cannot give rise to a cause of action. While this is true in a **negligence** suit it is not true in any cause of action in which **nominal damages** can be recovered, such as in the case of intentional torts (assault and battery) and actions for **breach of contract.**

INJURIA NON EXCUSAT INJURIAM *(ĭn-jû'-rē-á nŏn ĕx-kū'-sät ĭn-jû'-rē-äm)*- Lat: one wrong does not justify another.

INJURY any wrong or damage done to another, either in his person, rights, representation, or property. 24 So. 2d 623, 626. Unlike the ordinary meaning of injury (that which damages the body), a LEGAL INJURY is any damage resulting from a violation of a legal right, and without which no **action** at law is maintainable. See 33 A. 1, 2. See **damnum absque injuria; irreparable injury.** Compare **damages.**

IN KIND of the same kind; to return something of the same or similar type or quality to that which was received, though not necessarily the identical article.

IN LOCO PARENTIS *(ĭn lō'-kō pä-rĕn'-tĭs)*-Lat: in the place of a parent; "according to its generally accepted common law meaning, refers to a person who has put himself in the situation of a lawful parent by assuming the obligations incident to the parental relation without going through the formalities necessary to legal adoption. It embodies the two ideas of assuming the parental status and discharging the parental duties." 159 F. 2d 683, 686. The term is commonly used with reference to the relationship between a minor and a residential institution such as a boarding school.

INNUENDO that part of a **pleading** in an **action** for **libel** which explains words spoken or written and annexes to them their proper meaning. 41 A. 781, 782. The plaintiff in a libel action cannot enlarge or change original language by innuendo, since the purpose of innuendo is to explain the application of words used, and words which are not libelous in themselves cannot be made so by innuendo. See 81 N.Y.S. 2d 920, 921.

IN OMNIBUS *(ĭn ŏm'-nĭ-būs)*—Lat: in all things; in all the world; in all nature, in all respects.

IN PAIS *(ĭn pĕ'-ĭs)*—Fr: applies to a transaction handled outside the court or without a legal **proceeding**.

IN PARI DELICTO *(ĭn pä'-rē dĕ-lĭk'-tō)*- Lat: in equal fault. The term is used with reference to an exception to the general rule that illegal transactions or contracts are not legally enforceable; thus, where the parties to an illegal agreement are not "in pari delicto," the agreement may nevertheless be enforceable at **equity** by the innocent or less guilty party. 23 A. 2d 607. Such a situation may arise where one party's consent to the arrangement is made under **duress**, see (Id.) or is obtained **fraudulently**, see 113 P. 2d 190; or where one party is but an instrument in the hands of another, see 39 P. 270; or where the law violated by the agreement was one designed especially for the protection of one class of persons from oppression by another, see 70 N.E. 258. The term may also be used with reference to liability in tort, where the party most negligent may be required to bear the entire burden of the loss or injury. 178 F. 2d 628 See **clean hands**.

IN PARI MATERIA *(ĭn pä'-rē mä-tär'-ē-ā)*-Lat: on like subject matter. "**Statutes** in pari materia are those which relate to the same person or things. In the **construction** of a particular statute, or in the interpretation of any of its provisions, all acts relating to the same subject, or having the same general purpose, should be read in connection with

it, as together constituting one law." 43 Okl. 652, 653.

IN PERPETUITY to exist forever; perpetually.

IN PERSONAM *(ĭn pĕr-sō'-näm)*—Lat: into or against the person; in pleading, an action against a person or persons, founded on personal **liability**, and requiring **jurisdiction** by the court over the person sought to be held liable, i.e., the defendant; actions whereby "the plaintiff either seeks to subject defendant's general **assets** to execution in order to satisfy a money **judgment**, or to obtain a judgment directing defendant to do an act or refrain from doing an act under sanction of the court's contempt power." 237 So. 2d 592, 594. An action **in rem** is distinguished from an action **in personam**; "in an action 'in rem' a valid judgment may be obtained so far as it affects the **res** without personal **service** of **process**, but in an action to recover a judgment 'in personam, process must usually be personally served or there must be a compliance with the substituted service specifically provided by some statute. A judgment in rem is conclusive upon all who may have or claim any interest in the subject matter of the litigation." 267 S.W. 2d 18, 22.

IN PRAESENTI *(ĭn prā-sĕn'-tē)*—Lat: in the present; e.g., when a grant of land is made **in praesenti**, "it imports the transfer, subject to the limitations mentioned, of a present interest in the lands designated." 106 U.S. 360, 365. Compare **in futuro**.

IN QUANTUM MERUIT see **quantum meruit**.

INQUEST a judicial inquiry; an inquiry made by a coroner to determine the cause of death of one who has been killed, has died suddenly, has died under suspicious circumstances, or has died in prison. Generally, it is "a trial of an issue of fact where the plaintiff alone introduces testimony [and which] does not necessitate a jury." 6 How. Prac. 118, 119.

IN RE *(ĭn rā)*—Lat: in the matter of; usually used to signify a legal proceeding where there is no opponent, but rather some judicial disposition of a thing, or **res**, such as the **estate** of a decedent.

IN REM *(ĭn rĕm)*—Lat: signifies actions which are against the **res**, or thing, rather than against the person. "A proceeding 'in rem' is one taken against property, and has for its object the disposition of the property, without reference to the title of individual **claimants**." 71 A. 2d 911, 914. Compare **in personam**.

INSANITY not mentally responsible, to some degree depending on the legal transaction in relation to which it is employed. 232 F. Supp. 255, 257. It may refer to lack of criminal responsibility, commitment to a mental institution, inability to transact business, inability to stand trial (i.e., unable to assist in one's own defense). See 214 A. 2d 393, 405. "In criminal law, 'insanity,' by whatever test it may be ascertained, may be said to be that degree or quantity of mental disorder which relieves one of the criminal responsibility for his actions." 316 P. 2d 917, 919. Compare **incompetence**. See also **non compos mentis**.

The most modern and current statement of the rule in criminal law, where the original **M'Naghten Rule** has been displaced by statute or court decision, is the test proposed by the American Law Institute as part of the Model Penal Code: "A person is not responsible for criminal conduct if at the time of such conduct as a result of mental disease or defect he lacks substantial capacity either to appreciate the criminality [or alternatively, wrongfulness] of his conduct or to conform his conduct to the requirements of law." Model Penal Code §4.01(1) (Approved Draft 1962). The ALI provision further provides that "the terms 'mental disease or defect' do not include an abnormality manifested only by repeated criminal or otherwise anti-social conduct." Id. at § 4.01(2). The ALI test or some version thereof has been adopted by most federal courts and many state courts and legislatures. See, e.g., 471 F. 2d 969 (adopting the ALI test over its own **Durham Rule** test).

IN SE *(ĭn sā)*—Lat: in and of itself, e.g., **malum in se** refers to that which is evil in and of itself.

INSIDER §16(a) of the Securities and Exchange Act, 15 U.S.C. §78p(a) (1964), defines an insider as every officer and director of a **corporation** and any person who owns more than 10% of the **stock** of that corporation.

Under federal law, such insiders are forced to return to the corporation the "SHORT SWING" PROFITS which they made on the sale or exchange of corporate stock. Such profits are defined under the federal statute as those made by the insider through sale or other disposition of the corporate stock within six months after purchase.

Both federal securities acts and state **blue sky laws** regulate the stock transactions of individuals who have access to inside information concerning a corporation. The reason for these laws is that insider trading may cause the general investing public to hesitate in the purchase of securities because of their concern that the price of these securities has been artificially inflated or deflated by insider trading.

INSOLVENCY a financial condition in which one is unable to meet his obligations as they mature in the ordinary course of business or in which one's liabilities exceed his assets at any given time. 317 P. 2d 182. In the absence of statutory definition, the former description of insolvency is the more widely recognized, Id.; however, statutory definition is common today. See, e.g., 11 U.S.C.A. §1(1)(19) (Bankruptcy Act). See also **bankruptcy**.

INSOLVENCY PROCEEDINGS see **bankruptcy**.

IN SPECIE *(ĭn spē'-shē)*—Lat: in kind; in like form; e.g., to repay a loan "in specie" would be to return the same kind of goods to the lender as were borrowed.

INSPECTION OF DOCUMENTS right of parties in a **civil action** to view and copy documents in the possession of the court or of the **adverse party** essential to his **cause of action**. This is done as part of the **discovery** process before trial; but apart from the production for inspection a party may by the use of a **subpoena** "duces tecum" require the production of documents at the time of trial for the purpose of introducing them into **evidence**.

IN STATU QUO *(ĭn stă'-tū kwō)*—Lat: to place in the situation or condition which was; e.g., in a contract, "in statu quo [ante]" means "being placed in the same position in which a party was at the time of the inception of the contract which is sought to be **rescinded**." 28 P. 764, 767.

INSTRUCTION directions given by the judge to the **jury** prior to their deliberation, informing them of the law applicable to the facts of the **case** before them, which is to guide them in reaching a correct verdict according to law and evidence. See 155 S.W. 2d 550. An instruction to the jury is a "**charge**" to the jury, 47 S.W. 2d 443, 447; "and denotes more in the nature of a 'command' than request." 29 A. 2d 705.

INSTRUMENT in commercial law, a written document which records an act or agreement and which is regarded as the formal expression thereof; it thus provides the evidence of that act or agreement. 54 P. 2d 553.

In the law of evidence, the term "has a still wider meaning, and includes not merely documents, but witnesses, and things animate and inanimate, which may be presented for inspection" by the tribunal. 39 P. 783, 785.

INSURABLE INTEREST that relationship with a person or thing which will support the issuance of an insurance policy. "A person is usually regarded as having an insurable interest in the subject matter insured when he will derive pecuniary benefit or advantage from its preservation, or will suffer pecuniary loss or damage from its destruction. . . ." 255 S.W. 2d 990, 991. Ownership or other possessory interest is not necessary, 54 So. 2d 764; so long as there is a reasonable expectation of pecuniary advantage. 15 P. 2d 483.

An insurable interest in the life of another requires that the person holding the insurance be "so connected with [the other] as to make the continuance of [his] life a matter of some real interest" to the insuring party. 94 U.S. 457, 460. The connection may be pecuniary in nature (such as when a **creditor** in-

sures the life of his **debtor**), or it may consist of familial or other such ties of affection. Id.

INSURANCE the benefit arising from an agreement by one party (insurer) to provide the other (insured), for a **consideration**, money or some other benefit in the event of the destruction or loss of, or injury to, a specified person or thing in which the other has an interest. 30 A. 2d 44. Thus, payment under the agreement by the insurer is based entirely on contingencies, 155 F. Supp. 612; which may include loss or injury not only of a specified subject, but also from a specified peril. See 172 P. 2d 4. "[T]here must be a risk of loss to which one party may be subjected by contingent or future events and an assumption of it by legally binding arrangement by another." 107 F. 2d 239, 245.

INTANGIBLE PROPERTY property which has value not in itself, but which simply represents value, such as **stock certificates**, **bonds**, **promissory notes**, **franchises** (contracts giving right to manufacture certain items), etc. 60 F. 2d 827, 828.

INTEGRATION the process by which the parties to an agreement adopt a writing or writings as the full and final expression of their agreement, see 3 A. 2d 180; also, the writing or writings so adopted. Restatement, Contracts, §228. Thus, where the parties to a contract have agreed to it as an integration, **parol evidence** is not admissibile to supplement or vary its terms. 436 P. 2d 561.

INTENT a state of mind wherein the person knows and desires the consequences of his act which, for purposes of criminal **liability**, must exist at the time the offense is commited. 473 P. 2d 169, 170. The existence of this state of mind is often impossible to prove directly; consequently, it must be determined from reasonable deductions, such as the likelihood that the act in question would result in the consequent injury. See 262 S.W. 2d 748, 751. Two general classes of "intent" exist in the criminal law: GENERAL INTENT, which must exist in all crimes, and SPECIFIC INTENT, which is essential to certain crimes and which, as an essential element of the crime, must be proved beyond a reasonable doubt. See 261 P. 2d 614. **Assault** is a general intent offense requiring only the general **mens rea** common to any offense; "assault with intent to **rape**" is a specific intent offense requiring in addition to the general mens rea for an assault a special mens rea consisting of intent to rape the victim.

INTER ALIA (ĭn'-tèr ä'-lē-à)–Lat: among other things, as in, "the statute provides inter alia . . . ."

INTEREST in commercial law, **consideration** or **compensation** paid for the use of money loaned or forebearance in demanding it when due. Interest is a means of compensation. 133 F. 2d 442, 444, 445. The term expresses a formula containing three elements consisting of amount charged (a percentage), the amount loaned, and the time involved. 36 A. 2d 33, 36.

In practice, the term connotes concern for the advantage or disadvantage of parties to the cause of action, 42 So. 2d 445, 446; or bias, 165 So. 2d 294, 297. Its existence is a factor affecting the credibility of witnesses. The having of such a concern is a requirement for the **intervention** of third party in a lawsuit; it is also a ground for disqualifying judge or juror.

In real property, the broadest term applicable to claims in or on **real estate**, including any right **title**, or **estate** in or **lien** on real property, 268 N.W. 665, 667; the legal concern of a person in the property, or in the right to some of the benefits or uses from which the property is inseparable. 107 So. 103, 104.

EXECUTED INTEREST an interest presently enjoyed and possessed by a party.

EXECUTORY INTEREST interest which may become actual at some future date or upon the happening of some contingency.

SHIFTING INTEREST a future interest arising in derogation of or out of a preceding interest.

SPRINGING INTEREST a future interest arising from an estate in the grantor.

VESTED INTEREST one in which there is a present fixed right of present or future enjoyment. See 95 A. 510.

INTERIM ORDER a temporary order, made until another or **final order** takes its place or a specific event occurs. 39 N.W. 2d 809. See also **interlocutory**.

INTERLOCUTORY provisional; temporary; not final, 507 P. 2d 530, 532. "An order or judgment is interlocutory if it does not determine the **issues** (at trial) but directs some further **proceeding** preliminary to a final **decree**. Such an order or judgment is subject to change by the court during the pendency of the action to meet the exigencies of the case." 120 S.E. 2d 82, 91.

INTERLOCUTORY DECREE see **decree**.

INTERLOCUTORY ORDER order determining an intermediate issue, made in the course of a pending litigation which does not dispose of the case, but abides further court action resolving the entire controversy. See 205 S.W. 2d 612, 614. Such orders are not generally appealable until after the entire matter has been disposed of by final order or judgment. 28 U.S.C. §§1291-1293.

INTER PARES (ĭn'-tèr pär'-ās) — Lat: among peers; among those of equal rank.

INTER PARTES (ĭn'-tèr pär'-tās)—Lat: between the parties.

INTERPLEADER an equitable action in which a debtor, not knowing to whom among his creditors a certain debt is owed, and having no claim or stake in the fund or other thing in dispute other than its proper disposition, will petition a court to require that the creditors litigate the claim among themselves. The person interpleading is called the STAKE-HOLDER. "Interpleader" is used to avoid double or multiple liability on the part of the debtor. See Green, Basic Civil Procedure 74 (1970). Interpleader is a procedure used often by insurance carriers, which will deposit the proceeds of a policy in court where several persons with conflicting rights have made claims. Compare **cross-claim**; **impleader**; **joinder**.

INTERROGATION informal term used to describe the process by which **suspects** are rigorously questioned by police; must be preceeded by "**Miranda** warnings."

INTERROGATORIES in **civil actions,** a pretrial **discovery** tool in which written questions are propounded by one party and served on the adversary, who must serve written replies thereto under oath. 149 A. 761. "Interrogatories" can only be served on **parties** to the action, and while not as flexible as **depositions,** which include opportunity of cross-examination, they are a good and inexpensive means of establishing important facts held by the adversary.

INTERSTATE COMMERCE intercourse and traffic between citizens or inhabitants of different states; includes not only the transportation of persons and property and navigation of public waters for that purpose, but also the purchase, sale, and exchange of commodities. U.S.C.A. Const. Art. 1, Sec. 8, Cl. 3. 57 F. Supp. 57, 62.

INTERVENING CAUSE see **cause.**

INTER VIVOS(*ĭn'-tẽr vẽ'-vōs*)—Lat: between the living; transactions made "inter vivos" are those made while the parties are living, and not upon death (such as in the case of **inheritance**) or upon contemplation of death [**causa mortis**]. A **deed,** therefore, is an **instrument** which **conveys** inter vivosly a present **interest** in land, or which conveys the **corpus** of a **trust** to the **trustees** [a **deed of trust**]. Gifts are either inter vivos, by **will,** or causa mortis.

INTESTATE (INTESTACY) to die without leaving a valid **will.** "Intestate property" (i.e., **undevised property**) is that which a **testator** has failed to dispose of by will. 33 A. 2d 322, 326. Thus, an "intestate estate" is that left upon the death of a **devisee** to whom a testator willed a **life estate** without providing for the **remainder.** 47 N.E. 2d 454, 456.

INTESTATE SUCCESSION the disposition of property according to the laws of **descent** and distribution upon the death of a person who has left no will or who has left a portion of his **estate**

unaccounted for. 116 N.E. 2d 439, 441. See **intestate; heirs.**

IN TOTO (*ĭn tō'-tō*)—Lat: in entirety; in total; e.g., to repay a debt **in toto.**

INTOXICATION state of drunkenness or inebriation. In the criminal law, voluntary intoxication is no **defense** against crimes of "general **intent,**" but may operate to refute the existence of **mens rea** necessary for crimes of "specific intent." Intoxication may also be a mitigating factor reducing punishment meted out for certain crimes. Involuntary intoxication will render an actor's conduct involuntary and thereby allow him to avoid criminal **liability.** Compare **incompetence.**

INTRINSIC FRAUD see **fraud.**

INURE to take effect, to operate; to serve to the use, benefit or advantage of someone; in property, to **vest.** 154 S.W. 2d 961, 964.

INVEST to place **capital** in such a way that it will (hopefully) secure income or profit for the investor. See 12 F. Supp. 245, 247.

INVITEE one who comes upon the land of another by the other's invitation, 23 A. 2d 917, 918; whether express or implied. 189 P. 2d 442, 444. In tort law, the occupier is not an insurer of the safety of invitees, but he owes a duty to them to exercise reasonable care for their protection of latent defects. Prosser, Torts 392 (4th ed.). Compare **licensee; trespass.**

INVOLUNTARY BAILMENT see **bailment.**

IPSE DIXIT (*ĭp'-sā dĭx'-ĭt*)—Lat: he himself said it; an assertion by one whose sole authority for it is the fact that he himself has said it.

IPSO FACTO(*ĭp'-sō făk'-tō*)—Lat: by the fact itself; in and of itself, 270 N.Y.S. 737; e.g., "the sale of his property should 'ipso facto' end any interest he may have in it."

IPSO JURE (*ĭp'-sō jû'-rā*)—Lat: by the law itself; merely by the law.

IRREPARABLE INJURY (HARM) a type of injury for which no remedy at law suffices, and which thus requires equitable intervention, often by way of an **injunction**. In fact, a showing of imminent "irreparable injury" is ordinarily a prerequisite to a request for an injunction. It is any "injury of such a nature that the injured party cannot be adequately compensated therefore in **damages**, or that damages which may result therefrom cannot be measured by a definite, certain or usable pecuniary standard." 317 S.W. 2d 260, 263. An irreparable injury may not be necessarily very large or beyond the possibility of repair; it can also be an injury which is consta y recurring. See 130 N.E. 2d 758, 7 ; 297 N.E. 2d 557, 561. See **injury**.

ISSUE   in general, to put into circulation; to send out, as to a buyer. See 73 F. 2d 799, 803 In the law of **real property**, "issue' are descendants. All persons who are descendant from a common ancestor may be regarded as issue but in some contexts the term has a more restricted meaning and may refer to **heirs** only as a term of limitation [see **words of limitation**]. See 24 A. 297. See also **failure of issue; fee tail**.

In practice, an issue is a single, certain point of fact or law disputed between **parties** to the **litigation**, generally composed of an affirmative assertion by one side and a denial by the other. See 249 F. 285, 287.

J

JOBBER   a "middleman" in the **sale of goods,** 119 N.Y.S. 325; typically, one who buys goods from a "wholesaler" and then sells them to a "retailer." See 66 F. Supp. 555. A jobber is distinguished from a **broker** or **agent**, who sells goods on another's behalf; a jobber actually purchases the goods himself, and then resells them. Compare **wholesaler**.

JOINDER   uniting of several **causes of action** or **parties** in a single **suit**. In fed-

eral practice, a party "may join, either as independent, or as alternative **claims**, as many claims, legal, **equitable**, or **maritime**, as he has against the opposing party." Fed. R. Civ. Proc. 18(a). S.C. See also id. at Rules 19-23. See **class action; cross-claim; counterclaim; impleader; interpleader; real party in interest**.

COMPULSORY JOINDER   mandatory coupling of a certain person who must be made a party with others in an action under certain circumstances because his participation is necessary for a just adjudication of the controversy. Fed. R. Civ. Proc. 19(a). A party must join all of his related claims against another or face the possibility of being barred from litigating them separately on the grounds that such action constitutes **multiplicity of suits**. If a defendant, a party must raise related claims as **compulsory counterclaims** in an analogous situation.

PERMISSIVE JOINDER   the joining of persons under certain circumstances, as plaintiffs or defendants, in an action until such persons can sue or be sued separately. See Fed. R. Civ. Proc. 20. The interests of "judicial economy" encourage a party to raise as many unrelated claims in a single law suit as he may have against another party, with the court "severing" those which ought not to be tried together. Likewise, a defendant may plead in his answer, any PERMISSIVE COUNTERCLAIMS he may have against the plaintiff.

JOINT   united, combined, not solitary in interest or action.

JOINT ACCOUNT   a bank account with two or more names, consisting of funds held in **joint tenancy**.

JOINT AND SEVERAL   condition in which rights and **liabilities** are shared among a group of people collectively and also individually. Thus, if **defendants** in a **negligence suit** are jointly and severally liable, all may be sued together or any one may be sued for full satisfaction to the injured party. See 108 F. Supp. 386, 387. Compare **severally**.

JOINT ENTERPRISE   enterprise or undertaking founded on consensual agreement of parties. Its essential elements are agreement, common purpose, community of interest, and equal right of control. 466 P. 2d 413, 418. Those who engage in a joint enterprise may be liable as **joint tortfeasors**, accessories, or conspirators.

JOINT LIABILITY such shared **liability** as results in the right of any one party sued to insist that others be sued jointly with him. See 38 F. Supp. 404, 407.

JOINT STOCK COMPANY see **company**.

JOINT TENANCY property in which there is a single **estate** in land or other property owned by two or more persons, created under one **instrument** and at one time, all such persons having an equal right to share in the use and enjoyment of the property during their respective lives. On the death of a joint tenant, the rights in the property pass to the survivors, and finally goes to the last survivor. 309 P. 2d 1022, 1025. The property can be conveyed by a **deed** joined in by all the co-tenants or by a forced judicial **partition**. See **unities**.

JOINT TORT-FEASORS two or more persons who owe to another the same **duty** and whose **negligence** results in injury to such other person, thus rendering the tort-feasors both jointly and severally [individually] liable for the injury, 194 N.W. 2d 564, 565; 277 F. Supp. 457, 461; the parties must either act in **concert** or must by independent acts unite in causing a single injury. See also **contribution**.

JOINTURE an **estate** or **property** secured to a prospective wife as a marriage settlement, to be enjoyed by her after her husband's decease. See 74 N.W. 1077, 1078. The estate existed under the **common law** as a means of protecting the wife's future, upon the death of her husband, in lieu of **dower**. See also **curtesy**.

JOINT VENTURE a business undertaking by two or more parties in which profits, losses and control are shared. See 447 P. 2d 609. Though the term is often considered synonymous, in a general sense, with **"partnership,"** a joint venture may connote an enterprise which is of a more limited scope and duration, though it gives rise to the same sort of mutual **liability**. See 27 N.Y.S. 785. Compare **corporation**.

JUDGE-MADE LAW law made in the **common-law** tradition; that law arrived at by judicial **precedent** rather than by statute; also, judicial **construction** of statutes so different from their original legislative intent that the resulting application of them can be attributed to the **judiciary**, rather than to the legislature. See **stare decisis**.

JUDGMENT the determination of a court of competent **jurisdiction** upon matters submitted to it, 30 N.E. 2d 994, 995; the last word in a judicial controversy; a final determination of the rights of the **parties**. 28 N.W. 2d 567, 568. See **default judgment; summary judgment**.

ESTOPPEL BY JUDGMENT **estoppel** brought about by the judgment of a court. The essence of estoppel by judgment is that some like question or fact in dispute has been determined by a court of competent jurisdiction between the same parties or their **privies**. 117 F. 2d 672, 678.

JUDGMENT BY DEFAULT see **default**.

JUDGMENT IN REM one which is pronounced upon the status of some particular subject matter, property, or thing, as opposed to one pronounced upon persons. See 259 P. 2d 953, 954. See **in rem**.

JUDGMENT N.O.V. see **n.o.v.**

JUDGMENT OF CONVICTION the **sentence** in a criminal case formally entered in the clerk's records.

JUDGMENT ON THE MERITS judgment determined by analysis and adjudication of the factual issues posted, rather than by a technical or **procedural** defect requiring one party to prevail. A judgment on the merits is binding and issues so judged become subject to the force of **res judicata** and **collateral estoppel**.

JUDGMENT CREDITOR a **creditor** who has obtained a **judgment** against a **debtor** [called a JUDGMENT DEBTOR] through which he can obtain the sum now due him. **Notice** of the creditor's **action** must be given the debtor before the judgment may be enforced. See 345 U.S. 361. The effect of becoming a judgment creditor is to create certain **priority** against creditors who have not reduced their claim to judgment, see U.C.C. §9-301(3); and to extend the life of the claim under the **statute of limitations** so that the judgment debt may be sued upon for a much longer period of time than would be possible regarding a debt upon which a judgment had not been rendered. See **levy**; **writ of execution**.

JUDICATURE that department of government which it was intended should interpret and administer the law, 11 N.W. 424, 426; the judiciary and all those connected with the practice of law.

JUDICIAL DISCRETION see **discretion**.

JUDICIAL NOTICE a process whereby the court takes note of certain facts which are capable of being known to a veritable certainty by consulting sources of indisputable accuracy, thereby relieving one party of the burden of producing **evidence** to prove these facts. 187 N.W. 2d 845, 847. A court can use this doctrine to admit as "proved" such facts which are common knowledge to a judicial professional or to an average, well-informed citizen. See 322 S.W. 2d 916, 924. Thus, the Court could take judicial notice that regular mail is not delivered on New Year's Day or that a given day was a certain day of the week (by resort to a calendar).

JUDICIAL SALE see **sale**.

JUMP BAIL colloquial expression meaning to leave the **jurisdiction** or to avoid **appearance** in a criminal trial after **bail** has been posted, thus causing a forfeiture of bail; to **abscond** after the posting of bail. See also **flight**.

JURAT (*jûr'-ät*)—Lat: the clause appearing at the end of an **affidavit** reciting the date, location, and person before whom the statement was sworn.

JURISDICTION the power to hear and determine a case. 147 P. 2d 759, 761. Jurisdiction may be over subject matter or over parties. In addition to having the power to adjudicate, a valid exercise of jurisdiction requires fair notice and an opportunity to be heard. The lack of any essential element of jurisdiction (power or notice) will render the judgment unenforceable. See Restatement of Judgments §6; 389 P. 2d 7, 9.

The word "jurisdiction" is also used to refer to particular legal systems, as in "the law varies in different jurisdictions," and in the sense of territory (coupled with authority to reach conduct within the territory) as in "within the jurisdiction of X state."

"With respect to the power aspect of jurisdiction, a distinction is made between actions **in personam** and actions **in rem**. In the ACTION IN PERSONAM the plaintiff seeks either to subject defendant's general **assets** to **execution** in order to satisfy a money **judgment**, or to obtain a judgment directing defendant to do an act or refrain from doing an act, under sanction of the court's **contempt** power." James, Civil Procedure 612 (1965).

ACTIONS IN REM "those which seek not to impose personal liability but rather to affect the interests of persons in a specific thing (or **res**). A few such actions purport to affect the interests of all persons ('all the world') in the thing; most of them seek to affect the interests of only certain particular persons in the thing. Typical modern examples are actions for **partition** of, or **foreclosure** of a lien upon, or to **quiet title** to, real estate. The concept of in rem actions has been extended to those which seek to affect status (e.g., divorce actions), the status being given a situs (e.g., where one of [the] spouses is domiciled)." Id. at 612-613.

"There is also a third category, commonly known as ACTIONS QUASI IN REM. These are actions based on a claim for money damages begun by **attachment** or **garnishment** or other seizure of property 'where the court has no jurisdiction over the person of the defendant but has jurisdiction over a thing belonging to the defendant or over a person who is indebted or under a duty to the defendant.' "

Id. at 613 (citing Restatement of Judgments §§8-9).

The state can exercise jurisdiction in personam over persons within its territory and jurisdiction in rem with respect to things within its territory. In both instances **due process** requirements of notice and opportunity to be heard must be satisfied. The usual manner of obtaining jurisdiction over a person within the court's territorial jurisdiction is by personal service of process within such territorial jurisdiction. See also **long-arm statutes.**

APPELLATE JURISDICTION the power vested in a superior **tribunal** to correct legal errors of an inferior tribunal and to revise their judgments accordingly. See 106 S.W. 326, 331.

CONCURRENT JURISDICTION equal jurisdiction; that jurisdiction exercised by different courts at the same time, over the same subject matter and within the same territory, and wherein litigants may, in the first instance, resort to either court indifferently. 242 Ill. App. 139.

DIVERSITY JURISDICTION that jurisdiction in federal courts brought about by the fact that opposing parties come from different states. See **diversity of citizenship.**

SUBJECT MATTER JURISDICTION refers to the competency of the court to hear and determine a particular category of cases. See 257 F. Supp. 219, 224. Sometimes used to refer to in rem jurisdictions insofar as specific subject matter property is involved in the litigation.

See also **ancillary jurisdiction; federal question jurisdiction; original jurisdiction; pendent jurisdiction.**

JURIS IGNORANTIA EST CUM NOSTRUM IGNORAMUS *(jŭ'-rĭs ĭg-nō-rän'-shē-ā ĕst kŭm nōs'-trŭm ĭg-nō-rä'-mŭs)* Lat: it is ignorance of the law when we are unfamiliar with our own rights.

JURISPRUDENCE the science of law; the study of the structure of legal systems, i.e., of the form, as distinguished from the content, of systems of law; also, a collective term denoting the course of judicial decision, i.e., case law, as opposed to legislation; sometimes used simply as a synonym for "law." See Pound, 1 Jurisprudence 7-9 (1959).

JURIST a legal scholar; one versed in law, particularly the **civil law** or the law of nations; also sometimes used to refer to a judge.

JUROR person sworn as member of a **jury**; also, a person selected for jury duty, but not yet chosen for a particular case. 144 N.E. 338, 340.

JURY a group of people summoned and sworn to decide on the facts in issue at a trial; a jury is composed of the peers or a cross-section of the community. See 328 U.S. 217; 407 U.S. 493. See **grand jury; petit jury.**

GRAND JURY a body of persons summoned and sworn to determine whether the facts and accusations presented by the prosecutor warrant an indictment and eventual trial of the accused. Called grand because of the relatively large amount of jurors impaneled (traditionally twenty-three) as compared with a **petit jury.** See also **grand jury.**

PETIT (PETTY) JURY ordinary trial jury, as opposed to a **grand jury.** Its function is to determine issues of fact in civil and criminal cases and to reach a verdict in conjunction with those findings. Petit juries have been composed traditionally of 12 members, whose verdict was required to be unanimous. This remains the case in most jurisdictions today, but 6 person juries, 399 U.S. 78 (1970); and less than unanimous verdicts have been held constitutionally permissible in state (but not federal) criminal proceedings. 406 U.S. 404 (1972).

JURY OF THE VICINAGE literally, a jury from the neighborhood where a crime was committed. 82 S.W. 643, 644.

JUST COMPENSATION with regard to a taking of property under the power of **eminent domain,** "full indemnity or remuneration for the loss or damage sustained by the owner of the property taken or injured," 319 S.W. 2d 930, 934; it consists of a "settlement with a citizen which leaves him no poorer and no richer than he was before the property was taken." 40 F. Supp. 811, 819. The measure generally used is the fair **market value** of the property at the time of taking, 418 P. 2d 1020; which means the value which the land could have if put to the most profitable use for which it is adapted. 33 F. Supp. 519. "Just compensation" need not take account of anticipated or possible future profitability, 155 F. 2d 905; or of sentimental or other non-objective values, but is to be based on the property's value to a willing seller and a willing buyer. 150 F. Supp. 347.

JUS TERTII *(yūs tĕr'-shē)*—Lat: the right of a third; the legal right of a third. The term often appears in the context of actions involving claims of **title** to **real property**, wherein it is said that because a possessor's title is good against all the world except those with a better title, one seeking to **oust** a possessor must do so on the strength of his own title, and may not rely on a jus tertii, or the better title held by a third party.

JUSTICE OF THE PEACE a judicial officer of inferior rank, who presides in a court of statutorily limited **civil jurisdiction** and who is also a conservator of the peace with limited jurisdiction in criminal **proceedings, prosecutions,** and commitments of offenders as fixed by statute. 94 S.W. 2d 632.

JUSTICIABLE capable of being tried in a court of law or equity. "Justiciability" is generally a question of feasibility, i.e., whether it is feasible for a court to carry out and enforce its decision, as opposed to **jurisdiction**, which is a matter of whether a court has the power or authority to hear a case. A court can have jurisdiction, but at the same time have a "non-justiciable" **issue** before it.

JUSTICIABLE CONTROVERSY a real and substantial controversy which is appropriate for judicial determination, as distinguished from a hypothetical, contingent or abstract dispute, 155 S.E. 2d 618, 621; a dispute which involves legal relations of parties who have real adverse interests, and upon which judgment may effectively operate through a decree of conclusive character. 249 So. 2d 908, 918. See **controversy; political question.**

JUSTIFIABLE HOMICIDE see **homicide.**

JUSTIFICATION showing of a suffi-

cient reason in court why defendant did what he is called upon to answer to, so as to excuse **liability**; just cause or excuse; just, lawful excuse for an act; reasonable excuse. 342 F. Supp. 1048, 1062.

The defense of justification [also called NECESSITY] in criminal and tort law excuses the defendant from an otherwise criminal or tortious act when he has unavoidably been forced to make a "choice of evils;" e.g., intentionally setting fire to "real property of another for the purpose of preventing a raging forest fire from spreading into a densely populated community." New York Penal Law § 35.05, Commentary (McKinney ed. 1967). See Model Penal Code §3.02 (Final Draft 1962). In tort law a PUBLIC NECESSITY will provide a complete justification while a PRIVATE NECESSITY will provide a more limited **privilege.** Prosser, Torts §24 (4th ed. 1971) See also **duress; mistake.**

JUVENILE COURTS judicial systems first established in the United States in the late 1800's and designed to treat youthful offenders separately from adult persons accused. Fashioned after the Chancery Court of Crime of England, the framework was intended to place the state through the presiding judge in the position of **parens patriae** and to remove the adversary nature of normal proceedings and replace it with a paternal concern for the child's well-being. Because of this changed atmosphere, the minimal procedural due process requirements guaranteed to adult offenders through the **Bill of Rights** were not afforded to the young persons coming before such courts. Offenders were referred to as "delinquents" rather than "criminals," although the allowable period of incarceration in detention homes to which they were liable was often longer than that to which an adult would be subject. The landmark decision of the Supreme Court in the case of *In Re Gault*, 387 U.S. 1 (1967), found that the **due process** clause of the Fourteenth Amendment requires that persons before such courts facing possible incarceration be assured of timely notice of charges, right to counsel, the privilege against **self-incrimination,** and the opportunity to cross-examine witnesses. See 18 Crime and Delin. 68-78 (1972).

JUVENILE DELINQUENT term used to describe minors who have committed an offense ordinarily punishable by criminal processes, but who are under the age, set by statute, for criminal responsibility. When a juvenile commits an offense it is considered an act of JUVENILE DELINQUENCY. See juvenile court.

K

KIDNAPPING [KIDNAPING] unlawful taking and carrying away of a person against his will. 178 S.E. 2d 407, 411. Kidnapping is **false imprisonment** with the extra element of removal of the victim to another place. See 174 N.E. 162, 163.

"A distinctive feature of the original common law offense was the requirement that the victim be sent out of the country, a requirement echoed in American legislation that speaks of taking out of the state, county. A very substantial displacement was contemplated. . . . Various circumstances and forces led to an expansion of the original concept. It [was] soon apparent that distance and isolation could be achieved within the realm, and that even distance was not essential to isolating a victim from the law and his friends, e.g., by 'secret' confinement in the immediate vicinity." Model Penal Code, Tent. Draft No. 11 at 12 (1960). Kidnapping was only a **misdemeanor** at common law, 4 Bl. Comm. *219; but is a serious **felony** in the United States. Simple kidnapping is often distinguished from the more aggravated forms involving ransom demands or child-stealing. Compare **abduction**. See also **false arrest**.

KING'S [QUEEN'S] BENCH Court of King's Bench or Court of Queen's Bench (depending on who is the reigning monarch); the highest English **common law** court, both civil and criminal, so called because the king or queen formerly presided; now known as the King's Bench or Queens Bench Division of the High Court of Justice, embracing the jurisdiction of the former **Courts of Exchequer** and Courts of Common Pleas.

KNOWINGLY see **mens rea.**

L

LABOR UNION any association of workers which exists for the purpose, in whole or in part, of bargaining on behalf of workers with employers about the terms of employment. Originally, in England, unions were indictable as criminal **conspiracies**. When statutes were enacted freeing them from this criminal **liability** they were still condemned by the courts as being organizations in restraint of trade, and therefore not deserving of legal enforcement of their rights. This attitude was carried over and for a time persisted in the United States. 28 Am. D. 501. Today labor unions are recognized in full by the law and are subject to regulation by the federal government under the National Labor Relations Act. See 29 U.S.C. §§151-168. Compare **cooperative association.**

LACHES an **equitable defense** doctrine which asserts that long-neglected rights cannot be enforced. Laches signifies not only undue lapse of time in enforcing a right of **action**, and **negligence** in failing to act more promptly, 100 A. 110, 113; but also that the negligence has led the **adverse party** into changing his condition as to the **property** or right in question, making it inequitable to allow the negligent party to be preferred in his legal right. 118 S.W. 324, 326. The consequent precluding of the negligent party's action constitutes a species of equitable estoppel known as ESTOPPEL BY LACHES. See **estoppel** (ESTOPPEL IN PAIS).

LAND broadly, any ground, soil, or

earth. More specifically, the term refers to **real estate** or **real property**, 42 P. 2d 292; or to any tract which may be **conveyed** by **deed**. 125 F. 2d 430, 434. "Land" may comprehend an **estate or interest** in real property. 161 S.E. 2d 163, 166. It often refers not only to the soil and earth itself, but also to things of a permanent nature found there or affixed thereto. 166 S.E. 570, 580.

LANDLORD one who leases **real property**. See **lease**.

LARCENY the taking of another's **property** unlawfully, with the intention of depriving the owner of its use; "the **felonious** taking and carrying away from any place the **personal property** of another, without his consent, by a person not entitled to the **possession** thereof, with the intent to deprive the owner of the property and to convert it to the use of the taker or some person other than the owner." 53 So. 2d 533, 536. In some modern penal statutes, "larceny" includes common-law larceny by **trespassory** taking, common-law larceny by trick, **embezzlement**, and obtaining property by false pretenses; it may also include acquiring lost property by any means, and issuing a bad **check**. See New York Penal Law §155.05

Larceny was classified by an early statute as either GRAND larceny or PETIT larceny (now often spelled "petty"). If the value of the property taken did not exceed 12 pence it was termed petit larceny and the death penalty was not exacted. Statute of Westminster I, c. 15 (1275). Today the distinction based on value is retained in the present criminal codes with the frequent addition of automobile theft and larceny by extortion added to the dollar value as aggravating factors leading to grand larceny classification and a higher sanction range. The dollar amount varies by statute from a common low of $50 to $200–250. Some states have more than one degree of grand larceny, again according to the value of property taken or the method used or both. Compare **burglary; robbery**.

LAST ANTECEDENT DOCTRINE in statutory **construction**, under the last antecedent doctrine, relative or modi-

fying phrases are to be applied only to words immediately preceding them, and are not to be construed as extending to more remote phrases, 195 P. 2d 82, 84; unless such is clearly required by the context of the statute or the reading of it as a whole. 272 N.W. 50, 52.

LAST CLEAR CHANCE the doctrine in some jurisdictions that a defendant may still be liable for the injuries he caused, even though the plaintiff was guilty of **contributory negligence**, if the defendant could have avoided injury to the plaintiff by exercising ordinary care; "the essential elements of the doctrine are: the plaintiff by his own **negligence** placed himself in a position of danger; that the plaintiff's negligence had ceased; that the defendant, seeing the plaintiff in a position of danger, or by the exercise of **due care** should have seen the plaintiff in such position, by exercising due care on his part had a clear chance to avoid injuring the plaintiff; that the defendant failed to exercise such due care; and as a result of such failure on the defendant's part plaintiff was injured." 470 P. 2d 748, 753.

LAST WILL AND TESTAMENT see **will**.

LATENT DEFECT a defect which is hidden from knowledge as well as from sight and one which would not be discovered even by the exercise of ordinary and reasonable care. 202 A. 2d 560, 563. A **landlord** may not be liable for injuries to **tenants** resulting from latent defects in the **leased** premises, since the landlord's duty with respect thereto extends only to making a reasonably careful inspection, which would not have been sufficient to avoid the risk of the injury in the event of a latent defect. See 261 N.W. 354. The same may be true of a host's liability to an **invitee** injured on the host's **premises**. But a defect may be latent to the tenant though known to the landlord, in which case the landlord would have a duty to warn the tenant as to that known latent defect. Prosser, Law of Torts 392, 401 (4th 1971). Compare **patent defect**. See also [WARRANTY OF HABITABILITY].

LAW the legislative pronouncement of the rules which should guide one's actions in society; "the aggregate of those rules and principles of conduct promulgated by the legislative authority, [court decisions], or established by local custom. Our laws are the [result] derived from a combination of the divine or moral laws, the laws of nature, and human experience, as such . . . has been evolved by human intellect influenced by the virtues of the ages. Human laws must therefore of necessity continually change as human experience shall prove the necessity of new laws to meet new evils, or evils which have taken upon themselves new forms, or as the public conscience shall change, thus viewing matters from a different moral viewpoint." 123 N.W. 504, 508.

LAW MERCHANT a body of commercial law governing merchants in England, with similar rules existing in other European states. These laws were first enforced by special English mercantile courts, and later enforced in **common law courts of law** and **equity**. It is particularly noted for contributions to the law of **negotiable instruments**; the modern doctrine of **holder in due course** had its genesis in the law merchant.

The law merchant was the common law's recognition of usages and procedures that had developed over a long period of time among merchants in England and other European countries. As part of the common law of England, it was incorporated into American law and has largely been supplanted by common law evolution and statutory enactment.

LAW OF ADMIRALTY see **maritime law**.

LAW OF THE CASE doctrine whereby courts will refuse to consider those matters of law which have been **adjudicated** in prior **appeal**. This doctrine reflects the courts' unwillingness generally to reopen **issues** already finally determined and is applied even when the **appellate court** considers the prior decision **erroneous**. 132 P. 2d 471, 474. Some courts have permitted exceptional reexamination. 492 P. 2d 686, 691. "The doctrine of 'the law of the case' permits, wisely, of a change of decision, where, among other things, intervening between a first and second appeal, there has been a material change in the situation either as to the facts or in the applicable law."

143 F. 2d 484, 486. See **res judicata**; **collateral estoppel**.

LAW OF THE LAND phrase first used in Magna Carta referring to the then established law of the Kingdom as opposed to Roman or **civil law**. 56 Cal. 229, 238. Refers today to fundamental principles of justice commensurate with **due process** of law those rights which the legislature cannot abolish or significantly limit, because they are so fundamental to our system of liberty and justice; also refers to law as developed by the courts or in statutes in pursuance of those principles or rights. The United States Constitution establishes itself, and laws made under its authority, and treaties of the United States, as the "supreme law of the land." Art. 6 §2.

LAW SUIT see **suit**.

LEADING QUESTION a question posed by a trial lawyer which is ordinarily improper on direct examination because it suggests to the **witness** the answer he is to deliver, or in effect produces answers that are to be given irrespective of actual memory. See 223 So. 2d 843, 847, 274 A. 2d 742, 745. Leading questions may be asked on cross-examination and in general of a witness who is hostile to the party examining him. McCormick, Evidence 10-11 (1954).

LEASE an agreement whereby one party (called the **landlord**) relinquishes his right to immediate possession of property while retaining ultimate legal ownership (title). "Ordinarily when a lease is made we find an agreement by the owner-**lessor** to turn over specifically-described premises to the exclusive possession of the **lessee** for a definite period of time and for a **consideration** commonly called **rent**. Although no absolute requirement exists for the use of particular words, the instrument is usually studded with the terms such as 'lease,' 'let,' 'demise,' 'grant,' and the like." 197 A. 2d 176, 182.

The difference between a lease and a **license** (or permit, privilege, limited custodial use) is that a lease gives exclusive possession of the premises against all the world, including the owner, while a license confers a privilege to occupy under the owner. A license, or similar status is generally revocable at the pleasure of the owner (except if there has been detrimental reliance upon the granting of the license, see 83 P. 808) and gives occupancy only so far as necessary to engage in the agreed acts or the performance of agreed services; while a lease gives the right of exclusive possession for all purposes not prohibited by its terms. See 197 A. 2d 176, 182. The difference may be vital inasmuch as the lease must ordinarily be in writing under the **statute of frauds** (at least if for a long term) while a mere license may be valid although only orally agreed to. See 18 N.E. 2d 362.

A lease creates an estate in real property (called a **copyhold estate**) and although contractual in form it is governed more by property doctrine than by contract doctrine, although the contractual nature of the lease is gaining increasing recognition by the courts. Burby, Real Property 112-113 (3rd ed. 1965). If a tenant vacates his leasehold interest before his term expires he does not, for example, affect his estate and rent is still due periodically unless the lease specifically provides (as most do) that vacating the premises before the end of the term accelerates the entire term rental. Id. Modern law now permits in some jurisdictions a rent set-off for certain essential repairs that the landlord has failed to make although the older property doctrine held that the various covenants (to pay rent and to make essential repairs) were not dependent and hence a landlord's breach did not permit the rent set-off. 56 N. J. 130, 141-146.

LEASEHOLD the estate in **real property** of a **lessee**, created by a **lease**. See 299 P. 838, 841. It generally refers to an estate whose duration is fixed, see 10 S.E. 2d 901; but may also be used to describe a "**tenancy** at will", 151 A. 81, 83, a month-to-month tenancy, periodic tenancy, etc.

LEGACY a disposition by **will** of personal **property**. 118 S.E. 546, 549. The term is generally viewed as being synonymous with **bequest** and is properly distinguished from the term **devise**, which connotes a disposition of **real property**. Id.

LEGATEE   recipient of personal property by virtue of a will—i.e., the recipient of a "legacy."

LEGAL CONSIDERATION   see **consideration**.

LEGAL DISCRETION   see **discretion**.

LEGAL DUTY "that which the law requires be done or forborne by a determinate person." 278 N.E. 2d 504, 510. **Breach** of a legal duty owed another is an element of **negligence** and is the essence of most actions in **tort**. Legal duties not otherwise imposed may be created by a **contract** or by one's entering into some other such relationship (landlord-tenant, host-invitee, etc.). See **duty**.

LEGAL ESTATE   see **estate**.

LEGAL IMPOSSIBILITY   see **impossibility**.

LEGATEE   one who takes a **legacy**.

LESSEE   one who holds an estate by virtue of a lease, 253 P. 553, 554; the **tenant** of a landlord. See **lease**.

LESSER-INCLUDED   OFFENSE "one which is necessarily established by proof of the greater offense and which is properly submitted to the jury, should the **prosecution's** proof fail to establish **guilt** of the greater offense charged, without necessity of multiple **indictment**," 407 F. 2d 1199, 1228; also defined as that offense committed "when it is impossible to commit a particular crime without concomitantly committing, by the same conduct, another offense of lesser grade or degree," which latter offense is, in respect to the former, the "lesser-included offense." See New York Criminal Procedure Law §1.20 (37). For example, **larceny** is necessarily lesser-included in the crime of **robbery**, just as **assault** is ordinarily a lesser-included element of **murder**. See also **graded offense**.

Criminal cases are often disposed of by a **plea bargain** in which the prosecutor accepts a **plea** of guilty to a lesser-included offense and the more serious charge is dismissed.

LESSOR   one who grants a **lease** to another, 252 P. 2d 624, 626; thereby transferring to him an exclusive right of **possession** of certain land, subject only to rights expressly retained by the lessor in the lease agreement. 18 N.W. 2d 88. See **landlord**.

LET to **lease**; to grant the use of **realty** for a compensation; to hire out for compensation. 118 S.W. 881, 883. The term does not always connote the act of "leasing," but may simply involve the granting of a **license**. See 119 N.Y.S. 222, 223.

LETTERS ROGATORY see **rogatory letters**.

LEVY to raise or collect; to seize; to assess, as to levy a tax; a seizure or levying, as of land or other property or rights through lawful process or by force. When one levies or places a levy upon some property, right, or a **chose in action**, it is seized and may be sold to satisfy a **judgment**. See **writ of execution**.

LEX LOCI CONTRACTUS see **conflict of laws**.

LEX LOCI DELICTI see **conflict of laws**.

LIABILITY an obligation to do or refrain from doing something; a duty which eventually must be performed; an obligation to pay money; signifies money owed, as opposed to **asset**; also used to refer to one's responsibility for his conduct, such as contractual liability, tort liability, criminal ilability, etc. See **strict liability**; **vicarious liability**.

LIABILITY WITHOUT FAULT see **strict liability**.

LIABLE to be responsible for; to be obligated in law. See **liability**.

LIBEL refers to a false and malicious publication printed for the purpose of defaming one alive or marring the memory of one dead; (spoken defamation is called **slander**). "Libel" includes "any unprivileged, false and **malicious** publication which by printing, writing, signs or pictures tends to expose a person to public scorn, hatred, contempt or ridicule . . . and also embraced therein is any such publication that relates to a person's office, trade, business or employment, if the publication imputes

to him some incapacity or lack of due qualifications to fill the position, or some positive past misconduct which will injurously affect him in it." 252 A. 2d 755, 772. The truth of the published statement creates a valid **defense** to an **action** for libel.

The First Amendment protects the press against certain libel actions unless malice or **reckless** disregard for truth is shown. 376 U.S. 254 (public officials); 388 U.S. 130 (public figures). The constitutional limitation does not apply to **defamation** by a newspaper of private persons, where only some degree of fault on the part of the newspaper is required. 42 U.S.L.W. 5123. Compare **slander**.

LIBERTY, CIVIL see **civil rights**.

LICENSE a right granted which gives the grantee permission to do something which he could not legally do absent such permission; "leave to do a thing which the LICENSOR [the party granting the license] could prevent. . . . [G]enerally speaking, [it] means a grant of permission to do a particular thing, to exercise a certain privilege, or to carry on a particular business or to pursue a certain occupation." 160 P. 2d 37, 39. Licenses may be granted by private persons or by governmental authority, such as in the case of a driver's license, liquor license, etc. See **franchise**; **monopoly**.

In the law of property, a license is a personal privilege or permission with respect to some use of land, and is revocable at the will of the landowner. 230 S.W. 2d 770, 775. The privilege attaches only to the party holding it and not to the land itself since, unlike an **easement**, a license does not represent an **estate** or **interest** in the land. 41 A. 2d 66, 68. For the same reason, a license is distinguished from a **lease**, which is an estate that includes an exclusive right of possession. 5 F. Supp. 435, 437.

Because a license represents only a personal right, it is generally not **assignable**. 34 N.Y.S. 693.

LICENSEE one to whom a license has been granted; in property, "a person who is neither a customer, nor a servant, nor a **trespasser**, and does not stand in any contractual relation with the owner of the **premises**, and who is permitted expressly or impliedly to go thereon merely for his own interest, convenience, or gratification." 118 S.E. 697, 698. In tort law one's status as a licensee may affect the **duty** of care owed to him. Typically, "the law places those who come upon the premises of another in three classes: **invitees** are those who are expressly or impliedly invited, as a customer to a store; licensees are persons whose presence is not invited, but tolerated; **trespassers** are persons who are neither suffered nor invited to enter. The duty of the owner toward an invitee is to exercise reasonable care to keep the premises in a safe condition, but licensees take the premises as they find them, the only duty of the occupier being to give notice of traps or concealed dangers [of which the occupier himself has knowledge]. Toward trespassers the occupier need only refrain from willful or wanton injury as modified by the 'attractive nuisance' line of cases." 282 N.W. 389, 392. Some jurisdictions have abandoned the tort law distinction between invitees and licensees. See Prosser, Law of Torts §62 (4th ed. 1971).

LICENSOR see **license.**

LIEN a charge, hold or claim upon the **property** of another as security for some **debt** or charge, 227 A. 2d 423, 426; not a **title** to property but rather a charge upon it; the term connotes the right which the law gives to have a **debt** satisfied out of the property, 429 S.W. 2d 381, 382; by the sale of the property if necessary. 170 S.W. 86, 89.

MECHANIC'S LIEN one "created . . . for the purpose of securing priority of payment of the price or value of work performed and materials furnished in erecting or repairing a building or other structure, and as such attaches to the land as well as buildings and improvements erected thereon." 142 U.S. 128, 130. Statutes according priority to the satisfaction of the debt represented by a mechanic's lien are found in most jurisdictions and extend to automobiles and other **goods** as well as to structures; as applied to automobiles, sometimes called GARAGEMAN'S LIEN. 20 F. Supp. 465, 466.

LIEN JURISDICTIONS those jurisdictions in which **title** to **mortgaged premises** remains with **mortgagor** pending payment of the mortgage price. See **mortgage; title jurisdiction.**

LIFE ESTATE an **estate** whose duration is limited to or measured by the life of the person holding it or that of some other person [per autre vie], 282 P. 2d 141, 143. It is a **freehold interest** in land, whereas a right of HOMESTEAD includes only right of occupancy and use of the surface of the land. 291 S.W. 757, 759.

LIMITATIONS, STATUTE OF see **statute of limitations.**

LIMITED PARTNERSHIP see **partnership.**

LINEAL refers to descent by a direct line of **succession** in ancestry. See 87 A. 2d 485, 486.

LIQUIDATE to settle; to determine the amount due, and to whom due, and having done so, to extinguish the indebtedness. See 29 N.C. 143, 61 N.E. 2d 801. Although the term more properly signifies the adjustment or **settlement** of debts, "to liquidate" is often used simply to mean "to pay." 68 N.W. 628.

LIQUIDATE A BUSINESS "to assemble and mobilize the **assets**, settle with the **creditors** and **debtors**, and apportion the remaining assets, if any, among the stockholders or owners." 281 N.W. 172, 175.

LIQUIDATE A CLAIM "to determine by agreement or **litigation** the precise amount" of the claim. 298 F. 125.

LIQUIDATED DAMAGES an amount stipulated in the **contract** which the **parties** agree to as a reasonable estimation of the **damages** owing to one in the event of a **breach** by the other. 151 F. 534. In order for such a provision to be enforceable as a measure of damages the liquidated damages provision must constitute a reasonable forecast of the damages likely to actually result from the breach. 134 A. 252. Where these conditions are met, the amount thus provided for establishes a maximum limitation on the defaulting party's **liability.** 25 F. Supp. 478. If the provision does not meet these conditions, or if it otherwise appears that inclusion of the provision was motivated by a desire to deter a breach rather than by a **good faith** effort to estimate probable damages, the provision will be considered a "penalty" and will be unenforceable; recovery will then be limited to actual damages, if any. 72 A. 2d 233. See U.C.C. 2-718.

LIQUIDATION DIVIDEND   see **dividend.**

LIS PENDENS *(lēs pĕn'-dĕns)*—Lat: a suspended **lawsuit;** a pending lawsuit. "In a legal sense the term is equivalent to the maxim that pending the suit nothing should be changed . . .; and the doctrine of lis pendens is that one who acquired any **interest** in **property** during the pendency of **litigation** respecting such property from a party to the litigation, takes subject to the **decree** or **judgment** in such litigation and is bound by it." 288 N.W. 832.

NOTICE OF LIS PENDENS may be required in some jurisdictions to warn persons (such as prospective purchasers) that the **title** to the property is in litigation and that they will be bound by the possibly adverse judgment. See 33 P. 153. See also **pendente lite.**

LITE PENDENTE   see **pendente lite.**

LITIGANTS   the parties involved in a **lawsuit;** those involved in **litigation;** refers to all parties whether **plaintiffs** or **defendants.** The term is usually limited to those actively involved in the suit.

LITIGATION   a controversy in a court; a judicial contest through which legal rights are sought to be determined and enforced. The term refers to **civil actions.** 34 F. Supp. 274, 280. See also **action; case; suit.**

LITIGIOUS   most commonly used to refer to one's fondness for or propensity to become engaged in **litigation.** Thus, a citizen who repeatedly sues his neighbor over various issues would be called "litigious." Compare **malicious prosecution.** See also **vexatious litigation.**

LIVERY OF SEISIN   an ancient ceremony signifying an **alienation** of land by **feoffment.** "It consisted of a formal delivery of **possession** on the **premises,** symbolized by the manual **delivery** of a clod or piece of turf from the land, all

of which was done in the presence of **witnesses."** 140 P. 242, 244. See **seisin.**

LOBBYIST   one engaged in the business of persuading legislators to pass laws which are favorable, and to defeat those which are unfavorable, to their interests or the interests of their clients. The activities of lobbyists are regulated by statute in most jurisdictions; at the federal level such activities are subject to the provisions of the Lobbying Regulation Acts. U.S.C. 1964 Title 2, §§261-270.

LOCO PARENTIS   see **in loco parentis.**

LOCUS *(lō'-kŭs)*—Lat: the place.

LOCUS DELICTI   *(dĕ-lĭk'-tē)*   the place where the wrong occurred. Where the "defendant's conduct occurs in one state and the **injury** is done in another; . . . the locus delicti is taken by courts in this country to be the state where the last event necessary to make the actor **liable** occurs." 242 S.W.2d 285, 288.

LOCUS IN QUO   *(ĭn kwō)*   the place in which or where, as referring to the locale where an offense was committed or a **cause of action** arose.

LOCUS POENITENTIAE *(pō-ā-nĭ-tĕn'-shē-ī)* a place for repentance; the opportunity for one to change his mind as to certain things, such as the revoking of a gift **inter vivos;** or **withdrawing** or **renunciating** before the consummation of a crime.

LOG ROLLING   schemes used by legislators to force the passage of desired **bills** without actually convincing their colleagues concerning the merits of their proposals. One type of log rolling is the inclusion of several sub-bills under one bill, each sub-bill of which probably would not have been approved if voted on singly. See 36 P. 2d 549, 552. Another practice is for two (or more) legislators to agree to vote on each other's bills, even if neither has any interest in the other's bill.

LOITER   to linger idly by; to move slowly about; to be dilatory, particularly in a public place, around a school, or near a transportation facility. Criminal prohibitions against "loitering" include proscription of such behavior as remaining or wandering around a public place for purposes of begging, gambling, soliciting another to engage in sexual intercourse, or for the purpose of selling or using drugs; being masked or disguised in an unusual manner; or simply not being able to give a satisfactory explanation of one's behavior. See New York Penal Law §§240.35-240.36. Loitering statutes are often quite vague and may operate to permit **arrest** for mere suspicion. In either instance the law will be unconstitutional. See 405 U.S. 156; 347 N.Y.S. 2d 33. See **probable cause; void for vagueness.**

LONG-ARM STATUTES statutes which allow local **forums** to obtain **jurisdiction** over nonresident **defendants** when the **cause of acton** is generated locally and affects local **plaintiffs.** The Supreme Court, in *International Shoe Co.* v. *State of Washington*, 236 U.S. 310, 316, authorized such expanded jurisdiction where "the contacts of the nonresident defendant with the forum are such that the exercise of jurisdiction does not offend our traditional notions of fair play and substantial justice." Green, Basic Civil Procedure 31 (1972). Such statutes are commonly employed to allow a local court to exercise jurisdiction over nonresident motorists who cause automobile accidents within the state. See also **service** [CONSTRUCTIVE SERVICE].

LONG-TERM CAPITAL GAIN see **capital.**

LOST PROPERTY **property** with which the owner involuntarily has parted through neglect, carelessness or inadvertence, 284 S.W. 2d 333, 335; **mislaid property**, on the other hand, is property which the owner intentionally has placed where he could again resort to it, but then forgot where he placed it. Id. at 336. Compare **abandonment.**

MAGISTRATE "a public civil officer, invested with some part of the legisla-

tive, executive, or judicial power. [In this sense] the President of the United States is chief magistrate of the nation; the governors are the chief magistrates of their respective states. In a narrower sense, the term only includes inferior judicial officers, such as justices of the peace," etc. 16 S.W. 903, 905.

MAIL BOX RULE a rule which provides that an **acceptance** which is made in response to an offer is valid and forms a binding **contract** at the time of its dispatch, as when it is placed in the mail box, if that method of accepting is a reasonable response to the offer. It originated in the case of *Adams* v. *Lindsell*, 1 Barn. & Ald. 681 (King's Bench 1818). The so-called "deposited acceptance rule" was necessitated by the situation in which an **offeror**, after making his **offer**, dispatched to the **offeree** a **revocation**, but before receiving the revocation, the offeree sent by mail an **acceptance** of the offer. It became necessary, therefore, to determine the point at which each of these communications assumed legal validity—upon dispatch, or upon receipt. According to the Mail Box Rule, it is the former; and this rule generally prevails today provided that the means chosen for communication of the acceptance are reasonable. Restatement, Contracts §64; U.C.C. 1-201(38), 2-206(1)(a).

MAIN PURPOSE RULE see **statute of frauds.**

MAJORITY, AGE OF the age when a person is considered legally capable of being responsible for all his activities, e.g., he can no longer **rescind** a **contract** on the grounds of being a minor. In most states, the age of majority was traditionally 21 but is rapidly becoming 18, due at least in part to the enactment in 1972 of the 26th Amendment to the United States Constitution, allowing those 18 years of age to vote in federal elections.

MAJORITY OPINION see **opinion.**

MAKER in commercial law, he who **executes** a **note**; anyone who **endorses** a note before its delivery to the **payee**, 172 S.W. 1147. The making of a note thus creates an absolute obligation to make payment on the part of the maker; it is therefore distinguished from an **indorsement**, which involves a conditional obligation. 10 Cal. 282.

MALFEASANCE the doing of an act which is wrongful and unlawful; "a wrongful act which the actor has no legal right to do . . . as any wrongful conduct which affects, interrupts or interferes with the performance of official duty; . . . as an act for which there is no authority or warrant of law; . . . as an act which a person ought not to do at all. . . ." 97 S.E. 2d 33, 42. See **misfeasance; nonfeasance.**

MALICE the state of mind which accompanies the intentional doing of a wrongful act without **justification** or excuse. 99 A. 2d 849, 854. It refers to an "intent to cause the very harm that results or some harm of the same general nature, or an act done in **wanton** or **wilful** disregard of the plain and strong likelihood that some such harm will result. It requires also on the negative side the absence of any circumstance of justification, excuse or recognized mitigation." 118 N.W. 2d 422, 425. It denotes "a reckless disregard of human life which proceeds from a heart and mind devoid of a just sense of social duty and fatally bent on mischief." 234 A. 2d 442, 443. It may be express or implied from acts that manifest a reckless disregard for human life. See 75 Cal. Rptr. 430, 435.

With respect to **slander** and **libel**, it is the mental state that accompanies the making of a false statement when the maker knows it to be false or when the maker recklessly disregards the truth or falsity of it. See 362 F. 2d 188, 195.

In cases of **malicious prosecution**, it embodies an intent to institute a **prosecution** for a purpose other than "bringing an offender to justice." 164 So. 2d 745, 750. It includes any prosecution "undertaken from improper wrongful motives or [in] reckless disregard of the rights of the plaintiff." 461 P. 2d 557, 559. See also **malice aforethought.**

MALICE AFORETHOUGHT the distinguishing state of mind which may render an unlawful homicide **murder** at common law; it is characterized by a "man-endangering" mental disposition for which there is no justification or excuse and as to which no mitigating circumstances exist. See Perkins, Criminal Law 49 (2d ed. 1969).

" 'Malice aforethought' is the characteristic mark of all murder, as distinguished from the lesser crime of **manslaughter** which lacks it. It does not mean simply hatred or particular ill-will, but extends to and embraces generally the state of mind with which one commits a wrongful act. It may be discoverable in a specific deliberate intent to kill. It is not synonymous with **premeditation**, however, but may also be inferred from circumstances which show a wanton and depraved spirit, a mind bent on evil mischief without regard to its consequences." 362 F. 2d 770, 774.

Malice aforethought is not "malice in its ordinary understanding alone, a particular ill-will, a spite or a grudge. Malice is a legal term, implying much more. It comprehends not only a particular ill-will but every case where there is a wickedness of disposition, hardness of heart, cruelty, recklessness of consequences, a mind regardless of social duty, although a particular person may not be intended to be injured. Murder, therefore, at common law embraces cases where no intent to kill existed, but where the state or frame of mind termed malice, in its legal sense, prevailed." 58 Pa. 9, 15.

MALICIOUS ARREST the arresting of a person on a criminal **charge** without **probable cause**, or with knowledge that that person did not commit the offense charged. See **malicious prosecution**. Compare **false arrest.**

MALICIOUS PROSECUTION an action for recovery of damages which have resulted to person, **property** or reputation from previous unsuccessful **civil** or criminal **proceedings** which were prosecuted without **probable cause** and with **malice**. 52 N.W. 2d 86, 90. See also **false arrest.**

MALUM IN SE (*mǎl'-lŭm ĭn sā*)—Lat: evil in itself; "naturally evil, as adjudged by the sense of a civilized community." 259 P. 893, 898. It refers to an "**act or case** involving illegality from the very nature of the transaction, upon principles of natural, moral and public law."

373 S.W. 2d 90, 93. For example, murder is "malum in se" because even without a specific criminal prohibition the community would think it to be an evil and wrongful act. Compare **malum prohibitum**.

MALUM PROHIBITUM *(mă'-lŭm prō-hĭ'-bĭ-tŭm)*—Lat: wrong because it is prohibited; made unlawful by statute for the public welfare, but not inherently evil and not involving moral turpitude. See 223 N.E. 2d 755, 757. It refers to an act which is wrong only because it is made so by statute. See 262 F. 2d 245, 248. It is contradistinguished from **malum in se**. For example, "speeding" along the highway is malum prohibitum because it has been so designated by statute as a result of a determination that it is dangerous to the community, though it may not be inherently dangerous; whereas, reckless driving would be regarded as malum in se.

MANDAMUS an extraordinary **writ** issued from a court to an official compelling performance of an act which the law recognizes as a duty. It is extraordinary in the sense that it is used only when all other judicial remedies have failed or are inadequate. 9 F. Supp. 422, 423. It is an emergency writ. 74 P. 695, 501. See **ministerial act**.

MANDATE a judicial command; especially, an official mode of communicating the **judgment** of the **appellate court** to the lower court, 151 P. 228, 230; also, a **bailment** of something for the performance of some **gratuitous** service with respect to it by the bailee. 190 P. 12, 16.

MANDATORY INJUNCTION see **injunction**.

MANSLAUGHTER an unlawful killing of another person without malice aforethought. See La Fave and Scott, Criminal Law 75 (1972). The crime of manslaughter was developed as an alternative to murder with its attendant death penalty, for homicides which were not as extreme and were explainable. Most jurisdictions distinguish between voluntary and involuntary manslaughter. In general VOLUNTARY MANSLAUGHTER is an intentional killing committed under circumstances which, although they do not justify the homicide, mitigate it. The classic example of voluntary manslaughter is where the accused killed in the heat of passion caused by the deceased's provocation. See, e.g., 59 N.J. 515. The defendant must have been in a heat of passion, such as rage, fright, terror, or wild desperation when he killed the victim. 80 A. 571; 325 P. 2d 97. The heat of passion must have been provoked by the deceased. This provocation, to mitigate the intentional homicide sufficiently to reduce it to manslaughter, must be a provocation which would cause a reasonable man to lose his normal self-control. Voluntary manslaughter is also committed when the killing, although unintentional, resulted from an unreasonable and grossly reckless conduct.

The class of homicide called INVOLUNTARY MANSLAUGHTER consists of "criminally-negligent homicide" and "unlawful-act manslaughter." A typical example of criminally negligent homicide is where a death results from the negligent operation of an automobile. See Anno., 99 A.L.R. 756; 160 A.L.R. 515. The standard form of the offense exists where the defendant has killed someone as the consequence of his gross negligence or recklessness. The conduct of the defendant under the circumstances must have involved an unreasonable and high degree of risk of death or serious bodily injury. See 59 N.J. 515. The cases differ, however, as to whether the defendant must be conscious that his conduct produces an unreasonable and high degree of risk. See 55 N.E. 2d 902.

Unlawful-act manslaughter occurs when someone dies as the result of the defendant's doing of an unlawful act, usually a **misdemeanor**. The unlawful act referred to can be any act prohibited by law. See 75 S.E. 523. Unlawful acts which are **malum in se**, and which cause a death, constitute involuntary manslaughter. Unlawful acts that are **malum prohibitum** and have death as a foreseeable consequence of committing the act also constitute involuntary manslaughter. La Fave and Scott §79 (1972). Thus, misdemeanor-manslaughter is analogous to **felony-murder**. Many states have been leaning towards the abolition of the unlawful-act doctrine. See, e.g., N.Y. Penal Law § 125.15.

MARITAL DEDUCTION an **estate tax** deduction under 26 U.S.C. §2056 (1970), the Federal Estate and Gift Tax Statute, permitting a spouse to take, tax free, up to ½ of the value of the decedent spouse's gross **estate.**

The marital deduction is a means used by Congress to permit property to pass to the surviving spouse without being depleted by the federal estate tax. It was enacted in order to give all taxpayers tax treatment similar to that enjoyed by surviving spouses in the several **community property** states, where ½ of the decedent's gross estate was presumed by law to already belong to the surviving spouse and hence was not subject to an estate tax.

MARITIME LAW the traditional body of rules and practices particularly relating to commerce and navigation, to business transacted at sea or relating to navigation, ships, seamen, harbors, and general maritime affairs, 318 U.S. 36; it "is entirely distinct from the municipal law of the land. It is, and always has been, a separate and distinctive **jurisprudence.** The Constitution of the United States transferred this jurisprudence from the sovereignty of the states to that of the nation. The maritime law proper finds its expression now only in the national will." 73 F. 350, 351. See **admiralty and maritime jurisdiction.**

MARKETABLE TITLE one which a reasonably well informed purchaser would, in exercise of ordinary business prudence, be willing to accept. See 172 S.W. 472, 473. "A **title**, to be marketable, need not be perfect, (that is to say, free from every possible technical criticism), but it must be reasonably safe. . . ." 136 P. 849. See also **good title.**

MARKET VALUE the price which goods or **property** would bring in a market of willing buyers and willing sellers, in the ordinary course of trade. See 27 F. Supp. 65. It cannot be determined on the basis of a price which would be acceptable to a buyer or seller operating under pressures or constraints. See 63 F. 2d 241.

For **condemnation** purposes, to determine **just compensation,** market value is not to be based necessarily on the use to which the land is presently put, but on the best and most profitable use to which it is reasonably adaptable. 470 P. 2d 967.

Market value is generally established on the basis of sales of similar goods or property in the same locality, but where there have been no such prior sales, there is no single measure of value, and other evidence of value must be looked to. 108 F. 2d 95. Market value is generally regarded as synonymous with AC-TUAL VALUE, CASH VALUE, and FAIR MARKET VALUE. 288 F. 2d 232; 216 A. 2d 439.

MARRIED WOMEN'S ACTS see **tenancy.**

MARSHAL "an officer of the peace, appointed by authority of a city or borough, who holds himself in readiness to answer such calls as fall within the general duties of a constable or sheriff." 9 S. 7, 10. An officer in each federal district who performs the same duties as the sheriffs do for the states.

MARSHALING [MARSHALLING] arranging or ranking in order. In the sense in which it is used in **courts of equity,** "to marshall" means "so to arrange different funds under administration that all parties having equities therein may receive their due proportion. The principle applied in such cases is that he who has a right to resort to two funds, in one of which alone another has a subsidiary interest, shall be compelled to exhaust the one to which the other cannot resort, before coming upon the one in which both have an interest." 47 A. 128.

MARSHALING ASSETS a rule of ranking assets that seeks to achieve an equitable distribution of assets among as many claims as possible according to the equities of the different parties. "Broadly defined, the rule of marshaling assets is one which courts of equity sometimes invoke to compel a **creditor,** who has the right to make his **debt** out of either of two funds, to resort to that one of them which will not interfere with or defeat the rights of another creditor who has recourse to only one of these funds. It is not a **vested** right or **lien** founded on **contract**, but rests upon equitable principles called into action by the benevolence of the Court." 192 N.Y. 266, 282, 283. See also 81 N.Y.S. 2d 404.

Probate courts marshall assets to meet the stated wishes of a **testator** (testatrix) in a **will** when appointed property (i.e., property disposed of in the will by the exercise of a **power of appointment**) would because of technical impediments pass into an inappropriate **residuary** clause rather than within the intended disposals. Marshaling of assets in probate courts to achieve this objective is also called SELECTIVE ALLOCATION.

MARSHALING LIENS "doctrine whereby one claiming a **lien** against two or more classes of property, one of which is also subject to a junior lien [a lien inferior to another] will be required to exact satisfaction from the property not subject to the junior lien. Thus, the junior lien is preserved where other assets exist sufficient to satisfy the senior lien." 171 F. Supp. 655, 660.

MARSHALING REMEDIES "where one creditor has security on two funds of his debtor, and another creditor has security for his debt on only one of those funds, the latter has a right in equity to compel the former to resort to the other fund, if [such an action] is necessary for the satisfaction of both creditors, provided it will not prejudice the rights or interests of the party entitled to the double fund, nor do injustice to the common debtor, nor operate inequitably on the interests of other persons," 27 A. 2d 166, 174.

MARTIAL LAW law of military necessity, where the military exercises great control over civilians and civilian affairs, usually because of the existence of war. "When instituted, [it] is complete and represents the arbitrary will of the commander, controlled only by consideration of strategy, tactics and policy and subject only to the orders of the President. Under martial law the commander can seize men and hold them in confinement without trial. He can try them before a military commission for a vio-

lation of the laws of war or his own regulations. Finally, he can legislate and bind citizens and others by rules established by him and governing their conduct in the future." 48 F. Supp. 40, 49. Under a constitutional government, martial law can come into existence only when utter necessity so compels it. See also **court-martial**.

MASTER (MASTER IN CHANCERY; SPECIAL MASTER) a judicial officer appointed by **courts of equity** to hear **testimony** and make reports which, when approved by the presiding judge, become the **decision** of the court.

MATERIAL important, necessary; relating to a given matter; "[g]enerally speaking, any evidence is relevant and material which tends to prove or disprove any ultimate **issue** made by the **pleadings**, or to make the proposition at issue more or less probable, or which can throw any light on the transaction involved." 155 S.W. 2d 624, 625.

In contract law a material **breach** excuses further performance by the **aggrieved** party and gives rise to an action for **breach of contract**.

MATTER OF FACT see **question of fact**.

MATTER OF LAW see **question of law**.

MATURITY term used to describe the date at which legal rights in an entity ripen; e.g., in the context of **commercial paper [negotiable instruments]** it is the "time when the paper becomes due and demandable, that is, the time when an action can be maintained thereon to enforce payment." 221 F. 2d 402, 405.

McNABB-MALLORY RULE renders incriminating statements inadmissible in federal court if they are obtained from a suspect while he is being held in violation of the speedy **arraignment** provisions of federal law, i.e., if there is a delay in arraignment that is unreasonable. This doctrine is a matter of judicial policy based on federal law and is not constitutionally mandated. See Fed. R. Crim. Proc. 5(a); 318 U.S. 332, 341, 345; and 354 U.S. 449, 453, 456. The Omnibus Crime Control and Safe Streets Act of 1968 states that a voluntary confession is admissible if it is made within 6 hours following arrest **or**

detention; if the delay in arraignment is longer than 6 hours, a voluntary confession is admissible if the delay was reasonable in view of the means of transportation and the distance to be travelled to the nearest magistrate. See 18 U.S.C. §3501(c).

MECHANICS LIEN   see **lien.**

MEDIATE DATA   facts from which **ultimate facts** may be inferred for purposes of **collateral estoppel.** See 246 F. Supp. 19, 21.

MEDIATELY   indirectly; deduced from proven facts.

MEETING OF MINDS   in reference to the parties to a **contract,** a mutual manifestation of assent to the same terms. It is one of the traditional rules of contract law that the agreement between contracting parties which is legally enforceable is exclusively that which has been expressed by the terms of the contract they create; for therein lies the requisite "meeting of the minds," and a hidden or private intent on the part of either party will not change the effect of the agreement as expressed. 200 F. 287. Where, however, there has been a **mutual mistake,** Id., or where the circumstances indicate that one party knew or should have known of the other's undisclosed intent, that intent might no longer be considered "hidden" and might affect interpretation of the contract. 84 S.E. 2d 516.

MEMORANDUM   an informal record; "a brief note, in writing, of some transaction or an outline of some intended instrument; an instrument drawn up in brief and compendious form." 43 P. 896, 899.

MEMORANDUM OF LAW   an argument by an **advocate** in support of his position much like a **brief** but in less formal style without argument headings, tables of cases, etc.

OFFICE MEMORANDUM   an informal discussion of the merits of a matter pending in a lawyer's office; usually written by a law clerk or junior associate for the benefit of a senior associate or partner.

MEMORANDUM CHECK   see **check.**

MENACING   see **assault.**

MENS REA   a guilty mind. Mens rea is the mental state accompanying a forbidden act. To be a criminal offense, the act usually must be illegal and accompanied by a requisite mental state. Generally, there are four criminal states of mind: (1) intentionally; (2) knowingly; (3) recklessly; and (4) grossly [criminally] negligent. See Model Penal Code §2.02 (Proposed Official Draft 1962). The mens rea may be GENERAL, i.e., a general intent to do the prohibited act or SPECIFIC which means that a special mental element is required for a particular offense such as "**assault** with intent to rape" or **larceny** which requires a specific intent to appropriate another's property. In a criminal prosecution, the state must prove beyond a reasonable doubt that the required mental state coexisted with the doing of the proscribed act. Defenses of insanity, intoxication and mistake may either nullify or mitigate the existence of a SPECIFIC MENS REA. Crimes that are **malum prohibitum** often do not require any specific mens rea. See, e.g., 343 U.S. 790. These are usually crimes of **strict liability.**

MENTAL ANGUISH   compensable **injury** embracing all forms of mental, as opposed to mere physical, pain, including deep grief, distress, anxiety and fright. See 114 So. 529. Compare **pain and suffering.**

MENTAL CRUELTY   a ground for **divorce,** consisting of a course of behavior by one spouse toward the other such as imperils the mental and physical health of the other to the extent that continuing the marriage relationship is rendered unbearable. 102 So. 2d 837, 838.

Although probably intended to reach only the most extreme cases when divorce was morally objectionable to most persons, the term has been given an expansive and liberal construction by courts willing to permit divorces practically upon request, even where specific no-fault divorce reform legislation has not yet been enacted. See Clark, Law of Domestic Relations §12.4 (1968).

MERCANTILE LAW   the branch of law (often called commercial law) which deals with the rules and institutions of commercial transactions. It is derived from the **law merchant.**

MERCHANTABLE salable and fit for the market; "the quality of being reasonably fit for the general purpose for which an article is manufactured and sold," 242 N.W. 895, 896; having at least an average or ordinary quality, in light of the quality of the same or similar products produced previously or elsewhere. See U.C.C. §2-314.

MERCHANTABLE TITLE see **marketable title.**

WARRANTY OF MERCHANTABILITY see **warranty.**

MERGER in criminal law, the process by which, when a single criminal act constitutes two offenses, the **lesser-included offense** "merges" or becomes a part of the more serious or higher offense. See 90 S.W. 440, 444.

In the law of **corporations**, a merger is effected when one (or more) corporation(s) become(s) a part of or merge(s) with another corporation; the former corporation(s) cease(s) to exist but the latter corporation continues to exist. In a merger, the company that continues to exist retains its name and identity and acquires the assets, liabilities, franchises and powers of the corporation(s) that cease(s) to exist. By contrast, in CONSOLIDATION, two or more corporations unite to form a new corporation and the original corporations cease to exist. Thus, in the merger of A and B corporation, one will survive; but in consolidation of A and B, a new corporation, C, will be formed. In both merger and consolidation, the surviving or consolidated corporation acquires the assets of the former corporations, assumes their liabilities, and issues its shares or pays fair consideration for the shares of the former corporation. See Henn, Law of Corporations, 713 (2d 1970); 272 N.E. 2d 105, 108.

In practice, "merger" is used to describe the effect of a **judgment** in plaintiff's favor. "Such a judgment extinguishes the entire **claim** or **cause of action** which was the subject of the former action and merges it in the judgment. . . . Plaintiff may no longer sue on the original cause of action or any item thereof even if that item was omitted from the original action." James, Civil Procedure 550 (1965). Thus, a judgment in plaintiff's favor

merges and puts an end to all issues he raised or could have raised in the cause of action litigated. A marital separation agreement may either merge into the judgment of divorce or "survive" (i.e. not merge) that judgment according to the intention of the parties and the law of the jurisdiction. The same is true of representations made and agreements entered into prior to the delivery of the executed deed in a real property conveyance. So, if the seller and buyer agreed in the contract of sale that the seller was to provide **warranties (covenants)** of title, of **quiet enjoyment**, against encumbrances, and of further assurances, but the deed delivered at closing of title was not a full warranty but instead a **quitclaim** deed, the buyer could not then, after he accepted the deed, sue on the warranties, as they merged into and were extinguished by the deed. An agreement to landscape the property which by the terms of the contract was to survive the delivery of the deed will not merge into that executed deed.

The term also applies to the process by which, since the **Statute of Uses**, equitable ownership becomes legal ownership as well, and a conveyance of the former is effective to convey the latter.

MERGER CLAUSE see **parol evidence rule.**

MERITS the various elements which enter into or qualify plaintiff's right to the relief sought, see 271 U.S. 228, or defendant's right to prevail in his defense; the substance of a **litigant's** claim or refutation of a claim; the totality of the elements of a party's claim which tend to establish or refute the validity or credibility of his cause; the grounds of an action or defense. 112 F. 2d 886, 887. See also **judgment** (JUDGMENT ON THE MERITS).

MESNE intermediate; between two extremes.

MESNE LORD in English law, a lord who held lands under authority of the King and who then gave others inferior in class to himself the right to use those lands, and thus became a lord to those **grantees**. See **feoffment, servitudes.**

MESNE PROFITS those profits which are obtained from the land by one who has no legal right to the land and holds it against the true owner.

METES AND BOUNDS a method of describing the territorial limits of property by means of measuring distances and angles from designated landmarks and in relation to adjoining properties. See 177 S.W. 2d 231, 234.

MINISTERIAL ACT those acts which are performed, according to explicit directions (often embodied in a statute), by a subordinate official; "the term 'ministerial' . . . is generic rather than specific, and ministerial acts may be divided into two classes: (1) those which are ministerial solely and involve no judgment or discretion; and (2) those which are quasi-judicial . . . . A purely ministerial act . . . is one which a person performs on a given state of facts in a prescribed manner, in obedience to the mandate of legal authority, without regard to or the exercise of his own judgment upon the propriety of the act being done." 139 N.W. 83, 88. A public servant or official may be compelled to perform ministerial acts through a **mandamus** proceeding, while **discretionary** acts may be outside the scope of such a proceeding, at least unless a clear **abuse of discretion** can be demonstrated. See Id; 102 P. 2d 970, 973; and 157 N.E. 792, 794.

MINORITY not of legal age. "In the context of the constitutional guarantee of **equal protection**, 'minority' does not have a merely numerical denotation; rather it refers to an identifiable and specially disadvantaged group." 343 F. Supp. 704, 730. See **incompetency; majority, age of.**

MIRANDA RULE [WARNINGS] the requirement that a person receive certain warnings relating to his privilege against **self-incrimination** (right to remain silent) and his right to the presence and advice of an attorney before any custodial **interrogation** by law enforcement authorities takes place. The actual rule was enunciated in *Miranda* v. *Arizona*: "[t]he prosecution may not use statements, whether exculpatory or inculpatory, stemming from custodial interrogation of the defendant unless it demonstrates the use of **procedural** safeguards effective to secure the privilege against self-incrimination. By custodial interrogation, we mean questioning initiated by law enforcement officers after a person has been taken into custody or otherwise deprived of his freedom of action in any significant way. As for the procedural safeguards to be employed, unless other fully effective means are devised to inform accused persons of their right of silence and to assure a continuous opportunity to exercise it, the following measures are required. Prior to any questioning, the person must be warned that he has a right to remain silent, that any statement he does make may be used as **evidence** against him, and that he has a right to the presence of an attorney, either retained or appointed. The defendant may waive effectuation of these rights, provided the waiver is made voluntarily, knowingly, and intelligently. If, however, he indicates in any manner and at any stage of the process that he wishes to consult with an attorney before speaking there can be no questioning. Likewise, if the individual is alone and indicates in any manner that he does not wish to be interrogated, the police may not question him. The mere fact that he may have answered some questions or volunteered some statements on his own does not deprive him of the right to refrain from answering any further inquiries until he has consulted with an attorney and thereafter consents to be questioned." 384 U.S. 436, 444-45.

Statements and evidence obtained in violation of this rule are not admissible in the defendant's criminal **trial** and are grounds for federal constitutional challenge to any **conviction** obtained thereby.

MISAPPLICATION [MISAPPROPRIATION] OF PROPERTY the use of funds or property for a wrongful purpose; it implies a conscious misappropriation or illegality. See 66 A. 420, 424. "Misapplication" and "misappropriation" particularly apply to the acts of a **fiduciary** [one in a position of trust], including public servants as well as private **trustees.** The terms can include the misapplication of funds intended for another purpose, e.g., the misapplication of public money, or the **conversion** of another's funds for one's own benefit. See 147 F. 349, 357. Thus **embezzlement** is included as a type of misapplication or misappropriation. See 64 P. 692, 693. Compare **larceny.**

MISCARRIAGE OF JUSTICE prejudice to the rights of one **party** to an **action** that is sufficiently substantial to require **reversal.** "It has no hard and fast definition. It seems assured, however, that where errors have been committed, and where the **appellate court** finds that upon the record it is seriously doubtful that without such errors the **defendant** would have been **convicted,** then it may well be that errors which otherwise would not be considered to be seriously prejudicial, will require a reversal." 71 P. 2d 220, 253-54.

MISCEGENATION a mixing of the races; usually referred to marriage between a caucasian (white) and a member of any of the other races; "the mixture of races in marriage or [the] living together in a state of **adultery** or **fornication** by a white person and a Negro, or descendant of a Negro." 129 So. 306.
Such marriages can no longer be validly proscribed nor deemed criminal. 379 U.S. 184; 388 U.S. 1.

MISDEMEANOR a class of criminal offenses which consists of those less serious offenses than **felonies** and which are sanctioned by less severe penalties. It is generally distinguished from a felony by the duration or place of imprisonment and the general severity of the possible or actual punishment. See 121 N.W. 2d 457, 459; 402 P. 2d 998, 1000. At common law, "misdemeanors" applied to all indictable offenses below felonies. In a jurisdiction where there are no "felonies" the more serious misdemeanors are called HIGH MISDEMEANORS. See N.J.S.A. 2A:85-6.
The distinction between felony and misdemeanor may be important in various ways depending upon the state or locality of the occurrence. **Burglary,** under the common law, could only be committed by entering a dwelling house at night with the intent to commit a felony. In criminal procedure, an alleged felon may have to be tried by a

state rather than municipal court, he may have to be **indicted** by a **grand jury,** while a misdemeanant may receive less in the way of procedural safeguards. Outside these areas, the distinction may also matter. The convicted felon may be disqualified from holding office or from serving on a jury or from engaging in particular licensed occupations, while one convicted of a misdemeanor may not be similarly handicapped. LaFave and Scott, Criminal Law 27-28 (1972).

MISFEASANCE the doing of an act in a wrongful or injurious manner; the improper performance of an act which might have been lawfully done. See **malfeasance; nonfeasance.**

MISJOINDER the joining together of distinct counts in a single **indictment** or **complaint,** which counts ought not to be tried together. See Fed. R. Civ. Proc. 42(b). "The charging in separate counts, of separate and distinct offenses arising out of wholly different transactions having no connection or relation with each other." 13 F. 2d 11, 12. Also, the improper consolidation of separate indictments, or actions. The term may also be used with reference to the improper joining of parties in a single action. See Fed. R. Civ. Proc. 19-21. See **joinder** (COMPULSORY JOINDER, PERMISSIVE JOINDER).

MISLAID PROPERTY property which owner has intentionally placed where he can resort to it, but which place is then forgotten. See 284 S.W. 2d 333, 335. The finder of mislaid property acquires no **interest** or right to **possession,** and thus the proprietor of the place in which the mislaid object is found is the only one entitled to retain possession pending the search for the true owner. Compare **lost property.**

MISNOMER a term applied to a mistake in the word or combination of words constituting a person's name and distinguishing him from other individuals. See 1 A. 2d 178, 181. The MISNOMER RULE, which affords relief from the **statute of limitations,** "applies to situations in which the **plaintiff** has actually sued and **served** the correct party, the party he intends to sue, but merely mistakenly used the wrong name of the **defendant.**" 284 F. Supp. 635, 641.

MISPRISION OF FELONY at common law, the **misdemeanor** of seeing a **felony** and failing to prevent it, or of knowing about a felony and failing to disclose the fact of its occurrence, or concealing the felony without any previous agreement with or subsequent assistance to the **felon** as would make the concealer an **accessory** before- or after-the-fact. See 217 A. 2d 432, 433. The offense of misprision of felony has not been accorded general recognition in the United States. Perkins, Criminal Law 651 (2d ed. 1969). Today, in order to be guilty of the federal crime of "misprision of felony," in addition to knowing about a felony and failing to disclose information about it, one must take an affirmative step to conceal the felony. See 38 F. 2d 515, 517. Compare **accomplice; conspiracy**.

MISTAKE "an act or omission arising from ignorance or misconception," 31 Ohio Dec. 130, which may, depending upon its character or the circumstances surrounding it, justify **rescission** of a **contract**, or exoneration of a defendant from tort or criminal **liability**.
Commercial law distinguishes two types of mistake:

MUTUAL [BILATERAL] MISTAKE signifies error on the part of both parties regarding the same matter, i.e., "where both parties understood that the real agreement was what one party alleges it to be, but had unintentionally prepared and executed one which did not express the true agreement." 237 P. 879, 880. In the event of such a mistake, the contract may be subject to **rescission** (i.e., it may be **voidable**, 423 S.W. 2d 427), or **reformation**, 160 S.E. 2d 833, by either of the parties. See Restatement, Contracts, §§502, 504.

UNILATERAL MISTAKE a mistake on the part of only one of the parties. It can never justify reformation or alteration of the contract, though such a mistake may be the basis for rescission if the parties can be restored to their original positions (**status quo ante**) and one party is seeking an unconscionable advantage over the other. 140 A. 749.
A further distinction is drawn between a MISTAKE OF LAW and a MIS-TAKE OF FACT. With respect to a contract, the latter is the sort that may justify rescission, subject to the mistake's **materiality** to the transaction. See 24 S.E. 677. However, a mistake of law—which consists of one's ignorance of the legal consequences of his conduct, though he is fully cognizant of the facts and substance of that conduct—is not generally regarded as sufficient to justify rescission or reformation of a contract, unless the mistake is a mutual one concerning private legal rights of one of the parties, which rights the contract was expected to secure. 47 N.E. 2d 284.

The criminal law has traditionally recognized the same dichotomy, allowing a mistake of fact in some cases to constitute a valid defense to a criminal prosecution, but relying on the maxim, "ignorance of the law is no excuse," with regard to mistakes of law. LaFave and Scott, Criminal Law 347 (1972). [see **ignorantia legis non excusat**.] The more modern and far less confusing, rule is that either type of mistake supplies a valid defense if it necessarily negates the **culpable** mental state (intent, knowledge, etc.) required by the criminal statute for one to be guilty of the crime in question. Model Penal Code §2.04(1)(a). Nevertheless, he could be guilty if what he erroneously *thought* he was doing also constitutes a crime. Id. §2.04(2).

MISTRIAL a trial which has been terminated and declared void prior to the jury's returning a **verdict** (or the judge's declaring his verdict in a non-jury trial) due to some extraordinary circumstance (such as death or illness of a necessary juror or of an attorney), or because of some fundamental error prejudicial to the defendant which cannot be cured by appropriate instructions to the jury (such as the inclusion of highly improper remarks in the prosecutor's summation), or most commonly because of the jury's inability to reach a verdict because it is hopelessly deadlocked in its deliberations (**hung jury**). It does not result in a **judgment** for any party, but merely indicates a failure of **trial**. See 157 S.W. 2d 879, 881. Mistrials in a criminal prosecution may prevent retrial under the doctrine of **double jeopardy**, unless due to manifest necessity or required by the interests of public justice. 400 U.S. 470; 410 U.S. 458.

MITIGATING CIRCUMSTANCES those circumstances which, while not completely exonerating the person charged, at least reduce the penalty connected to the offense, or the **damages** arising from the offense; e.g., **murder** may be reduced to **manslaughter** where there were present mitigating circumstances, i.e., that the killing was committed in a sudden heat of passion caused by legally adequate provocation. See 407 P. 2d 917, 920. Mitigating circumstances may also influence the choice of sanction by the court so that a defendant pleading mitigating circumstances might receive a more lenient **sentence**. See **comparative negligence.**

MITIGATION OF DAMAGES a requirement that one injured by reason of another's **tort** or **breach** of an agreement exercise reasonable diligence and ordinary care to avoid aggravating the injury or increasing the **damages**. 236 So. 2d 57. The term also refers to a defendant's request to the court for a reduction in damages owed to the plaintiff, a request which the defendant justifies by reason of some evidence which shows the plaintiff not entitled to the full amount which might otherwise be awarded to him. 360 F. 2d 643.

DUTY TO MITIGATE DAMAGES not actually a duty at all in the sense that its breach will give rise to a **cause of action** against the person who violates it. Rather it expresses the general rule that one who was wronged must act reasonably to avoid or limit losses because he cannot recover damages which could reasonably have been avoided. Thus, if a wrongfully discharged employee failed to look for alternative work and work was readily available of the same kind that was the subject of the breached contract, the employer would be allowed to deduct what the earnings could have been from the damages claimed. In this sense the rule has been termed a "rule of avoidable consequences" rather than a duty to mitigate damages. McCormick, Damages, §§33, 160 (1935).

MIXED NUISANCE see **nuisance.**

M'NAGHTEN RULE the **common law** test of criminal responsibility first announced by the judges to the House of Lords in 1843, 8 Eng. Rep. 718, under which a person was not responsible for criminal acts and was thus entitled to an "**acquittal** by reason of **insanity**" if as a result of a mental disease or defect he did not understand what he did or that it was wrong, or if he was under a delusion (but not otherwise insane) which, if true, would have provided a good **defense**. Thus, if one did not understand what he was doing at all or did not know that it was wrong, he was excused. He was likewise excused if due to an insane delusion he thought he was acting in self-defense or carrying out the will of God. This is called the RIGHT AND WRONG TEST because it is often said that one was not insane under M'Naghten if he could distinguish right from wrong. Some courts added an IRRESISTABLE IMPULSE dimension to reach the case where the actor knew his conduct was wrongful but was unable to resist forces driving him psychologically to commit the prohibited act. 7 Metc. 500, 502 (Mass. 1844). The test has been much criticized as too restrictive and has been replaced in many jurisdictions with broader tests. See **insanity.** See also **Durham Rule.**

The defendant in the M'Naghten case may have spelled his name "M'Naughten," 1957 1 W.L.R. 1122, or "McNaughton," 74 L.Q. Rev. 1 (1958), but as Justice Frankfurter has asked, "to what extent is a lunatic's spelling even of his own name to be deemed an authority?" 74 L.Q. Rev. 321 (1958). The spelling "M'Naghten" has become the accepted spelling for the name of the case and the rule it generated. See 357 F. 2d 606, 608 n. 2.

M.O. see **modus operandi.**

MODUS OPERANDI (*mō'-dŭs ŏp'-ėr-än'-dē*)—Lat: the manner of operation; the means of accomplishing an act; "characteristic method employed by defendant in performance of repeated criminal acts," 249 C.A. 2d 81; e.g., the modus operandi of the murderers was suffocation by a pillow; abbreviated M.O.

MOIETY denotes the half part, in contrast to **entirety** which denotes the whole. 9 N.Y.S. 275. To hold a moiety is to hold a half part.

MOLLITER MANUS IMPOSUIT *(mō'-lĭ-tèr mä'-nŭs ĭm-pō'-zū-ĭt)*-Lat: the gentle laying of hands upon; in a **tort** action, refers to assertion by one of the **parties** that he used only such force as was necessary to protect himself or his **property** from injury by the other party. See also **self-defense.**

MONOPOLY "where all or so nearly all of an article of trade or commerce within a community or district is brought within the hands of one man or set of men, as to practically bring the handling or production of the commodity or thing within . . . single control, to the exclusion of competition or free traffic therein." 18 N.W. 2d 905, 908.

"The offense of monopoly under §2 of the Sherman Act has two elements: 1) the **possession** of monopoly power in the relevant market, and 2) the willful acquisition or maintenance of that power as distinguished from growth or development as a consequence of a superior product, business acumen, or historical accident." 384 U.S. 563, 570-71.

The term also comprehends a privilege or **license** granted to a group or company which gives it the sole authority to deal in produce, or provide a product or service in a specified area. For example, utilities are usually lawful monopolies within their assigned areas.

MOOT CASE a case "which seeks to determine an abstract question which does not rest upon existing facts or rights, or which seeks a **judgment** in a pretended controversy when in reality there is none, or one which seeks a decision in advance about a right before it has actually been asserted or contested, or a judgment upon some matter which when rendered for any cause cannot have any practical effect upon the existing controversy." 32 N.W. 2d 190, 192. See also **advisory opinion.** Compare **declaratory judgment.**

MOOT COURT a fictitious court which is established for the purposes of arguing a case which is moot, such courts usually being found in law schools as an instrument of learning. See **moot case.**

MORAL CERTAINTY to be reasonably certain or certain beyond a **reasonable doubt;** "a reasonable certitude or conviction based on convincing reasons and excluding all doubts that a contrary or opposite conclusion can exist based on any reasons." 104 N.W. 2d 379, 382. A juror is said to be morally certain of the truth of a fact sought to be proved when he would act in reliance upon its truth in matters of the greatest importance to himself.

The term is sometimes used to express the criminal law standard of proof [proof "beyond a reasonable doubt"] but may also be used to indicate an even higher standard, as in regard to an allegation that an unlawful **homicide** has been committed when the victim's body is missing. [1955] 1 Q.B. 388. Compare **preponderance.**

MORAL CONSIDERATION see **consideration.**

MORAL TURPITUDE baseness, vileness, or dishonesty of a high degree. See 44 So. 2d 802. Conviction of a crime of "moral turpitude" may lead to disqualification from office, loss of licensed employment, and deportation of immigrants. See, e.g., 8 U.S.C. §1251(a)(4) (deportation). The term lacks precision but has been held not unconstitutionally vague. 450 F. 2d 1022, 1024. A crime of "moral turpitude" is one demonstrating depravity in the private and social duties which a man owes to another and society at large, contrary to what is accepted and customary. See 99 S.W. 2d 1079. This category of offenses is sufficiently broad to have been found to include such relatively commonplace crimes as bribery, 187 F. Supp. 753, and larceny, 112 F. Supp. 324.

MORTGAGE at **common law,** a **conveyance** of a **conditional fee** of a **debtor** to his **creditor,** intended as a security for the repayment of a loan, usually the purchase price (or a part thereof) of the **property** so conveyed. The transfer was to be **void** upon repayment, i.e., the property reverted to the debtor upon the discharge of the mortgage by the timely payment of the sum loaned. Since the mortgage actually conveyed the legal **title,** the creditor had all of the incidents of legal ownership including the right to **possession** itself. But the **courts of equity** recognized the security nature of the transaction and protected the debtor's right of possession. See Osborne, Mortgages 8-22 (2d ed. 1970).

In American jurisdictions three theories of mortgages are recognized: title theory, **lien** theory, and hybrid theory. The TITLE THEORY is the modern version of the common law mortgage under which the creditor has the legal right to possession (though in fact the debtor remains in possession of his property). Under the HYBRID THEORY the creditor's right to possession arises only upon default by the debtor. Under the LIEN THEORY, the **mortgagee** (creditor) takes only a lien on the property, and is not entitled to possession until he has pursued his remedy in **foreclosure** and the mortgaged **premises** have been sold; i.e., the right to possession arises only when the **equity of redemption** has been foreclosed. See Id. at 23-26. In the mortgage relationship, the debtor is called the **mortgagor** and the creditor is called the mortgagee. In most home purchase transactions the buyer is the mortgagor who gives a mortgage in the home he is purchasing either to the bank or to the seller (and sometimes to both parties if there are first and second mortgages upon the same property). The bank (or the seller) is the mortgagee. Compare **deed of trust.**

CHATTEL MORTGAGE conveyance of a present interest in **personal property**, also generally made as security for the payment of money, such as the purchase price of the property, or for the performance of some other act. Like a mortgage of **real property**, "it operates in some states to pass title to the mortgagee, but in other states merely to create a lien," 162 P. 2d 754, 755; but in either case the mortgagor retains possession. It is thus distinguished from a **pledge**, which establishes a **bailment** and which therefore establishes the pledgee as **bailee** and grants him possession of the **personalty**.

EQUITABLE MORTGAGES "usually defined as security transactions which fail to satisfy the requirements of legal mortgages but nevertheless are treated as mortgages in equity. Stated thus broadly they include cases in which the **interest** in the property in the hands of the creditor is the full legal ownership and the aid of equity is necessary to cut it down to a security interest and to establish the rights of the debtor as a mortgagor." Id. at 32. Also included are cases where the transaction is technically insufficient to create a mortgage at law, but where equity intervenes to protect the mortgagee.

MORTIS CAUSA see **causa** [CAUSA MORTIS].

MORTMAIN literally, "dead hand;" "applies to all **property** that, from the nature of the purposes to which it is devoted, or the character of the **ownership** to which it is subjected, is for every practical purpose in a dead or unserviceable hand." 9 Barb. 324, 333 (N.Y.). In England, Mortmain Acts restricting any **alienation** of property which would limit its free circulation by means of the **possession** or control by one **corporation** perpetually, constituted a response to such possession and control over lands by the Church and other ecclesiastical bodies; but the concept has been used with reference to any sort of corporation which may hold property in perpetuity, and thus with a "dead hand." 259 P. 2d 49.

MOTION an application to the court requesting an order or rule in favor of the applicant. See 347 S.W. 2d 211, 216. Motions are generally made in reference to a pending action and may be addressed to a matter within the discretion of the judge, or may concern a point of law as in the case of a MOTION TO DISMISS which tests the adequacy of the **pleadings**. Motions may be made orally, or, more formally, in writing, by a NOTICE OF MOTION.

MOTION IN ARREST OF JUDGMENT application made by defendant after verdict to withhold judgment. The motion, like a **demurrer**, must point out some fatal defect arising as a matter of law from the record. See 112 F. 972, 983.

MOTION IN ERROR same as **writ of error,** except no notice to opponent is required, since both parties are before the court when a motion in error is made. 21 Conn. 283, 284.

MOTION TO SET ASIDE JUDGMENT exactly like motion in arrest of judgment, except that while a motion to
arrest must be made during term of
court which renders judgment, a motion to set aside judgment can be
made at any time within the applicable **statute of limitations**. Both motions must be based on a legal defect
appearing on the face of the **record**.
See 121 S.E. 648, 649.

MOTOR VEHICLE CODE   see **code**.

MOVANT   the moving party; applicant
for an **order** by way of **motion** before
a court.

MOVE   to make a **motion**; to make application to a court or other tribunal for
a ruling, **order**, or particular **relief**.

MULTIFARIOUS   a bill [**suit**] wherein
"distinct and independent matters are
improperly **joined** . . ., and thereby con-
founded—as for example, where several perfectly distinct and unconnected
matters against one **defendant** are united
in one bill," 69 N.E. 912, 913; also refers to **misjoinder** of **causes of action**
and misjoinder of **parties** in a suit. See
65 S.E. 656, 658. Modern practice favors **joinder** of distinct claims in the interest of judicial economy. See **counterclaim**.

MULTIPARTITE   consisting of two or
more parts or parties, as where several
nations join in a treaty.

**MULTIPLICITY OF SUITS (OR AC-
TIONS)**   a ground for **equity jurisdiction**, consisting of the existence of several separate **actions** at law brought against
the same defendant to **litigate** the same
right. In exercise of its equity powers,
the court can enjoin the proceedings at
law and hear all of the claims at a single
proceeding. A mere multitude of suits
is not sufficient to invoke the jurisdiction. The court must find that the remedy at law is not sufficient and that the
proceedings will be vexatious for the
defendant and wasteful for the courts.
51 N.E. 2d 436, 438-440. See also
litigious; malicious prosecution.

MUNICIPAL COURT   city court which
administers the law within the city.
These courts generally have exclusive

jurisdiction over violations of city **ordinances**, and may also have jurisdiction
over criminal cases arising within the
city and over certain civil cases. See 82
N.E. 521, 523. They are thus inferior
courts of limited jurisdiction.

MURDER   a common law offense of
unlawful homicide; unlawful killings of
another human being with **malice aforethought**. This requires a premeditated
intent to kill plus an element of hatred.
See LaFave and Scott, Criminal Law
§67 (1972). The development of the
law of the crime led to several other
categories of murder such as intentional
killings in the heat of an unreasonable
passion; **felony-murder**, where the defendant unintentionally kills another
person in the commission of a **felony**;
and where the defendant kills another
while intending to do him only serious
bodily harm.

Today, legislatures have distinguished
between the different degrees of homicide in order to limit the possible infliction of the death penalty to the most
aggregious form, "first degree" murder. The modern classification of murder includes first degree murder and
second degree murder. MURDER IN THE
FIRST DEGREE has been often defined as
an unlawful killing that is willful, deliberate and premeditated, see e.g.,
N.J.S.A. 2A:113-2; willfulness being
the requirement of intent, deliberation
requiring a conscious consideration of
the decision to kill, and premeditation
requiring that the intent to kill be fashioned prior to the killing. Each one of
the requisite elements can be formed
within a time of a moment's duration.
First degree murder also includes the
category of felony-murder.

SECOND DEGREE MURDER is the unlawful killing of another with malice
aforethought but without deliberation
and premeditation. Such malice may be
in the form of express malice as the actual intention to kill, or of implied
malice where there is no intent, but
where death is caused by an act which
discloses such a reckless state of mind
as to be equivalent to an actual intent
to kill, such as where the accused
shoots into a crowd. See 222 S.W. 244.

It is often said that all unlawful killings with malice aforethought are pre-

sumed to be second degree murder, with the burden of proof upon the prosecutor to prove murder in the first degree and the burden upon the defendant to prove a lesser degree of homicide. See, e.g., 51 N.J. 444.

MUTE see **standing mute.**

MUTUALITY OF ESTOPPEL see **estoppel.**

MUTUALITY OF OBLIGATION term used to describe the responsibilities imposed on each of the parties to a contract, which must be mutual and by which each must be bound. Unless each party is bound to perform in some way the agreement will lack **consideration.** "[A] promise whose performance depends upon the mere will of the promisor imposes no obligation upon him and is insufficient consideration to support the promise of the other party to the supposed contract." 159 F. 2d 642, 643. See **illusory promise.**

MUTUAL MISTAKE see **mistake.**

N

NATURAL LAW law "which so necessarily agrees with the nature and state of man, that without observing its maxims, the peace and happiness of society can never be preserved . . . [K]nowledge of [natural laws] may be attained merely by the light of reason, from the facts of their essential agreeableness with the constitution of human nature." 11 Ark. 519, 527. Natural law exists regardless of whether it is enacted as **positive law.** See also **positivism.**

NATURAL LAW THEORY in jurisprudence, the view that the nature and value of any legal order is best understood by studying how the **positive law** of that legal order agrees or contrasts with **natural law.** See d'Entreves, Natural Law (1951), for a full discussion.

NATURAL PERSON a human being, as opposed to artificial or fictitious "persons" such as **corporations.** See 209 F. 749, 754; 104 N.Y.S. 510, 511. The phrase "natural person" does not include corporate entities, but the phrase "person" without qualification may or may not include artificial persons, depending on the context. Thus, the phrase "no person" in the Fourteenth Amendment's **equal protection** clause has been held to include natural and artificial persons, see 118 U.S. 394, 396, but the same phrase "no person" in the Fifth Amendment's "privilege against **self-incrimination**" clause has been held to include only natural persons and not corporations since the privilege is personal and may not be asserted by an artificial person. See 201 U.S. 43.

N.B. nota bene.

NECESSARY IMPLICATION see **implication.**

NECESSARY INFERENCE inference or deduced fact that "is inescapable, or unavoidable from the standpoint of reason; an inference is not inescapable or unavoidable if another and a different inference may be reasonably drawn from the facts as stated." 9 So. 2d 644, 646. Compare **presumption.**

NECESSARY PARTY see **party.**

NECESSITY, DEFENSE OF see **justification.**

NEGATIVE PREGNANT refers to a **denial** which implies an affirmation of a substantial fact and hence is beneficial to opponent. Thus, when only a qualification or modification is denied while the fact itself remains undenied, the denial is "pregnant" with the affirmation. See 115 S.W. 2d 330.

NEGLIGENCE failure to exercise that degree of care which a person of ordinary prudence (a **reasonable man**) would exercise under the same circumstances. The term refers to conduct which falls below the standard established by law for the protection of others against unreasonable risk of harm. It does not comprehend conduct recklessly disregardful of the interests of others. Restatement, Torts §287; nor does it include intentional infliction of injury on another. Unless the actor is a child, the standard of conduct to which he must conform to avoid being negligent is that of a reasonable man under like circumstances. See Id. §283. Negligent conduct may involve either a) an act which the actor as a reasonable man should recognize as involving an unreasonable risk of causing an invasion of an interest of another, or b) a failure to do an act which is necessary for the protection or assistance of another and which the actor is under a duty to perform. See Id. §284.

In the law of torts, the degrees of negligence, in general, are: SLIGHT NEGLIGENCE, which is failure to use great care; ORDINARY NEGLIGENCE, which is failure to use ordinary care; and GROSS NEGLIGENCE, which is failure to use even slight care. Prosser, Torts 181 (4th ed. 1971).

COMPARATIVE NEGLIGENCE the proportional sharing between plaintiff and defendant of compensation for injuries, based on the relative negligence of the two; the reduction of the damages to be recovered by the negligent plaintiff in proportion to his fault. See Id. §407.

CONTRIBUTORY NEGLIGENCE conduct on the part of the plaintiff which falls below the standard to which he should conform for his own protection, and which is a legally contributing cause cooperating with the negligence of the defendant in bringing about the plaintiff's harm. Id. §483. As an **affirmative defense**, the defendant has the **burden of proof** on this issue. Prosser, Torts 416 (4th ed. 1971). Compare **assumption of risk**.

CRIMINAL [CULPABLE] NEGLIGENCE such negligence as is necessary to incur criminal liability; in most jurisdictions, culpable [criminal] negligence is something more than the slight negligence necessary to support a civil actions for damages. 133 N.Y.S. 2d 423, 427. Thus, culpable negligence, "under criminal law, is recklessness or carelessness resulting in injury or death, as imports a thoughtless disregard of consequences or a heedless indifference to the safety and rights of others." 85 S. E. 2d 327, 332; see also Perkins, Criminal Law 755 (2nd ed. 1969).

NEGLIGENCE PER SE negligence as a matter of law, 3 Cal. Rptr. 274, 275; an act or omission that is recognized as negligent either because it is contrary to the requirements of the law or because it is so opposed to the dictates of common prudence that one could say without hesitation or doubt that no careful person would have committed the act or omission. See 278 S.W. 2d 466, 470; 31 F. 755, 756. "The distinction between negligence and 'negligence per se' is the means and method of ascertainment. The first must be found by the jury from the facts, the conditions, and circumstances disclosed by the evidence; the latter is a violation of a specific requirement of law or ordinance; the only fact for determination by the jury being the omission or commission of the specific act inhibited or required." 196 N.E. 274, 278.

In a considerable minority of jurisdictions the violation of a statutory duty of care creates only evidence of negligence which the jury may accept or reject. See Prosser, Torts §36 (4th ed. 1971). Even in the majority of jurisdictions the per se negligence doctrine operates only to create a mandatory finding of negligence leaving open as a defense lack of **proximate causation**, contributory negligence, and assumption of risk. See Id.

NEGOTIABLE INSTRUMENT a writing which is signed by the **maker** or **drawer**, contains an unconditional promise or order to pay a sum certain in money, is payable on demand or at a definite time, and is payable to **order** or to **bearer**. A **draft, check, certificate of deposit**, and **note** may or may not be a negotiable instrument depending upon whether the above elements of negotiability are satisfied. See U.C.C. §3-104.

A negotiable instrument is transferred to a **holder** who takes free of most claims which the maker may have against his **payee** if he takes it as a **bona fide purchaser**. Such a holder is called a **holder in due course.**

NEMO EST SUPRA LEGIS (nā'-mō ĕst sū'-prȧ lāg'-ĭs)—Lat: nobody is above the law. See *Nixon* v. *U.S.* 94 S. Ct. 2962.

NET ESTATE that **estate** which under federal and state statute is subject to an **estate tax;** generally that estate remaining after all debts of decedent, funeral and administrative expenses, and/ or other deductions prescribed by law, have been deducted from the **gross estate** [total valuation of the estate's assets at decedent's death]. See 136 N.Y.S. 2d 923, 925. The term thus refers generally to that estate left to be distributed after all deductions have been made. See 225 N.Y.S. 190.

NET INCOME the gross [total] income less the deductions and exemptions allowed by law, 221 S.W. 2d 51; "gross income less the legitimate expenses of realizing same." 240 F. 2d 324.

NEW MATTER matters raised by defendant which go beyond mere denials of plaintiff's allegations. It involves new issues, with new facts to be proved, and purports to show that the alleged **cause of action** never did exist and that material allegations are not true. See 3 P. 2d 768, 769.

NIHIL *(nĭ'-hĭl)* nothing, not, not at all, in no respect. NIL is an often-used form to express the noun. Describes a sheriff's **return** after an unsuccessful attempt to **serve** a **summons** or otherwise gain **jurisdiction** over an individual.

NIL see **nihil.**

NISI PRIUS *(nē'-sē prē'-ŭs)*—Lat: in American law, sometimes used to describe any court where a case is first heard by a **judge** and **jury,** distinguishing such courts from the **appellate courts.** Literally translated it means "unless the first", i.e., unless it is the original or first **forum** it is not a "nisi prius" court. See **original jurisdiction.**

NOLO CONTENDERE *(nō'-lōkôn-těn'-dĕrā)*—Lat: I do not wish to contend, fight or maintain (a **defense**); "not strictly a **plea** at all, but a statement that the **defendant** will not contend [a] **charge** made by the government."119 F. Supp. 288. Like a **demurrer** to an **indictment,** it admits all facts stated in the indictment for the purposes of a particular **case,** but it cannot be used as an **admis-**sion elsewhere, as it is an implied **confession** only of the **offense** charged. See 139 P. 2d 682. Thus, corporations often plead "nolo contendere" in order to avoid any collateral civil effects from their plea in criminal **antitrust** cases. The plea of nolo contendere is equivalent to a plea of guilty for the purposes of the criminal matter and is accepted only in the discretion of the trial court, which must be satisfied that it is voluntarily and intelligently entered and that there is a factual basis to support it. See, e.g., Fed. R. Crim. Proc. 11.

NOMINAL DAMAGES see **damages.**

NOMINAL PARTY see **party.**

NON COMPOS MENTIS *(nŏn kŏm'-pōs měn'-tĭs)*—Lat: not having control over the mind or intellect. Not sound of mind; insane. See 108 A. 2d 820, 822. In certain circumstances its effect is lessened to mean only "not legally competent." See 1 S.E. 2d 768, 770. Compare **incompetent; non sui juris.**

NON-CONFORMING USE a **use** of land "which lawfully existed prior to the enactment of a **zoning** ordinance and which may be maintained after the effective date of the ordinance" although it no longer complies with the use restrictions applicable to the area. 508 P. 2d 190, 192. Continuation of the existing use comprehends preservation of both the functional use of the land and the physical structures thereon, and neither of these aspects of "use" may be extended or enlarged once the zoning restriction has taken effect. 102 A. 2d 84. Only actual uses are protected by this doctrine, and not merely uses for which the land might be suitable. 86 A. 2d 74. The protection may extend to a use which is not yet in existence, but whose development has reached a certain stage. 508 P. 2d. 190. Compare **variance.**

NON-CUSTODIAL SENTENCE see **sentence.**

NONFEASANCE in the law of agency, "the total omission or failure of an **agent** to enter upon the performance of some distinct duty or undertaking which he has agreed with his **principal** to do." 191 N.E. 2d 588, 591. Also, it is the "substantial failure [of an officer] to perform a duty, or, in other words, the neglect or refusal, without sufficient excuse, to do that which it [is an] officer's legal duty to do." 115 N.W. 2d 411, 413. It differs from **misfeasance**, which is the improper doing of an act that one might lawfully do, and from **malfeasance**, which is the doing of an act that is wholly wrongful and unlawful. See 323 P. 2d 301, 309.

NON-REBUTTABLE PRESUMPTION see **presumption**.

NON SEQUITUR *(nŏn sĕ'-kwĭ-tûr)*–Lat: it does not follow; it does not come after (in time). "Non seq." is an often-used abbreviated form. When an action or decree is non sequitur it is unrelated to the preceding events. A non sequitur is something which has no logical or temporal purpose for its place in the progression of events; it is logically, temporally and spatially incoherent.

NON SUI JURIS *(nŏn sū'-ē jū'-rĭs)*–Lat: not by his own authority or legal right. This maxim refers to those who are not legally **competent** to manage their own affairs as regards **contracts** and other causes in which this **incompetency** restricts their granting **power of attorney** or otherwise exercising self-judgment. Compare **non compos mentis**.

NONSUIT a **judgment** rendered against a **plaintiff** who "fails to proceed to trial, or is unable to prove his case." 12 S.E. 2d 553, 554. Since the adjudication is made when the **complainant** has simply failed to provide evidence sufficient to make out a case, it does not decide the **merits** of his **cause of action**, 78 P. 2d 1010, and thus does not preclude his bringing it again. 42 S.E. 2d 648. The term is sometimes broadly applied to various terminations of an action which do not amount to a **judgment on the merits**. 78 P. 2d 1010.

NOTA BENE *(nō'-tà bā'-nā)*–Lat: note well; written as the original note N.B. to indicate an important portion of the text to be studied.

NOTARY PUBLIC a public officer under civil and commercial law, authorized to administer oaths, to attest to and certify certain types of documents, to take **depositions**, and to perform certain acts in commercial matters, such as **protesting commercial paper**. See 164 A. 253, 254. The seal of a "notary public" authenticates a document. Id. In some jurisdictions an attorney admitted to practice within the jurisdiction can act as a notary public. In many jurisdictions private persons can apply for and receive authority to act as notaries to witness documents. Thus, secretaries in law offices, bank officers, insurance and real estate agents, small town grocery clerks, drug store clerks, etc. are often licensed notaries.

NOTICE "information concerning a fact, actually communicated to a person by an authorized person, or actually derived by him from a proper source." 215 F. 2d 415, 417. Notice to a **defendant** of a **lawsuit** which has been instituted against him or of an **action** in which he may have an interest to defend is accomplished by **service of process** on him.

AVERMENT OF NOTICE a statement included in the **pleadings** that a **party** to an action has received proper notice thereof.

CONSTRUCTIVE NOTICE that notice which is presumed by law to have been acquired. 226 P. 697. It is often accomplished by the posting of notices or by the mailing of notification to the defendant. Green, Basic Civil Procedure 44 (1972).

INQUIRY NOTICE with respect to one who claims to have been a **bona fide purchaser** without notice, "information from whatever source derived, which would excite apprehension in an ordinary mind and prompt a person of average prudence to make inquiry." 311 P. 2d 676, 678.

JUDICIAL NOTICE see **judicial notice**.

NOTICE BY PUBLICATION method of bringing a lawsuit to the attention of parties which may have an interest therein by publishing notification of it in a newspaper of general circulation. This type of notice is permissible only where specifically allowed by statute, and is generally limited to actions involving land, estates, or status. Green, Civil Procedure §6 (1972).

NOTICE OF LIS PENDENS see **lis pendens.**

NOTICE OF MOTION see **motion.**

NOTORIOUS POSSESSION possession of **real property** that is open, undisguised, and conspicuous to the point where such possession is generally known or recognized. See 108 S.W. 2d 489, 493. The term is used as one of the elements in defining and/or determining the existence of **adverse possession,** which involves a claim of right to property not by **title** but by possession for a statutory period of time; such possession is required to be "actual," "continuous," "notorious," and "hostile," in order that the title owner without actual **notice** of such possession may be legally presumed to have notice. 14 So. 805, 806. See also **hostile possession.**

N.O.V. [NON OBSTANTE VERDICTO] —Lat: notwithstanding the verdict. A judgment n.o.v. is one which reverses the determination of the jury, and is granted when it is obvious that the jury **verdict** had no reasonable support in fact or was contrary to law. See 170 S.W. 2d 303, 306. The motion for a judgment n.o.v. provides a second chance for the trial court to render what is, in effect, a **directed verdict** for the moving party. See, e.g., Fed. R. Civ. Proc. 50(b).

NOVATION the substitution of another **party** for one of the original parties to a contract with the consent of the remaining party. The result is that the old contract is extinguished, and a new contract, with the same content but with at least one different party, is created. See 248 N.Y.S. 89. It often involves a transaction whereby the original debtor is discharged from liability to his creditor by the substitution of a second debtor. If an **assignment** or a **lease** is consented to by the **landlord,** it will amount to a novation and the original lessee will be discharged from further liability under the lease agreement.

NUDUM PACTUM *(nū'-dŭm päk'-tŭm)* —Lat: a bare **contract** or agreement which amounts to merely a naked **promise.** See 22 S.E. 2d 186. "A contract, naked of any obligation or duty on one side, a 'nudum pactum' is not enforceable." 151 P. 270. Contracts must generally be supported by a **consideration** on each side. A naked contract is one that is bare of a valid consideration on one side and hence unenforceable.

NUGATORY void; of no effect; invalid. For example, **judicial proceedings** in a court that lacks **jurisdiction** are sometimes considered "nugatory." See 121 S.E. 828, 829. Compare **voidable.**

NUISANCE in tort law, it is a broad concept characterizing "the defendant's interference with the plaintiff's interests." Prosser, Law of Torts 571 (4th ed. 1971); "anything which annoys or disturbs the free use of one's property, or which renders its ordinary use or physical occupation uncomfortable. . . . [I]t extends to everything that endangers life or health, gives offense to the senses, violates the laws of decency, or obstructs the reasonable and comfortable use of property." 391 S.W. 2d 5, 9. It thus refers to "a wrong arising from an unreasonable or unlawful use of property to the discomfort, annoyance, inconvenience or damage of another, and usually comprehends continuous or recurrent acts." 483 S.W. 2d 633, 637.

ABATABLE NUISANCE a nuisance "which is practically susceptible of being suppressed, or extinguished, or rendered harmless, and whose continued existence is not authorized under the law." 113 S.W. 996, 1000.

ABATEMENT OF A NUISANCE the removal, termination or destruction of a nuisance.

ATTRACTIVE NUISANCE see **attractive nuisance.**

MIXED NUISANCE a nuisance which is both a public nuisance [see below] and a private nuisance [see below] at the same time; it interferes with a right of the general public and also interferes with a particular person's use and enjoyment of his land. See 132 A. 2d 445, 448.

PRIVATE NUISANCE " an actionable interference with a person's interest in the private use and enjoyment of his land." 212 N.W. 2d 505, 508.

PUBLIC [COMMON] NUISANCE "an unreasonable interference with a right common to the general public. . . . It is behavior which unreasonably interferes with the health, safety, peace, comfort or convenience of the general community." 299 A. 2d 155, 158. A public nuisance offends the public at large or a segment of the public, a private nuisance offends only a particular person or persons. See 303 A. 2d 544, 567.

NULLITY "in law, a void act or an act having no legal force or validity—invalid—null." 64 F. Supp. 865, 870. It is "the highest degree of an irregularity, . . . and is such a defect as renders the proceeding in which it occurs totally null and void, of no avail or effect whatever and incapable of being made so; . . . a proceeding that is essentially defective, or that is expressly declared to be a nullity by statute." 4 N.W. 220, 222.

NUNC PRO TUNC *(nŭnk prō tŭnk)*— Lat: now for then.

NUNC PRO TUNC ORDER an **order** used by the courts to correct the **record**. It supplements a prior **judgment** or order in any matter over which the court originally had **jurisdiction**. If the time for taking an appeal has expired, the party may seek leave to file a notice of appeal "out-of-time." If it is permitted, the notice would be filed nunc pro tunc and thus render the appeal timely.

O

OATH an affirmation of truth of a statement which, if made by one who knows it to be false, may subject one to a prosecution for perjury or other legal proceedings. Writings, (e.g., **affidavits**) as well as oral testimony may be made "under oath."

OBITER DICTA *(ō'-bĭ-tèr dĭk'-tà)*—Lat: passing or incidental statements; statements made or decisions reached in a court opinion which were not necessary to the disposition of the case. It is the plural of "obiter dictum." See **dictum.**

OBLIGATION OF A CONTRACT "the civil obligation, the binding efficacy, the coercive power, the legal duty of performing the contract." 25 U.S. 212. Thus the term refers not to any duty which rises out of the contract itself, but to the legal requirements which bind the contracting parties to the performance of their undertaking. 71 P. 301. But, except where **specific performance** is available as a remedy, one cannot be compelled to actually perform a contract obligation; rather, he merely subjects himself to liability in **damages** if he fails to honor the obligation of a contract.

IMPAIR THE OBLIGATION OF A CONTRACT "to weaken [the contract], or lessen its value, or make it worse in any respect or in any degree. . . . Any law which changes the intention and legal effect of the original parties, giving to one a greater and to the other a less interest or benefit in the contract, impairs its obligation." 115 A. 484, 486. "The extent of the change is immaterial. Any deviation from its terms by hastening or postponing the time of performance which it prescribes, or imposing conditions not included in the contract, or dispensing with the performance of those that are included . . . impairs the obligation of a contract." Id. Impairment is also said to exist where the right to enforce a contract is eliminated or substantially lessened. See 185 A. 401. State statutes which do so are prohibited by Art. I, §10 of the United States Constitution.

OBSCENE MATERIAL material which, taken as a whole, appeals to the prurient interest and lacks serious literary, artistic, political or scientific value. Matter so classified is not protected by the "free speech" guarantee of the First Amendment. 354 U.S. 476. Guidelines for determining obscenity have changed through the years, but as of 1974, material is "obscene" when a) the subject as a whole appeals to the prurient interest of the average person, using contemporary community standards, b) the work depicts or describes in a patently offensive way sexual conduct specifically denied by state statute, and c) the work as a whole lacks serious literary, artistic, political or scientific value; but note that the former test of "utterly without redeeming social value" is rejected. See 413 U.S. 15. Evidence of **pandering** may be used to establish obscenity. 383 U.S. 463, 474.

The issue of how "local" the community must be by whose standards obscenity is to be determined is largely a statutory matter. It has been held that "contemporary community standards" is a sufficient jury instruction without specifying the geographical extent of the community. 94 S.Ct. 2750.

OBSTRUCTION OF JUSTICE the "impeding or obstructing [of] those who seek justice in a court, or those who have duties or powers of administering justice therein." 214 S.W. 788. It was an offense at common law. Id. at 789. It includes acts such as attempting to influence, intimidate or impede any juror, witness or officer in any court regarding the discharge of his duty, as well as the actual impeding or obstructing of the due administration of justice. See 16 A. 2d 642, 644. When the statute reaches beyond interference with the judicial process and proscribes as well interference with police officers and other such administrative officials, it is sometimes called "obstruction of governmental administration." See, e.g., N.Y. Penal Law §195.05.

OCCUPANT one who "takes **possession**; one who has the actual use or possession, or is in possession of, a thing. One who holds possession and exercises dominion (or control) over it," 77 N.Y.S. 2d 732, 734; one who has actual possession, such as a tenant, in contrast to a landlord, who retains legal **ownership**. See 67 N.W. 2d 481, 487.

OCCUPATIONAL DISEASE "a disease which is the natural incident or result of a particular employment, usually developing gradually from the effects of long-continued work at the employment." 176 S.W. 2d 471, 476. It is a disease that results from the conditions of a particular employment that involve a risk of contracting the disease greater than the risk that exists in employment and living conditions in general. See 418 P. 2d 769, 777. See also **employers' liability acts; workmen's compensation.**

OCCUPATIONAL HAZARD a risk which is peculiar to a particular type of employment or workplace, and which arises as a natural incident of such employment or of employment in such a place.

OCCUPYING THE FIELD see **pre-emption.**

OFFER a "manifestation of willingness to enter into a bargain, so made as to justify another person in understanding that his assent to that bargain is invited and will conclude it," Restatement, Contracts (2d) §24; "a promise, a commitment to do or refrain from doing some specified thing in the future. The offer creates a power of **acceptance** permitting the offeree by accepting the offer to transform the offeror's promise into a contractual obligation." Calamari and Perillo, Contracts 17 (1970).

A communication addressed to numerous persons will not generally be an offer but will rather be considered an invitation for offers (which may then become **contracts** through acceptance). This is the case in most mail-order settings and in newspaper advertisements. If, however, there is a "principle of selection" among the offerees (such as "first-come, first-served," "first ten persons," etc.) then the "ad" may amount to an offer that generates a power of acceptance and which by acceptance may lead to a contract. See, e.g., 86 N.W. 2d 689.

To constitute an offer there must be "language of promise" (i.e. "I may" or "I want" is not as likely to be construed as an offer as a communication using the language "I will . . .") and a sufficiently definite statement of terms so that an acceptance may be made without suggesting new terms. The U.C.C. permits an offer, if intended to operate as such, to be missing many terms (such as price, time of delivery) provided that there is a reasonable basis for framing a remedy in the event of a **breach** of contract. See U.C.C. §§2-305, 2-308, 2-309 and 2-204.

OFFICER a person invested with the authority of a particular position or office. The term embraces the idea of **tenure**, duration, **emoluments** and duties, the latter being continuing and permanent and not occasional or temporary, 99 U.S. 508; and, in light of those characteristics, it is distinguished from "employee." An officer may be either public or private in that the office which he occupies may or may not be invested with a public trust. The term is often used to designate corporate personnel who are appointed by the directors and are charged with the duty of managing the day-to-day affairs of the **corporation.**

OFFICIAL IMMUNITY   see **immunity.**

OFFICIOUS INTERMEDDLER   one who performs an act that confers a benefit upon another, although he had neither a contractual duty to do the act nor a legally recognized interest in seeing to it that the act was done, and who may nevertheless expect payment or **restitution** for the benefit conferred. See 153 F. 2d 798, 799.

OFFSET   see **set-off.**

OLIGOPOLY   an industry in which a few large sellers of substantially identical products dominate the market, see 118 F. Supp. 41, 47; e.g., the automobile industry is an oligopoly. An oligopolistic industry is more concentrated than a competitive one but is less concentrated than a **monopoly.**

OLOGRAPHIC   see **holographic will.**

OMISSION   a "neglect or failure to do something; that which . . . is left undone," 175 So. 358, 364; the "neglect to perform what the law requires." 109 N.E. 2d 385, 387. An act of omission will not give rise to liability unless there is a **duty** to act. Thus a parent owes a duty of protection to his child and if he fails to do what is required to protect the child, he may face criminal liability; a nurse who neglects a patient may face tort and/or criminal liability. Thus, an omission, though it consists of a failure to act, will constitute the **actus reus** which is a component of criminal liability.

OMNIBUS CLAUSE   a clause in an automobile liability insurance policy which serves the purpose of giving "additional assureds, other than the person named in the liability policy as assured, with certain specified limitations, the benefit of the policy. . . . It extends protection to one 'permitted' to use the car, although the 'assured' may not be liable for the accident under the doctrine **respondeat superior.** The object of such clause is to cover the liability of the operator of the car as unnamed assured, and to protect any person so injured by giving him a **cause of action** against the insurer for injuries deemed by law to have been caused by the operation of the car." 30 So. 2d 123, 125. Statutes have been passed in some jurisdictions requiring the inclusion of omnibus clauses for the protection of automobile accident victims. See 84 N.W. 2d 84.

ON DEMAND   when requested; when asked for. For example, a note payable "on demand" is payable when the sum is requested. Such a note is called a **demand note** if no due date is stated in the obligation.

ON THE MERITS   refers to a decision or **judgment** based upon the essential facts of the case rather than upon a technical rule of practice, such as a failure of proper **service** or other **jurisdictional** defect. See 2 Wyo. 465, 472. A decision on the merits is rendered by the **trier of fact** after a full presentation of the evidence and determines finally the rights of the party, barring subsequent relitigation. 133 P. 2d 15, 17. A **summary judgment** may also be on the merits. See **res judicata.**

OPEN COURT   "a court [that] is formally opened and engaged in the transaction of judicial affairs, to which all persons who conduct themselves in an orderly manner, are admitted." 43 Ill. App. 573, 574. Most legal proceedings take place in open court except where confidentiality is a recognized interest (e.g., matrimonial, adoption, or juvenile delinquency proceedings, etc.).

OPEN POSSESSION   see **notorious possession.**

OPERATION OF LAW   by or through law; refers to the determination of rights and obligations through the automatic effects of the law and not by any direct act of the party affected. Thus, when one dies without leaving a valid **will** [**intestate**], his **heirs** take according to the statute of descent and distribution "by operation of law." So too, in certain instances the law will impose a constructive **trust** upon a transaction "by operation of law" to protect certain classes of persons.

OPINION the reason given for a court's judgment, finding, or conclusion, as opposed to the **decision**, which is the judgment itself. See 107 P. 2d 1104, 1106, 1107. An opinion of a court implies its adoption by a "carrying vote" of the judges. See 123 S.W. 2d 83, 85. Opinions are usually written by a single judge and if there were more than one judge deciding the matter, as in an appeal to a three-member appellate tribunal, other judges will join in the opinion. If a majority joins in the opinion, it is a MAJORITY OPINION or simply "the opinion," while a PLURALITY OPINION is one agreed to by less than a majority of the court, but which is concurred in for the result only so that the **appellate court** can dispose of the matter in accordance with the majority wishes of the court with respect to result if not with respect to the reasoning. A plurality opinion carries less weight under **stare decisis** than does a majority opinion.

CONCURRING OPINION one which is basically in accord with the majority opinion, but which is written to express a somewhat different view of the issues, to illuminate a particular judge's reasoning, to expound a principle which he holds in high esteem, etc. An opinion which concurs "in the result only" is one which entirely rejects the reasoning and conclusions concerning the law and/or the facts on the basis of which the majority reached its decision, but which expresses a different view which has coincidentally led the judge or justice writing it to recommend the same disposition of the case (affirmance, dismissal, remand, etc.) as was agreed upon by the majority (or plurality).

DISSENTING OPINION one which disagrees with the disposition made of the case by the court, the facts or law on the basis of which the court arrived at its decision, and/or the principles of law announced by the court in deciding the case. Opinions may also be written which express a dissent "in part."

PER CURIAM OPINION an opinion "by the court," which expresses its decision in the case but whose author is not identified.

"Opinion" also refers to the conclusions reached by a witness which are drawn from his observations of the facts; such an "opinion" is not conclusive. See 129 N.W. 2d 393, 396; 13 So. 2d 669, 672. See also **expert witness**.

ORAL CONTRACT   see **contract**.

ORDER a direction of the court on some matter incidental to the main proceeding which adjudicates a preliminary point or directs some step in the proceeding. See 420 S.W. 2d 530, 533. A FINAL ORDER is an appealable order. "If an order closes the matter and precludes future hearing and investigation it is final; but an order which does not completely dispose of the subject matter and settle the rights of the **parties** is not final." 146 N.W. 2d 450, 452. See **interlocutory order; restraining order**.

ORDERED LIBERTY   concept in constitutional law first announced by Justice Cardozo that the **due process** requirements applicable to the states through the Fourteenth Amendment to the United States Constitution do not incorporate all the provisions of the first eight amendments (the so-called **Bill of Rights**), but only those measures essential for the preservation of a scheme of "ordered liberty." "All that is meant is that due process contains within itself certain minimum standards which are 'of the very essence of a scheme of ordered liberty.'" 332 U.S. 46, 65 n. 28 quoting 302 U.S. 319, 325.

The restrictive view of due process expressed by this doctrine has been largely replaced today by a broader view of incorporating nearly all of the Bill of Rights as a national standard of fundamental fairness. If a right embodied in the Bill of Rights is "fundamental to the American scheme of justice," it will today be regarded as applicable to the states through the due process clause of the Fourteenth Amendment. See 391 U.S. 145. Thus, the right to trial by jury, recognized almost universally in American law, has been held applicable to the states in all but petty cases, which have been defined as those involving possible sanctions involving less than six months imprisonment. New York City alone in the nation defined petty in terms of one year and this was held to be an impermissible deviation from the national norm. See 399 U.S. 66.

ORDER PAPER a **negotiable instrument** which is payable to order, i.e., payable to whomever the payee directs in his **indorsement**. An instrument will be negotiable only if it is payable to order or to bearer [see **bearer paper**]. U.C.C. §3-104 (1) (d).

ORDINANCE a local law that applies to persons and things subject to the local jurisdiction. See 90 F. 2d 175, 177. Usually it is used in its municipal law context to mean an act of a city council or similar body that has the same force and effect as a law when it is duly enacted; it differs from a law in that laws are enacted by a state or federal legislature and ordinances are passed by a municipal legislative body. See 7 S.E. 2d 896, 898. Ordinances are enacted to regulate zoning, highway speed, parking, refuse disposal, and other matters typically and traditionally of local concern. Some criminal violations (such as loitering) are based on ordinances rather than state penal law, though the more serious offenses are covered by state laws. See **pre-emption**; **home rule**.

ORDINARY NEGLIGENCE see **negligence**.

OSTENSIBLE AUTHORITY see **apparent authority**.

OUSTER the wrongful dispossession of a person, or exclusion of him from property, usually associated with the acts of a co-tenant which exclude other co-tenants from their legal right to share **possession**. See 91 Cal Rptr. 170. The ouster of co-tenants with proper notice will commence the running of the **statute of limitations** for purposes of **adverse possession**. See 226 S.W. 2d 484, 486.

OUTPUT CONTRACT see **contract**.

OVERBREADTH a term used to describe a situation where a statute proscribes not only what may constitutionally be proscribed, but also forbids or inhibits conduct which is constitutionally protected, e.g., by the First Amendment's safeguards of freedom of speech and press. See 305 F. Supp. 842, 851. A statute which is overbroad may be challenged by another who, though engaging himself in so-called CORE CONDUCT which falls clearly within the permitted scope of the statute, will be permitted to argue the rights of those "chilled" by the existence of the overbroad statute. See **chilling effect**.

OVERREACHING in commercial law, the taking of an unfair advantage over another through cunning, cheating, or generally fraudulent practices, see 112 So. 2d 838, 841; synonymous with **fraud**. See 285 N.Y.S. 648, 670. Contracts which are the product of overreaching in an unequal bargaining context may be unenforceable today under modern concepts of fraud or the **unconscionability** doctrine. See U.C.C. §2-302.

OVERRULE to overturn or make void the **holding** of a prior **case**. This is generally accomplished by a court in a different and subsequent case, when it makes a decision on a point of law exactly opposite the decision made in the prior case. A decision can only be overruled by the same court or a higher court within the same **jurisdiction**. The overruling of a decision generally destroys its value as **precedent**. The term should be distinguished from **reverse**, which applies to a higher court's overturning of a lower court's decision in the same case, though sometimes the distinction is not made.

Overrule also applies to a court's denial of any **motion** or point raised to the court, such as in "overruling a motion for a new trial" or "objection overruled."

OVERT ACT open act; "in criminal law, . . . an outward act done in pursuance of [a] crime and in manifestation of an intent or design, looking toward the accomplishment of [a] crime." 275 F. 2d 813, 817. An "overt act" is required to find criminal liability for **at-**

tempt, **conspiracy**, or **treason**. In the case of a conspiracy, the existence of an "overt act" is necessary to establish criminal liability, but the act need not be itself an illegal act. See 175 P. 2d 724, 732.

OWNERSHIP "one's exclusive right of possessing, enjoying, and disposing of a thing." 72 So. 891. The term has been given a wide range of meanings, but is often said to comprehend both the concept of **possession** and, further, that of **title** and thus to be broader than either. See 139 N.W. 101.

ALLODIAL OWNERSHIP free ownership, not subject to the restrictions or obligations associated with **feudal** tenures. See 28 Wis. 367.

TENURIAL OWNERSHIP the holding of land subject to specific **services** or obligations owed to another.

OYER AND TERMINER In English law, special tribunals empowered to hear and determine cases within their criminal **jurisdiction**, commissioned by the King when the delay involved in ordinary prosecution could not be tolerated, as in the case of sudden insurrection. The term is sometimes used in American law as high courts of criminal jurisdiction in some states.

P

PACTUM *(päk'-tūm)*—Lat: pact, **contract**, agreement. An agreement which is unenforceable because it lacks **consideration** is said to be **nudum pactum**, meaning a naked or bare agreement.

PAIN AND SUFFERING a species of **damages** that one may recover for physical or mental "pain and suffering" that result from a wrong done or suffered. The loss of ability or capacity to work for reasons of physical pain or emotional or mental suffering is a species of pain and suffering and a proper element of compensation. See 48 S.E. 2d 137. Recovery for the pain and suffering of

a deceased person is sometimes permitted, by such person's personal representative, though some states by statute forbid such a recovery. See 217 F. 2d 344, 348, and 37 A. 571, 572. See **survival statute**.

PANDER to pimp, to cater to the lust of another; a PANDERER is thus a pimp, procurer, male bawd, one who caters to the lust of others. See 209 S.W. 2d 99, 100. "Pandering" is the crime of inducing any female to become an inmate of a den of prostitution. See 158 S.W. 1120, 1125. With reference to obscenity, "pandering" is the promotion of obscene literature or movies by appeals to prurient interests and such conduct is not protected by the First Amendment. See *Ginsburg* v. *U.S.*, 383 U.S. 463. See also **aid and abet**; **solicitation**.

PAR equal to the established value. Used in connection with **negotiable instruments** to denote the face amount of the instrument, and not the actual value it would receive on the open market.

Par is equal. The word is used to denote a state of equality or equal value. Bills of exchange, stocks and the like are at par when they sell at their nominal value, above or below par when they sell for more or less. 17 S.E. 49, 53.

PARAMOUNT TITLE a **title** which will prevail over another asserted against it. 231 S.W. 49. It signifies an immediate right of **possession**, and is generally referred to as the basis for **eviction** of a **tenant** by one with a right of possession superior to that of the tenant, i.e., his eviction by one with a "paramount title." 1 Nev. 433.

PARAMOUR a lover; one who stands in the place of a husband or wife, but without the legal rights attached to the marital relationship. See 292 S.W. 2d 74.

PARCENER at common law, one who, jointly with others, holds an **estate** by virtue of **descent** (i.e., **inheritance**). 27 Mo. App. 218. The **holding** of a parcener is generally known as an "estate in coparcenary," see 56 S.W. 2d 783, and usually refers to the estate held by each inheritor before the inheritance has been divided (i.e., **partitioned**). See 147 N.E. 602. The term is no longer widely used, since it is now said to be indistinguishable from a **tenancy in common**. See 194 N.E. 2d 921.

PARDON "an exercise of the sovereign prerogative of mercy, relieving the person on whom it is bestowed from further punishment and from legal disabilities because of the crime named." Rubin, The Law of Criminal Correction 555 (2d ed. 1973). Its effect is that of "relaxing the punishment and blotting out the existence of guilt, so that in the eyes of the law the offender is as innocent as if he had never committed the offense." 17 F. 2d 534, 535. But the majority of cases hold that a pardon does not obliterate the conviction or restore the defendant's good character. Most civil rights lost due to the conviction are, however, restored. See Id. at 690. "An unconditional pardon goes no further than to restore the accused to his civil rights and remit the penalty imposed for the particular offense of which he was convicted in so far it remains unpaid." 127 P. 2d 257, 259. The pardoning power is usually vested in the chief executive with few restrictions on its use. The only frequent exceptions in state constitutions are treason and a judgment on impeachment. See Rubin, supra at 679.

CONDITIONAL PARDON   any pardon imposing some condition, precedent or subsequent, that is not illegal, immoral, or impossible of performance. See 65 So. 2d 721, 722.

See **amnesty; commutation; executive clemency.**

PARENT CORPORATION see **subsidiary.**

PARI DELICTO see **in pari delicto.**

PAROLE in criminal law, a conditional release from imprisonment which entitles the person receiving the "parole" to serve the remainder of his term outside the prison if he satisfactorily complies with all the terms and conditions connected therewith. See 76 A. 2d 150, 153. Compare **probation.**

PAROL EVIDENCE evidence which is given verbally, rather than in written form.

PAROL EVIDENCE RULE a rule of substantive law (not an evidence rule) concerning the legal effect of the expression of an agreement in a final, fully integrated contract; it declares that when the terms of a contract have been embodied in a writing [called the **integration** of the agreement] to which both parties have assented as the final expression of their agreement, parol [oral] evidence of contemporaneous or prior oral agreements is not admissible for the purpose of varying or contradicting the written contract. Agreements relating to different subject matter and all subsequent agreements (whether oral or written), regardless of their effect on the writing, are not subject to the rule. A subsequent written or oral agreement discharges and supercedes prior agreements, whether oral or written. Prior agreements and understandings, oral or written, are not affected by a subsequent written contract if they are not inconsistent in meaning and operation even though they deal in some way with the same subject matter unless there is a MERGER CLAUSE stating that the written agreement is intended as exclusive (or a finding by the court to that effect, see U.C.C. §2-202(b)).

All relevant evidence is admissible to determine whether the agreement is final and exclusive, including parol evidence. Moreover, the parol evidence rule does not exclude evidence offered to prove **fraud, duress, mistake,** misrepresentation, illegality, special communications necessary to establish liability for consequential **damages, conditions precedent,** or evidence offered for the purpose of **rescission** or **reformation.** Parol evidence may be offered to show that the written contract does not accurately reflect the intention of the parties. See generally 3 Corbin, Contracts §§573-596 (1960); Restatement, Contracts 2d §§235-244 (Tent. Draft No. 5, May 1970).

PARTIAL ACTUAL EVICTION see **eviction.**

PARTIAL BREACH see **breach.**

PARTIAL DENIAL see **denial.**

PARTIALLY DISCLOSED PRINCIPAL see **principal.**

PARTICULARS, BILL OF see **bill of particulars.**

PARTITION a judicial separation of the respective interests in land of joint owners or **tenants in common** thereof, "so that each may take **possession** of, enjoy, and control his separate estate at his own pleasure." 23 N.E. 2d 57, 59. Partition is thus the dissolution of the **unity** of possession existing between common owners, 30 A. 2d 574, with the result that the parties hold their estates in **severalty.** 77 S.W. 2d 1086. Partition is available whenever desired by any co-tenant in a tenancy in common. A **joint tenancy** can be destroyed by either the **sale** or the **mortgaging** of a joint owner's interest in the estate and the resultant tenancy in common is then subject to partition, thus defeating the **survivorship** rights of other joint tenants in the subject of the sold or mortgaged property. A joint tenancy is not subject to partition until and unless the joint tenancy is destroyed; but partition is a matter of right and such right is not affected by the difficulty of the partition or any inconveniences which may result to the other tenants. 48 A. 384. When partition is not feasible, a court may order a sale, in which case the proceeds from the sale are distributed in the same proportion as interest held in the realty.

PARTNERSHIP "a contract of two or more competent persons to place their money, effects, labor and skill, or some or all of them, in lawful commerce or business, and to divide the profit and bear the loss in certain proportions; ... [an] association of two or more persons to carry on as co-owners a business for profit." 187 S.W. 2d 941, 944. Partners are individually liable for the debts of the partnership and assets individually owned will be subject to execution to satisfy any such debt when partnership assets are insufficient. Crane and Bromberg, Law of Partnership Chap. 6 p. 342 (1968). An essential element of partnerships is the agreement to share profits and to make good any losses. See 12 N.Y.S. 2d 464. Compare **corporation; joint venture.**

LIMITED PARTNERSHIP generally, "an entity in which one or more persons, with unlimited liability (called GEN-ERAL PARTNERS) manage the partnership, while one or more other persons only contribute capital; these latter partners (called LIMITED PARTNERS) have no right to participate in the management and operation of the business and assume no liability beyond the capital contributed." 243 A. 2d 130, 133.

PART PERFORMANCE see **Statute of Frauds.**

PARTY in a judicial proceeding, a litigant (plaintiff or defendant); a person directly interested in the subject matter of a case; one who could assert a claim, make a defense, control proceedings, examine witnesses, or appeal from the judgment. See 55 A. 2d 705, 708. The term also refers to a person or entity which enters into a contract, lease, deed, etc.; sometimes called "the party of the first part," "the party of the second part," etc. A POLITICAL PARTY is a group of persons uniting to pursue common political goals, specifically including the election of their members to public office.

INDISPENSABLE PARTY one whose interest in the subject matter of a controversy is of such a nature that his interests will be affected thereby or without whose **joinder** in the action complete relief cannot be granted, so that the suit cannot in equity and good conscience proceed without him. See Fed. R. Civ. Proc. 19(b). See also **indispensable party.**

NECESSARY PARTY one whose interests will be affected by the suit or without whom complete relief cannot be granted, but who will not be joined if doing so would deprive the court of **jurisdiction** in the case. See Fed. R. Civ. Proc. 19(a).

NOMINAL PARTY party appearing on the **record** not because he has any real interest in the case, but because technical rules of **pleading** require his presence in the record. See 134 S.W. 2d 850, 852. See **real party in interest.**

PARTY WALL see **party wall.**

PROPER PARTY one who has an interest in the subject matter of the litigation, but without whom, unlike a "necessary party," a substantial decree may nevertheless issue, though such decree will not settle all questions at issue in the controversy with respect to such party.

REAL PARTY IN INTEREST   see **real party in interest.**

THIRD PARTY   someone other than the parties directly involved in the action or transaction; an outsider with no legal interest in the matter.

PARTY TO BE CHARGED   see **Statute of Frauds.**

PARTY-WALL   a dividing wall between adjoining landowners. 94 N.E. 2d 55. It exists for the common benefit of both properties which it separates, and any use may be made of it by either party, so long as such use is not detrimental to the other. 34 N.Y.S. 2d 445. The two landowners own the wall as **tenants in common,** 106 N.W. 357, where the wall stands upon ground which is itself held in common, 94 N.E. 2d 55, or where it stands partly upon each of the two adjoining properties. 131 A. 290. A party-wall may be constructed wholly upon property belonging to one of the parties, 220 N.Y.S. 2d 752, or it may be owned entirely by only one of them, in which case it is said to be subject to an **easement** or right in the other to have it maintained. 43 N.Y.S. 1016. A party-wall is often one which provides support for one or more separately owned structures. 79 A. 2d 382; 222 S.W. 2d 197.

PASSIVE USE   see **use.**

PATENT   evident; obvious; a **patent defect** is one which is so obvious that it should have been discovered by the exercise of ordinary prudence.

PATENT OF INVENTION   (often called simply "a patent") a grant of right to exclude others from the making, using or selling of an invention during a specified time; it constitutes a legitimate **monopoly.** See 304 F. Supp. 357, 367.

PATENT PENDING   (often abbreviated PAT. PEND.) a notice to others that the product on which this notice is ascribed has been the subject of an application for patent protection and that if a patent does issue those with notice will be subject to the applicant's prior rights.

PATENT OF LAND   an instrument by which the government conveys a **fee simple** interest in land to another; it may or may not be accompanied by **warranties.** See 70 U.S. 478; 144 P. 499, 503.

PATENT DEFECT   a defect which could be recognized upon reasonably careful inspection or through the use of ordinary diligence and care. See 83 S.E. 2d 26, 29. Compare **latent defect.**

PATENT INFRINGEMENT   "the act of trespassing upon the incorporeal rights secured by a **patent.** . . . Any person who, without legal permission, [makes, uses, or sells] to another to be used, the thing which is the subject matter of any existing patent, is guilty of an infringement, for which **damages** may be recovered at law . . . or which may be remedied by a **bill in equity** for an **injunction.**" 273 F. 698, 704.

"The test of infringement is whether the accused device does substantially the same work in substantially the same way and accomplishes the same result. One appropriating the principle and mode of operation of a patent, and obtaining its results by the same or equivalent means, may not avoid infringement by making a device different in form, even though it be more or less efficient than the patented device." 79 F. 2d 685, 692.

Copyrights and **trademarks** can also be the subject of infringement action.

PATERNITY SUIT   a suit initiated to determine the paternity of a child born out of wedlock and to provide for the support of that child once paternity is proved. They are known in law as BASTARDY PROCEEDINGS. 234 P. 412.

PAT. PEND.   see **patent** [PATENT PENDING].

PATRICIDE   the killing of one's own father.

PAWN   to give **personal property** to another as security for a loan; "property deposited with another as security for the payment of a **debt.**" 42 S.E. 474, 475.

PAYABLE TO BEARER   see **bearer paper.**

PAYABLE TO ORDER   see **order paper.**

PEACEABLE POSSESSION possession which is continuous and which is not interrupted by adverse **suits** or other hostile action intended to **oust** the possessor from the land. 472 S.W. 2d 825. The term often refers to parties in **adverse possession** of land, and thus has nothing to do with actual **ownership**. 167 P. 2d 390. "Peaceable possession" does not preclude the existence of adverse claims, so long as no actual attempt to dispossess is made. 57 So. 706. Actions to **quiet title** generally require a showing of peaceable possession by the one bringing the action. See 47 So. 202.

PEACEFUL ENJOYMENT see **quiet enjoyment**.

PECULATION "the fraudulent **misappropriation** by one to his own use of money or goods intrusted to his care." 164 S.E. 375, 378. See also **embezzlement; larceny**.

PECUNIARY relating to money and monetary affairs, 136 N.E. 2d 550, 554; consisting of money or that which can be valued in money. Many **wrongful death statutes** limit recovery to PECUNIARY LOSS, i.e., a loss of money or of something which can be translated into an economic loss. The loss of affections that a parent suffers by the negligent death of a child is not such a loss, whereas the loss of actual or anticipated financial support by the deceased child is pecuniary loss.

PENAL INSTITUTION any place of confinement for convicted criminals. See 230 N.E. 2d 536, 541. Penal institutions include local and county jails and workhouses, reformatories, penitentiaries, prison camps and farms, as well as the modern CORRECTIONAL INSTITUTION (new nomenclature used to describe many penal institutions previously called "prisons").

PENAL LAW a law enacted to preserve the public order, which defines an offense against the public and inflicts a penalty for its violation. See 191 N.Y.S. 2d 54, 57. Statutes which grant a private [civil] **action** against a wrongdoer are not considered penal, but remedial in nature. See 218 S.W. 2d 75, 78; 59 S.W. 952, 953.

PENDENTE LITE *(pĕn-dĕn'-tā lē'-tā)*— Lat: suspended by the **lawsuit**; pending the lawsuit. Matters which are pendente lite are contingent upon the determination of a pending lawsuit. Thus, funds may be deposited with the clerk of the court, pendente lite, i.e., so that those funds can be used to make payment to the opposing party in the event that the depositing party loses the lawsuit. The term may also be written "lite pendente." See also **lis pendens**.

PENDENT JURISDICTION federal court doctrine whereby a plaintiff may rely upon both federal and non-federal bases for the **relief** which is sought in a **complaint**; i.e., the plaintiff joins a federal claim with a state law claim based on closely related or identical conduct of the defendant. Whether the federal court will hear and determine the state law claim should it dismiss the federal claim (and thus be without an independent jurisdictional basis for proceeding with the adjudication of his suit) is discretionary with the district court, although current practice would seem to favor retaining jurisdiction and deciding the state law claim. See 383 U.S. 715. Compare **ancillary jurisdiction**.

PER ANNUM *(pĕr ǎn'-nŭm)* — Lat: through the course of a year; annually. Anything (e.g., interest, wages, rent, etc.) which is calculated "per annum" is calculated on the basis of a year in time; sometimes a per annum rate will be fixed at 1/360th (or 1/364th) per day.

PER (PUR) AUTRE VIE *(pĕr(pûr) ô'-tr vē)*—Fr: for or during the life of another. An estate pur autre vie is a **life estate** measured by the life of a third person rather than the life of the **grantee**.

PER CAPITA *(pĕr kǎp'-ĭ-tä)* — Lat: through the head, top, summit; through the leader or capital (of country); "defined by the heads or polls; according to the number of individuals, share and share alike." 32 S.E. 2d 291. Anything which is figured per capita is calculated by the number of heads (people) involved and is divided equally among each individual. Compare **per stirpes**.

PER CURIAM see **opinion** [PER CURIAM OPINION].

PER DIEM *(pĕr dē'-ĕm)*—Lat: through the course of a day. As used in relation to compensation, wages or salary, it describes pay for a day's services. See 160 S.E. 596, 599. Government and private business travel allowances are often allocated on a "per diem" basis.

PEREMPTORY "absolute, conclusive, final, positive, not admitting of question or appeal," 178 S.W. 2d 274, 279; e.g., a peremptory trial date may be established by the court on its own **motion** or at the request of a **party** to insure a timely disposition of the case. In the selection of a jury each side has a right to a fixed number of PEREMPTORY CHALLENGES to the seating of potential jurors.

PEREMPTORY WRIT at common law, an original writ requiring the presence of the defendant in **civil actions** for certain cases including **trespass**.

PEREMPTORY PLEA see **plea.**

PERFECTED completed, executed, enforceable, merchantable; refers especially to the status which is ascribed to **security interests** after certain events have occurred. The necessary events in order to achieve PERFECTION can be broken down into two categories.

Certain security interests are perfected by no more than the creation of the security interest itself. See U.C.C. §9-302. An example of such an automatically perfected security interest is a purchase money security interest in consumer goods.

Other security interests require the creditor to take certain steps to perfect. Perfection of a security interest may occur by the taking of possession of the collateral by the creditor, see U.C.C. §9-305, or by filing. See Id. at §9-304.

There are many consequences which flow from perfection. The most important one is that a perfected security interest has **priority** over an unperfected interest. The date of perfection is also the time from which courts judge priority contests with other perfected creditors.

PERFORMANCE the fulfillment of an obligation, or a promise kept, 42 S.E. 2d 910; refers especially to completion of one's obligation under a contract.

See **specific performance; substantial performance.**

PERIODIC TENANCY see **tenancy.**

PERJURY criminal offense of making false statements under oath; at **common law,** only a willful and corrupt sworn statement made without sincere belief in its truth, and made in a judicial **proceeding** regarding a material matter, is perjury. Today, statutes have broadened the offense so that in some jurisdictions any **false swearing** in a legal instrument or legal setting is perjury, even if it is not material and even though it is not presented in a judicial proceeding. See Perkins, Criminal Law 454 (2d ed. 1969); N.Y. Penal Law, §210.05. See also **subornation of perjury.**

PERMANENT FIXTURE see **fixture.**

PERMANENT INJUNCTION see **injunction.**

PERMISSIVE COUNTERCLAIM see **counterclaim; joinder.**

PERMISSIVE JOINDER see **joinder.**

PERMISSIVE WASTE see **waste.**

PER MY ET PER TOUT *(pĕr mē ā pĕr tū)*—Law Fr: by half and by whole. In joint **tenancy,** each tenant's share is the whole, for purposes of **tenure** and **survivorship** [tout], and each share is an **aliquot** portion for purposes of **alienation** [my]. 1 Washburn, Real Property 528 (5th ed. 1902).

PERPETUITIES, RULE AGAINST see **Rule Against Perpetuities.**

PERPETUITY see **in perpetuity.**

PER QUOD *(pĕr kwōd)*—Lat: through which; by which; whereby. "False imputations may be **actionable per se,** that is, in themselves, or per quod, that is, on allegation and proof of **special damage.**" 161 F. 2d 335. In a **libel** and **slander** action words used which are not on their face, in their usual and natural usage, injurious, but which become so as a consequence of extrinsic facts and which require an innuendo, are actionable per quod. See 121 So. 459.

PER SE *(pĕr sā)*—Lat: through itself, by means of itself; not requiring extraneous evidence or support to establish its existence; e.g., **negligence per se** refers to acts which are inherently negligent, i.e., which implicitly involve a **breach** of duty, obviating the need to expressly allege the existence of the duty.

PERSON "in law, an individual or in corporated group having certain legal rights and responsibilities." 124 N.E. 2d 39, 41. This has been held to include foreign and domestic **corporations**. See 134 U.S. 594. Precise definition and delineation of the term has been necessary for purposes of ascertaining those to whom the 14th Amendment to the U.S. Constitution affords its protection, since that Amendment expressly applies to "persons." Compare **natural person.**

PERSONAL JUDGMENT judgment imposed on defendant requiring sums to be advanced from whatever assets he has within the **jurisdiction** of the issuing court, as opposed to a judgment directed against particular property (called an **in rem** judgment) or a judgment against a **corporate** entity. See **jurisdiction** (IN PERSONAM JURISDICTION).

PERSONAL JURISDICTION see **juris-diction.**

PERSONAL PROPERTY see **personalty.**

PERSONAL SERVICE see **service.**

PERSONALTY personal property; "chattels personal, things movable" as distinguished from **real property** or things attached to the **realty**. See 3 Ill. App. 275, 279. However, things attached to the realty may be considered personalty if by their nature they are severable without injury to the realty. See 25 S.E. 2d 315. See **fixture**. The term embraces both tangible and intangible property. 84 N.E. 2d 99.

PER STIRPES *(pĕr stûr'-pāz)*—Lat: "through or by roots or stocks, by representation." 282 S.W. 2d 478. The essential characteristic of a distribution of an **intestate's estate** per stirpes is that each distributee takes in a representative capacity and stands in the place of a deceased ancestor. See 82 N.E. 2d 866. "A distribution per stirpes is a division with reference to the intermediate course of descent from the ancestor. It is literally a distribution according to 'stock'. It gives the beneficiaries each a share

in the property to be distributed, not necessarily equal, but the proper fraction of the fraction to which the person through whom he claims from the ancestor would have been entitled. The gist of this is expressed in the words . . . 'by right of representation.'" 63 N.W. 2d 352. It is distinguished from a distribution **per capita**, which is "an equal division of the property to be divided among the beneficiaries, each receiving the same share as each of the others, without reference to the intermediate course of descent from the ancestor." Id.

PER TOUT ET NON PER MY *(pĕr tū ā nŏhn pĕr mē)*—Fr: by the whole and not by half; describes the type of **seisin** that exists in a **joint tenancy** or **tenancy by the entirety**; i.e., the joint tenants or man and wife who own property by the entirety own an **undivided interest** in the whole of the property but not an individual interest in half the property. In a tenancy by the entirety one spouse cannot seize or end the tenancy by his acts alone. See Cribbet, Principles of the Law of Property 93 (1962). See **partition; tenancy** [TENANCY IN COMMON].

PETITION "a formal written request or **prayer** for a certain thing to be done." 104 S.W. 1009, 1010. As related to **equity** procedure, the petition is the functional equivalent of a **complaint** at law; it "connotes an application in writing addressed to a court or judge, stating facts and circumstances relied upon as a cause for judicial action, and containing a prayer [formal request] for relief." 110 S.E. 2d 909, 911.

PETITIONER one who presents a petition to a court or other body either in order to institute an **equity** proceeding or to take an **appeal** from a **judgment**. The adverse party is called the **respondent.**

PETIT JURY see **jury.**

PETIT LARCENY see **larceny.**

PETTY JURY see **jury.**

PETTY LARCENY see **larceny.**

PHYSICAL WASTE see **waste.**

PICKETING the practice, often used in labor disputes, of patrolling, usually with placards, to publicize a dispute or to secure support for a cause. It is a constitutionally protected exercise of free expression when done peaceably, see 63 N.Y.S. 2d 860, 862, but may be prohibited when violent or dangerous to public safety, see 100 P. 2d 339, 343, or when done to propagandize falsely. See 139 P. 2d 963, 971.

PIERCING THE CORPORATE VEIL a term given to the process of disregarding the corporate entity and imposing liability for corporate activity on a person or entity other than the offending **corporation** itself.

For the most part, the corporate form isolates both individuals and **parent corporations** [see **subsidiary**] from liability for corporate misdeeds. This is not always the case, however, and there are times (such as when incorporation itself was accomplished to perpetrate a **fraud**) when the court will ignore the corporate entity and strip the organizers and managers of the corporation of the limited liability which they usually enjoy. See 93 Cal. Rptr. 338, 341; and Henn, Law of Corporations §§143, 146 (1961).

PLAGIARISM appropriation of the literary composition of another and passing off as one's own the product of the mind and language of another. 25 N.Y.S. 2d. 899. The offense of plagiarism is known in the law as INFRINGEMENT OF COPYRIGHT and comes into being only when the work allegedly copied is protected by **copyright**.

PLAINTIFF the one who initially brings the **suit**; "he who, in a personal **action**, seeks a remedy in a court of justice for an injury to, or a withholding of, his rights." 147 F. 44, 46. See also **complainant**; **defendant**; **petitioner**.

PLAINTIFF IN ERROR one who appeals from a judgment against him in a lower court, whether he was plaintiff or defendant in that court. See **defendant** [DEFENDANT IN ERROR].

PLAIN VIEW an exception to the general requirement of a valid **search warrant** to legitimize a **search or seizure**. "A search implies a prying into hidden places for that which is concealed, and it is not a search to observe that which is open to view." 193 N.E. 202, 203. The

courts have limited this exception somewhat by protecting those areas in which an individual has a reasonable expectation of privacy. See 389 U.S. 347. In all cases there must be a legal justification to be in the position in which seizable property is observed. "The plain view doctrine may not be used to extend a general exploratory search from one object to another until something incriminating at last emerges." 403 U.S. 443, 466.

PLEA in **equity**, a special answer showing or relying upon one or more things as a cause why the **suit** should either be dismissed, delayed, or barred, Story, Equity Pleading §649; at law, broadly, any one of the common law **pleadings**; technically, the defendant's answer by matter of fact to the plaintiff's **declaration**, as distinguished from a **demurrer** which is an answer by a matter of law. In criminal procedure, the defendant will enter a plea at the **arraignment**, of not guilty, guilty, or in some jurisdictions, **nolo contendere** or non vult [meaning "no contest"]. Pleas are either dilatory or peremptory.

DILATORY PLEAS those which tend to defeat the actions to which they refer by contesting grounds other than the **merits** of plaintiff's case. Hence, they go to issues such as improper **jurisdiction**, wrong defendant, or other procedural defects. [See also **dilatory plea**.]

PEREMPTORY PLEA, on the other hand, is one which answers the plaintiff's material contention.

PLEA IN ABATEMENT one which does not deny the truth of plaintiff's contention, but which introduces **new matter** to avoid the effect of his failure to deny plaintiff's allegations.

PLEA BARGAINING the process whereby the accused and the prosecutor negotiate a mutually satisfactory disposition of the case. "The disposition of criminal **charges** by agreement between the prosecutor and the accused, sometimes loosely called 'plea bargaining,' is an essential component of the administration of justice. Properly administered, it is to be encouraged. . . . Disposition of charges after plea discussions is not only an essential part of the process but a highly desirable part for many reasons. It leads to prompt and largely final disposition of most criminal cases; it avoids much of the corrosive impact of enforced idleness during pretrial confinement for those who are denied release pending trial; it protects the public from those accused persons who are prone to continue criminal conduct even while on pretrial release; and, by shortening the time between charge and disposition, it enhances whatever may be the rehabilitative prospects of the guilty when they are ultimately imprisoned." 404 U.S. 257, 260-261.

Plea negotiations can center around the defendant's pleading guilty to a lesser offense, or to only one or some of the counts in a multi-count **indictment**. In return, the defendant seeks to obtain concessions as to the type and length of his **sentence** or reduction of counts against him. The recognition of plea bargaining has led to the promulgation of standards for the conduct of the negotiations. See, e.g., ABA Minimum Standards For Criminal Justice—Standards Relating to Pleas of Guilty (1968). Many states now require that all plea bargains be placed upon **record** in **open court** at the time that the guilty plea is entered. Furthermore, a judge has discretion as to whether to accept the plea and its attendant bargain. See, e.g., N.J. Court Rule 3:9-2. However, once the guilty plea is accepted, the state must adhere to the terms of the bargain. See 404 U.S. 257.

PLEAD to make any **pleading**; to answer **plaintiff's common law declaration**; in criminal law, to answer to the **charge**, either admitting or denying guilt.

PLEA IN ABATEMENT see **dilatory plea**.

PLEADING BURDEN see **burden of proof**.

PLEADINGS statements, in logical and legal form, of the facts which constitute **plaintiff's cause of action** and **defendant's** ground of defense. They are either allegations by the parties affirming or denying certain matters of fact, or other statements by them in support or derogation of certain principles of law,

which are intended to have the effect of disclosing to the court or jury the real matter in dispute. 77 S.W. 2d 464, 469. At common law, pleadings were a rigorous process of successive statements the aim of which was to progressively narrow the issue. The common law pleadings were the plaintiff's declaration, the defendant's plea, the plaintiff's replication, the defendant's rejoinder, the plaintiff's surrejoinder, the defendant's rebutter, the plaintiff's surrebutter. Modern code procedure often includes only a **complaint**, an **answer**, and where necessary, a **reply** to the answer. See, e.g., Fed R. Civ. Proc. 7(a). Pleadings may be on the **merits**, and thus **peremptory**, or else they may be based on some other ground which prevents the case from going to the jury, in which case they are referred to as **dilatory pleas**.

PLEADING THE FIFTH AMENDMENT see **self-incrimination**.

PLENARY "literally, . . . full, entire, complete, absolute, perfect or unqualified; but with reference to judicial proceedings, it denotes a [complete, formally pleaded suit wherein] a **bill** or **petition** or **complaint** filed by one or more persons against one or more other persons who file an **answer** or a response." 315 S.W. 2d 521, 525. Compare **summary proceeding**.

PLURALITY OPINION see **opinion**.

POLICE COURT usually, an inferior municipal court with limited jurisdiction in criminal cases. See 91 P. 147, 148. Minor cases can be disposed of by such courts but otherwise they generally have the power only to arraign the prisoner and set **bail**.

POLICE POWER the power incident to state and local governments to impose those restrictions upon private rights which are reasonably related to the promotion and maintenance of the health, safety, morals, and for the general welfare of the public. See 57 N.W. 331. "Police power must be confined to such restrictions and burdens as are thus necessary to promote the public welfare, or, in other words to prevent the infliction of public injury." See 71 N.W. 400. "In the exercise of its police powers a state is not confined to matters relating strictly to the public health, morals, and peace, but, there may be interference whenever the public interest demands it; and in this particular, a large discretion is necessarily vested in the legislature, to determine not only what the interests of the public require, but what measures are necessarily for the protection of such interests." 9 N.W. 2d 914, 919.

POLITICAL ASYLUM see **asylum.**

POLITICAL CORPORATION see **corporation; public corporation.**

POLITICAL PARTY see **party.**

POLITICAL QUESTION a question which is not subject to judicial determination (i.e., which is not **justiciable**) because resolution of it is committed exclusively to the jurisdiction of another branch of government (legislature or executive) or because adequate standards for judicial review are lacking or because there is no way to insure enforcement of the court's judgment. Jurisdiction is not lacking, since the court has the power to decide political questions but chooses not to. Cases challenging the composition of state legislative bodies had been held political and nonjusticiable, 328 U.S. 549, until the Court determined that no other remedy existed and an **equal protection** of the laws violation was found, resulting in the formulation of the "one-man-one-vote" remedy. See 369 U.S. 186.

POLL TAX a capitation tax; a tax "of a fixed amount upon all the persons, or upon all the persons of a certain class, resident within specified territory, without regard to their property or the occupation in which they may be engaged." 88 So. 4, 5.
State laws requiring the payment of a poll tax to register or vote in federal elections are now barred by the Twenty-Fourth Amendment; as to state elections, required payment of a poll tax as a prerequisite to registration or voting has been held to discriminate against poor persons and thus violate the Fourteenth Amendment's guarantee of **equal protection of the laws**. 383 U.S. 663.

POLYGAMY in criminal law, the offense of having more than one husband or wife at one time. So important was the community's insistence upon monogamy (having only one wife or husband at a time), a polygamy conviction of a member of the Mormon faith was found not to violate the First Amendment guarantee of **free exercise** of religion even though the accepted doctrine of the defendant's church then imposed upon its male members the duty to practice polygamy. 98 U.S. 145.

POSITIVE FRAUD see **fraud** [FRAUD IN FACT].

POSITIVE LAW existing law created by legally valid procedures; ". . . law set by political superiors to political inferiors." Austin, The Province Of Jurisprudence Determined 9 (1954 ed.)

POSITIVISM in jurisprudence, the view that any legal system is best studied by concentrating on the **positive law** of that system; formed in reaction to **natural law theory**. See Hart, The Concept of Law (1961), for a full discussion.

POSSE COMITATUS *(pŏ'-sā kŏm'-ĭ-tä'-tŭs)*—Lat: to be able to be an attendant. "In a proper case the sheriff may summon to his assistance any person to assist him in making an **arrest** for a **felony**. A posse comitatus, i.e., those called to attend the sheriff, may be summoned verbally. The mode is immaterial, so long as the object is to require assistance. A person so summoned is neither an officer nor a mere private person, but occupies the legal position of a posse comitatus and while acting under his orders is just as much clothed with the protection of the law as the sheriff himself. It is not essential for a posse comitatus to be and remain in the actual physical presence of the sheriff; it is sufficient if the two are actually endeavoring to make the arrest and acting in concert with a view to effect their common design." 449 S.W. 2d 656, 661.

POSSESSION dominion and control over **property**; "the having, holding, or detention of property in one's power or command." 50 N.Y. 518. When distinguished from mere **custody**, it is said to involve custody plus the assertion of a right to exercise dominion and control. See 488 P. 2d 316.

ACTUAL POSSESSION immediate and direct physical control over property. 426 F. 2d 992. With regard to **real property**, it involves actual occupation of the property, see 92 S.E. 550, or direct appropriation of the benefits it yields. See 175 P. 247.

CONSTRUCTIVE POSSESSION though not being in direct control of or actually present upon the property, knowingly having both the power and the intention at any given time to exercise dominion and control over it. 426 F. 2d 992.

POSSESSORY ACTION a lawsuit brought for the purpose of obtaining or maintaining possession of real property. In a common instance, a landlord will bring a possessory action to evict **holdover tenants**, praying that the court will issue a writ of possession against the holdover tenants.

POSSESSORY INTEREST a right to exert control over certain land to the exclusion of others, coupled with an intent to exercise that right. Restatement, Property §7. It is this "privilege of exclusive occupation" which distinguishes possessory from non-possessory interests. Restatement, Property, Div. V, Part I, Introductory Note. One holding a non-possessory interest is subject to specific restrictions with respect to the use he may make of the land, but the holder of a possessory interest is limited only by the rights of others (including co-owners, neighbors, **remaindermen**, etc.). Id. Examples of non-possessory interests include **easements**, **remainders**, the rights retained by the **grantor** of a **life estate**, etc. Restatement, Property §7 Comment.

POSSIBILITY OF A REVERTER the possibility of the return of an **estate** to the **grantor**, should a specified event occur or a particular act be performed in the future. It is thus a **reversionary** interest subject to a **condition** precedent. 108 N.W. 2d 548. The possibility does not itself constitute an estate, present or future. 2 So. 2d 344. It describes the interest remaining in the **grantor** who conveys a **conditional** or **determinable fee**. 106 S.E. 2d 913. Distinguish **right of re-entry** for condition broken in which cases the grantor must assert his

right by judicial process before the preceding estate is terminated. Upon the occurrence of the condition in a determinable fee situation the estate is terminated automatically without any further act of the grantor. This construction works a forfeiture with less protection to the grantee and thus is disfavored in law.

POST-CONVICTION REVIEW PROCEEDINGS [PCR ACTIONS] a statutory or court rule procedure whereby a defendant may challenge collaterally a **judgment** of **conviction** which has otherwise become final in the normal **appellate** review process. [See **collateral attack**.] The availability of a PCR avenue of relief generally operates to preclude state or federal **habeas corpus**. The federal PCR statute is 28 U.S.C. §2255, enacted by Congress in 1948. The remedy has been interpreted as providing "a remedy exactly commensurate with that which had been available by habeas corpus." 368 U.S. 424, 427. A federal petitioner complaining of a federal judgment of conviction must bring a 2255 action rather than a writ of habeas corpus unless the 2255 remedy would be "inadequate or ineffective to test the legality of his detention." 28 U.S.C. §2255. The rules governing a 2255 motion are very much like those governing federal habeas, with the exception that the motion is brought not in the district of confinement, but in the sentencing court. See 373 U.S. 1.

Many states have adopted similar PCR statutes (or court rules) that encompass all constitutional challenges to the judgment of conviction, 381 U.S. 336, 338 (Brennan, J. concurring), but some statutes limit the scope of the remedy and the timeliness with which a motion for relief must be made (e.g., not more than five years after the conviction). A **writ of coram nobis** is available in some states as a form of PCR relief and in others an out-of-time motion for a new trial to correct a miscarriage of justice services this function. See generally ABA, Minimum Stds. for Criminal Justice, Post-Conviction Remedies (App. Draft 1968).

POST FACTO see **ex post facto**.

POST MORTEM (*pōst môr´-tĕm*)—Lat: after death. The term generally refers to the examination of the body of a deceased for the purpose of determining the cause of death; but it may comprehend only such examination as that undertaken by a **coroner** and may consequently not extend to a true medical determination of the cause of death involving **autopsy** and dissection. See 31 N.Y.S. 865, 866.

POWER OF APPOINTMENT "a power or authority given to a person to dispose of **property**, or an **interest** therein, which [property or interest] is **vested** in a person other than the donee of the power." 202 P. 2d 259, 265. The power may be created by **deed** or by **will**. . . . The authority thus granted must be to do an act which the grantor of the authority might himself lawfully do. 292 N.Y.S. 276. **Title** to the property or interest passes to the appointee thereof directly from the donor of the power; the donee of the power [the party having the power of appointment] thus acts merely as a conduit through which title passes. 92 S.E. 2d 503. A power of appointment does not itself constitute an **estate** or **interest**, and without more is therefore termed a "naked power;" but the donee of the power may also be granted, in the same instrument, a present or **future interest** in the subject or property over which the power is to be exercised; he is then said to have a POWER COUPLED WITH AN INTEREST. 227 P. 2d 670.

Powers of appointment are either general or special and are exercisable **inter vivos** or by **testamentary disposition**. A GENERAL POWER may be exercised by the donee in favor of any person(s) he chooses, including himself or his estate. The donee of a special power is limited in the choice of beneficiaries by the donor of the power, and so must appoint in favor of member(s) of the class specified in the instrument creating the power. There are tax consequences, Rule Against Perpetuities considerations and creditor's rights considerations incident to the different types of powers and how, or whether, they are exercised.

POWER OF ATTORNEY "an instrument in writing by which one person, as principal, appoints another as his agent and confers upon him the authority to perform certain specified acts or kinds of acts on behalf of the principal. The primary purpose of a power of attorney is not to define the authority of the agent as between himself and his principal, but to evidence the authority of the agent to third parties with whom the agent deals." 248 A. 2d 446, 448.

PRAYER [FOR RELIEF] request contained in **complaint** or **petition** which asks for relief to which plaintiff thinks himself entitled, see 256 P. 195, 196; that part of the **pleading** in which relief is requested.

In addition to whatever specific kinds of **relief** or **remedy** (e.g., money **damages, injunction**, etc.) the party may request, it is common to add a general "and such other and further relief as to the court may seem just and proper" prayer to enable the court to grant whatever relief it feels is appropriate.

PREAMBLE an introductory clause in a constitution, statute, or other legal **instrument** which states the intent of that instrument; "a prefatory statement or explanation or a finding of facts by the power making it, purporting to state the purpose, reason, or occasion for making the law to which it is prefixed." 177 P. 742, 744. Compare **purview**.

PRECATORY advisory or in the form of a recommendation or request rather than a positive command. See 284 P. 2d 1080, 1083. The term is applied to language, usually in a **trust** or a **will**, by which the **settlor** or **testator** expresses a wish or a desire to benefit another but does not impose an enforceable obligation upon any party to carry out this wish.

"Where a testator uses precatory rather than mandatory language, the courts frequently speak of PRECATORY TRUSTS. The phrase is ambiguous. It is not clear whether it is intended to denote a trust which is enforceable in spite of the mildness of the language used to create it, or whether it is intended to indicate a disposition which is not enforceable as a trust because of the mildness of the language used. In the earlier law the courts were very ready to find that a trust was created in spite of the precatory character of the language of the testator." Scott, Abridgment of the Law of Trusts §25-25.1 (1960). The earlier courts found a trust if the testator's desired disposition was clear enough to create a valid trust and found an absolute **gift** if his instructions would have created an invalid trust. Id. at § 25.1. Under more recent authority the question is, "Did the testator not only desire that the legatee should make a particular disposition of the property, but did he intend to impose a legal obligation upon him to make the disposition?" Id. at §25.2.

PRECEDENT previously decided case which is recognized as authority for the disposition of future cases. At common law, precedents were regarded as the major source of law. A precedent may involve a novel question of common law or it may involve an interpretation of a statute. In either event to the extent that future cases rely upon it or distinguish it from themselves without disapproving of it, the case will serve as a precedent for future cases under the doctrine of **stare decisis**.

PRECEDENT CONDITION see **condition**.

PRECEDING ESTATE a prior estate upon which a **future interest** is limited. Thus, a **remainder** is said to **vest** upon the termination of a preceding estate, such as a **life estate**.

PRE-EMPTION a doctrine concerning federal judicial treatment of state legislation which is related to the same subject matter as federal [congressionally-enacted] legislation; it "rests upon the **supremacy clause** of the federal constitution, and deprives a state of jurisdiction over matters embraced by a congressional act regardless of whether the state law coincides with, is complementary to, or opposes the federal congressional expression." 398 P. 2d 245, 246. State legislatures may also "pre-empt" local governments in the same manner. When Congress legislates in an area of federal concern, it may specifically pre-empt all state legislation (thus, OCCUPYING THE FIELD), or may bar only inconsistent legislation; where Congress does not directly indicate its intention in this regard, the court will determine that intention based on the nature and legis-

lative history of the enactment. See 312 U.S. 52; 350 U.S. 497.

At common law, the term expressed the King's right to buy provisions and other necessaries for the use of his household in preference to others. In international law, it expresses the right of a nation to detain goods of a stranger in transit so as to afford its subjects a preference of purchase.

PREFERENCE the paying or securing by an **insolvent** debtor, to one or more of his creditors, the whole or a part of their claims, to the exclusion or detriment of other creditors. See 157 P. 392, 394. Under the Bankruptcy Act of 1898, 11 U.S.C.A. §96(a); a **bankrupt** is deemed to have given a preference if within four months preceding the filing of his petition for bankruptcy he procures or suffers a judgment against him or makes a transfer of any of his assets, and the effect of this is to give a creditor a greater percentage of his debt than any other creditor of the same class.

Section 60B provides that, if a person receiving a preference has reasonable cause to believe a preference was intended, it shall be "voidable" by the **trustee** in bankruptcy, who shall then recover the property or its value from such person. See 104 N.W. 1. To constitute a voidable preference, as outlined above, it is immaterial whether the bankrupt intended the transfer to unduly benefit the recipient. See 181 So. 320, 321. See **insolvency**.

PREFERRED DIVIDEND see **dividend**.

PREFERRED STOCK A class of stock entailing certain rights beyond those attached to common stock; "corporate stock having preference rights. It represents a contribution to the capital of the corporation and is in no sense a loan of money. . . . By general definition preferred stock is stock entitled to a preference over other kinds of stock in the payment of **dividends**. The dividends come out of earnings [income] and not out of **capital**. Unless there are net earnings there is no right to dividends." 41 N.W. 2d 571, 575.

PREJUDICE see **dismissal** [DISMISSAL WITH PREJUDICE, DISMISSAL WITHOUT PREJUDICE].

PREJUDICIAL ERROR see **reversible error.**

PRELIMINARY HEARING in criminal law, a means of determining the question of whether or not **probable cause** for the arrest of a person existed, which is held prior to the issuing of an **indictment**; "the sole purpose of a preliminary hearing . . . is to determine whether there is sufficient **evidence** to warrant the **defendant's** [continued] detention [and whether submission of such evidence to the **grand jury** is justified] and the filing of the indictment conclusively establishes probable cause for such detention, thereby eliminating the necessity for a preliminary hearing." 42 F.R.D. 421, 423. Compare **arraignment.** See also **fair hearing.**

PREMEDITATION forethought; the giving of consideration to a matter beforehand "for some length of time, however short." 56 S.E. 2d 678, 681. As one of the elements of first-degree murder, the term is often equated with **intent** and "deliberateness," though it is said that premeditation should require more substantial contemplation and should be confined to instances of "real and substantial reflection." Perkins, Criminal Law 92 (2d ed. 1969). See also **mens rea.**

PREMISES land and its appurtenances, see 98 So. 444; land or a portion thereof and the buildings and structures thereon. See 131 S.E. 11. The term is an elastic one whose meaning depends on the context in which it is used. See 97 So. 2d 828. It is generally said to include a tract of land in the context of conveyancing, or to signify the right, title, or interest conveyed. See 71 N.E. 22. For purposes of insurance on a building, or in defining the crime of **burglary**, the scope of the term may be restricted so as to embrace only a building. See 287 S.W. 2d 714. The range of the term may be very unclear with respect to **search warrants**. See 1 R.I. 464. With respect to the **Workmen's Compensation Acts**, "premises" may include any place where the employee may go in the course of his employment. See 270 So. 2d 104.

PREPONDERANCE OF THE EVIDENCE general standard of **proof** in civil cases. "Evidence preponderates where it is more convincing to the trier [of fact] than the opposing evidence." McCormick, Evidence 793 (2nd ed. 1972). It thus refers to proof which leads the **trier of fact** to find that the existence of the fact in issue is more probable than not. Compare **reasonable doubt.**

PREROGATIVE WRIT writs formerly issued by the King. Today, these are a class of writs issued by courts in furtherance of its discretionary powers, and are not granted as a matter of right. See 12 P. 879, 884. The prerogative writs are the writ of procedendo, the writ of **mandamus**, the **writ of prohibition**, the writ of **quo warranto**, the writ of **habeas corpus**, and the writ of **certiorari**.

PRESCRIPTION a means of acquiring an **easement** in or on the land of another by continued regular use over a statutory period. See 81 A. 2d 137. Requisite elements are similar to those of **adverse possession**, except that acquisition by prescription does not require **hostile possession** or use and therefore, an easement can be acquired through permissive use (i.e., without an assertion of right). This is not inconsistent with the common-law notions concerning adverse possession, since a non-**freehold**, non-possessory interest, called an **incorporeal hereditament**, rather than the possessory interest in the land that had been enjoyed by the person(s) from whom the adverse possessor's interest is acquired. 85 N.Y.S. 561.

PRESENTMENT in criminal law, "a written accusation of crime made and returned by the **grand jury** upon its own initiative in the exercise of its lawful inquisitorial powers." 487 S.W. 2d 672, 675. In formal terms a "presentment" is the result of the grand jury's "investigation on its own without the consent or participation of a prosecutor. The grand jury holds broad power over the terms of charges it returns, and its decision not to bring charges is unreviewable. Furthermore, the grand jury may insist that prosecutors prepare whatever accusations it deems appropriate and may return a DRAFT INDICTMENT even though the government attorney refuses to sign it." 370 F. Supp. 1219, 1222. "A presentment is in the form of a bill of **indictment** and . . . is [usually] signed individually by all the grand jurors who return it, whereas only the Grand Jury Foreman signs an indictment." 487 S.W. 2d 672, 675.

In commercial law, presentment is "the production of a **bill of exchange** or **promissory note** to the party on whom the former is drawn for his acceptance, or to the person bound to pay for payment. . . . Where the instrument has been **executed** and the parties bound thereby, presentment means presentment for payment, as distinguished from presentment for acceptance which must be made before the instrument is due." 141 S.E. 394, 395.

PRESUMPTION an assumption of fact resulting from a rule of law which requires such fact to be assumed from another fact or set of facts. The term "presumption" indicates that certain weight is accorded by law to a given evidentiary fact, which weight is heavy enough to require the production of further evidence to overcome the assumption thereby established. It thus constitutes a rule of evidence which has the effect of shifting either the **burden of proof** or the burden of producing evidence. Compare **inference**.

CONCLUSIVE (NON-REBUTTABLE) PRE-SUMPTION one which no evidence, however strong, no argument, or consideration, will be permitted to overcome. See 2 S.E. 2d 343, 348. Since a presumption always properly refers to a rebuttal assumption of a fact, when the term presumption is used in this conclusive sense, it is not a true presumption but is merely a statement by the court of a rule of law. See McCormick, Evidence 804 (2d ed. 1972).

REBUTTABLE PRESUMPTION an ordinary presumption which must, as a matter of law, be made once certain facts have been proved, and which is thus said to establish a certain conclusion **prima facie** once those facts have been adduced; but it is one which may be rebutted or overcome, and if it is not overcome through the introduction of contrary evidence, it becomes conclusive. See 145 A. 2d

289, 293; 114 P. 975, 976. After rebutting evidence is introduced, the prevailing doctrine is that the competing facts are weighed on their own merits, without further reference to the presumption. See McCormick, Evidence 821 (2d ed. 1972).

PRESUMPTIVE EVIDENCE evidence which is indirect or **circumstantial; prima facie** evidence or evidence which is not conclusive and admits of explanation or contradiction; evidence which must be received and treated as true and sufficient until and unless rebutted by other evidence, i.e., evidence which a statute says shall be presumptive of another fact unless rebutted. See 166 S.W. 2d 828. See **presumption**.

PRICE FIXING under the federal **antitrust** laws, "a combination or **conspiracy** formed for the purpose and with the effect of raising, depressing, fixing, pegging or stablilizing the price of a commodity in interstate commerce. The test is not what the actual effect is on prices, but whether such agreements interfere with the freedom of traders and thereby restrain their ability to sell in accordance with their own judgment." 235 F. Supp. 705, 720.

HORIZONTAL PRICE FIXING price fixing engaged in by those in competition with each other at the same level. 133 N.Y.S. 2d 908, 924.

VERTICAL PRICE FIXING price fixing engaged in by members of different levels of production, such as manufacturer and retailer. These agreements, unlike horizontal price fixing, are legal under the Fair Trade or Sherman Anti-Trust Acts. See 19 A. 2d 454, 458.

PRIMA FACIE (prī'-mä fā'-shē-à; prē' mä fā'-shē-à)–Lat: at first view, on its face; not requiring further support to establish existence, validity, credibility, etc.

PRIMA FACIE CASE a case sufficient on its face, being supported by at least the requisite minimum of **evidence**, and being free from palpable defects; state of facts which entitles a party to have his case go to the jury, see 105 N.E. 2d 454, 458; one that will usually prevail in the absence of contradictory evidence; "one in which the evidence is sufficient to support but not to compel a certain conclusion and does no more than furnish evidence to be considered and weighed but not necessarily to be accepted by the trier of the facts." 185 N.E. 2d 115, 124. See **prima facie.**

PRIMOGENITURE *(prē-mō-jĕn'-ĭ-tûr)*— ancient common law of **descent** in which the eldest son takes all property of decedent father. The opposite of primogeniture, BOROUGH ENGLISH, existed under local custom in at least one jurisdiction even while primogeniture prevailed elsewhere in England; the youngest son inherited on the death of the father. Under the local custom of GAVELKIND all sons took equally. In the event all **issue** of the **decedent** were daughters, they took equal shares in **coparceny.** See generally, 2 Pollack and Maitland, History of English Law 261-266 (2nd Ed. 1903).

PRINCIPAL most important; manifest ranking. In the criminal law, one who commits an offense or an accomplice who is present actually or constructively during the commission of the offense. "A principal is any person concerned in the commission of a criminal offense, regardless of whether he profits from such involvement." 111 P. 1096. A PRINCIPAL IN THE FIRST-DEGREE is "one who with the requisite mental state, engages in the act or omission concurring with the mental state which causes the criminal result." LaFave and Scott, Criminal Law 496 (1972). A PRINCIPAL IN THE SECOND DEGREE is one who is actually or constructively present at the commission of a criminal offense and who aids, counsels, commands, or encourages the principal in the first-degree in the commission of that offense. See Id. at 497.

In commercial law, the principal is the amount which is received, in the case of a loan, or the amount from which flows the interest. See 154 A. 315, 316.

In the law of agency, a principal is "one who has permitted or directed another to act for his benefit and subject to his direction or control." Seavey, Law of Agency §3 (1964). Master is a species of principal. Id. "In a transaction conducted by an **agent,** the principal is DISCLOSED if the other party has notice of his identity; he is PARTIALLY DISCLOSED if the other party has notice of his existence but not his identity; he is UNDISCLOSED if the other party has no notice that the agent is acting for a principal." Id. at §4.

PRIORITY preference; the condition of coming before, or of coming first; e.g., in a **bankruptcy** proceeding, the right to be paid before other **creditors** out of the assets of the bankrupt party. The term may also be used with reference to a **prior lien,** prior **mortgage,** etc.

PRIOR LIEN a first or superior **lien,** though not necessarily one antecedent to others. 231 F. 205, 210.

PRIVATE CORPORATION see **corporation.**

PRIVATE DWELLING see **dwelling house.**

PRIVATE NECESSITY see **justification.**

PRIVATE NUISANCE see **nuisance.**

PRIVILEGE an advantage not enjoyed by all; "a particular or peculiar benefit enjoyed by a person, company, or class beyond the common advantages of other citizens; an exceptional or extraordinary exemption; or an immunity held beyond the course of the law. And, again, it is defined to be an exemption from some burden or attendance, with which certain persons are indulged, from a supposition of the law that their public duties or services, or the offices in which they are engaged, are such as require all their time and care, and that therefore, without this indulgence, those duties could not be performed to that advantage which the public good demands." 55 S.E. 820, 823.

PRIVILEGE AGAINST SELF-INCRIMINATION see **self-incrimination, privilege against.**

PRIVILEGED COMMUNICATIONS communications which occur in an air of legal or other recognized professional confidentiality. The fact that certain communication is termed privileged allows the speakers to resist legal pressure to disclose its contents. See McCormick, Evidence, §72 (2d ed. 1972). When communications are termed privileged, a

breach of the concurrent confidentiality can result in a **civil suit** in **tort**. There are several forms of privileged communications: (1) communications in the sanctity of the marital relationship; (2) communications between a physician and his patient; (3) communications of psychological counselors and their clients; (4) priest-and-penitent communications; and (5) in some jurisdictions, the communications between a journalist and his sources. See N.J. Rule of Evidence, 26-29. See generally McCormick, supra, §§78-113. The usual effect of the legal determination of privileged communication is that the participants can not be forced under legal compulsion to state the substance of the communication. Furthermore, one of the participants can enjoin the other from disclosing.

PRIVITY a relationship between parties out of which there arises some mutuality of interest. 443 P. 2d 39, 43.

In the law of judgments, the doctrine of **res judicata** is said to apply not only to one who was a party to the **litigation**, but also to those "in privity" with him, since their mutual or subsequently-acquired interests can be considered so related to the interest of the actual party litigant that it is proper to hold them bound by the judgment as well. 200 N.W. 2d 45, 47. Privity in this context is said to exist, and to invoke res judicata, especially where a party has, subsequent to the rendition of the judgment, acquired an interest in the subject matter affected by the judgment, 289 N.E. 2d 788, 793, or where one not a named party to an action controls it, or where one has his interest protected by a party to an action (e.g., in **class actions**). Green, Basic Civil Procedure 213 (1972).

PRIVITY OF CONTRACT "the relationship that exists between two or more contracting parties. It is essential to the maintenance of an **action** on any contract that there should subsist a privity between the plaintiff and defendant in respect to the matter sued on." 47 A. 929, 935. This requirement has been abrogated in the area of **products liability**. See U.C.C. § 2-318; Prosser, Torts §§96, 100 (4th ed. 1971).

PRIVITY OF ESTATE denotes mutual or successive relation to the same right in property. "A privy in estate is one who derives from another **title** to property, by contract or law." 60 S.E. 404, 405.

PRIVY persons connected together, or having mutual interest in the same action or thing, by some relation other than that of actual **contract** between them. 274 N.Y.S. 875. See **privity**.

PROBABLE CAUSE a requisite element of a valid **search and seizure** or **arrest**, which consists of the existence of facts and circumstances within one's knowledge and of which one has reasonably trustworthy information, which are sufficient in themselves to warrant a man of reasonable caution in the belief that a crime has been committed [in the context of an arrest] or that property subject to seizure is at a designated location [in the context of a search and seizure]. See 267 U.S. 132. The issue of whether there is probable cause to search must be determined on the basis of an independent judgment of a "detached magistrate;" it must be based on **affidavits**, in support of a request for a search warrant or; if the police officer conducts a warrantless search, the issue of probable cause may be later determined by a judge at a hearing if a **motion** is filed to suppress the **evidence** as illegally obtained.

Probable cause can be established in many ways. It may be established on the basis of the cumulative knowledge of the investigating officers. See 380 U.S. 102, 111. However, probable cause cannot be based on facts which are completely innocent in themselves. See 393 U.S. 410. Furthermore, the fact that the suspect has been previously involved in similar crimes is not of important value. See 393 U.S. 410. Probable cause must be based on particular facts in the affidavit and not by mere conclusions. See 378 U.S. 108. Particularly difficult problems in determining probable cause arise when an informer is the source of information. An informer's tip standing alone does not create probable cause. It must be corroborated by the informer's reliability or by the cumulative effect of other information and observations made by the police. See 393 U.S. 410.

Probable cause is required at the time of the arrest or search, see 287 U.S. 206, and may not be created by the fruits of a successful search or arrest.

PROBATE the act of proving that an **instrument** purporting to be a **will** was signed and otherwise executed in accordance with legal requirements, and of determining its validity thereby, see 301 S.W. 2d 310; also, the combined result of all the procedural acts necessary to establish the validity of a will. See 22 N.E. 2d 679. In some jurisdictions a PROBATE COURT is a special court having jurisdiction of proceedings incident to the settlement of a decedent's **estate**. See 169 N.E. 2d 591.

PROBATION a procedure whereby a **defendant** found guilty of a crime upon a **verdict** or **plea** of guilty is released by the court without imprisonment, subject to conditions imposed by the court, under the supervision of a probation officer. A VIOLATION OF PROBATION can lead to REVOCATION OF PROBATION and the imposition of a custodial [prison] sentence. One of the conditions permitted in some jurisdictions as a condition of probation is a short period of incarceration. This is called a SPLIT SENTENCE since part of it is served in a jail and the balance on probation. Under the federal statute no more than 6 months imprisonment may be imposed as a condition of probation. 18 U.S.C. §3651.

Probation is part of the sentencing process and the defendant is entitled to be represented by counsel under the Sixth Amendment of the United States Constitution. 389 U.S. 128. Compare **parole** which, unlike probation, is not part of the sentencing process, but is the supervised release from confinement of a prisoner who is permitted to serve part of a custodial sentence in the community and who is subject to REVOCATION OF PAROLE by the parole board should he violate the terms and conditions of his release. Neither a probation nor a parole revocation proceeding is part of the sentencing process, but the defendant will nevertheless be entitled to procedural **due process** safeguards, including a **hearing** with **notice** and an opportunity to be heard, but not including appointed counsel [at state expense] unless the issues are complex or fundamental fairness otherwise requires that he have the aid of counsel to be dealt with justly. 408 U.S. 471; 411 U.S. 778.

PROBATIVE tending to prove a particular proposition; having the tendency of persuading one as to the truth of an allegation.

PROBATIVE FACTS matters of evidence required to prove ultimate facts; "facts from which the ultimate and decisive facts may be inferred . . . are probative." 21 S.E. 2d 873.

PROBATIVE VALUE the relative weight of particular evidence. For example, if a trial involves the question of whether the defendant was driving at an excessive rate of speed through a school zone, evidence tending to prove that he was going 50 miles an hour less than a block from the school zone would be of very high probative value; evidence that he was going 50 miles an hour two blocks away (without an intervening stop sign) would have less but still high probative value; evidence that he was going 50 miles an hour six blocks away in a residential zone would have even less but still some probative value; evidence that he was speeding several miles away or that he ran a traffic signal the previous day would have very little probative value. Whatever value the traffic violation the previous day may have would be outweighed by its prejudicial impact upon the jury and it would likely be excluded. See **admissible evidence.**

PRO BONO PUBLICO *(prō bŏ'-nō pŭb'-lē-kō)*—Lat: for the public good or welfare. When attorneys take on cases without compensation to advance a social cause, they are said to be representing the party "pro bono publico."

PROCEDURAL DUE PROCESS see **due process of law.**

PROCEDURE legal method; the machinery for carrying on the **suit,** including pleading, process, evidence and practice. The term thus refers to the mechanics of the legal process—i.e., the body of rules and practice by which justice is meted out by the legal system—rather than the substance and content of the law itself.

PROCEEDING the succession of events constituting the process by which judicial action is invoked and utilized, see 80 A. 2d 100, 102; the form in which actions are to be brought and defended, the manner of intervening in suits, of conducting them; the mode of deciding them, of opposing and of executing judgments. 37 F. 470, 488. It is thus broader in meaning than the term **action**, 136 F. 2d 790, 791.

PROCESS "a formal writing [**writ**] issued by authority of law," 38 F. Supp. 142, 143; any "means used by the court to acquire or to exercise its **jurisdiction** over a person or over specified property," 282 N.E. 2d 452, 456; usually refers to the method used to compel the attendance of a **defendant** in court in a **civil** suit. 283 N.E. 2d 456, 458. See **service of process.**

PROCTOR one who manages another's affairs, acting as that person's **agent**; an attorney who is admitted to practice in a **probate, admiralty,** or ecclesiastical court. Compare **administrator.**

PRODUCTION BURDEN see **burden of proof.**

PRODUCTS LIABILITY a relatively recent development in the law of **torts** which dictates that "a manufacturer is **strictly liable** in tort when an article he places in the market, knowing that it is to be used without inspection for defects, proves to have a defect that causes injury to a human being." 377 P. 2d 897, 900. This theory of liability has been accepted by the Second Restatement of Torts, §402A: "(1) One who sells any product in a defective condition unreasonably dangerous to the user or consumer or to his property is subject to liability for physical harm thereby caused to the ultimate user or consumer, or to his property, if (a) the seller is engaged in the business of selling such a product, and (b) it is expected to and does reach the user or consumer without substantial change in the condition in which it is sold. (2) The rule stated in subsection (1) applies although

(a) the seller has exercised all possible care in the preparation and sale of his product [i.e., has not been **negligent**], and (b) the user or consumer has not bought the product from or entered into any contractual relation with the seller [i.e., without regard to **privity of contract**]." See **strict liability.**

PRO FORMA (*prō fôr'-mä*)—Lat: for the sake of form; as a matter of form. In an appealable **decree** or **judgment**, the term usually means "that the decision was rendered, not upon intellectual conviction that the decree was right, but merely to facilitate further proceedings." 267 F. 564, 568.

PROHIBITION see **writ of prohibition.**

PROMISE a declaration of one's intention to do or to refrain from doing something. 119 S.E. 235, 236. See also **contract; covenant.**

BREACH OF PROMISE see **breach of promise.**

ILLUSORY PROMISE see **illusory promise.**

PROMISSORY ESTOPPEL an equitable doctrine which declares that "a promise which the promisor should reasonably expect [will] induce action or forbearance on the part of the promisee or a third person and which does induce such action or forbearance is binding if injustice can be avoided only by enforcement of the promise. . . ." See Restatement 2d, Contracts §90. The promisor, having induced **reliance** on his promise by the other party, is said to be "estopped" from denying the existence of a contract, though in fact one has not been made. Thus, promissory estoppel departs from traditional contract law in that no bargain is involved. A typical situation wherein the doctrine of promissory estoppel is invoked, is that in which a pension is promised to an employee and at the fruition period, the promise is not honored.

Promissory estoppel is a recognized alternative to the requirement of **consideration** in appropriate cases. However, some jurisdictions do not accept it and demand that the traditional requirements of **consideration** be met. See also **estoppel; waiver** (EXECUTORY WAIVER).

PROMISSORY NOTE a kind of **negotiable instrument** wherein the **maker** agrees (promises) to pay a sum certain at a definite time.

PROOF the quantity of evidence which tends to establish the existence of a fact in issue; the persuasion of the **trier of fact** by the production of evidence of the truth of a fact alleged. See also **burden of proof; inference; moral certainty; preponderance of evidence; presumption; reasonable doubt.**

PROOF BEYOND A REASONABLE DOUBT see **reasonable doubt.**

PROOFS the evidence offered to prove or disprove a fact in issue.

PROOF TO A MORAL CERTAINTY see **moral certainty.**

PROPER PARTY see **party.**

PROPERTY "every species of valuable right or interest that is subject to **ownership**, has an exchangeable value, or adds to one's wealth or **estate.**" 107 A. 2d 274, 276. "Property" describes one's exclusive right to possess, use, and dispose of a thing, 202 P. 2d 771, as well as the object, benefit, or prerogative which constitutes the subject matter of that right. 331 U.S. 1.

COMMON PROPERTY that which belongs to the citizenry as a whole, 7 P. 2d 868; property owned by **tenants in common,** 108 P. 2d 377, or in some jurisdictions where designated by statute, that owned by husband and wife. 3 Cal. 83. Compare **community property.**

PERSONAL PROPERTY see **personalty.**

REAL PROPERTY see **real property.**

PROPRIETARY INTEREST "any right in relation to a **chattel** which enables a person to retain its **possession** indefinitely or for a period of time." Restatement, Torts, § 223 (Comment on Clause (d)).

PRO RATA *(prō rä'-tä)*—Lat: according to the rate, i.e., in proportion; "according to a measure which fixes proportions. It has no meaning unless referable to some rule or standard." 39 A. 134, 135. Thus, a lease terminated by agreement before the expiration of the full term may call for the payment of rent on a pro rata basis for the expired term of the lease; an adjudicated bankrupt, after establishing **insolvency,** is relieved of liability to all listed creditors after engaging in a pro rata distribution of his assets among those creditors.

PRO SE *(prō sā)*—Lat: for himself; in one's own behalf; e.g., one represents himself "pro se" in a legal **action** when he does so without counsel.

PROSECUTION the act of pursuing a law suit or criminal trial; also, the party initiating a criminal suit, i.e., the state. Where the civil **litigant,** or the state in a criminal trial, fails to move the case towards final resolution or trial as required by the court schedule, the matter may be dismissed for "want of prosecution."

PROSECUTOR a public official who prepares and conducts the prosecution of persons accused of crime, who may be either elected or appointed. In certain cases, the legislature may appoint a special prosecutor to conduct a limited investigation and prosecution. The state prosecutors are usually called district attorneys or county prosecutors. The federal prosecutor is known as the United States Attorney for a certain federal district. Each chief prosecutor has several assistant prosecutors.

The basic role of the prosecutor is to seek justice and not convictions. His office is charged with the duty to see that the laws of his jurisdiction are faithfully executed and enforced. In the enforcement of the laws, the prosecutor has the responsibility of making a decision of who and when to prosecute, a decision with respect to which the prosecutor has broad discretion. See generally, ABA Minimum Standards Relating to the Prosecution Function and the Defense Function §§1.1-3.9 (Approved Draft 1971).

PROSECUTORIAL DISCRETION see **discretion.**

PRO TANTO *(prō tän'-tō)*—Lat: to such extent; for so much; as far as it goes; "to the extent, but only to the extent." 104 N.W. 2d 462, 466.

PROVISIONAL REMEDY see **remedy.**

PROVISO a condition or stipulation. Its general function is to "except something from the basic provision, to qualify or restrain its general scope, or to prevent misinterpretation." 108 F. 2d 936, 940.

PROXIMATE CAUSE see **cause**.

PROXY a term given to an individual who is the recipient of a grant of authority to act or speak for another. "A proxy is one permitted to vote in place of a **stockholder** of a **corporation**, and is presumably voicing the judgment and the will of his principal." 59 A. 778, 783. Sometimes used to identify the instrument used to grant this authority.

The ultimate control of any corporation rests in the hands of the stockholders. These stockholders exercise this power by means of voting their shares at duly constituted stockholders' meetings. Because many stockholders are unable to attend such meetings they delegate their authority to vote these shares through the issuance of proxies to individuals whom they feel will represent their interests. Such proxies are revocable until they are voted, unless there is a specific contractual agreement to the contrary. Compare **voting trust**.

Association by-laws sometimes permit voting by proxy on stated issues. The absent voting member actually casts a written vote and delivers it to the chairman in advance of the meeting. If he can ultimately attend or if the issues at the meeting differ from that voted upon by the written proxy, the proxy becomes ineffective. This is to distinguish from the instances in which one authorizes another, the proxy, to vote on his behalf (with or without confidential instructions).

PUBLIC CORPORATION see **corporation**.

PUBLIC DOMAIN "comprehends all lands and waters in the possession or ownership of the United States, and including all lands owned by the several states, as distinguished from lands possessed by private individuals or corporations." 143 F. 740, 748.

"Information, the source of which is available to anyone, . . . and not subject to **copyright**" is considered to be in the "public domain." 46 F. Supp. 468, 471.

PUBLIC EASEMENT any easement enjoyed by the public in general, e.g., the right of passage of the public over the surface of streets, alleys, highways, etc. It is also called a DEDICATION, meaning that the use of the land has been devoted for such purposes by the owner of the **fee**. A "public easement" carries with it the right to construct and properly maintain the passageway, and includes necessary light and air space above the surface. See 42 A. 583, 584, 134 A. 77, 79.

PUBLIC NECESSITY see **justification**.

PUBLIC NUISANCE see **nuisance**.

PUBLIC PROPERTY that which is dedicated to the use of the public, see 84 P. 685, and/or that over which the state has dominion and control. See 173 S.W. 2d 631. Thus the term may be used either to describe the use to which the property is put, or to describe the character of its ownership. 25 Ohio St. 229. See also **public domain**.

PUBLIC SALE see **sale**.

PUBLIC SECURITIES see **securities**.

PUBLIC USE see **use**.

PUR AUTRE VIE see **per autre vie**.

PURCHASE-MONEY SECURITY INTEREST see **security interest**.

PURLOIN to steal; to commit **larceny**.

PURSUASION BURDEN see **burden of proof**.

PURVIEW the enacting part or body of the act, as distinguished from other parts of it, such as the preamble. 173 N.E. 229, 231. Conduct is said to be "within the purview" of a statute when it properly comes within its scope, purpose, operation, or effect.

PUTATIVE alleged; supposed; commonly used in family law, e.g., a "putative" marriage is one which is actually null, but which has been contracted in good faith by the two parties, or by one of the parties. See 136 S.W. 1145, 1148. The "putative father" in a **paternity suit**

is the person alleged to have fathered the child whose parentage is at issue in the suit.

QUAERE see **query.**

QUANTUM MERUIT *(kwän'-tŭm mĕ'-rū-ĭt)*—Lat: as much as he deserved. Historically, it was a common count in the action of **assumpsit,** allowing recovery "for services performed for another on the basis of a **contract** implied in law or an implied promise to pay the performer for what the services were reasonably worth." 121 N.W. 2d 744, 746. To recover today under quantum meruit, the **plaintiff** must have performed valuable services or furnished materials for the person sought to be charged; and those materials or services must have been accepted, used and enjoyed by him under such circumstances as reasonably notified the person sought to be charged that the plaintiff expected to be paid when he performed the services or furnished the materials. See 459 S.W. 2d 691, 694. It involves **liability** for a contract implied in law, which "arises not from the consent of the parties but from the law of natural justice and equity, and is based on the doctrine of **unjust enrichment.**" Thus, where a physician renders emergency services to an unconscious accident victim, the consent of the injured party is implied in law, so that the physician may bring an action in quantum meruit to recover the reasonable value of his services. 432 P. 2d 386, 390. Compare **officious intermeddler.** See also **quasi-contract.**

QUARE CLAUSUM FREGIT *(kwä'-rā klŏw'-sŭm frä'-gĭt)*—Lat: wherefore he broke the close. An early form of **trespass** designed to obtain **damages** for an unlawful entry upon another's **land.** The **form of action** was called "trespass quare clausum fregit," or "trespass qu. cl. fr." in its abbreviated form. **Breaking a close** was the technical **common law** expression for an unlawful entry upon land. Even without an actual fence the **action** would **plead** that the "defendant with force and arms broke and entered the close of the **plaintiff,**" 182 S.E. 156, 157, since in the eyes of the common law, every unauthorized entry upon the soil of another was a trespass.

QUASH to annul, overthrow, or vacate by judicial decision. 162 S.E. 1, 2. Oppressive and unreasonable **subpoenas** can be "quashed," as can **injunctions, orders,** etc.

QUASI *(kwä'-sī; kwä'-sē)*—Lat: as it were, so to speak; about, nearly, almost, like.

QUASI-CONTRACTS those which, "unlike true **contracts,** are not based on the apparent intention of the **parties** to undertake the **performances** in question, nor are they promises. They are obligations created by law for reasons of justice." Restatement of Contracts § 5. "The doctrine of quasi-contracts is based upon the principle that a party who has received a benefit, which he desired, under circumstances which render it inequitable for him to retain it without making compensation, must do so." 298 P. 184. See **quantum meruit; unjust enrichment.**

QUASI-CRIMINAL refers to a **proceeding** which though not actually a criminal **prosecution** is sufficiently similar in terms of the "grievous loss" (civil fine, loss of employment, loss of license, suspension from school, etc.) or the stigma to be attached to warrant some of the special **procedural** safeguards of a criminal proceeding. A **parole** revocation is not a criminal proceeding, but it is quasi-criminal in the sense that the parole board must accord substantial procedural **due process** to the parolee facing revocation. 408 U.S. 471.

QUASI IN REM "proceedings which are not strictly and purely **in rem** but [which] are brought against the **defendant** personally, although the real object is to deal with the particular property," 71 A. 2d 914; "actions based on a claim for money **damages** begun by **attachment,** or **garnishment** or other **seizure** of property where the court has no **jurisdiction** over the person of the defendant but has jurisdiction over a thing belonging to the defendant or over a person who is indebted or under a duty to the defendant." James, Civil Procedure §12.1 (1965).

QUASI CORPORATION see **corporation.**

QUEEN'S BENCH see **King's Bench.**

QUERY question; indicates the proposition or rule it introduces is unsettled or open to some question. Thus, a law professor might say, "Query: whether a **pardon** can reach pre-**indictment** offenses of a public official?"

QUESTION OF FACT disputed factual contention which is traditionally left for the jury to decide. In a **battery** case, a question of fact would be whether A touched B. The legal significance of the touching of B by A is left for the judge to decide since it amounts to a **question of law.**

The distinction between fact and law is often nebulous. However, the way an issue is characterized in this regard can trigger many different legal consequences. There are different standards of review for findings of fact and findings of law. The doctrine of **res judicata, collateral estoppel** and **stare decisis** often center on this problem.

QUESTION OF LAW disputed legal contentions which are traditionally left for the judge to decide. The occurrence or non-occurrence of an event is a **question of fact**; their legal significance is a question of law.

The resolution of a question of law is paid less deference in an **appeal** than is a determination of fact. It must be noted that often the line between fact and law is impossible to objectively determine. In those situations, there may be a compound conclusion of law and fact.

QUIA EMPTORES, STATUTE OF English statute in 1290 which terminated the process of **subinfeudation** [Creation of new manors by the subject of a lord]. After that date, only the King was able to infeudate. The statute's practical effect on land transactions and ownership was that after the land was sold, the

seller had no further connection with it. See Cheshire, The Modern Law of Real Property (6th ed. 1949). Thus subinfeudation was replaced by strict **alienation.**

QUID PRO QUO *(kwĭd prō kwō)*—Lat: what for what; something for something; in some legal contexts, synonymous with **consideration,** see 209 S.W. 2d 851; sometimes referred to simply as the "quid" and always indicating that which the party receives or is promised in return for something he promises, gives, or does, e.g., a defendant's willingness to testify for the state may be the quid pro quo for the government's willingness to accept a **plea** of guilty to a lesser offense.

QUIET ENJOYMENT the right to unimpaired use and enjoyment of **property leased** or **conveyed.** As to leased premises a guarantee of quiet enjoyment is usually expressed by a **covenant** of quiet enjoyment in a written lease, but such a covenant may be implied today from the landlord-tenant relationship where it is not so expressed. This covenant is violated if the tenant's enjoyment of the premises is substantially disturbed either by wrongful acts or omissions of the landlord or by persons claiming a **paramount title** against the landlord. The covenant does not extend to interference with **possession** by a stranger, i.e., a person not claiming under the lessor or under a title paramount to the lessor's. 128 P. 222. The covenant may be and often is included in the **deed** conveying title to property, but in this context it does not arise by implication. If it is present in a deed, the **grantor** is obligated to protect the estate of his **grantee** against lawful claims of ownership by others. Burby, Real Property 315, (3d ed. 1965). See **constructive eviction.**

QUIET TITLE an **equitable action** to determine all adverse claims to the property in question; a **suit** in **equity** brought to obtain a final determination as to the **title** of a specific piece of **property;** such a suit is usually the result of various individuals asserting contradictory rights to the same parcel of land. "It is made use of where a person has a right which may be controverted by various persons at different times, whereupon the Court will, to prevent a **multiplicity of suits**, direct an issue to determine the right and ultimately issue an **injunction**." 164 N.W. 338, 341. It is distinguished from an action brought to REMOVE CLOUD ON TITLE, which refers to determining and resolving problems of **instruments** conveying a particular piece of land, rather than resolving the claims to that land themselves.

QUITCLAIM DEED   a **deed** which conveys only that right, **title**, or **interest** which the **grantor** has, or may have, and which does not require that the grantor thereby pass a **good title**. A quit claim deed may be purchased for a small sum as protection against the possibility that the grantor has a substantial interest unknown to him. The grantor of a quit claim deed does not represent that he has any interest whatever in the property for which he gives the deed—merely that whatever interest he may have he **conveys** to the grantee. Compare **warranty deed**.

QUORUM   the number of members of any body who must necessarily be present in order to transact the business of that body. "A quorum is such a number of officers or members of any body as is sufficient to transact business." 179 P. 2d 870, 873. Usually, but not necessarily, it requires a majority.

A quorum is required to render legitimate any actions voted on or taken by any limited membership body. While a quorum is usually a majority of either the total membership or the members present, this general principle can be altered by the body to require or permit that more or less than a majority of the body is necessary to transact business.

QUOTATION   in commercial usage, a statement of the price of an item; it also refers to the price stated in response to an inquiry, see 2 Cal. Rptr. 310, 314; more generally, the word for word repetition of a statement from some authority, case, or law. See also **citation**.

QUO WARRANTO *(kwō wär′-răn-tō)*— Lat: by what right or authority; an ancient **common law writ**, which was "an original writ issuing out of **chancery** in the nature of a **writ of right** for the king against one who claimed or usurped any

office, **franchise** or liberty, to inquire by what authority he asserted a right thereto in order that it might be determined." 38 N.E. 2d 2, 5. "Formerly a criminal method of **prosecution**, it has long since lost its criminal character, and is now a **civil proceeding**, expressly recognized by statute, and usually employed for **trying the title** to a corporate franchise or to a corporate or public office." 234 S.W. 344, 347.

"Quo warranto" proceedings may be brought against **corporations** where the company has abused or failed for a long time to exercise its franchise; in the case of an official it may be brought to cause him to forfeit an office for misconduct. If in these cases a quo warranto proceeding determines that a company no longer properly holds a franchise or that an officer no longer properly holds his office, it will oust the wrongdoer from enjoying the franchise or office. The purpose of the writ is not to prevent an improper exercise of power lawfully posssessed; its purpose is to prevent an official, corporation, or persons acting as such from usurping a power which they do not have. See 148 S.W. 2d 527, 530.

R

RACE   see **recording acts**.

RAPE   the act of unlawful sexual intercourse between persons not married to each other accomplished through the use of force or fear of force by the man and implying lack of consent and resistance by the woman. An essential element of the common law offense of rape was penetration, however slight. In the absence of penetration, only an **attempt** can be established. See Perkins, Criminal Law 155 (2d ed. 1969).

In many jurisdictions a valid conviction for rape requires that certain material elements (e.g. force, penetration, identity) be corroborated by evidence other than the testimony of the victim, although the modern trend is to repeal such special requirements.

CARNAL KNOWLEDGE was the original term for the act itself and is retained in many statutes which proscribe "carnal knowledge of a child," regardless of her purported consent. This offense is often called STATUTORY RAPE.

RATIO DECEDENDI *(rä'-shē-ō dā-sē-děn'-dē)*—Lat: the principle which the case establishes; the reason for the decision.

RATIO LEGIS *(rä'-shē-ō lāg'-ĭs)*—Lat: the underlying principle; reasoning; grounds; scheme; theory, doctrine or science of the law. Thus, the ratio legis of a loitering statute is to allow law enforcement officers more latitude in attempting to prevent crime rather than relying solely on apprehension and sentencing as a deterrence.

RAVISH generally, synonymous with **rape**. Literally, to "ravish" is to seize or snatch by force. Traditionally, a valid **indictment** for rape required the use of the term "ravished," which implied the element of force or violence; it would thus constitute an "essential word in all indictments for rape, [importing] not only force and violence on the part of the man but resistance on the part of the woman." 6 Minn. 279, 285. Also, it "includes the meaning of the phrase 'carnally known by force and against her will.'" Id.

REAL ESTATE every possible **interest** in land, except for a mere **chattel** interest; signifies the interest which one has in land; "every estate, interest, and right, legal and equitable, in lands, tenements, and hereditaments." 4 S.W. 56, 59.

REAL PARTY IN INTEREST the person who will be entitled to the benefits of the action if successful; one who is actually and substantially interested in the subject matter, as opposed to one who has only a nominal, formal or technical interest in or connection with it. See 167 P. 619, 620. For example, if an insurance company pays its insured for damage done his automobile under a collision insurance provision of his policy and if the insurance company attempts to collect its loss from the responsible party, the suit may be brought in the name of the insured, but the "real party

in interest" will be the insurance company. See **nominal party**.

REAL PROPERTY "not only land and whatever is erected or growing thereon, or affixed thereto, but also rights issuing out of, annexed to, and exercisable within or about, the land." 280 P. 350.

Originally, the distinction between real and personal property depended not on the nature of the property but on the nature of the **action** by which rights were vindicated. This later evolved into a distinction between real property, which is land, and personal property, which consists of **chattels** (movables). The former distinction, however, has persisted to a large extent in treating a **lessor's** interest, (not being a **freehold**) as a **chattel**, and hence recoverable in an action for **breach of contract** only. Today, however, "leasehold interests in land are for many purposes treated as personalty." See Brown, The Law of Personal Property 12 (2d ed. 1955).

REALTY an interest in land; another word for **real property**.

REASONABLE DOUBT refers to the degree of certainty required of a juror for a legally valid determination by him of the guilt of a criminal **defendant**. These words are used in **instructions** to the jury in a criminal trial to indicate that innocence is to be presumed unless guilt is so clearly proved that the jury can see that no "reasonable doubt" remains as to the guilt of the person charged. The term "reasonable doubt" does not signify a mere skeptical condition of the mind. It does not require that the proof should be so clear that no possibility of error can exist, for if that were the case no criminal prosecution would prevail. It means simply that it must be so conclusive and complete that all reasonable doubts of the fact are removed from the mind. See 25 F. 556, 558. See also **moral certainty**; **preponderance**.

REASONABLE MAN [PERSON] a phrase used to denote a hypothetical person who exercises "those qualities of attention, knowledge, intelligence and judgment which society requires of its members for the protection of their own interest and the interests of others." Restatement Torts § 283(a). Thus, the test of **negligence** is based on a failure to do "something which a reasonable man, guided by those considerations which ordinarily regulate the conduct of human affairs, would do, or [the doing of] something which a reasonable and prudent person would not do." 43 S.W. 508, 509. The phrase does not apply to a person's ability to reason, but rather the prudence with which he acts under the circumstances. See id. Similar phrases include: "reasonably prudent person," "ordinarily prudent man," etc.

REBUTTABLE PRESUMPTION see **presumption.**

REBUTTAL EVIDENCE "any evidence that repels, counteracts or disproves evidence given by a witness," 158 P. 2d 799, 803; "that which explains away, contradicts, or otherwise refutes the adverse party's evidence 'by any process which consists merely in diminishing or negating the force' of it." 202 N.W. 896, 898. Rebuttal evidence is offered to contradict other evidence or to rebut a **presumption** of fact.

REBUTTER a form of **common law** pleading which was a defendant's answer of fact to the plaintiff's response to the defendant's **surrejoinder.** See **pleadings.**

RECEIVER a neutral person with respect to the parties in or to a **cause of action** who is appointed by the court to receive and preserve the property or fund that is the subject of the **litigation** during the period of litigation, see 115 S.W. 2d 1212, 1216; a "person appointed by a court or judicial officer to take charge of property during the pendency of a **civil action,** suit, or proceeding, or upon a judgment, decree, or order therein, and to manage and dispose of it as the court or officer may direct." 76 P. 774, 775. The court takes possession of the property in controversy through its **agent,** the receiver, during the litigation or after the decree or judgment, for the benefit of the people entitled to the property, when the court does not deem it proper that either party should have control of it during

that time. 76 P. 774, 775. Although the "receiver" is the custodian of the assets involved in the litigation, title to the assets remains in the owners who are parties to the litigation and the receiver manages the property for the benefit of the parties. See 275 N.E. 2d 724, 728.

In criminal law, one who obtains possession of property which he knows or believes to have been stolen is a "receiver" [colloquially called a "fence"] of stolen property and commits an offense thereby.

RECEIVERSHIP an equitable remedy whereby property is by order of the court placed under the control of a **receiver** so that it may be preserved for the benefit of affected parties. A failing company may be placed in receivership in an action brought by its creditors. The business is often continued but is subject to the receiver's control. A receivership is ancillary to or in aid of the main **relief** sought in an action; it is sometimes used to carry out an **order** or **decree** but is generally used for the purpose of preserving property during **litigation** involving rights in the property. See 60 F. Supp. 716, 719; 175 N.E. 2d 655, 659. The term is also used to refer to the status of property affected by this remedy. For example, property is said to be "in receivership." Compare **bankruptcy.**

RECESS an adjournment of a trial or hearing which is temporary and which occurs after commencement of the trial or hearing; it may be very short, for lunch, overnight, or for a few days. If it amounts to a substantial delay in the proceedings it is called a **continuance.** It refers also to "the intermission between sittings of the same [legislative] body at its regular or adjourned session, and not . . . the interval between the final adjournment of one body and the convening of another at the next regular session. . . . A temporary dismissal, and not an adjournment **sine die.**" 74 S.W. 298.

RECIDIVIST term used to describe an "habitual criminal," who is often subject to extended terms of imprisonment under **habitual offender** statutes.

RECIPROCITY generally, a relationship

between persons, corporations, states, or countries whereby favors or privileges granted by one are returned by the other. Thus, if state A certifies engineers already certified by state B to work in state A, "reciprocity" exists when state B similarly certifies engineers previously certified by state A. Reciprocity does not involve a **vested right** that would exist without it. See 103 S.E. 2d 205, 208. See also **comity**.

RECKLESS careless, heedless, inattentive to duty. The word "reckless" has a wide range of meaning, that may vary in color and content according to the circumstances and the time in which it is used. Some cases hold that the term implies more than carelessness, that it implies willfulness, and is in fact the equivalent of "willful." In this sense, the term may be used as meaning "foolishly heedless of danger; headlong; impetuously or rashly adventurous; indifferent to consequences; mindless; not caring or noting; . . . rash; . . . or very negligent." 26 P. 2d 573.

In the criminal area the modern trend is to define "recklessly" with regard to a material element of an offense as conscious disregard of a "substantial and unjustifiable risk that the material element exists or will result from his conduct. The risk must be of such a nature and degree that the actor's failure to perceive it, considering the nature and purpose of his conduct and the circumstances known to him, involves a gross deviation from the standard of care that a reasonable person would observe in the actor's situation." Model Penal Code §2.02 (App. Draft 1962). Thus, recklessness in this sense imports wanton indifference to the consequences of one's acts. Compare **negligence**.

RECKLESS DISREGARD refers to "an act or conduct destitute of heed or concern for consequences; especially, foolishly heedless of danger; headlong, rash; wanton disregard or indifference to consequences. This implies a consciousness of danger and a willingness to assume the risk." 305 P. 2d 752, 757. The phrase is often associated with **guest statutes** and refers to the actions of a driver. "Reckless disregard" is more severe than ordinary **negligence**, but

does not necessarily require a criminal intent to harm, either in general, or a victim in particular. See 404 P. 2d 677, 678.

RECOGNIZANCE, ONE'S OWN see **release on recognizance**.

RECORD to preserve in a writing or printing, or by film, tape, etc. It often refers to "a precise history of a suit from its commencement to its termination, including the conclusions of law thereon drawn by the proper officer for the purpose of perpetuating the exact state of facts." 159 N.E. 591, 592. The RECORD ON APPEAL consists of those items introduced in evidence in the lower court; thus, if an **appellant** attempts to base his argument on facts other than those presented in the court below, he will be going "outside the record" (**hors the record**) which he ordinarily cannot do.

RECORDING ACTS in real property law, statutes that afford a means of giving **constructive** notice of **ownership** respecting **estates** or **interests** in land by providing for recording the existence of that estate or interest. These statutes generally provide for recording **deeds**, **mortgages**, **executory contracts** of **sale**, and **leases** of specified duration. When one's interest or ownership in land is recorded, the recording prevents a subsequent purchaser or mortgagee of the land from qualifying as a **bona fide purchaser** for value without notice, because the instrument recorded would provide at least *constructive* notice of another's prior ownership or interest in the land. Usually recording acts apply to derivative titles and not to original titles, so that anyone who obtains an original title by **adverse possession** will continue to hold title even if the record holder of title conveys his interest to one who is a **bona fide purchaser** for value and without notice. See Burby, Real Property § 130 (3rd ed. 1965).

The different types of recording acts are "pure race," "race-notice" (with or without a period of grace) and "notice" (with or without a period of grace). Under the RACE type of recording act, the person who records first takes in preference to other persons who receive an interest from the same source, even if the first recorder had notice of a prior unrecorded conveyance. A RACE-NOTICE type of act operates in the same way as the race statute, but only if the first recorder had no notice of the prior unrecorded conveyance.

NOTICE type recording acts provide that a bona fide purchaser is favored even though a prior purchaser is the first to record, so long as the second purchaser had no knowledge of the prior conveyance at the time he made his purchase. Of course, this can happen only where the first purchaser has failed to record his deed at the time the second purchase is made, since the act of recording puts all subsequent purchasers on constructive notice of the recorded conveyance, depriving them of the right to assert that they are bona fide purchasers.

Where there is a GRACE PERIOD provided by a recording act, a prior conveyee is protected as against a subsequent conveyee even if he doesn't record first, as long as he records within the period of grace defined by the recording act. See Cribbet, Principles of Law of Property 220 (1962); Smith and Boyer, Survey of the Law of Property 324 (2d ed. 1971). See also **chain of title**.

RECOUPMENT the right of **defendant** to have **plaintiff's** award of **damages** against defendant reduced; a right of deduction from the amount of the plaintiff's claim by reason of either a payment thereon or some loss sustained by the defendant by reason of the plaintiff's wrongful or defective **performance** of the **contract** out of which his **claim** originated. It has been defined to be "a keeping back of something which is due because there is an equitable reason for withholding it. . . ." The word is nearly if not completely synonymous with "discount" or "deduction" or "reduction." 143 F. 929, 936. See also **counter-claim; set-off**.

RECOVERY "the establishment of a right by the judgment of a court." 18 F. 2d 752, 753. Thus a person who is successful in a suit to obtain a judgment "recovers" that which the court deems him to have lost, though recovery does

not necessarily imply a return to whole or normal. See 347 F. Supp. 955, 962; 429 P. 2d 379, 381. It also refers to the amount of the judgment as well as the amount actually collected pursuant to it. See 167 N.Y.S. 217, 219.

REDEMPTION "to purchase back; to regain possession by payment of a stipulated price; repurchase," 139 N.W. 802, 803; the "process of cancelling and annulling a defeasible **title**, such as is created by a **mortgage** or tax sale, by paying the **debt** or fulfilling other obligations." 253 P. 2d 957, 960.

RIGHT OF REDEMPTION statutory right in some jurisdictions to redeem property that has been forfeited because the mortgagor defaulted on the mortgage payments; it can be exercised only after the **foreclosure** and sale of the property; it is a personal privilege and not an interest or **estate** in land, and it can be exercised only by the persons and on the condition named in the statute that grants the right. This right arises only after the **equity of redemption** period ends. See 133 F. 2d 287, 289; 156 P. 1085, 1086. It is frequently found with reference to tax foreclosure statutes.

REDUCTIO AD ABSURDUM *(rā-dŭk'-tē-ō äd äb-sûr'-dŭm)*—Lat: to reduce to the absurd, e.g., to disprove a legal argument by showing that it ultimately leads to an absurd position.

RE-ENTRY [RIGHT OF] the assumption of **possession** pursuant to a right reserved when the former possession was parted with. It was a remedy given by the feudal law for nonpayment of rent, and also refers to a right reserved in the conveyance of a **fee** which is subject to a **condition** subsequent. Under the common law the grantor was permitted to exercise the right through **self-help**. Contemporary decisions usually deny a right to use self-help even though the right is formally reserved in the instrument of conveyance. A suit to **quiet title** is preferred. In the landlord-tenant relationship the right can be exercised only when it "is expressly reserved in the lease, for without such reservation the remedy of the **lessor** under the lease . . . is confined to an action on the covenant. The method of exercising the right is by an action of **ejectment** to recover possession of the demised premises." 62 N.E. 425, 427.

REFEREE a quasi-judicial officer appointed by a court for a specific purpose, having the power to take **testimony**, determine issues of factual dispute, and report the findings to the court upon which the court can enter judgment. See 46 N.W. 193, 76 Cal. Rep. 803, 806. "Referee" derives from "refer," i.e., the matters before the referee have been "referred" to him by the court. See **master.**

REFORMATION the re-writing of a contract, under **equitable** principles, in cases where the written terms of the contract do not express what was actually agreed upon. Thus, reformation is generally only decreed upon a **clear and convincing** showing of mutual **mistake**, for "[i]f only one party was mistaken, reformation will not be decreed unless the mistake on one side was caused by the other party's **fraud.**" Simpson, Contracts 200 (1965). **Parole evidence** is admissible for its **probative value** in establishing that a mistake has been made. 100 F. 2d 294.

Because reformation deals with written contracts incorrectly stating a prior agreement, it is not an action for the removal of provisions to which a party had never agreed. See Corbin, Contracts 395 (one vol. ed. 1952). Compare **rescission.**

REGISTER to record formally and exactly; to enroll; to enter precisely in a list or the like. 452 P. 2d 930, 933.

REGISTRY (OF DEEDS) serves to give notice to all third parties that there has been a change in the ownership of property effected by a **conveyance** of that property. See 54 A. 397, 398. See **Recording Acts.**

REGULATORY OFFENSE those crimes which are not inherently evil but are wrong only because prohibited by legislation. See 51 S.E. 945, 946. "Generally a crime involving 'moral turpitude' is **malum in se,** but otherwise it is **malum**

prohibitum." LeFave, and Scott, Criminal Law 29 (1972). Some examples of regulatory offenses are: "driving over the speed limit, . . . sale of intoxicating liquors, public intoxication, hunting without permission, carrying a concealed weapon, shooting in a public place, keeping slot machines, and passing through a toll gate without paying the toll." Id. at 30. Regulatory offenses are also called STATUTORY OFFENSES and often impose **strict liability** upon defendants for their violation.

REHEARING a retrial or reconsideration of the issues by the same court or body; "a new hearing and a new consideration of the case by the court [or other body] in which the suit was originally heard, and upon the **pleadings** and **depositions** already in the case." 14 A. 490, 494.

REHEARING EN BANC see **en banc.**

REJOINDER in pleadings, at **common law,** an answer to **plaintiff's replication** by some matter of fact, in an **action at law.**

RELATION BACK the principle that an act done at a later time is deemed by law to have occurred at a prior time. Thus, in practice, an amended **complaint** will relate back to the time of the filing of the initial complaint for the purpose of the statute of limitations. See Fed. R. Civ. Proc. 15(c).

RELEASE the act or writing by which some **claim,** right or interest is given up to the person against whom the claim, right or interest could have been enforced. See 149 N.E. 137, 138; 20 S.W. 1081, 1085. For example, a person may sign a "release" that ends his right to sue someone for an injury caused by that person.

In the law of property, the holder of a fee simple may convey to another a term of years and then subsequently "release" his **reversionary** interest (LEASE AND RELEASE) to the possessor of the term of years; conversely, should the possessor of the term of years quit the premises before the end of the term, he may be said to have "surrendered" the remainder of the term to the grantor.

RELEASE ON RECOGNIZANCE (ROR)

a condition under which an individual is released in lieu of **bail**, i.e., upon his promise to appear and answer a criminal charge. See, e.g., 18 U.S.C. §3146. Bail is intended to assure the defendant's appearance when required by the trial court. The ROR procedure permits his release on non-monetary conditions, generally involving only his promise to appear but sometimes involving special conditions (e.g., remaining in the custody of another, abiding by travel restrictions, etc.).

In determining whether to permit ROR, the court must "take into account the nature and circumstances of the offense charged, the weight of the evidence against the accused, the accused's family ties, employment, financial resources, character and mental condition, the length of his residence in the community, his record of convictions, and his record of appearance at court proceedings or of flight to avoid prosecution or failure to appear at court proceedings." Id. at §3146(1) (b).

RELEVANT MARKET a term used by the courts in determining whether a violation of an **antitrust statute** has occurred. Identification of the relevant market "takes into account not only the product (the line of commerce) but also its geographic area of distribution (the section of the country). . . . A geographic market must include commercial realities and at the same time be economically significant."345 F. Supp. 117, 120-121. "[C]ommodities reasonably interchangeable by consumers for the same purposes make up that 'part of the trade or commerce' monopolization of which may be illegal." 351 U.S. 395.

RELIANCE dependence, confidence, trust, repose of mind upon what is deemed sufficient support or authority. DETRIMENTAL RELIANCE involving reliance by one party on the acts, representations, or promises of another which cause the first party to allow or to effect a change for the worse in his position, is an important element in many legal contexts. If such a detrimental change of position is established, and if the reliance appears to have been justified under the circumstances, it may preclude revocation of an offer of waiver, may support a promise as a **contract** even without **consideration** [see **promissory estoppel**], and is a necessary ingredient in an action to recover upon a claim of **fraud**.

RELICTION the gradual and imperceptible withdrawal of water from land which it covers "by the lowering of its surface level from any cause." 91 N.W. 2d 57, 58. If the retreat of the waters is permanent—i.e., not merely seasonal—the owner of the contiguous property acquires ownership of the dry land thus created. See 152 N.W. 796. See **dereliction**; see also **accretion, avulsion.**

RELIEF the redress or assistance awarded to a **complainant**, by the court, especially a court of equity, including such remedies as **specific performance, injunction, rescission** of a contract, etc.; but the term generally does not comprehend an award of money **damages**. Thus the term **affirmative relief** is often used to indicate that the gist of relief is protection from future harm rather than compensation for past injury.

In feudal property law, "a relief was a sum payable to the lord by the **heir** of a deceased **tenant** for the privilege of succeeding to his ancestor's lands." Moynihan, Introduction to the Law of Real Property 18 (1962). Thus, it operated as a kind of inheritance tax. Because inheritance was a privilege to be paid for, the lord possessed unlimited discretion in fixing the price payable by the tenant for the privilege. Abuses of this prerogative led to the charging of exorbitant reliefs, which effectively disinherited the tenant's descendant, and therefore inspired many ingenious efforts to avoid them. Inheritance later became a matter of right, but the payment of relief to the lord continued.

The term more generally refers to the assistance which society gives to those in need, usually that which is administered by a branch of the government. Relief in this sense is often called public assistance or more simply "welfare."

RELIEF TO LITIGANTS see **contempt of court**.

RELINQUISHMENT see **abstention**.

REMAINDER that part of an **estate** in

land which is left upon the termination of the immediately preceding estate and which does not amount to a **reversion** to the original grantor or his heirs. The legal conditions for a remainder are that "there must be a precedent particular estate, whose regular termination the remainder must await; the remainder must be created by the same conveyance, and at the same time, as a particular estate; the remainder must **vest** in right during the continuance of the particular estate . . . [and that] no remainder can be limited after a **fee simple**." 57 S.W. 584, 599. Thus, "if A, being the owner of land [in fee simple] gives it by deed or will to B for life, and after the death of B, to C in fee, the estate given to C is called a 'remainder,' because it is the remnant or remainder of the estate or title which is left after taking out the lesser estate [life estate] given to B." 101 N.W. 195, 197.

CONTINGENT [EXECUTORY] REMAINDER "any remainder which is created in favor of an ascertained person but is subject to a **condition** precedent; is created in favor of an unborn person; or is created in favor of an existing but unascertained person. It was not, according to the older common law definition, an estate, but merely the possibility of an estate. . . . A contingent remainder becomes a **vested** remainder if any condition precedent is fulfilled and if the **remainderman** is ascertained before the termination of the preceding estate. Thus, A conveys to B for life, then to C and his heirs if C marries. At the time of the conveyance C is unmarried. The state of the title at that time is: life estate in B, contingent remainder in fee simple in C, reversion in fee simple in A. C marries while B is yet living. C's remainder becomes vested immediately on his marriage and all of the characteristics of a vested remainder attach thereto. The vesting of C's remainder operates to divest the **reversion** in A." Moynihan, Real Property, §18, p. 123 (1962).

EXECUTED REMAINDER a remainder interest which is **vested** as of the present, though the enjoyment of it is withheld until a future date.

VESTED REMAINDER "a remainder lim-

ited to a person in existence and ascertained who is given the right to immediate possession whenever and however the preceding estate or estates come to an end. It is an estate the owner of which is entitled to immediate possession subject only to the existence of a prior right to possession in another person which created the remainder," Moynihan, Real Property, §16, p. 116 (1962), e.g., A, owner in fee simple of Blackacre, conveys Blackacre to B for life, then to C and his heirs. C has a vested remainder of which he can take possession upon the death of B.

REMAINDERMAN one who has an interest in land **in futuro**; one who has an interest in an estate which becomes possessory at some point in the future after the termination, by whatever reason, of a present possessory interest. "Remainderman" usually refers to one who holds an interest in a **remainder** whether **vested** or **contingent**. It may also refer to one who holds an interest in an executory limitation.

REMAND to send back, as for further deliberation; "to send back to the tribunal [or body] from which it was appealed or moved." 155 N.W. 2d 507, 511. When a judgment is **reversed**, the **appellate court** usually remands the matter for a new trial to be carried out consistent with the principles announced by the appellate court in its opinion which ordered the remand. Sometimes the court will simply direct that "the matter be remanded [to the lower court] for further proceedings not inconsistent with this opinion."

REMEDY "the means employed to enforce or redress an injury." 272 F. 538, 539. The most common remedy at law consists of money **damages**.

EXTRAORDINARY REMEDY a **remedy** not usually available in an action at law or in **equity**, and ordinarily not employed unless the evidence clearly indicates that such a remedy is necessary to preserve the rights of the party. See 39 N.E. 2d 162, 166. Examples include an appointment of a **receiver**, a decree of **specific performance**, the issuing of a writ of mandamus or **writ of prohibition**, etc.

PROVISIONAL REMEDY a proceeding incidental to and in connection with a regular **action**, invoked while the primary action is pending in order to assure that the claimant's rights will be preserved or that he will not suffer irreparable injury. Its connection to the primary action is termed **collateral**. Examples include **attachment**, temporary **restraining orders**, preliminary **injunctions**, **appointment of receivers**, **arrest** and **bail**, etc.

REMITTER the act by which a person, who has a good title to land, and enters upon the land with less than his original title, is restored to his original good title, see 3 Bl.Comm.* 19; the doctrine whereby the law will relate back from a defective title to an earlier valid title.

REMITTITUR *(rē-mĭt'-tĭ-tûr)*— Lat: "in its broadest sense, the **procedural** process by which the **verdict** of a jury is diminished by subtraction. . . . The term is used to describe generally any reduction made by the court without the consent of the jury." 116 S.E. 2d 867, 871. "The theory of **additur** is a corollary to that of remittitur, the former to increase an inadequate verdict, the latter to decrease an excessive verdict. It is a universal rule . . . that a remittitur may not be granted by a court in lieu of a new trial unless consented to by the party 'unfavorably affected thereby.'" 258 F. 2d 17, 30.

REMOVAL refers to a change in place or position, as the removal of a **proceeding** to another court.

REMOVE CLOUD ON TITLE see **quiet title**.

RENT a profit in money, goods, or labor issuing yearly out of land and **tenements**, constituting a periodic return for the privilege of use, 262 N.Y.S. 217; the compensation, a return of value given at stated times for the possession of lands and tenements corporeal. 282 N.Y.S. 282.

RENVOI *(rähn'-vwä)*—Fr: "rule in some jurisdictions that in a **suit** by a nonresident upon a cause arising locally, his capacity to sue will be determined by looking to the law of his **domicile** rather than to the local law," 174 A. 508, 511; . . . the problem of renvoi is nothing more than the question whether the whole law including its **conflict of laws** or the internal law of a foreign state is looked to for solution when a reference is made to the law of another state. If the reference is to the whole law, as is often the case, an application of the renvoi concept is involved. . . . Take, for example, the case of a citizen of the United States permanently residing in France who dies leaving movables in New York. Assuming the New York conflict of laws rule to be that the law of the **decedent's domicile** will govern this matter, the New York **forum** would look to the "law" of France. If the forum should look to the law applicable to a Frenchman dying in France leaving movables there, the court would be rejecting the use of renvoi. If, however, the forum looks to the whole law, i.e., including the French conflicts rule, this is using the renvoi. See 181 N.Y.S. 336, 342.

RENUNCIATION in criminal law, the voluntary and complete abandonment of criminal purpose prior to the commission of a crime, or an act otherwise preventing its commission; in some jurisdictions it is an **affirmative defense** to inchoate offenses such as **attempts**, **conspiracy**, **solicitation** or offenses dependent upon the conduct of another (i.e., accessorial crimes). "Renunciation" is "not voluntary if it is motivated, in whole or in part, by circumstances, not present or apparent at the inception of the actor's course of conduct, which increase the probability of detection or apprehension or which make more difficult the accomplishment of the criminal purpose. Renunciation is not complete if it is motivated by a decision to postpone the criminal conduct until a more advantageous time or to transfer the criminal effort to another but similar objective or victim." Model Penal Code § 501(4) (Proposed Official Draft 1962). Compare **withdrawal**.

REORGANIZATION refers to the situation where substantially all the assets of an old **corporation** are transferred to a newly-formed corporation. The **stock-**

holders of the old corporation generally hold the same proportion of stock in the new corporation. See 207 F. 2d 495. The term is most often used to mean reorganization under Chapter X of the Federal Bankruptcy Act. See Henn, Law of Corporations at 827 (2d ed. 1961).

REPEAL abolish, rescind, annul by legislative act; "the abrogation or annulling of a previously existing law by the enactment of a subsequent statute, which either declares that the former law shall be revoked and abrogated, or which contains provisions so contrary to or irreconcilable with those of the earlier law that only one of the two can stand in force; the latter is the 'implied' repeal . . . the former, the 'express' repeal." 139 S.W. 443, 445.

REPLEVIN an **action** which lies for the recovery of the thing taken, rather than for the value of that thing; a possessory remedy; "a legal form of action ordinarily employed only to recover possession or the value of specific personal property unlawfully withheld from the plaintiff plus **damages** for its detention. . . . It is primarily a possessory action in which the issues ordinarily are limited to the plaintiff's title or right to possession of the goods." 182 A. 2d 219, 221. Compare **trespass; trover.**

REPLEVY to deliver to the owner; to redeliver goods which have been kept from the rightful owner. See 30 So. 788, 789. See **replevin.**

REPLICATION the plaintiff's answer or reply to the defendant's **plea** or **answer.** See 6 So. 374, 375. See **pleadings.**

REPLY a defensive **pleading,** its sole purpose being to interpose a **defense** to **new matter** pleaded in the **answer.** 255 S.W. 935, 937. In modern practice a reply is an extraordinary pleading and is not permitted except to respond to a **counterclaim** or by leave of court to an answer or third-party answer. See, e.g., Fed. R. Civ. Proc. 7(a).

REPRIEVE in criminal law, "the withdrawing of a **sentence** for an interval of time whereby the execution is suspended. . . . It is merely the postponement of the sentence for a time. It does not and

cannot defeat the ultimate execution of the judgment of the court, but merely delays it." 131 S.W. 2d 583, 585. Reprieves are most commonly granted by the Governor or President to postpone the execution of a death sentence. If the death sentence is to be modified, the action will be a **commutation** or **pardon.** See also **executive clemency.**

REQUIREMENTS CONTRACT see **contract.**

RES *(rās)*—Lat: the subject matter of **actions** that are primarily **in rem,** i.e., actions that establish rights in relation to an object, as opposed to a person, or **in personam.** See 42 N.Y.S. 626, 628. For example, in an action which resolves a conflict over **title** to **real property,** the land in question is the res. Tangible **personal property** can also be a "res," as in the corpus of a trust. In a **quasi in rem proceeding,** land or **chattels** that are seized and **attached** at the beginning of the action, in order that they may later be used to satisfy a personal **claim,** are the res of such suits. The term refers as well to the status of individuals. Thus, in a divorce suit, the marital status is the res. The purpose of a res is to establish a court's **jurisdiction,** i.e., if the property lies within the state where the action is brought, or an individual in a divorce action is a **domiciliary** of the state, then jurisdiction is established.

RES AJUDICATA see **res judicata.**

RESCIND to abrogate a **contract,** release the parties from further obligations to each other and restore the parties to the positions they would have occupied if the contract had never been made. See 163 N.W. 2d 35, 38. For instance, in "rescinding" a sales contract, any monies paid or goods received would usually be returned to their original holders though the parties could agree otherwise.

RESCISSION the cancellation of a **contract** and the return of the parties to the positions they would have occupied if the contract had not been made. Rescission may be brought about by the mutual consent of the parties, by the conduct of the parties, or by a **decree** to that effect by a **court of equity.** For instance, there is a "recission" of a contract if both parties expressly or by their actions implicitly agree not to go through with the contract before their positions have been altered by the performance of their duties under contract.

RESCUE DOCTRINE tort rule which holds a **tortfeasor** liable to his victim's rescuer, should the latter injure himself during a reasonable rescue attempt; "one who had, through his **negligence**, endangered the safety of [himself or] another, may be held liable for injuries sustained by a third person [who attempts] to save such other from injury." 393 S.W. 2d 48, 57. The doctrine derives from the fact that "the original wrong which imperils life is not only a wrong insofar as the imperiled victim is concerned, but is a wrong also to his rescuer." 146 A. 2d 705, 712. One who attempts such a rescue cannot be charged with **contributory negligence**, provided his rescue attempt was not rash or reckless. See 188 P. 2d 121, 123, 124.

RESERVATION a clause in any **instrument** of **conveyance**, such as a **deed**, which creates a lesser **estate**, or some right, interest, or **profit** in the estate granted, to be retained by the **grantor**. See 214 P. 2d 212, 214, 85 A. 2d 775, 778.

Also refers to a tract of land, usually substantial, set aside for specific purposes such as military grounds, parks, Indian lands.

In practice, the term refers to the act of a court or other body in delaying decision on a point of law. The court may "reserve decision" and proceed with the matter or may adjourn the proceedings pending its decision. When the court "takes the matter under advisement" it in effect reserves decision, often so that it may render a written decision.

RES GESTAE *(räs gĕs'-tī)*—Lat: the thing done; "the circumstances which are the undesigned incidents of the **litigated** act, which are admissible [as **evidence**] when illustrative of such act. These incidents may be separated from the act by a lapse of time more or less appreciable . . . Their sole distinguishing feature is that they should be the necessary inci-

dents of the litigated act,—necessary in this sense: that they are part of the immediate preparations for, or emanations of, such act, and are not produced by the calculated policy of the actors." 63 A. 2d 28, 31. Declarations which are subject to the **hearsay rule**, may be admissible if they qualify as res gestae; i.e., if they constitute a part of "the thing done," under a recognized exception to the hearsay rule. See 89 S.W. 2d 801, 809.

RESIDENCE broadly, any place of abode that is more than temporary. See 88 Cal. Rptr. 628, 630. The term is often used as being synonymous with **domicile**, since a person's residence is usually also his domicile and since the two terms have been held equivalent in judicial construction of some statutes. However, in a strict sense, "residence" applies to the mere fact of a person dwelling in a particular abode, while "domicile" is a person's legal home, or the place that the law presumes is his permanent residence, regardless of temporary absence. See 67 A. 2d 273, 275. Traditionally, one may have more than one residence, but only a single domicile.

RESIDENT ALIEN   see **alien.**

RESIDUARY BEQUEST   see **bequest.**

RESIDUARY CLAUSE clause in a **will** which conveys to the beneficiary of a **residuary legacy** (residuary legatee) everything in a **testator**'s **estate** not **devised** to a specific **legatee**; "includes in its gift any property or interest in the will which, for any reason, eventually falls into the general residue. It will include **legacies** which were originally **void**, either because the disposition was illegal, or because for any other reason it was impossible that it should take effect; and it includes such legacies as may lapse by events subsequent to the making of the will. [But see **antilapse statutes.**] It operates to transfer to the **residuary legatee** such portion of his property as the **testator** has not perfectly disposed of." 20 N.E. 602, 604.

RESIDUARY ESTATE that part of a **testator**'s estate which remains undisposed of after all of the **estate** has been discharged through the satisfaction of all claims and specific legacies with the exception of the dispositions authorized by the residuary clause; "that portion of the estate which remains after the payment of debts and other classes of legacies; it is conditional upon something remaining after the paramount claims on the testator's estate are satisfied." 43 N.E. 2d 769, 775.

RESIDUARY LEGACY "a general legacy into which fall all the assets of the estate after the satisfaction of other legacies and the payment of all debts of the estate and all costs of administration." 44 S.E. 2d 659, 664.

RES IPSA LOQUITUR *(rās ēp'-sȧ lō'-kwĭ-tûr)*—Lat: the thing speaks for itself; "a rule of evidence whereby **negligence** of the alleged wrongdoer may be inferred from the mere fact that the accident happened, provided: (1) the character of the accident and the circumstances attending it lead reasonably to the belief that in the absence of negligence it would not have occurred, and (2) the thing which caused the injury is shown to have been under the [exclusive] management of the alleged wrongdoer." 484 S.W. 113, 115. The rule may not apply when direct evidence of negligence exists. See 270 So. 2d 900, 904. "The gist of it, and the key to it, is the inference, or process of reasoning by which the conclusion is reached. This must be based upon the evidence given, together with a sufficient background of human experience to justify the conclusion. It is not enough that plaintiff's counsel can suggest a possibility of negligence. The evidence must sustain the **burden of proof** by making it appear more likely than not." Prosser, Torts 212 (4th ed. 1971). The procedural effect of successful invocation of the doctrine is to shift the **burden** of going forward with the evidence, which normally attaches to the plaintiff, to the defendant, who is thereby charged with introducing evidence to refute the presumption of negligence which has been created.

RESISTING ARREST common law offense involving physical efforts to oppose a lawful arrest: "In every case where one person has a right to arrest

or restrain another, the other can have no rights to resist, since the two rights cannot coexist. . . . No right of **self-defense** can arise out of such a circumstance." 173 P. 1076, 1080-1081. Most often, the person attempting to make the arrest is a police officer in whose presence an offense has occurred, and the resistance is classified as an **assault** and **battery** upon the officer. See, e.g. 274 S.W. 17.

RES JUDICATA a thing decided; a matter adjudged. Doctrine by which "a final judgment by a court of competent **jurisdiction** is conclusive upon the **parties** in any subsequent **litigation** involving the same cause of action. . . . The policy underlying the doctrine of res judicata is one of repose, the same policy which is reflected in the **statute of limitations** with state claims." Green, Civil Procedure 201 (1972). Compare **collateral estoppel**. See also **bar; merger**.

RESPITE a delay, postponement, or **forebearance** of a **sentence**, not comprehending a permanent suspension of execution of the judgment, see 237 P. 525, 527; also, a delay in repayment, granted to a debtor by his creditor. See **grace period**.

RESPONDEAT SUPERIOR *(rā'-spôn-dā'-ät sū-pĕr'-ē-ôr)*—Lat: let the superior reply. This doctrine is invoked when there is a master-**servant** relationship between two parties. The "respondeat superior" doctrine stands for the proposition that when an employer, dubbed "master," is acting through the facility of an employee or **agent**, dubbed "servant," and tort **liability** is incurred during the course of this agency due to some fault of the agent, then the employer or master must accept the responsibility. Implicit in this is the **common law** notion that a duty rests upon every man to conduct his affairs so as not to injure another, whether or not in the management of his affairs he employs agents or servants. See 143 P. 2d 554, 556. This doctrine is **civil** in its application. See 9 N.W. 2d 518, 521. See **scope of employment**. Compare **vicarious liability**.

RESPONDENT in **equity**, the party who answers a **bill** or other **pleading**. "Anyone who answers or responds may properly be called a 'respondent'." 158 N.W. 2d 809, 812. The term also refers to the party against whom an **appeal** is brought.

RESTATEMENT an attempt by the American Law Institute ". . . to present an orderly statement of the general **common law** of the United States, including in that term not only the law developed solely by judicial decision, but also the law that has grown from the application by the courts of statutes. . . ." Restatement, Torts viii, ix (1st ed). Restatements are compiled according to subject matter; those compiled include contracts, torts, property, trusts, agency, conflict of laws, judgments, restitution, security, and foreign relations.

The policy of the A.L.I. in the Restatements 2nd has turned away from a mere head-count of the jurisdictions in determining what the general state of the law is and has taken into account other factors, namely, what influential jurisdictions and well-thought out opinions reveal about the modern trend of the law. See Wechsler, The Course of the Restatements, 55 A.B.A.J. 147 (1969).

RESTITUTION act of making good, or of giving the equivalent for, any loss, damage or injury; **indemnification.** 3 A. 2d 521, 525. As a remedy it is available to prevent **unjust enrichment,** to correct an erroneous payment, and to permit an **aggrieved party** to recover deposits advanced on a contract. Under the Uniform Commercial Code an aggrieved party is entitled to restitution and **damages** for a breach to the extent the latter can be proved. See U.C.C. § 2-711. At common law the plaintiff would have to elect between restitution and damages. See 22 Pick. 457 (Mass. 1839). As a contract remedy, restitution is limited to the value of a performance rendered by the injured party, see Restatement, Contracts §347, and ordinarily requires that both parties to a transaction be returned to the **status quo** ante. See 22 Pick. 457.

In criminal law, restitution is sometimes ordered as a condition of a **probationary sentence.** See, e.g., N.Y. Penal Law §65.10(2)(f).

RESTRAINING ORDER an order granted without notice or hearing, demanding the preservation of the **status quo** until a hearing can be had to determine the propriety of **injunctive relief,** temporary or permanent. A restraining order is always temporary in nature inasmuch as it is granted pending a hearing and thus is often called a T.R.O. [temporary restraining order]. The restraining order is made upon application of a plaintiff which requests the court to forbid an action or threatened action of defendant; the form of request will generally be upon an order to show cause why the injunctive relief the plaintiff seeks ought not be granted. After a hearing a preliminary or permanent injunction may issue.

Although sometimes used interchangeably, a restraining order is distinguished from an injunction in that the restraining order issues without a hearing whereas the injunction will follow a hearing.

RESTRAINT OF TRADE [UNREASONABLE] as used in the Sherman Antitrust Act, illegal per se "restraints" interfering with free competition in business and commercial transactions, which tend to restrict production, affect prices, or otherwise control the market to the detriment of purchasers or consumers of goods and services. Ordinarily reasonable restraints of trade are made unreasonable if they are intended to accomplish the equivalent of an illegal restraint. 255 F. 2d 214, 230. This term means the same thing in the trust laws as it means at common law. 182 F. 2d 158, 167.

RESTRAINT ON ALIENATION restriction on the ability to **convey real property** interests, any attempt at which was in derogation of the **common law** policy in favor of free alienability; interests thus created were void or voidable as an unlawful restraint on alienation.

Although fees on condition subsequent and fee simple determinables are, in general, permissable **estates,** a condition which states, "but if any attempt is made to alienate the land, the **grantor** and his **heirs** reserve the right to re-enter and declare the estate forfeit," would be against the policy. As a consequence, a rule exists which requires that there be a person capable of transferring absolute interest in possession within a certain period of time. See 201 P. 2d 69, 73. See **alienation; rule against perpetuities**. However, in **estates** created by short-term **leases** such restraints are permissible. The determination of validity is based upon the nature and quality (duration) of the restraint, the type of estate in question, and the penalty imposed for violation of the restraint.

RESTRICTIVE COVENANT a promise existing as part of an agreement restricting the use of **real property** or the kind of buildings that may be erected thereupon; the promise is usually expressed by the creation of an express **covenant**, reservation, or exception in a **deed**. In order for a grantor to enforce the covenant against remote grantees [i.e., subsequent owners who take title from the first grantee], the covenant must "**run with the land**." Restrictive covenants that discriminate racially, e.g., by limiting the use of the property or its transfer to white persons, may be unenforceable since a court will be unable, consistent with the **equal protection clause** of the Fourteenth Amendment, to lend its support to enforcement. See 334 U.S. 1; 346 U.S. 249. It matters not that a racially restrictive covenant is expressed as a condition and thus purports to automatically cause a **reversion** to the grantor. See 316 P. 2d 252; but see 388 S.E. 2d 114. See also 382 U.S. 296.

RESTRICTIVE INDORSEMENT see **indorsement**.

RESULTING TRUST see **trust**.

RESULTING USE see **use**.

RETAINER compensation paid in advance to an attorney for services to be performed in a specific case. A "retainer" includes fees "not only for the rendition of professional services when requested, but also for the attorney taking the case, making himself available to handle it, and refusing employment by [the client's] adversary." 201 S.E. 2d 794, 796. A retainer may represent the whole sum to be charged (plus expenses) but more often is in the nature of a deposit, with the attorney rendering from time to time or at the conclusion of the matter a statement of amounts owed by the client for services rendered.

RETIRE in reference to **bills of exchange**, "to recover, redeem, regain by the payment of a sum of money; . . . to withdraw from circulation or from the market; to take up and pay." 110 F. 2d 878, 879. For example, the federal government retires a Series E bond when the holder turns it in for cash upon **maturity**.

The term also refers to the voluntary withdrawal from office, a public station, business, or other employment. See 131 A. 2d 512, 515.

A **jury** is "retired" at that point when the judge has submitted the case for its consideration and **verdict**. See 192 S.W. 922, 923.

RETRACTION to withdraw a **renunciation**, declaration, **accusation**, promise, etc. As to a **defamation**, "it has been held that a retraction . . . can be effected only if it is a full and unequivocal one which does not contain lurking insinuations or hesitant withdrawals. It must, in short, be an honest endeavor to repair all the wrong done by the defamatory imputation." 123 A. 2d 473, 477.

RETROACTIVE refers to a rule of law, whether legislative or judicial, which relates to things already decided in the past. "Retroactive" includes both RETROSPECTIVE and **ex post facto**, the former technically applying only to **civil** laws, the latter to criminal or penal laws. A retrospective law is one that relates back to a previous transaction and gives it some different legal effect from that which it had under the law when it occurred, and, in the sense in which it is constitutionally objectionable, is one that impairs **vested** rights acquired under existing laws, or creates a new obligation or attaches a new disability with respect to past transactions. Similarly, in respect to **ex post facto** laws, "retroactivity" refers to the imposition of criminal liability on behavior that took place prior to the enactment of the criminal statute. State constitutions may prohibit their legislatures from enacting retrospective laws; ex post facto laws are prohibited by the Constitution of the United States. It should be noted, however, that judicially created law (common law) is often "retroactive" in its effect, the court's decision being made on the basis of a previously existent fact pattern wherein the actors could not possibly have predicted at the time the court's eventual interpretation of the law but are nevertheless held accountable to it.

In constitutional law, decisions announcing new or different rights for criminal defendants are often given full retroactive effect so as to permit a **collateral attack** on previously finalized judgments. Because of the tremendous impact on the administration of justice the Court has held some of these decisions not to be retroactive where the integrity of the fact-finding process was not challenged by the new rules and where there has been reliance by law enforcement authorities upon the former practice. Compare 393 U.S. 5 (holding fully retroactive a right to counsel) with 384 U.S. 719 (holding that the new **Miranda** rights applicable only to trials not yet begun when that decision was handed down) and 394 U.S. 244 (holding new search and seizure rules applicable only to searches not yet conducted).

RETROSPECTIVE   see **retroactive.**

RETURN   a report from an official, such as a sheriff, stating what he has done in respect to a command from the court, or why he has failed to do what was requested. See Bl. Comm.* 287. A **false return** is a false or incorrect statement by the official which acts to the detriment of an interested party. See 70 S.W. 192.

The term may also refer to a report from an individual or corporation as to its earnings, etc. for tax or other governmental purposes.

REVERSAL   as used in opinions, judgments, and mandates, the setting aside, annulling, vacating or changing to the contrary the decision of a lower court or other body. Compare **overrule; remand.** See also **affirm.**

REVERSIBLE ERROR   error substantially affecting **appellant's** legal rights and obligations which, if uncorrected,

would result in a miscarriage of justice and which justifies reversing a judgment in the court below; synonymous with prejudicial error. See 314 P. 2d 973, 976. Compare **harmless error.**

REVERSION   an **interest** created by operation of law by a **conveyance** of property but not transferred by that conveyance which thus remains in the **grantor;** "a **future estate** created by operation of law to take effect in possession in favor of a **lessor** or a **grantor** or his **heirs,** or their heirs of a **testator,** after the natural termination of a prior particular estate leased, granted or **devised.**" 30 A. 2d 57. Compare **remainder.**

REVERTER   see **reversion.** See also **possibility of a reverter.**

REVIEW   judicial re-examination of the proceedings of a court or other body; a reconsideration by the same court or body of its former decision; often used to express what an **appellate court** does when it examines the **record** of a lower court or agency's determination which is on appeal before the court.

REVISED   STATUTES   statutes that have been changed, altered, reorganized, or simply reenacted. Their enactment is generally regarded as repealing and replacing the former laws. See 171 S.W. 2d 41 at 45.

REVOCATION   the recall of a power or authority conferred, or the cancellation of an **instrument** previously made, 300 N.Y.D. 351, 361; often used to signify the cancellation of an offer by the offeror, which, if effective, terminates the offeree's power of **acceptance.**

REVOCATION OF PAROLE   see **probation.**

REVOCATION OF PROBATION   see **probation.**

REVOKE   to recall a power or authority previously conferred, vacate an **instrument** previously made, or annul, repeal, **rescind** or cancel privileges. 67 N.E. 2d 570, 572. For example, in many states motorists who receive more than a specified number of points for motor vehicle moving violations may have their licenses revoked.

RIGHT OF ACTION see **cause of action.**

RIGHT OF FIRST PUBLICATION see **copyright.**

RIGHT OF REDEMPTION see **redemption.**

RIGHT OF RE-ENTRY see **re-entry, right of.**

RIGHT OR WRONG TEST see **M'Naghten Rule.**

RIGOR MORTIS *(rĭ'-gôr môr'-tĭs)*–Lat: medical terminology depicting the stiffness, numbness or hardness, of the muscles which occurs after death. "Medcal authorities agree that it is not possible to fix the time of death from the onset of rigor mortis. . . . 'A period of death may be assigned [based on rigor mortis] which is inconsistent with the proved facts, and thus give immunity to murderers [or] . . . help convict an innocent man'." 47 A. 2d 450, 456, 457.

RIPARIAN RIGHTS rights which accrue to owners of land on the banks of water ways, such as the use of such water, ownership of soil under the water, etc.; "rights not originating in grants, but [arising] by **operation of law**, and [which] are called 'natural rights,' because they arise by reason of the ownership of lands upon or along streams of water, which are furnished by nature, and the lands to which these natural rights are attached are called in law 'riparian lands.' Riparian lands, in the language of the cases and treatises, include by nature the lands over as [well as] those along which the stream flows, and riparian rights are incident to lands on the bank, as well as those forming the bed of the stream." 70 A. 472, 479.

RIPE FOR JUDGMENT doctrine in constitutional law under which the Supreme Court, in accordance with its policy of self-restraint, will not decide cases "in advance of the necessity of deciding them." 331 U.S. 549.

RISK OF NONPERSUASION see **burden of proof.**

ROBBERY forcible stealing; a common law offense defined as "the **felonious** taking of property from the person of another by violence or by putting him in fear. A felonious taking in his presence is a taking from the person when it is done by violence and against his will. . . . The violence or putting in fear must be at the time of the act or immediately preceding it." 152 F. 2d 808, 809. Thus, a person commits "robbery" when, "in the course of committing a **larceny**, he uses or threatens the immediate use of physical force upon another person for the purpose of: (1) preventing or overcoming resistance to the taking of the property or to the retention thereof immediately after the taking; or (2) compelling the owner of such property or another person to deliver up the property or to engage in other conduct which aids in the commission of the larceny." New York Penal Law § 160.00.

ROGATORY LETTERS "a formal communication from a court in which an **action** is pending, to a foreign court, requesting that the **testimony** of a **witness** residing in such foreign jurisdiction be taken under the direction of the court addressed and transmitted to the court making the request." 215 N.W. 21, 22. The term is applicable to interstate as well as to international affairs. See 269 N.W. 498, 499.

RULE AGAINST PERPETUITIES the rule that "no [contingent] **interest** is good unless it must **vest**, if at all, not later than twenty-one years after some life in being at the creation of the interest." Gray, Rule Against Perpetuities, 191 (4th ed., 1942).
The weight of authority is that the rule against perpetuities is aimed against the remoteness of vesting of **estates** or interests in property. The minority view is that a perpetuity involves the suspension of the power of **alienation** beyond the time permitted by law. See Burby, Real Property, 412 (3rd ed., 1965). "Its ultimate purpose is to prevent the clogging of title beyond reasonable limits in time by contingent interests and to keep land freely alienable in the market places." Smith & Boyer, Survey of the Law of Real Property, 112 (2d ed., 1971).

RULE IN SHELLEY'S CASE "When in the same **conveyance** an **estate** for life is given to the ancestor with **remainder** to the ancestor's **heirs**, then the ancestor takes the **fee simple** remainder estate and the heirs take nothing;" e.g., 'A,' fee owner, conveys "to 'B' for life, then to the heirs of 'B.' 'B' takes both the life estate and the remainder in fee simple." Smith & Boyer, Survey of the Law of Real Property, 102 (2nd ed., 1971). The rule, created in 1324, has been abolished in England and in a majority of American jurisdictions. Id. at 106.

RULE IN WILD'S CASE in property law, a rule of construction by which a devise to "B and his children," where B has no children at the time the gift **vests** in B, was read to mean a gift to B in **fee tail**, the words "and his children" thus being construed as **words of limitation** and not **words of purchase.** The popularity of the fee tail has declined and most American jurisdictions have repudiated the Rule in Wild's Case, construing the language quoted to be a gift of a **life estate** to B, with a **remainder** to his children. See Moynihan, Introduction to the Law of Real Property 46-47 (1962).

RULE NISI procedure by which one party by way of an **ex parte** application or an order to **show cause** calls upon another to show cause why the rule proposed in his order should not be made final by the court. If no cause is shown the court will enter an order rendering "absolute" [i.e., final] the rule, thereby requiring whatever was sought to be accomplished by the rule.

RUN WITH THE LAND a phrase used with respect to **covenants** in the law of real property meaning that "the burdens or benefits, or both, of the covenant pass to the persons who succeed to the **estate** of the original contracting parties, the idea being that the covenant runs because it is attached to the estate in the land as it is conveyed from one to another in the **chain of title.**" Smith and Boyer, Survey of the Law of Property 348 (2d ed. 1971). In order for a covenant to run with the land at law, the necessary formalities for creation of such a covenant must be met: the **covenant** must "touch and concern the land" [meaning that it must increase the use or value of the land benefitted, or it must decrease the use or value of the land burdened]; the parties must intend that the covenant will run with the land; and there must be **privity** of estate. See Id. Cribbet, Principles of the Law of Property 283 (1962). In some jurisdictions such a covenant can only be created at the time a conveyance of land takes place.

S

SALE a **contract** by which **property** real or personal, is transferred from the seller [vendor] to the buyer [vendee] for a fixed price in money, paid or agreed to be paid by the buyer. 172 F. 940, 942. "A 'sale' contemplates a free **offer** and **acceptance,** a seller and purchaser dealing at **arm's length,** and the fixing and payment of a purchase price." 46 N.E. 2d 184, 191.

ABSOLUTE SALE a sale wherein the property passes to the buyer upon completion of the agreement between the parties. See 32 A. 227, 228.

CONDITIONAL SALE "a sale in which the vendee receives the **possession** and right of use of the goods sold, but transfer of the title to the vendee is made dependent upon the performance of some condition, usually the full payment of the purchase price." 434 P. 2d 655, 657. The "conditional sale" becomes absolute on the occurrence of the condition. See 131 N.E. 816, 817. It also refers to a "purchase accompanied by an agreement to resell upon particular terms." Id.

EXECUTED SALE in contracts to an EXECUTORY SALE [see below], it exists when "nothing remains to be done by either party to effect a complete transfer of the title to the subject matter of the sale." 167 S.W. 2d 407, 411.

EXECUTION SALE see **sheriff's sale.**

EXECUTORY SALE in contrast to an EXECUTED SALE, it is an agreement to sell wherein "something remains to be done by either party before delivery and passing of title," 167 S.W. 2d 407, 411; an agreement to sell where something more remains to be done before all the terms of the agreement are performed.

PUBLIC SALE a sale upon notice to the public and in which members of the public may bid. See 99 N.W. 2d 885, 888. See also U.C.C. §2-706.

SALE IN GROSS as applied to a sale of land, a sale by the tract or as a whole, without regard to any warranty as to quantity (acres); sometimes referred to as a CONTRACT OF HAZARD. See 77 Va. 610, 616; 169 A. 203, 205.

SALE BY SAMPLE a sale of goods in existence in bulk, but not present for examination, where it is mutually understood that the goods not exhibited conform to the sample; such a sale carries with it an implied **warranty** that the bulk of the goods purchased conforms to the sample. See 83 S.W. 78, 81; 120 S.E. 427, 429; U.C.C. § 2-313 (I) (C).

SALE ON APPROVAL a transaction in which goods delivered primarily for use may be returned if the buyer is unsatisfied with them even though they may conform to the contract. U.C.C. §2-326 (1) (a); 175 S.W. 2d 218. If the goods are delivered primarily for resale, rather than for use, the transaction is termed a SALE OR RETURN. U.C.C. §2-326 (1) (b). Goods so consigned may be returned if unsold in a reasonable amount of time at the buyer's risk and expense. Id. at §2-327 (2) (b).

SALE WITH RIGHT OF REDEMPTION sale where seller reserves the right to take back title to property he has sold upon repayment of the purchase price; it is distinct from transactions where a purchaser grants an option to his seller to repurchase. See 263 So. 2d 96, 105.

SHERIFF'S SALE see **sheriff's sale.**

TAX SALE a sale of land for the non-payment of taxes. See 25 So. 105, 108. See **foreclosure.**

SANCTION a consequence or punishment for violation of accepted norms of social conduct, which may be of two kinds: those which redress **civil** injuries, i.e., civil sanctions; and those which punish crimes, i.e., penal sanctions. See 81 S.W. 526, 528. Also, to approve; "convey[s] the idea of sacredness, or of authority." 43 N.E. 80, 81.

SATISFACTION [OF A DEBT] a release and discharge of the obligation in reference to which it is given. 105 P. 2d 342, 345. See **accord; accord and satisfaction.**

SCIENTER *(sē'-ĕn-têr)* — Lat: knowledge; previous knowledge of an operative state of facts; frequently signifies "guilty knowledge." As used in **pleadings**, it signifies that "the alleged **crime** or **tort** was done designedly, understandingly, knowingly or with guilty knowledge," 211 N.W. 346; "a term usually employed in legal **issues** involving **fraud**, means knowledge on the part of a person making representations, at the time they were made, that they are false . . . the false statements must have been made intentionally to deceive or with what is recognized as the legal equivalent to a deliberately fraudulent intent to deceive." 444 S.W. 2d 498, 505. See also **culpable; mens rea.**

SCOPE OF EMPLOYMENT the range of activities encompassed by one's employment; refers to those acts done while performing one's job duties; "[t]he phrase . . . [was] adopted by the courts for the purpose of determining a master's **liability** for the acts of his **servants**, [and] has 'no fixed or technical meaning,' . . . 'the ultimate question is whether it is just that the loss resulting from the servant's acts should be considered one of the normal risks of the business in which the servant is employed which that business should bear.' " 145 So. 743, 745. The phrase is "a convenient means of defining those **tortious** acts of the servant not ordered by the master for which the policy of law imposes liability upon the master." 181 A. 2d 565, 569. The master (usually, the employer) is **vicariously liable** only for those torts of the servant (employee) which are committed within the scope of his employment. See **respondeat superior.** See also **Employers' Liability Acts; Workmen's Compensation Acts.**

SCRIP DIVIDEND see **dividend.**

SCRIVENER a term, not usually used in the United States, which signifies a writer or scribe, particularly one who draws legal documents. Also, one who acts as the **agent** for another, investing and managing that other's property, whether money or otherwise, for a fee.

SEAL at common law, an impression on wax, wafer, or other tenacious substance capable of being impressed. See 30 S.W. 132, 133. "The purpose of a 'seal' is to attest in a formal manner to the execution of an **instrument**." 42 So. 959, 960. "Among the forms of 'seal' that are in use in most of the states are wax, a gummed wafer, an impression in the paper itself, the word 'seal,' the letters 'L.S.' (signfying 'lacus sigilli'), [and] a pen scrawl." Corbin Contracts 3241 (one-volume ed., 1952).

A **seal** of a corporation is sometimes called a COMMON SEAL. See 65 A. 526, 527.

SEALED INSTRUMENT one that is signed and has the **seal** of the signer attached. "To render a **contract** a sealed instrument, it must be so recited in the body of the instrument and a seal or scroll must be placed after the signature." 16 S.E. 2d 502, 504. A sealed contract was a FORMAL CONTRACT (as opposed to a contract without a seal which was called a SIMPLE CONTRACT) and is often called a CONTRACT UNDER SEAL; such a contract did not require **consideration** at **common law**, Corbin Contracts §252 (1952); a deed under seal likewise required no consideration. Today any symbol, even the word "seal" or the letters "L.S." printed on a form, will, if so intended, constitute the necessary seal. Statutes have eliminated most of the special effects of sealed instruments at common law in most of the states though a number of states continue the common law significance of sealed instruments. Even in many states which have purported to abrogate these effects, longer periods for enforcing debts founded upon sealed instruments exist under their **statutes of limitations**. See Id. §254.

Under the Uniform Commercial Code the use of a seal is intended to have no effect upon the transaction; the use of a seal "does not constitute the writing a sealed instrument and the law with respect to sealed instruments does not apply." U.C.C. 2-203.

SEARCH AND SEIZURE a police practice whereby a person or place is searched and evidence useful in the investigation and prosecution of crime is seized. The search and seizure is constitutionally limited by the Fourth and Fourteenth Amendments to the United States Constitution and by provisions in the several state constitutions, statutes, and rules of court. A search and seizure must be reasonable. This reasonableness usually requires the existence of **probable cause** to believe that the item searched for was involved in criminal activity and will be located at the place to be searched. In most circumstances a **search warrant** is required prior to the search and seizure. However, there are several exigent circumstances where such warrants are not required: (1) searches that are incident to an arrest, see 267 U.S. 132, 399 U.S. 30, [which must be limited to the person and the immediately surrounding area, see 395 U.S. 752 (1969)]; (2) frisks conducted as part of an investigative stop [limited to the outer frisk for a weapon, see 392 U.S. 1]; (3) seizures of items in **plain view**, see 390 U.S. 234; (4) seizures of abandoned property, see 265 U.S. 57; (5) searches and seizures in exigent circumstances where it would be impossible or unwise to secure a warrant, see 387 U.S. 294; (6) searches where there is proper consent, see 255 U.S. 313; 412 U.S. 218; and (7) searches at international borders. See 413 U.S. 266.

If there is an unreasonable or otherwise unconstitutional search, the evidence seized will be excluded at any criminal proceeding where the defendant has **standing** to object to its introduction. See 367 U.S. 643. Furthermore, all fruits of the illegal search are excluded. See 251 U.S. 385. Victims of an illegal search may also bring a civil **tort** suit against the officers for the violation of their civil right of privacy. See 403 U.S. 388.

SEARCH WARRANT an order issued by a judge directing certain law enforcement officers to conduct a search of specified premises for specified things or persons, and to bring them before the court. It has long been a requirement of fundamental law that searches be conducted after the obtaining of a search warrant. The requirement was embedded in American law by the Fourth Amendment to the Constitution, which is now applicable to the states through the Fourteenth Amendment, see 338 U.S. 25 (1949), and requires that all searches be reasonable and that search warrants issue only upon **probable cause** supported by sworn allegations and that the warrant "particularly describe the place to be searched, and the persons or things to be seized." The paramount evil to which the Fourth Amendment is addressed was the use of GENERAL WARRANTS to be used by the government to conduct unreasonable searches. See 116 U.S. 612. Thus, general searches of the described premises and the seizure of things not described in the warrant, except in certain instances where the unmentioned thing is in **"plain view,"** have been proscribed by Supreme Court construction of the Fourth Amendment. See 403 U.S. 443.

The "reasonableness" requirement of the Fourth Amendment does not mean that a warrant is required for all searches since there are exceptional circumstances under which a warrant is not required, although probable cause may be required. See Cook, Constitutional Rights of The Accused, Pretrial Rights, §§43-58 (1971). A major exception to the warrant requirement is that a search of the person and the area within his control is permitted without warrant, incident to a valid **arrest** [i.e., one made upon probable cause]. See 414 U.S. 218.

In those cases where warrants are required, only a judicial officer can issue it, and only upon a showing of probable cause that the described item is located in the designated place and that it was involved in the planning or commission of a crime. See 333 U.S. 10, 403 U.S. 443.

SECUNDUM *(sĕ-kŭn'-dŭm)*—Lat: immediately after, beside, next to. In law publishing the second series of a treatise may be called secundum as in Corpus Juris Secundum (C.J.S.).

SECURED TRANSACTIONS see **credit, security interest.**

SECURITIES stock **certificates, bonds,** or other **evidence** of a secured indebtedness or of a right created in the holder to participate in profits or **assets** distribution of a profit-making enterprise; more generally, written assurances for the return or payment of money, 91 P. 2d 892, 895; **instruments** giving to their legal holders right to money or other property. They are therefore instruments which have value and are used as such in regular channels of commerce.

PUBLIC SECURITIES those certificates and other **negotiable instruments** evidencing the debt of a governmental body.

SECURITY DEPOSIT money which **tenant** deposits with **landlord** so as to insure landlord that tenant will abide by the lease agreements; "represents a fund from which the landlord may obtain payment for damages caused by the tenant during his occupancy." 172 So. 2d 26, 28. Leases sometimes provide that the landlord may retain the security deposit as **liquidated damages** in the event that the lease is terminated at the tenant's request prior to the expiration of the full term of the lease. In some jurisdictions the new legislation now requires that no more than a certain sum (often 1 or 1½ times the monthly rental) be required as security and that it be held separately from the landlord's other funds in an interest paying account. See, e.g., N.J.S. §46:8-19. Compare **surety.**

SECURITY INTEREST an **interest** in **real** or **personal property** which secures the payment of an obligation. Under the Uniform Commercial Code security interests are limited to personal property and **fixtures.** See U.C.C. 1-201 (37).

At common law, security interests are either consensual or arise by **operation of law.** Security interests that arise by operation of law include judgment **liens** and statutory liens. The U.C.C. excludes most interests that arise by operation of law.

The clearest examples of security interests are the **mortgage,** the **pledge** and the **conditional sale.** The mortgage involves the situation wherein the mortgagor gives the mortgagee a security interest in a specific asset, which is usually real property. The pledge deals with the situation wherein the creditor takes possession of the property. The conditional sale involves the situation wherein the seller gives credit and takes a security interest. The U.C.C. ignores differences of form and treats all secured interests in personal property simply as "security interests." See U.C.C. §9-102.

A PURCHASE-MONEY SECURITY INTEREST is one "taken or retained by the seller of the **collateral** to secure all or part of its price; or is one taken by a person who, by making advances or incurring an obligation, gives value in order to enable the debtor to acquire rights in or the use of collateral if such value is in fact so used." U.C.C. §9-107.

SEDITION illegal action which tends to cause the disruption and overthrow of the government. The United States had enacted an Alien and Sedition Act as early as the Adams administration (1798). Sedition acts were enacted during World War I prohibiting kinds of communication which advocated the overthrow of the government. In 1919 the Supreme Court held that seditious communications could be punished consistent with the First Amendment, if they presented a **clear and present danger** of bringing about an evil (violence) which the government had a right to prevent. See 249 U.S. 47.

The state governments also have the power to prevent harmful sedition. See 254 U.S. 325. However, the states cannot punish sedition against the United States where Congress has already **preempted** legislation in this area by "occupying the field" with legislation of its own. See 350 U.S. 497.

SEDITIOUS LIBEL in English law a misdemeanor involving the publishing of any words or document, with a seditious intention. "A seditious intention means an intention to bring into contempt or excite disaffection against the government or to promote feelings of ill will between the classes. If the seditious statement is published, the publisher is guilty of a seditious libel." Black, Constitutional Law 543 (2d ed. 1897). The law of seditious libel is now severely circumscribed in this country by the First Amendment to the Constitution.

SEDUCTION "[i]nducing a chaste, unmarried woman, by means of temptation, deception, acts, flattery, or a promise of marriage, to engage in sexual intercourse." 151 So. 2d 752, 757. Force is not an **element** of "seduction." At common law, seduction merely created a **civil** liability and in some states the woman could recover **damages** for her own seduction. In states where seduction is now a criminal offense, the chastity or reputation of chastity of the victim prior to seduction may be essential for conviction.

SEISED the condition of legally **owning** and **possessing realty**. Thus, one "seised of **real property** legally owns and possesses it. The phrase imports legal **title** as opposed to **beneficial ownership**. See 110 A. 770, 773. See **seisin**.

SEISIN in early English property law, the term which properly described the **interest** in land of one who held a **freehold estate**. The term "ownership" was not used, since the sovereign was considered, technically, the owner of all lands in England; a landholder was instead said to be "seised of" his estate. The concept embraced more than mere **possession**, involving as well some legal right to hold; an **ouster** effected a **disseisin** of the original holder, requiring the original holder to resort to self-help or the legal process to regain his land. A voluntary transfer of the holder's interest was accomplished by **livery of seisin**. See Cribbet, Principles of the Law of Property 14 (1962).

Today, "seisin" is generally considered synonymous with "ownership." See 83 U.S. 352, 361.

SEIZURE the act of forcibly dispossessing an owner of property, under actual or apparent authority of law; also, the taking of property into the **custody** of the court in **satisfaction** of a **judgment**, or in consequence of a violation of public law. See 94 N.W. 18.

In a **condemnation proceeding**, '[s]eizure is the initial step in proceeding against a thing. . . . It is absolutely essential to the existence of the **action**, to the **jurisdiction** of the court, to the validity of the condemnation." 93 P. 2d

455, 462. See **attachment; garnishment; in rem; levy; search and seizure.**

SELECTIVE ALLOCATION see **marshaling.**

SELF-DEALING synonymous with IN-SIDER TRADING; a type of trading in which a party acts upon secret information obtained by his or another's special position in the corporation. It may involve sale or purchase of stock by the director, officers and majority **shareholders** of a **corporation.** Under state law, most courts hold that insiders are under no **fiduciary** duty to disclose inside information to either purchaser or seller. See 383 F. 2d 157. Some jurisdictions follow the "special facts" rule under which disclosure is required if certain conditions are shown, see 213 U.S. 417, such as the existence of a relatively inexperienced purchaser or seller. Some states place an absolute duty on insiders to disclose inside information. See 155 S.E. 2d 601.

Federal law deals with the problem of insider trading in both Section 10b and 16 of the Securities Exchange Act. These actions are stricter than state law and present fewer procedural and evidentiary hurdles to the effective policing of such transactions.

SELF-DEFENSE the right which exists to protect one's person, or members of one's family, and, to a lesser extent, one's property, from harm by an aggressor. It is a valid **defense** to a criminal **charge** or to tort liability. The essential elements of self-defense are, "[f]irst , that the defendant must be free from fault, must not say or do anything for the purpose of provoking a difficulty, nor be unmindful of the consequences in this respect of any wrongful word or act; second, there must be no convenient mode of escape by retreat or by declining the combat; and, lastly, there must be a present impending peril . . . either real or apparent, [so] as to create the **bona fide** belief of an existing necessity." 23 So. 2d 19, 20. Whether or not retreat is required depends upon the jurisdiction and the circumstances.

There are two classes of self-defense, perfect and imperfect. "A perfect right of self-defense can only obtain and avail where the party **pleading** it acted from necessity, and was wholly free from ·

wrong or blame in occasioning or producing the necessity which required his action. If, however, he was in the wrong —if he was himself violating or in the act of violating the law—and on account of his own wrong was placed in a situation wherein it became necessary for him to defend himself against an attack made upon himself, which was superinduced or created by his own wrong, then the law justly limits his right of self-defense, and regulates it according to the magnitude of his own wrong. Such a state [is] . . . the imperfect right of self-defense." 162 U.S. 466, 472. See also **justification.**

SELF-INCRIMINATION, PRIVILEGE AGAINST the constitutional right of a person to refuse to answer questions or otherwise give **testimony** against himself which will subject him to a substantial likelihood of criminal incrimination. The Fifth Amendment rule (often called simply PLEADING THE FIFTH AMENDMENT) is now applicable to the states through the **due process** clause of the Fourteenth Amendment, 378 U.S. 1, and is applicable in any situation, civil or criminal where the state attempts to compel incriminating testimony. See 369 U.S. 556. The right may be waived where the defendant testifies, 356 U.S. 148, and the privilege does not preclude the use of voluntary **confessions,** 377 U.S. 201; 384 U.S. 436, provided that the requirements of the **Miranda rule** have been complied with.

The requisite compulsion will include any threat calculated to interfere with the unfettered free will of the suspect. Thus, the privilege has been held to bar the use in a criminal trial of the testimony of a policeman obtained after he was threatened with job dismissal if he did not testify. This was so even though the policeman could have been validly dismissed for refusing to testify, 392 U.S. 273, but the testimony could not validly be compelled by using such a threat to induce him to testify. 385 U.S. 493.

In general, only criminal sanctions are within the privilege and testimony can be compelled despite the personal, social, or economic costs to the witness. For example, a mother having no statutory evidentiary privilege could be compelled to testify against her child and would not be able to plead the privilege against self-incrimination unless she too feared a personal criminal sanction. If she persisted in her refusal to testify, she could be found in **contempt**. The Court has, however, held that a lawyer facing a disbarment proceeding may plead the privilege, 385 U.S. 511, and a juvenile facing **juvenile delinquency** charges enjoys the full protection of the privilege. 387 U.S. 1.

The "hit-and-run" statutes requiring that a motorist involved in an accident stop and identify himself and give certain information to the other motorist and to the police have been upheld on the ground that such forced disclosures are not incriminating in that they are all neutral acts, not intended to be probative of guilt and posing only an insignificant hazard of self-incrimination. Requiring a person to buy a gambling tax stamp, however, does identify such a person as participating in an activity illegal nearly everywhere and as such violates the privilege. 390 U.S. 39.

The privilege can be displaced by a grant of USE IMMUNITY which guarantees that neither the compelled testimony nor any fruits will be used against the witness. Given such immunity the witness can no longer fear criminal incrimination and thus cannot plead the privilege. 406 U.S. 441; 406 U.S. 472. Some states give such witnesses a broader form of TRANSACTIONAL IMMUNITY which protects them not merely from use of their testimony but from any prosecution brought about relating to transactions about which relevant testimony was elicited. See, e.g. N.Y. Crim. Proc. Law §50.10. Transactional immunity was previously the federal standard, 18 U.S.C. §2514, but was replaced in 1970 by testimonial immunity. 18 U.S.C. 6002.

The rule does not extend to non-testimonial compulsion. Thus, blood tests may be compelled from the accused because they are "non-communicative," i.e., the evidence is considered physical or real and not testimonial so as to invoke the protection of the privilege. On the same reasoning the Court has permitted compelled line-ups, 388 U.S. 218, and hand-writing exemplars. 388 U.S. 263.

SENILE DEMENTIA *(dĕ-mĕn'-shē-á)*— Lat: insanity which occurs as the result of old age and is progressive in character; "a progressive, incurable form of fixed insanity resulting in a total collapse of the mental faculties and, in its final state, necessarily deprives one of **testamentary** capacity. With that particular malady the victim is robbed of his power to think, reason or act sanely." 100 P. 2d 776, 784. See also **non compos mentis**.

SENTENCE the punishment ordered by a court to be inflicted upon a person convicted of a crime, usually either a NON-CUSTODIAL SENTENCE such as **probation** and/or a fine, or a CUSTODIAL SENTENCE such as a term of years of imprisonment or a number of months in a county jail. Such an order usually identifies the authority which must carry out the sentence and authorizes and directs such authority to execute the order. See 100 S.E. 2d 681, 683; 128 So. 814, 816.

CONCURRENT SENTENCE a sentence which overlaps with another for a period of time, as opposed to a consecutive [cumulative] sentence [see below] which runs by itself, beginning after or ending before the running of another sentence. See 255 P. 2d 782, 784; 456 P. 2d 415, 417. Two or more sentences running concurrently need not begin and/or end at the same time.

CONDITIONAL DISCHARGE SENTENCE see SUSPENDED SENTENCE below.

CONSECUTIVE [CUMULATIVE] SENTENCE a sentence which runs separately from one or more other sentences to be served by the same individual. The sentence is cumulative to the extent that it begins after an existing sentence has terminated either by expiration of the maximum term of the existing sentence, or by release from the present sentence through parole. If the consecutive sentence is a custodial one, the parole will be to the cell (called "cell parole") so that the consecutive sentence may be served during the period of the parole.

INDETERMINATE SENTENCE "a sentence for the maximum period prescribed by law for the particular offense committed, subject to the provision of the statute that it may be sooner terminated by the board of pardons." 284 P. 323, 325. The sentence may be terminated any time after the expiration of the minimum period required. See 97 F. 2d 182, 187.

INTERLOCUTORY SENTENCE a temporary or provisional sentence, one pending the imposition of a final sentence; a sentence on an ancillary question derived from the main cause of action.

SUSPENDED SENTENCE a sentence whose imposition or execution has been withheld by the court on certain terms and conditions. A defendant sentenced to six months in jail "suspended" is not required to serve that time in jail provided that he does not violate the express or implied conditions of his suspension. An implied condition is always that the defendant not commit a further violation of the law during a fixed period. Where no such period is fixed by the court the practical effect of the suspended sentence is similar to an UNCONDITIONAL DISCHARGE sentence, i.e. the matter is terminated without any real conditions whatsoever. A CONDITIONAL DISCHARGE is a suspended sentence on particular conditions for a period which is expressly fixed by the court or by statute at generally between one and three years after the sentence is imposed. See, e.g., New York Penal Law §65.05.

SEQUESTER to separate from as in to sequester assets or to sequester witnesses during a trial. See **sequestration**.

SEQUESTRATION in **equity**, the act of seizing or taking possession of the property belonging to another, and holding it "until the profits have paid the demand for which it was taken." 15 F. 6, 11.

In practice, at **common law, juries** (at least in capital cases) were always sequestered, i.e., kept together throughout the trial and deliberations and guarded from improper contact, until they were discharged. This common law right to demand jury sequestration has been replaced in most jurisdictions with a **discretion** in the trial court to grant sequestration "in the interests of justice." The modern view is that locking a jury up during the trial prejudices both the State and the **defendant**. See 117 A. 2d 473, 478. If a case is sensational and major the jury will likely be sequestered.

The sequestration of **witnesses** is frequently ordered by the court at the request of one of the parties in order to insure that the in-court testimony of each witness not be colored by what another witness said. The order of sequestration usually forbids the witnesses who have not yet testified from talking with witnesses who have testified. Sequestered witnesses are not kept together but rather kept apart from one another and outside the courtroom.

SERIATIM *(sĕr-ē-ā'-tĭm)*—Lat: in due order, successively; in order, in succession, individually; one by one; separately; severally.

SERVANT one who works for, and is subject to, the control of his master; a person employed to "perform services in the affairs of another and who with respect to the physical conduct in the performance of the services is subject to the other's control or right to control.

"In determining whether one acting for another is a servant or an independent **contractor**, the following matters of fact, among others, are considered: (1) the extent of control which, by the agreement, the master may exercise over the details of the work; (2) whether or not the one employed is engaged in a distinct occupation or business; (3) the kind of occupation, with reference to whether, in the locality, the work is usually done under the direction of the employer or by a specialist without supervision; (4) the skill required in the particular occuaption; (5) whether the employer or the workman supplies the instrumentalities, tools, and the place of work for the person doing the work; (6) the length of time for which the person is employed; (7) the method of payment, whether by the time or by the job; (8) whether or not the work is a part of the regular business of the employer; (9) whether or not the parties believe they are creating the relation of master and servant; and (10) whether the principal is or is not in business."

Restatement of Agency (2d) §220, pp. 485-87. A master is in many instances liable, under the theory of **respondeat superior,** for the torts of his servant, but not for those of an **independent contractor.** See also **agent.**

SERVICE delivery of communication of a **pleading,** notice, or other paper in a **suit,** to the opposite party, so as to charge him with the receipt of it and subject him to its legal effect. See 178 N.E. 870, 871. The bringing to notice, either actually or constructively. See 74 S.E. 2d 852, 854.

PERSONAL SERVICE actual delivery to the party to be served. There is some question whether mailing of service is "personal service." See 246 S.W. 196, 200 (yes), 228 F. 304 (no). Historically, personal service was an outgrowth of **capias,** and, as opposed to all other types of constructive service, is only achieved upon personal delivery. See James, Civil Procedure 621 (1965).

SERVICE BY PUBLICATION constructive service accomplished by publishing the notice to be served in a newspaper designated by the court and in some jurisdictions, by mailing that newspaper to the last known address of the party. See 243 U.S. 90.

SUBSTITUTED SERVICE contructive service accomplished by presenting service to a recognized representative or agent of the party to be served. See Fed. R. Civ. Proc. 4(d)(1); New York C.P.L.R. §308.

SERVICE OF PROCESS the communication of the substance of the **process** to the defendant, either by actual delivery, or by other methods whereby defendant is furnished with reasonable notice of the proceedings against him to afford him opportunity to appear and be heard. See 296 F. Supp. 1106, 1107. [For the types of service of process see **service.**]

SERVICES at common law, the acts done by an English **feudal tenant** for the benefit of his lord, which formed the **consideration** for the property granted to him by his lord. Services were of several types, including knight's service, military service, and the more varied kind of certain and determinate service called socage. See also **tenure.**

SERVIENT ESTATE in relation to an **easement,** that **estate** which is **burdened** by the **servitude,** i.e., that estate which is subject to use in some way by the owner of the **dominant estate;** also called SERVIENT TENEMENT.

SESSION LAWS laws bound in volumes in the order of their enactment by a state legislature, before possible codification. See **code.**

SET ASIDE to annul, or make **void,** as to "set aside" a judgment. When **proceedings** are irregular, they may be set aside on **motion** of the **party** whom they injuriously affect. See also **reverse.**

SET-OFF a **counter-claim** by **defendant** against **plaintiff** which grows from an independent **cause of action** and diminishes the plaintiff's potential recovery; "a counter-demand arising out of a transaction extrinsic to the plaintiff's cause of action. It, therefore, is not incompatible with the justice of the plaintiff's claim but seeks to balance it in whole or in part by a counter-obligation alleged to be due by the plaintiff to the defendant in another transaction." 67 F. Supp. 212, 215.

"Set-off, both at law and in equity, must be understood as that right which exists between two parties each of whom under an independent contract owes an ascertained amount to the other to set-off his respective debts by way of mutual deduction so that in any action brought for the larger debt, the residue only, after such deduction, shall be recovered." 16 A. 2d 804, 806. See also **recoupment.**

SETTLEMENT generally, the conclusive fixing or resolving of a matter; the arrangement of a final disposition of it. See 116 N.J. Super. 390, 397. A compromise achieved by the adverse parties in a **civil suit** before final **judgment,** whereby they agree between themselves upon their respective rights and obligations, thus eliminating the necessity of judicial resolution of the controversy. See **accord and satisfaction.** Compare **plea bargaining** in the criminal context.

SETTLOR one who creates a **trust** by giving **real** or **personal property** "in trust" to another (the **trustee**), for the benefit of a third person (the **benefici-ary**). One who gives such money is said to "settle" it on, or bring **title** to rest with, the trustee, and is also called the "donor" or "trustor." See 144 F. 2d 683, 690.

SEVERABLE CONTRACT one which, in the event of a **breach** by one of the parties, may be justly considered as several independent agreements which have been expressed in a single **instrument**. Where a contract is deemed "severable," a breach thereof may constitute a default as to only a part of the contract, saving the defaulting party from the necessity of responding in **damages** for a breach of the entire agreement.

A severable contract may in fact be a series of DIVISIBLE CONTRACTS so that each part may be supported by a separate consideration and involve separate suits for breach of contract. See U.C.C. §2-612; 410 P. 2d 751.

SEVERABLE STATUTE one the remainder of which, remains valid when a certain portion has been declared invalid, because the statute is one whose parts are not wholly interdependent. "After the invalid portion of the act has been stricken out, (if) that which remains is self-sustaining and is capable of separate enforcement without regard to that portion of the statute which has been cast aside," then such a statute is severable. 196 A. 73, 79.

SEVERALLY separate and apart from; e.g., in a **note**, each who "severally" promises to pay is responsible separately for the entire amount; and in a **judgment** against more than one defendant, arising out of one **action**, each may be **liable** for the entire amount of the judgment, thereby permitting the successful plaintiff to recover the entire amount of the judgment from any defendant against whom he chooses to institute a suit. Compare **joint; joint and several.**

SEVERALTY refers to the holding of property solely, separately, and individually. A tenant in severalty holds the land exclusively and solely for the duration of his or her **estate** without any other person holding joint rights. See 322 S.W. 2d 443, 444. Compare **joint; joint and several.**

SEVERANCE the act of separating; the state of being disjoined or separated. It refers especially to a process "by which the law provides for selecting the particular **charge** on which the **defendant** is currently to stand trial. . . . [It is] a severance of the charges of the **indictment** returned by the **grand jury** so that only one charge or only properly joined charges are before the **jury** in one trial." 167 P. 2d 970, 972. Severance may also refer to the disjoinder, for separate trials, of two or more defendants named in the same **indictment** or **information**, who would normally be tried together. It is a useful device especially where some prejudice might arise to one or more of the defendants if they were tried together.

Severance of claims is also available in **civil** trials to prevent prejudice or for the convenience of the parties. Not infrequently a court may sever the issue of **liability** from the issue of **damages** and direct that the question of liability be determined first. Once liability is established the parties may agree upon the question of damages, thereby avoiding a lengthy trial on that issue. See, e.g., N.J. Court Rules, R. 4:38-2(b).

SHAM PLEADING "one sufficient on its face, but so clearly and indisputably false that it presents no real **issue** of fact to be determined by a **trial**. Bad faith, however, is not necessary. . . . An **answer** will be stricken as sham only when it is clear and undisputed that the alleged **defense** is wholly unsupported by facts." 70 F. 2d 469, 472.

SHARE a portion of something; an **interest** in a **corporation**. See **stock certificate.**

SHELLEY'S CASE, RULE IN see **Rule in Shelley's Case.**

SHERIFF'S SALE a **sale** of **property** by the sheriff under authority of a court's **judgment** and **writ of execution** in order to satisfy an unpaid judgment, **mortgage, lien,** or other **debt** of the owner [**judgment debtor**]. An execution sale of **real property** has the same effect as a **conveyance** by **quitclaim deed,** in that only such **title** as the judgment debtor has at the time of the sale is passed. Any **after-acquired title** or interest is not conveyed. See 130 P. 2d 426, 429.

SHIFTING INTEREST see **interest.**

SHIFTING USE see **use.** See also **interest** [EXECUTORY INTEREST].

SHORT-SWING PROFIT see **insider.**

SHORT-TERM CAPITAL GAIN see **capital.**

SHOW CAUSE ORDER "an **order** [made upon the **motion** of one party] requiring a party to appear and show cause [argue] why a certain thing should not be done or permitted. It requires the [adverse] party to meet the **prima facie case** made by the applicant's verified **complaint** or **affidavit.**" 230 S.W. 2d 444, 447.

An order to show cause is an accelerated method of beginning a litigation by compelling the adverse party to respond in a much shorter period of time than he would normally have under a **complaint.** The order may or may not contain temporary restraints [see **restraining orders**] but will generally be "returnable" in a few days which means that the opposing party must prepare answering affidavits and persuade the court that an issue of a fact exists that requires a full, plenary trial proceeding or simply argue on the return date that even if the plaintiff's statements in his moving papers are true, they do not state a cause of action or justify the relief prayed for in the order to show cause.

SIMPLE CONTRACT see **sealed instrument.**

SINE DIE (*sē'-nā dē'-ā*)—Lat: without day, without time; "a legislative body adjourns 'sine die' when it adjourns without appointing a day on which to appear or assemble again." 300 S.W. 2d 806.

SINE QUA NON (*sē'-nā kwä nōn*)— Lat: without which not; that without which the thing cannot be, i.e., the essence of something; e.g., in **tort** law, the act of the defendant, without which there would not have been a tort. See **cause.**

SINKING FUND an accumulation, by a corporation or governmental body, of money invested for the purpose of repaying a **debt** or debts. In governmental bodies, a sinking fund is a fund arising from taxes, imposts or duties, which is appropriated toward the payment of interest due on a public loan and for the eventual payment of the **principal.** See 29 A. 387, 389.

SLANDER to make an oral defamatory remark about another; spoken words which tend to damage the reputation of another. See 260 S.W. 523, 525. Under modern legal and constitutional concepts, slander is limited to false remarks inasmuch as truth is an absolute **defense** to an **action** for slander.

Unlike **libel**, slanderous utterances may not be actionable without proof of actual temporal **damages.** Only where the words impute crime, loathsome disease or unchastity, or when they relate to an individual's business or profession is this requirement of proving "special damages" dispensed with. Prosser, Torts 754 (4th ed. 1971). Slander may take the form of either SLANDER PER SE or SLANDER PER QUOD. If the defamatory meaning is apparent on the face of the statement, then the statement is slanderous per se. If the defamatory meaning arises only from extrinsic facts, not apparent upon the face of the statement, then the statement is slanderous per quod. See Id. at 748. See also **defamation; fighting words.**

SLIGHT NEGLIGENCE see **negligence.**

SOCAGE in feudal England, a type of tenure founded upon certain and designated services performed by the vassal for his lord, other than military or knight's service. Where the services were considered honorable it was called FREE SOCAGE and where the services were of a baser nature it was called VILLEIN SOCAGE. By the statute 12 Car. 2, c. 24, most all tenures by knight-servants were converted into FREE AND COMMON SOCAGE. See 2 Bl. Comm.*79-80. See also **homage.**

SOCIAL GUEST see **guest.**

SODOMY crime against nature made a **felony** in the early sixteenth century by statute and thus considered a **common law** felony in the United States. It was originally only an ecclesiastical offense. Sodomy includes both **bestiality** and buggery [copulation per anus] and in many jurisdictions has been expanded to cover other acts of unnatural sexual intercourse. See Perkins, Criminal Law 389 (2d ed. 1969).

Sodomy can be either consensual, by forcible compulsion, or with a physically helpless person, and includes such acts with underaged persons.

Modern statutes may limit the scope of sodomy such as by defining deviate sexual intercourse as "sexual conduct between persons not married to each other consisting of contact between the penis and anus, the mouth and penis, or the mouth and vulva." New York Penal Law §§130.38, 130.00(2).

SOLICITATION an offense developed by the later common law courts to reach conduct whereby one enticed, incited, or importuned another to commit a **felony** or certain **misdemeanors** injurious to the public welfare. See 102 Eng. Rep. 269 (1801). The common law offense has been codified by only a small minority of American jurisdictions and is sometimes an element in an **attempt** liability. If the actor agrees to join the other in an offense, a **conspiracy** will be established and there will be no need for solicitation liability.

"The Model Penal Code defines solicitation broadly to include requesting another to commit any offense, and would generally make solicitation punishable to the same degree as authorized for the offense solicited. The theory is that 'to the extent that sentencing depends upon the anti-social disposition of the actor and the demonstrated need for a corrective sanction, there is likely to be little difference in the gravity of the required measures depending on the consummation or the failure of the plan.'" LaFave and Scott, Criminal Law 416 (1972) (quoting Model Penal Code § 5.05, Comment [Tent. Draft No. 10, 1960]).

SOLICITER see **barrister**.

SOLVENCY the ability to pay all **debts** and just claims as they come due; "gen-erally understood to mean that a person is able to pay his debts as they mature. . . . The term is used, too, in a sense importing that one's property is adequate to satisfy his obligations when sold under **execution.** Only clear solvency in the latter sense will uphold a voluntary conveyance against pre-existing debts." 91 S.W. 958, 961. In certain contexts, solvency may consist simply of an excess of assets over liabilities. See 9 S.W. 2d 688, 690.

SOUNDS IN has a connection or association with; is concerned with; thus, though a party to a lawsuit has **pleaded damages** in **tort,** it may be said that the **action** nevertheless "sounds in" **contract** if the elements of the offense charged appear to constitute a contract, rather than a tort, action. Whether the court will consider it a tort or a contract may influence the damage measure since, for example, **punitive damages** are recoverable in tort but not on contract. See Simpson, Contracts 394 (2d ed. 1965).

SOVEREIGN IMMUNITY a doctrine precluding the institution of a **suit** against the sovereign [government] without the sovereign's consent when the sovereign is engaged in a governmental function. The doctrine was originally based on the maxim "the King can do no wrong." Another rationale is that the "sovereign is exempt from suit, not because of any formal conception or obsolete theory, but on the logical and practical ground that there can be no legal right against the authority that makes the law on which the right depends." 205 U.S. 349, 353. The state may be liable where the injuring activity was "proprietary" rather than "governmental," i.e., where the injury was caused by the State acting in its capacity as a commercial entity rather than that of sovereign. 115 N.W. 2d 618, 621. Now a somewhat discredited doctrine, it has been abrogated in some states by judicial decision, 115 N.W. 2d 618, and in others by statutory enactment.

SPECIAL APPEARANCE see **appearance.**

SPECIAL INDORSEMENT see **indorsement.**

SPECIAL LEGISLATION acts of the legislature enacted in the form of private acts, for the benefit of a certain individual, as opposed to general legislation enacted for the general population. Examples include acts to provide recovery otherwise unavailable in the courts, and special laws enacted for a limited group of persons. Special laws may be constitutional if there is a rational basis for limiting the application of the statute to the special group. Several states have constitutional provisions allowing the enactment of special legislation affecting certain classes of persons, such as small municipalities, but usually only if enacted pursuant to a certain procedure. See, e.g., N.J. Const. Art. 4, §7, paras. 9, 10.

SPECIAL TRAVERSE see **traverse.**

SPECIE money which has an intrinsic value, e.g., gold and silver coins. These are coins made of scarce metals which are usually minted in various denominations differentiated by weight and fineness. Most often these coins are stamped with government seals and insignias signifying their value as currency. See 79 U.S. (12 Wall.) 687, 695. See also **in specie.**

SPECIFIC BEQUEST see **bequest.**

SPECIFIC INTENT see **intent.**

SPECIFIC MENS REA see **mens rea.**

SPECIFIC PERFORMANCE an **equitable remedy** available to an aggrieved party when his remedy at law is inadequate, which consists of a requirement that the party guilty of a **breach of contract** undertake to perform or to complete performance of his obligations under the contract. It is grounded on the equitable maxim that equity regards that as done which ought to have been done. Unlike money **damages** which are enforceable only by a judgment against property, a decree of specific performance requires that the party against whom the decree is directed do a particular act on pain of being imprisoned for contempt. Specific performance is available whenever the subject-matter of the contract is unique and "in other proper circumstances." U.C.C. §2-716

(1). Thus one can obtain a decree of specific performance for the purchase of a unique chattel such as a rare painting, and in all transactions involving land, which the law presumes to be unique. Restatement, Contracts §360. Once a purchaser of land has signed a contract he is said to have equitable title because he can enforce the contract through a decree of specific performance.

There are cases in which the court of equity will not specifically enforce a contract even though the remedy at law is inadequate. Personal service contracts and construction contracts are common examples, Restatement, Contracts §§ 371, 379, due to the difficulty of the court's overseeing proper performance by the defaulting party. In these instances a negative injunction can sometimes be obtained, preventing the defaulting party from doing the same act or service for anyone other than the aggrieved party. Also, where the defaulting party is a buyer, an aggrieved seller who has produced specially manufactured goods for the buyer or who is otherwise unable to sell the goods may enjoy a kind of "specific performance" at law by bringing an action for the price. See U.C.C. §2-709.

SPECIFIC RELIEF see **specific performance.**

SPENDTHRIFT TRUST a trust created to provide a fund for the maintenance of a beneficiary which is so restricted that it is secure against the beneficiary's improvidence, see 93 P. 2d 880, 883, and beyond the reach of his creditors. See 27 A. 2d 166, 172.

SPLIT SENTENCE see **probation.**

SPLITTING A CAUSE OF ACTION impermissible practice of bringing an **action** for only part of the **cause of action** in one **suit,** and initiating another suit for another part; consists in dividing a single or indivdual cause of acton into several parts or claims and bringing several actions thereon. See 59 N.W. 2d 74, 78. Under the general policy against the splitting of causes of action, "the law mandatorily requires that all **damages** sustained or accruing to one as a result of a single **wrongful act** must be claimed and recovered in one action or not at all." 10 So. 2d 432, 433. See also **multiplicity of suits.** Compare **joinder; misjoinder.**

SPRINGING INTEREST   see **interest.**

SPRINGING USE   see **use.** See also **interest** [EXECUTORY INTEREST].

STAKEHOLDER   "a third party chosen by two or more persons to keep in deposit **property** or money the right or **possession** of which is contested between them, and to be delivered to the one who shall establish his right to it." 162 S.E. 2d 765, 770.

STANDING   the legal right of a person or group to challenge in a judicial forum the conduct of another, especially with respect to governmental conduct. In the federal system, **litigants** must satisfy constitutional standing requirements in order to create a legitimate **case or controversy** within the meaning of Article III of the federal Constitution. Under the case of *Flast* v. *Cohen*, 392 U.S. 83 (1968), a taxpayer will have standing to challenge governmental conduct if the taxpayer can establish (1) "a logical link between that status and the type of legislative enactment attacked," and (2) "a nexus between that status and the precise nature of the constitutional infringement alleged." Id. at 102. "The gist of the question of standing,' is whether the party seeking relief has 'alleged such a personal stake in the outcome of the controversy as to insure that concrete adverseness which sharpens the presentation of issues upon which the court so largely depends for illumination of difficult constitutional questions.' " 94 S. Ct. 2962, 2963 (Powell, J., concurring). See **political question.**

In criminal procedure, under federal constitutional standards only persons aggrieved by a violation of the Fourth Amendment have standing to challenge the police conduct and its fruits. Thus, persons legitimately present upon premises, conversants in a conversation and the owner of premises and property have standing, but third parties not present do not have standing even though the evidence obtained is to be used against them. See 362 U.S. 257; 392

U.S. 364; 394 U.S. 165. California courts follow a rule of "vicarious standing" whereby any citizen can challenge the legality of the methods employed to obtain evidence against him. See 290 P. 2d 855.

STANDING MUTE   in a criminal trial, refusing to **plead**; today held equivalent to a **plea** of **not guilty.** See also **self-incrimination.**

STAR CHAMBER   an ancient court of England which received its name because the ceiling was covered with stars; it sat with no jury and could administer any penalty but death. The Star Chamber was abolished when its jurisdiction was expanded to such an extent that it became too onerous for the people of England. See Baker, An Introduction to English Legal History 51 (1971). See generally, Holdsworth, A History of English Law 155-214 (1924). The abuses of the star chamber were a principal reason for the incorporation in the federal constitution of the privilege against **self-incrimination.**

STARE DECISIS *(stǎ'-rā dě-sī'-sǐs)*—Lat: to stand by that which was decided; rule by which common law courts "are slow to interfere with principles announced in the former decisions and often uphold them even though they would decide otherwise were the question a new one." 156 P. 2d 340, 345. "Although [stare decisis] is not inviolable, our judicial system demands that it be overturned only on a showing of good cause. Where such a good cause is not shown, it will not be repudiated." See **precedent.**

STATU QUO   see **in statu quo.**

STATUS QUO   *(stǎ'-tǔs kwō)*—Lat: the postures or positions which existed; the conditions or situations which existed. The "status quo to be preserved by [a] temporary **injunction** is the last actual, peaceable, noncontested status which preceded the pending controversy." 498 S.W. 2d 42, 48. In a **breach of contract** setting, in order for the plaintiff to get **restitution** for the value of his performance he must return the value of the part performance he received from the defendant, since the purpose of the remedy of restitution is to restore the STATUS QUO ANTE, i.e., the situation which existed at the inception of the **contract**. In order to restore the status quo ante each party must be placed **in statu quo**, i.e., each party must be placed in the position he occupied at the inception of the contract. Placing each of the parties in statu quo means restoring each to the status quo; i.e., the position occupied at the making of the contract. See 5 Corbin, Contracts §114 (1964); Restatement, Contracts §349; 28 P. 764, 767. The status quo ante is in contradiction to the usual "benefit of the bargain" goal of placing the parties in the position they would have been in had the contract been fulfilled. See **damages.**

STATUTE an act of the legislature, adopted pursuant to its constitutional authority, by prescribed means and in certain form such that it becomes the law governing conduct within its scope. Statutes are enacted to prescribe conduct, define crimes, create inferior governmental bodies, appropriate public monies, and in general to promote the public good and welfare. Lesser governmental bodies adopt **ordinances;** administrative agencies adopt regulations. See **police power.** Compare **common law, judge-made law.**

STATUTE OF FRAUDS statutory requirement that certain contracts be in writing to be enforceable. Most such statutes are patterned after the English statute enacted in 1677. Contracts to answer to a **creditor** for the **debt** of another, contracts made in **consideration** of marriage, contracts for the sale of land or affecting any **interest** in land (except short-term **leases**) and contracts not to be performed within one year from their making, must be evidenced by a written memorandum, and signed by the PARTY TO BE CHARGED, [i.e., by the defendant in an action for **breach**]. Under a separate section of the English statute and as codified in the Uniform Commercial Code, a contract for the sale of goods where the contract price exceeds $500. must likewise be in writing. See U.C.C. §2-201.

Under the MAIN PURPOSE RULE, where one party has agreed to answer for the debt of another and the promisor undertaking the obligation has an independent interest of his own in so doing, such contract need not be in writing. Nor need a contract "in consideration of marriage" be in writing where it is actually only in contemplation of marriage and supported by other consideration. An oral contract that has been fully performed on both sides is "not within the statute," that is, not subject to its requirements. The statute does not apply to contracts implied by law or to **quasi-contracts.**

PART PERFORMANCE is another important exception and operates to take an oral contract "out of the statute," i.e., to render it enforceable. In the case of a sale of goods within the statute, acceptance of part or all of the goods by the buyer or payment of all or part of the purchase price by the buyer suffices as part performance as to that portion of the contract. See U.C.C. 2-201 (3)(c).

STATUTE OF LIMITATIONS "any law which fixes the time within which **parties** must take judicial action to enforce rights or else be thereafter barred from enforcing them," 116 S.E. 2d 654, 657.

Most every type of action at law, **civil** or **criminal**, has a statutory time beyond which the action may not be brought. A common exception is murder, which is generally not subject to a statute of limitations. Equity proceedings are governed by an independent equity doctrine called **laches**. These limitations are also an essential element of **adverse possession**, prescribing the time at which the adverse possessor's interest in the property becomes unassailable. The policy behind the enactment of such laws consists of the belief that there is a point beyond which a prospective defendant should no longer need to worry about the possible commencement in the future of an action against him, that the law disfavors "stale evidence," and that no one should be able to "sit on his rights" for an unreasonable amount of time without forfeiting his claims.

STATUTE OF QUIA EMPTORES see **Quia Emptores, Statute of.**

STATUTE OF USES An English statute (27 Hen. VIII) enacted in 1536, for the purpose of preventing the separation of legal and **equitable estates** in land, a separation that arose whenever a **use** was created at **common law**. The purpose was to unite all legal and equitable estates in the beneficiary [the holder of the equitable estates] and to strip the **trustee** [the holder of the legal **title**] of all interest. [See **use** for a discussion of statute's application.]

STATUTE OF WILLS   an early English statute prescribing the conditions necessary for a valid disposition through a **will**. Today, the term is used broadly to refer to the statutory provisions of a particular jurisdiction relating to the requirements for valid testamentary dispositions. See generally Atkinson, Law of Wills, ch. 7 (2d ed. 1953).

STATUTORY ARSON   see **arson**.

STATUTORY OFFENSE   see **regulatory offense**.

STATUTORY RAPE   see **rape**.

STAY   a halt in a judicial **proceeding** where, by its **order**, the court will not take further action until the occurrence of some event. Compare **adjournment**, **continuance**, **recess**.

STAY OF EXECUTION   process whereby a **judgment** is precluded from being executed for a specific period of time.

STIRPES   see **per stirpes**.

STOCK CERTIFICATE   written **instrument** evidencing a share in the ownership of a **corporation**. Although sometimes called a **security**, this is not technically accurate because it does not evidence a **debt**. See 21 So. 75.

STOCK DIVIDEND   see **dividend**.

STOCKHOLDER   one who is holder or proprietor of one or more **shares** of the stock of a **corporation**. To be a stockholder of an incorporated company is to be possessed of the evidence, usually **stock certificates**, that the holder is the real owner of a certain individual portion of the property in actual or potential existence held by the company in its name as a unit for the common bene-fit of all the owners of the entire **capital** stock of the company. See 77 Ill. App. 424, 433.

STOCKHOLDER'S DERIVATIVE ACTION "in legal effect, a **suit** by the **corporation** conducted by the **stockholders** as the corporation's representative. The shareholder is only a nominal **plaintiff**, and the corporation is the **real party in interest**." 452 S.W. 2d 75, 78. "One in which the grievance to be redressed has been suffered primarily by the corporation and normally it should institute the **action**." But where it fails or refuses to act after [a] demand [that it do so by the stockholders], . . . [their] ultimate interest in the corporation is sufficient to warrant the prosecution of . . . [an] . . . action [on behalf of the corporation which will] ultimately . . . effect the recovery for the corporation of the rights or property of which it has been deprived by the wrongdoer." 314 P. 2d 204, 207.

Such suits are the only civil remedy which a stockholder has for breach of a fiduciary duty on the part of those entrusted with the management and direction of their corporation. Many states have enacted statutes requiring small stockholders to provide security for the costs which may be incurred by the corporation in defending these suits in order to prevent the abuse of this remedy by small stockholders. See N.Y. Bus. Corp. L. §627. See **strike suits**.

STOCK OPTION   the granting to an individual of the right to purchase a corporate **stock** at some future date at a price which is specified at the time the option is given rather than at the time the stock is purchased. Such options involve no commitments on the part of the individual to purchase the stock and the option is usually exercised only if the price of the stock has risen above the price specified at the time the option was given.

Stock options are a form of incentive compensation. They are usually given by a corporation in an attempt to motivate an employee or **officer** to continue with the corporation or to improve corporate productivity in a manner which will cause the price of the corporation's stock to rise and thereby increase the value of the option. See also **stock dividend.**

STOP AND FRISK in reference to police conduct on the street, a limited search for weapons confined to outer clothing. See 475 P. 2d 702-705. Under the Fourth Amendment as judicially construed, a policeman may "stop and frisk" a person only if he has reason to believe that that person is an armed and dangerous individual. If so, he may make a reasonable search for weapons for his own protection regardless of whether he has **probable cause** to **arrest** the individual. The standard for judging if a "stop and frisk" was proper is based on whether a reasonably prudent person in the circumstances would be warranted in the belief that his safety or that of others was in danger; but due weight is also given to the reasonable inferences that a policeman is entitled to draw from the facts, in light of his professional experience. 392 U.S. 1, 27, 30. See also **search and seizure.**

STRAW MAN a colloquial expression designating those arguments in **briefs** or **opinions** created solely for the purpose of debunking or "discovering" them. Arguments so created are like "straw men" because they are, by nature, insubstantial.

The term is also sometimes referred to in commercial and property contexts when a transfer is made to a third party, the straw man, simply for the purpose of re-transferring to the transferror in order to accomplish some purpose not otherwise permitted. Thus, if a **covenant running with the land** must be included in the deed in the jurisdiction, such a covenant can be established subsequently by conveying the property to a straw man and obtaining from him a new grant with the desired covenant now in the deed.

STRICT CONSTRUCTION as to statutes, or contracts, an interpretation by adherence to the literal meaning of the words used. "Strict **construction** of a statute means simply that it must be confined to such subjects or applications as are obviously within its terms or purposes. . . . It does not require such an unreasonable technical construction that the words used cannot be given

their fair and sensible meaning in accord with the obvious intent of the legislature." 68 N.E. 2d 278, 282.

STRICT LIABILITY in tort and criminal law, liability without a showing of fault. It is often the case in tort law that one who engages in an activity that has an inherent risk of injury such as those classified as **ultrahazardous activities,** is liable for all injuries proximately caused by his enterprise, even without a showing of negligence. Thus, one who uses explosives or who harbors wild animals is liable for all resulting injuries even if he uses utmost care. The rationale of the tort law of strict liability is that it tends to discourage dangerous activities while not entirely prohibiting any social benefit they may have. Prosser, Torts 404 (4th ed. 1971). A recently developing area of strict liability concerns consumer **product liability.**

In the criminal law, offenses sometimes do not require any specific or general **mens rea.** The conduct itself, even if innocently engaged in, results in criminal liability. Because of the possible harshness of holding people strictly accountable in this way, the courts require strong evidence of a legislative intent to statutorily create strict liability before the usual requirement of mens rea will be dispensed with; and strict liability crimes are usually limited to minor offenses or **regulatory offenses** such as parking violations and violations of health codes. Penalties for strict liability crimes are usually minimal, except in certain instances such as drug and weapons offenses where the penalties may be quite substantial. In some jurisdictions, strict liability offenses are reduced to "violations" which carry only money fines (and short jail terms) and are not deemed "criminal" offenses. See, e.g., New York Penal Code §55.10 (3).

STRIKE SUITS "shareholder **derivative actions** begun with the hope of winning large attorney's fees or private settlements, and with no intention of benefitting the **corporation** on behalf of which **suit** is theoretically brought." 210 A. 2d 890, 894. See **stockholder's derivative action.**

SUA SPONTE *(sū'-à spŏn'-tā)*—Lat: of

itself or of one's self, i.e., without being prompted, as where the court moves to declare a **mistrial** "sua sponte," that is, through the court's own volition [on its own motion], without such a **motion** being made by either of the **adverse parties.**

SUB-CHAPTER S CORPORATION see **corporation.**

SUBCONTRACTOR one to whom principal contractor sublets part of, or all of, contract; also refers to portions obtained from other subcontractors. See 183 S.E. 914, 915. One who takes a part of a contract for the principal [general] contractor or another subcontractor.

SUBINFEUDATION the process which developed under **feudal** law whereby the **grantee** of an **estate** in land from his lord granted a smaller estate in the same land to another. In 1066, William the Conqueror claimed all the land of England for the crown. Subsequently, he granted land to barons for their use in exchange for **services,** but retained ultimate **ownership,** this grant process being called **infeudation.** Such barons held land **in capite.** Subinfeudation was the process by which barons further divided the land by making grants to knights in return for knight services, and the term also includes all subsequent grants and subdivisions by knights and their grantees. Owners under subinfeudation held land "in service" to their grantor and owed nothing directly to the king. See Cheshire, The Modern Law of Real Property 9-27 (6th ed. 1949).

Subinfeudation was made illegal by the statute, of **Quia Emptores,** 18 Edw. I.C.I., and was replaced by the modern concept of **alienation.** See also **servitudes.**

SUBJECT MATTER the thing in dispute; the nature of the **cause of action;** "the real **issue** of fact or law presented for **trial** as between those **parties,**" 62 P. 2d 1248, 1252; the object of a contract.

SUBJECT MATTER JURISDICTION see **jurisdiction.**

SUB JUDICE *(sŭb jū'-dĭ-sā)* —Lat: under a court; before a court or judge

for consideration. 12 East 409, 413. Thus, the "instant matter" or the "case at bar" will be called the "matter (case) sub judice."

SUBLEASE "a transaction whereby a **tenant** [one who has **leased premises** from the owner, or **landlord**] grants an **interest** in the leased premises less than his own, or reserves to himself a **reversionary** interest in the term." 390 S.W. 2d 703, 707. See **assignment,** which connotes the **conveyance** of the whole term of a lease.

SUBLET "to make a **sublease** accompanied by a surrender of the **premises** or at least a part thereof." 413 S.W. 2d 592, 601. See **let.** Compare **assignment.**

SUB MODO *(sŭb mō'-dō)*—Lat: under a qualification; subject to a condition or qualification.

SUB NOMINE *(sŭb nō'-mē-nā)*—Lat: under the name; used to indicate that the title of a case has been altered at a later stage in the proceedings, e.g., A v. B, aff'd sub. nom. C v. B.

SUBORNATION OF PERJURY a crime consisting of "the procurement of another to make a false oath." 272 A. 2d 794, 800. Proof of surornation of perjury requires proof of both **perjury** in fact and that the perjured statement was procured by the **accused.** Id. There must also be proof that the suborner knew or should have known that such oaths or **testimony** would be false. See 262 F. 2d 788, 794. See also **false swearing.**

SUBPOENA *(sŭ-pē'-nà)*—Lat: a **writ** issued under authority of a court to compel the **appearance** of a **witness** at a judicial proceeding, the disobedience of which may be punishable as a **contempt** of court. 183 N.Y.S. 2d 125, 129.

SUBPOENA AD TESTIFICANDUM *(ăd tĕs'-tĭ-fĭ-kän'-dūm)* subpoena to testify. It "is a technical and descriptive name for the ordinary subpoena." 12 A. 2d 128, 129. Compare **summons.**

SUBPOENA DUCES TECUM *(dū'-chĕs tā'-kūm)* under penalty you shall take it with you. Type of subpoena issued by a court at the request of one of the parties to a suit which requires a witness having under his control documents or papers relevant to the controversy to bring such items to court during the trial. 139 So. 794. See, e.g., Fed. R. Civ. Proc. 45(b).

SUBROGATION "the substitution of another person in the place of the **creditor** to whose rights he [the other person] succeeds in relation to the **debt**; one's payment or assumption of an obligation for which another is primarily liable." McClintock, Equity §123 (2d ed. 1948). "This doctrine is not dependent upon **contract**, nor upon **privity** between the parties; it is the creature of **equity**, and is founded upon principles of natural justice. . . . Subrogation has been generally classified as being either legal or conventional. Legal subrogation arises by **operation of law** where one having a **liability**, or right, or a **fiduciary** relation in the premises, pays a debt due by another under such circumstances that he is in equity entitled to the security or obligation held by the creditor whom he has paid. Conventional subrogation, on the other hand, arises where by express or implied agreement with the **debtor**, a person advancing money to discharge a prior **lien** might be substituted to the security of the prior lienee." 18 S.E. 2d 917, 920.

Subrogation typically arises when an insurance company pays its insured under a collision protection feature of an insurance policy; in that event the company is subrogated to the cause of action of its insured. So too, under **workmen's compensation acts** the board is subrogated to the injured worker's right (up to the amount of the board's payments) to sue the responsible party.

SUBROGEE one who, by **subrogation**, succeeds to the legal rights or claims of another.

SUBROGOR one whose legal rights or claims are acquired by another through **subrogation**.

SUBSIDIARY an inferior portion or capacity; usually used in describing the relationship between **corporations**.

SUBSIDIARY CORPORATION one in which another corporation owns at least a majority of the shares and thus has control, 153 A. 159, 160; it

has all of the normal elements of a corporation (charter, by-laws, directors, etc.) but its **stock** is controlled by another corporation known as the PARENT CORPORATION. This relationship of parent and subsidiary often becomes important for tax purposes and for determining whether a court will ignore the corporate existence of the subsidiary and **pierce the corporate veil.**

SUB SILENTIO *(sŭb sĭ-lěn'-shē-ō)*— Lat: under silence; silently. When a later opinion reaches a result contrary to what would appear to be controlling authority, it is said that the later case has overruled sub silentio the prior holding by necessary implication.

SUBSTANTIAL PERFORMANCE [COMPLIANCE] the performance of all the essential terms of a contract so that the purpose of the contract is accomplished; however, unimportant omissions and defects may exist in the strict performance of the contract, see 272 S.W. 616, 619; "that performance of a contract which, while not full performance, is so nearly equivalent to what was bargained for that it would be unreasonable to deny the promisee the full contract price subject to the promisor's right to recover whatever damages may have been occasioned him by the promisee's failure to render full performance." 247 So. 2d 72, 75. See **breach of contract.**

SUBSTANTIVE DUE PROCESS see **due process of law.**

SUBSTANTIVE LAW "the **positive law** which creates, defines and regulates the rights and duties of the **parties** and which may give rise to a **cause of action,** as distinguished from **adjective law** which pertains to and prescribes the practice and **procedure** or the legal machinery by which the substantive law is determined or made effective." 192 P. 2d 589, 593-594.

SUBSTITUTED SERVICE see **service.**

SUBTENANT one who **leases** all or part of rented **premises** from the original **lessee** for a term less than that held by the original lessee. 3 P. 2d 1042, 1043. The original lessee becomes the sublessor as to the subtenant. Most leases either prohibit subletting or require the lessor's permission in advance. The original lessee remains responsible for the subtenant's obligations to the lessor. Compare **assignment.**

SUCCESSION refers to the process by which the property of a **decedent** is taken through **descent** or by **will.** It is a word which clearly excludes those who take by **deed, grant, gift,** or any form of purchase or **contract.** 10 S.W. 505, 507. See **inheritance; intestate succession.**

SUE OUT "to petition for and take out, or to apply for and obtain" a **writ** or court **order,** as to "sue out" a writ in **chancery.** 21 S.W. 811, 812.

SUFFICIENT CONSIDERATION see **consideration.**

SUICIDE the voluntary and intentional killing of one's self; the completed act was a felony at **common law,** but modern statutory law is not unanimous in classifying it as a crime. There is no unanimity on the question of whether **attempted** suicide or **aiding and abetting** suicide is illegal, although the criminalization of aiding and abetting suicide is strongly favored by critical commentators. See Perkins, Criminal Law 86 (2d ed. 1969).

Suicide by one in possession of his mental faculties is ordinarily excluded from insurance coverage. See 9 S.W. 812, 815.

SUI JURIS *(sū-ē' jûr'-ĭs)*—Lat: of his own right; a term used to describe one who is no longer dependent, e.g., one who has reached the age of **majority,** or has been removed from the care of a guardian; signifies one capable of caring for himself. See 196 P. 2d 456, 461. See **emancipation; incompetence.**

SUIT "a very comprehensive [word], . . . understood to apply to any **proceeding** in a court of justice by which an individual pursues that **remedy** which the law affords. The modes of proceeding may be various; but, if a right is litigated in a court of justice, the proceeding by which the decision of the court is sought is a suit." 91 U.S. 367, 375. Formerly applied only to proceed-

ings in **equity,** and now applicable to proceedings in **courts of law** as well. May also be used in relation to criminal procedings, but this is a less proper usage than its more frequent appearance in reference to civil cases. See 144 N.W. 491. See also **action; litigation.**

CLASS SUIT   see **class action.**

(STOCKHOLDERS') DERIVATIVE SUIT   see **derivative action.**

SUMMARY JUDGMENT pre-verdict **judgment** rendered by the court in response to a **motion** by plaintiff or defendant, who claims that the absence of factual dispute on one or more **issues** eliminates the need to send those issues to the **jury;** a "device designed to effect a prompt disposition of controversies on their **merits** without resort to a lengthy trial, if in essence there is no real dispute as to salient facts or if only a question of law is involved." 172 S.E. 2d 816, 817. See Fed. R. Civ. Proc. 56. Also, a judgment issued from a **summary proceeding.** Compare **directed verdict.**

SUMMARY PROCEEDING a method by which the **parties** to a legal controversy may achieve a more expeditious disposition or determination of their case than is usual for the type of matter involved by use of simplified and foreshortened **procedural** rules, usually involving more limited **discovery** or factfinding than is normally permitted in the particular type of proceeding; "a form of **trial** in which the established course of legal **proceedings** is disregarded, especially in the matter of trial by **jury.**" 131 N.E. 82, 84. "In no case can the [matter] be tried summarily unless such proceedings are authorized by legislative authority, except perhaps in cases of contempts, for the common law is a stranger to such a mode of trial." Bouvier's Law Dict. 1066.

Summary proceedings have been commonly used in **arbitration, bankruptcy, landlord-tenant,** and unlawful entry and detainer cases.

SUMMONS "a mandate requiring the **appearance** of said defendant in said **action** under penalty of having **judgment** entered [against him] for failure so to do." 294 P. 499, 500, [which amounts to a **default judgment** since it is entered against the party due to his default]. The object of the summons is to notify the defendant that he has been sued. See 155 N.E. 254, 255. See **process, service.** Compare **subpoena.**

SUO NOMINE *(sū'-ō nō'-mē-nā)*—Lat: in his own name.

SUPERSEDING CAUSE see **cause.**

SUPERVENING CAUSE see **cause.** (IN-TERVENING CAUSE).

SUPRA *(sū'prà)*—Lat: above; in a written work, it refers the reader to a part which precedes that which he is presently reading, as compared with the command "infra" which directs the reader forward. See **infra.**

SUPREMACY CLAUSE popularized title for Article VI, Section [2] of the United States Constitution, which is the main foundation of the federal government's power over the states, providing in effect that the "acts of the Federal Government are operative as supreme law throughout the Union. They are self executing, since they prescribe rules enforceable in all courts of the land. The states have no power to impede, burden, or in any manner control the operation of the laws enacted by the Government of the nation. . . . [T]he full import of the Supremacy Clause was made clear after John Marshall became Chief Justice. In the Marshall interpretation, the clause meant essentially two things: (1) the states may not interfere in any manner with the functioning of the Federal Government; and (2) federal action (whether in the form of a statute, a treaty, a court decision, or an administrative act), if itself constitutional, must prevail over state action inconsistent therewith." Schwarz, Constitutional Law 39-40.

SURETY "one who undertakes to pay money or perform other acts in the event that his **principal** fails therein; the surety is directly and immediately liable for the **debt.**" 334 F. Supp. 1009, 1013. See also **indorsement.**

SURREBUTTER in **common law pleading,** a **plaintiff's** answer to the **defendant's rebuttal** [rebutter].

SURREJOINDER in **common law pleading,** a **plaintiff's** answer to the **defendant's rejoinder.**

SURROGATE a judicial officer of limited **jurisdiction,** who administers matters of **probate** and **intestate succession** and, in some cases, adoptions.

SURVIVAL STATUTE a statute which preserves for his **estate** a decedent's **cause of action** for infliction of **pain and suffering** and related **damages** suffered up to the moment of death. Such a statute is to be contrasted with a **wrongful death** act wherein the causing of the death is viewed not as a **tort** as to the decedent himself, but as a wrong with respect to the family, and which thus operates in favor of the decedent's immediate family for losses occasioned by his or her death, such as lost wages and lost companionship (**consortium**). One chief difference between a survival statute and a wrongful death statute is that "where death is instantaneous, or substantially so, there can be no cause of action under the survival acts, since the decedent has had no time to suffer any appreciable damages, and so no cause of action ever has vested in him." Prosser, Torts 902 (4th ed. 1971).

SURVIVORSHIP a right whereby a person becomes entitled to property by reason of his having survived another person who had an interest in it. 20 N.Y.S. 2d 59, 62. It is one of the elements of a **joint tenancy.** See also **survival statutes.**

SUSPECT CLASSIFICATION see **equal protection of the laws.**

SUSPENDED SENTENCE see **sentence.**

SUSTAIN to support; to approve; to adequately maintain; e.g., the judge "sustained" the **plea** because he found it to be true. 25 N.E. 2d 230; or the plaintiff "sustained" the **burden** of coming forward with the requisite evidence.

SYLLABUS a **head note** which precedes a reported case and which summarizes the principles of law as established in that case. See 47 N.E. 2d 627, 629. Under the practice of the United States Supreme Court the headnotes are prepared for the convenience of readers by the Reporter of Decisions; as such the syllabus constitutes no part of the opinion of the Court. 200 U.S. 321, 337.

SYMBOLIC DELIVERY see **delivery**.

T

TAIL, ESTATE IN see **fee tail**.

TAINTED EVIDENCE [TAINT] see **fruit of the poisonous tree doctrine**.

TANGIBLE PROPERTY property, either **real** or **personal**, capable of being **possessed**; such as is capable of being apprehended by the senses, which is accessible, identifiable, etc., see 228 S.W. 2d 882; 147 N.Y.S. 465, 469. "Tangible property" is corporeal, as distinguished from intangible property or incorporeal rights in property, such as **franchises**, **copyrights**, **easements**, etc. See 57 P. 2d 1022, 1028. For taxation purposes, "tangible property" generally refers to **personalty** [personal property], and is that movable property which has a value of its own, rather than merely the evidence or representative of value, and which has a visible or substantial existence. See 307 U.S. 357.

TAX a rate or sum of money assessed on a citizen's person or property for the support of the government, 86 S.E. 2d 672, 676, and commonly levied upon assets or real property (property tax), or income derived from wages, etc. (income tax), or upon the sale or purchase of goods (sales tax).

AD VALOREM TAX a tax on the value of the actual property subject to taxation laid as a percentage of that value, as opposed to a specific tax which is applied as a fixed sum to all of a certain class of articles. See 194 S.E. 151, 154.

CAPITAL GAINS TAX see **capital** [CAPITAL GAINS].

EXCISE TAX see **excise**.

ESTATE TAX tax upon the transfer of property, and not a tax on the prop-

erty itself. Estate taxes are based on the power to transmit or the transmission from the dead to the living, while **inheritance taxes** are based on the right to receive the property and are thus applied to the recipients thereof. 298 F. 803, 810. See also 244 N.Y.S. 2d 960, 964.

POLL TAX see **poll tax**.

TAX SALE see **sale**.

TEMPORARY INJUNCTION see **injunction**.

TEMPORE *(tĕm'-pō-rā)*—Lat: for the time of; thus, the "President pro tempore" of the United States Senate is the President for the present time (when the Vice President is not presiding over the Senate).

TENANCY a **tenant's** right to possess an **estate**, whether by **lease** or by **title**, deriving from the Latin "tenes," meaning "to hold." See 17 S.W. 546, 547. Tenancy refers generally to any such right to hold property, but in a more limited sense it refers to holding in subordination to another's title, as in the landlord-tenant relationship. The various types of tenancy include the following:

HOLDOVER TENANCY see TENANCY AT SUFFERANCE, below.

JOINT TENANCY "a single **estate** in **property**, real or personal, owned by two or more persons, under one **instrument** or act of the parties, [with] an equal right in all to share in the enjoyment during their lives; and on the death of a joint tenant, the property descends to the survivor or survivors and at length to the last survivor." 309 P. 2d 1022, 1025. Joint tenancy originally was a technical feudal estate in land, but now applies, through statutes, to **personalty** as well. It is particularly common in the purchase of **stocks** and **bonds** and in bank accounts. At common law, a joint tenancy was found to have been formed when there were the four **unities** of time, title, interest, and possession, and these "four unities" are still referred to as elements of a joint tenancy. The primary characteristic of a "joint tenancy" is the **right of survivorship**, which distinguishes it from a TENANCY IN COMMON [see be-

low]. Unlike a TENANCY BY THE EN-
TIRETY [see below], a joint tenancy
may be **partitioned** [divided] by one
joint tenant by a **sale** or **incumbrance**
(i.e., a joint tenant's interest may be
reached by his **creditors**), without the
consent of the other(s). When this
happens, a "tenancy in common" is
created, because (technically) the unities of time and title or interest are
broken. See 189 N.E. 576, 578.

TENANCY IN COMMON　an interest held
by two or more persons, each having
a possessory right, usually deriving
from a title (though also from a lease)
in the same piece of land. "Tenancy
in common" also applies in **personalty**. See 107 P. 2d 933, 934. At common law, a tenancy in common was
(and still is) characterized by unity
of possession. Though co-tenants may
have unequal shares in the property,
they are each entitled to equal use and
possssion. Thus, each is said to have
an "undivided interest" in the property. See 176 P. 2d 425, 427. An estate
held as a tenancy in common may be
partitioned, sold or incumbered. See
partition.

TENANCY BY THE ENTIRETY　the ownership of property, real or personal,
tangible and **intangible**, by a husband
and wife together. In addition to the
four **unities** of time, title, interest, and
possession, **unity of person** must exist.
The husband and wife are said to be
"seized as one person." See 155 N.E.
787. Neither is allowed to **alienate**
any part of the property so held without consent of the other. The survivor
of the marriage is entitled to the
whole estate. See 295 F. 429, 431. A
divorce severs the tenancies by the entirety and usually creates a tenancy
in common. See 168 S.W. 2d 1087,
1090. Under the MARRIED WOMAN'S
ACTS each tenant by the entirety is a
"tenant in common" of the **use**, and
therefore entitled to one-half of the
rents and profits while both are alive.
See 125 N.Y.S. 1071, 1072.

TENANCY IN CAPITE　tenancy-in-chief.
In feudal law, the holding of land directly from the crown.

TENANCY FOR YEARS　an estate in land
created by a lease which is limited to
endure for any specified and definite

term, whether in weeks, months or
years. It is **determinable** [i.e. it ends]
upon the expiration of that term, and
does not require **notice** of re-entry by
the **landlord** nor notice to quit by the
tenant. However, if the tenant stays
on, the tenancy may be converted
into a TENANCY AT SUFFERANCE [see
below], TENANCY AT WILL [see be-
low], or a PERIODIC TENANCY [see be-
low], determinable as tenancies of
those kinds. See 82 P. 20, 21, 178 A.
113, 115, 94 P. 2d 335, 337. A "tenancy for years" is **alienable**, subject to
lease restrictions against **assignment**
or **sublease**.

TENANCY FROM YEAR TO YEAR　see
PERIODIC TENANCY, below.

TENANCY FROM MONTH TO MONTH　see
PERIODIC TENANCY, below

PERIODIC TENANCY　in landlord-tenant
law, a **tenancy** for a particular period
(a week, month, year, or number of
years), plus the expectancy or possibility that the period will be repeated.
In contrast to a "tenancy for years,"
a periodic tenancy must be terminated by due notice to quit by either the
landlord or the tenant, unless one
party has failed to perform some part
of his obligation. A periodic tenancy
is considered a form of TENANCY AT
WILL [see below], and is created either
by express agreement or by implication from the manner in which rent
is paid. For example, if A holds B's
land with no express time limitation,
and rent is payable with reference to
divisions of a year, it will be deemed
a tenancy from year to year. See 3
S.E. 2d 484, 485. State statutes govern the time necessary for due notice
to be given. A periodic tenancy is also
alienable.

TENANCY AT WILL　in landlord-tenant
law, a leased estate which confers upon the tenant the right to possession
for an indefinite period such as is
agreed upon by both parties. See 284
P. 2d 580, 582. A tenancy at will is
characterized primarily by the uncertain term and the right of either party
to terminate upon proper notice. A
tenancy at will may arise out of an
express contract or by implication.
Because a tenancy at will is determin-

able at any time, the tenant cannot **assign** or **grant** his estate to another. See 55 Me. 33, 36.

TENANCY AT SUFFERANCE [HOLD-OVER TENANCY] in landlord-tenant law, a tenancy that comes into existence when one at first lawfully possesses land as under a lease, and subsequently "holds over beyond the end of one term of such lease or occupies it without such lawful authority. For example, if A has a tenancy for years for one month, at the end of that month, if A continues in possession, his becomes a tenancy at sufferance [or holdover tenancy]. Thus a tenancy at sufferance cannot arise from an agreement, which distinguishes it from a tenancy at will. A tenant at sufferance differs from a **trespasser** only in that he originally entered with the landlord's permission. See 228 P. 2d 705. The landlord has a right to establish a landlord-tenant relationship (i.e., extend the lease) of a tenancy at sufferance. Reciprocally, a tenant cannot be sued for trespass as a tenant at sufferance before the landlord enters and demands possession. See 32 A. 2d 247. A tenant at sufferance cannot grant such an estate to a third person.

TENANT one who holds land by any kind of **title** or right, whether permanently or temporarily; one who purchases an **estate** and is entitled to **possession**, whether exclusive or to be shared with others; also, one who **leases** premises from the owner (**landlord**) or from his tenant as a **sub-tenant**.

TENANT IN FEE [SIMPLE] "a tenant in fee simple who hath lands, tenements, or hereditaments to hold to him and his heirs forever; generally, absolutely and simply without mentioning what heirs, but referring that to his own pleasure, or to the disposition of the law." 78 P. 2d 905, 908. The "word 'fee' alone, without any qualifying words, serves to designate a **fee simple estate**, and is not infrequently used in that sense." Id. at 907.

TENDER an unconditional offer to **perform** coupled with a manifested ability to carry out the offer and production of the subject matter (money,

etc.) of the tender, 243 F. Supp. 741, 744; an offer of performance which, if unjustifiably refused, places the refusing party in default and permits the party making tender to exercise his remedy for **breach of contract.** 17 P. 2d 952, 953.

TENDER OFFER a public offer made to **stockholders** of a particular **corporation** to purchase a given number of shares at a given price. The price quoted in such an offer is payable only if the offeror is able to obtain the total amount of stock specified in the offer. The number is usually sufficient to give the offeror control of the corporation.

TENEMENT strictly, property of a permanent and fixed nature including both **corporeal** and **incorporeal real property.** In modern usage, "tenement" applies to any house, building or structure attached to land, and also to any kind of human habitation or dwelling inhabited by a **tenant.** See 203 S.W. 36, 37, 73 N.E. 241, 243. "Tenement" is frequently used to indicate inferior dwellings and/or those rented to the poor. See 75 N.Y.S. 768, 769. For example an early statutory definition of "tenement" was: "Any house, building, structure or portion thereof, occupied, or adapted for occupation, as a dwelling by more than three families living independently of one another and doing their cooking upon the premises, or by more than two families above the first story so living and cooking." Mass. Stat. 1907, C. 550, §42. Compare **premises.**

TENURE right to hold, 39 N.W. 2d 359, 360; in real property, an ancient hierarchical system of holding lands. See 187 N.Y.S. 216, 231.

The term also refers to a statutory right of certain civil servants and teachers in the public schools to retain their positions permanently, subject only to removal for adequate cause, or economic necessity; e.g., the abolition of a department where the enrollment eliminates the demand and the tenured teacher is not qualified to teach another subject taught by a non-tenured teacher. In addition, tenure is frequently guaranteed by contract for teachers and professors in private educational institutions. In these situations, the standard clause provides for termination of tenured faculty only for adequate cause or in extraordinary circumstances, in case of demonstrably or bona fide financial exigency. See American Assoc. of Univ. Professors, Statement of Principles on Academic Freedom and Tenure in AAUP Bulletin 44:290-293 (No. 1A, 1958). This is the standard statement of academic tenure for private institutions. See also C. Byse and L. Joughin, Tenure in American Higher Education 172-175 (1959).

Where dismissal is for cause, notice and a hearing according the teacher rudimentary **due process** is required both in the public and the private sector.

TENURIAL OWNERSHIP see **ownership**.

TERM OF COURT a definite time period prescribed by law for a court to administer its duties. See 190 N.E. 270, 272. "Term" and "session" are often used interchangeably, but technically, "term" is the statutory time prescribed for judicial business and "session" is the time a court actually sits to hear cases. 242 S.W. 993, 994. In general, terms of court no longer have any special significance, fixed periods of days having replaced the stated terms of court.

TESTACY the state or condition of leaving a **will** at one's death, as opposed to "**intestacy**" which is the condition of dying without having made a will.

TESTAMENT strictly, a testimonial or just statement of a person's wishes concerning the disposition of his **personal property** after death, in contrast to a **will**, which is strictly a **devise** of **real estate**. See 21 Wend., N.Y., 430, 436. Commonly, however, "will" and "testament" are considered synonymous. 74 P. 2d 27, 32. The law of "testaments" is statutory. 147 S.W. 2d 644, 647. The word is rarely used today except in the formal heading of one's will, which reads "This is the last will and testament of. . . ."

TESTAMENTARY DISPOSITION a gift of property which **vests** [takes effect] at the time of the death of the person making the disposition. It can be effected by **deed**, by an **inter vivos** transaction, or by **will**. See 17 Cal. Rptr. 744, 751. All instruments used to make testamentary dispositions must comply with the requirements of the **statute of wills**. See **causa mortis**.

TESTATOR [TESTATRIX] one who makes and executes a **testament** or **will**, "testator" applying to males, "testatrix" to females. See also **intestate; testacy; testament; testamentary disposition**. Compare **administrator; executor**.

TESTIMONY a statement made by a **witness**, under oath, usually related to a legal **proceeding**; "**evidence** given by a competent witness under oath or affirmation as distinguished from evidence derived from writing and other sources. . . . Evidence is the broader term and includes all testimony, which is one species of evidence." 470 S.W. 2d 679, 682. See **expert witness**.

THEFT see **larceny**.

THIRD PARTY see **party**.

THIRD-PARTY BENEFICIARY "persons who are recognized as having enforceable rights created in them by a **contract** to which they are not **parties** and for which they give no **consideration**. These persons can be loosely grouped into two classes; (1) donee beneficiaries, and (2) creditor (or obligee) beneficiaries. The third person is a DONEE BENEFICIARY if the promisee who buys the promise expresses an intention and purpose to confer a benefit upon him as a **gift** in the shape of the promised performance. He is a CREDITOR BENEFICIARY if the promisee, or some other person, is under an obligation (a duty or a liability) to him and the contract is so made that the promised performance or the making of the executory contract itself will discharge that obligation." Corbin, Contracts 727 (One Vol. ed. 1952). The contract must be primarily for the third person's benefit, so that an incidental beneficiary of a contract would not have sufficient interest under which to enforce the promise. Restatement of Contracts § 147.

A third person's interest may be cut off prior to **vesting** by **recission** between the contracting parties. Once a third person's rights are vested, he may sue the promisor in the event of a **breach**. This prevents the promisor from **unjust** enrichment and avoids multiple litigation in the case of a creditor beneficiary. Any defenses available to the promisor arising from the contract may be asserted against the beneficiary. Corbin, **supra**, §818.

TIDE LAND land over which the tide ebbs and flows, see 150 F. 840, 842; land covered and uncovered by ordinary tides. See 219 P. 197, 199. The limit of the tide land is usually the mean high tide. See **avulsion; reliction.**

TITHE in old English law, a right of the clergy to extract for the use of the Church one tenth of the produce of lands and personal industry of the people. These tithes have been compared to rent charges or **ground rents**. 3 Steph. Com. 731.

TITLE as used in property law, "a shorthand term used to denote the facts which, if proved, will enable a **plaintiff** to recover **possession** or a **defendant** to retain possession of a thing." Cribbet, Principles of the Law of Property 15 (1962). Having title to something means having the right to possess the thing. The term is used most often in connection with **real property**. As to the sale of goods, the Uniform Commercial Code limits the effect of title upon the rights, obligations, and remedies covered by the Code. U.C.C. §2-401.

ADVERSE TITLE a title asserted in opposition to another; one claimed to have been acquired by **adverse possession.**

CLEAR TITLE see **clear title.**

CLEAR TITLE OF RECORD a **title** which the record shows to be an indefeasible unincumbered **estate**. It differs from a **clear title** in that the latter can be demonstrated by evidence independent of the record. See 154 N.E. 920, 921.

COLOR OF TITLE see **color of title.**

EQUITABLE TITLE ownership which is recognized by a court of equity or founded upon equitable principles as opposed to formal legal title. The purchaser of real property can specifically enforce his contract for purhase and as a result, prior to the actual conveyance, he has an enforceable equitable title which can be terminat-

ed only by a **bona fide purchaser**. See **specific performance.**

MARKETABLE TITLE see **marketable title.**

QUIET TITLE see **quiet title.**

TITLE JURISDICTION a jurisdiction in which **title** to **mortgaged premises** passes to the **mortgagee**, and only passes back to mortgagor (home owner) when full payment is made. See **lien jurisdictions.**

TITLE SEARCH a search made through the records maintained in the public record office to determine the state of a **title**, including all **liens, encumbrances, mortgages, future interests,** etc., affecting the property; the means by which a **chain of title** is ascertained.

TITLE THEORY see **mortgage.**

TORT a wrong; a private or **civil** wrong or injury independent of contract, resulting from a **breach** of a legal **duty**. 256 N.E. 2d 254, 259. The essential elements of a tort are the existence of a legal duty owed by **defendant** to **plaintiff**, breach of that duty, and a causal relation between defendant's conduct and the resulting damages to plaintiff. See also **derivative tort.**

TORT-FEASOR one who commits a **tort.**

JOINT TORT-FEASORS those who act together or independently to commit a tortious act on a person, causing a single injury. See 267 F. 472, 475. See **joint tort-feasor.**

TORTIOUS adjective describing conduct that subjects the actor(s) to tort liability, 143 N.E. 2d 673, 680; unlawful. 68 N.Y.S. 744, 745.

TO WIT namely; that is to say.

TRACT INDEX see **chain of title.**

TRADE FIXTURE property placed on or annexed to rented **real estate** by a **tenant** for the purpose of aiding himself in the conduct of a trade or business. The law makes provisions for the tenant to remove such **fixtures** at the end of his tenacy though the tenant is responsible to the landlord for any damage to the premises resulting from such removal, unlike other fixtures which are considered **improvements** and which the tenant must leave intact. See 175 P. 2d 512, 518; 65 A. 2d 523, 526. See **waste.**

TRADEMARK "any mark, word, letter, number, design, picture or combination thereof in any form or arrangement, which (a) is adopted and used by a person to denominate goods which he marks and; (b) is affixed to the goods and (c) is not . . . a common or generic name for the goods or a picture of them, or a geographical, personal or corporate or other association name, or a design descriptive of the goods or their quality, ingredients, properties or functions and; (d) the use of which is prohibited neither by legislative enactment nor an otherwise defined public policy." Restatement, Torts §715.

Protection from an infringement upon a trademark is afforded by the common law action for "unfair competition" once the trademark in question has been sufficiently identified with the goods, see 175 F. 2d 795, and by an action under state law in those states which permit one to register trademarks and which impose civil and criminal penalties for their unlawful infringement, see, e.g., 267 N.Y.S. 2d 269, or by an action under federal law which standardizes the common law action and registers trademarks for persons engaged in interstate commerce. See 15 U.S.C. §1051.

TRANSACTIONAL IMMUNITY see **self-incrimination.**

TRANSFER "to convey or remove from one place, person, etc., to another; pass or hand over from one to another; specifically, to take over the **possession** or control of, e.g., to transfer **title** to land; sell or give."25 N.E. 999, 1001.

TRANSFERRED INTENT a recognized concept in **tort,** and, to a lesser extent, in criminal law, which states that if defendant intends harm to A but harms B instead, the "intent" is said to be "transferred" to the harm befalling the actual victim as far as defendant's liability to B in tort is concerned. This is only a "fiction," or a legal conclusion, created in order to accomplish the desired result in terms of liability. See

Prosser, Torts 33 (4th ed., 1971). In criminal law, the doctrine has limited usefulness, see Id. at 822-828, but is chiefly applied to a situation wherein "if A by **malice aforethought** strikes at B and missing him strikes C whereof he dies, though he never bore any **malice** to C yet it is **murder;** and the law transfers the malice to the party slain." 1 Hale P.C. 466; 297 P. 2d 1053.

TRAVERSE a common law pleading which denies the opposing party's **allegations** of fact; "a denial by a party of facts alleged in an adverse **pleading** . . . [or] a denial that he has sufficient knowledge or information to form a belief concerning them." 9 S.W. 281.

GENERAL TRAVERSE a blanket denial, stated in general terms, intended to cover all the allegations.

SPECIAL TRAVERSE a denial which is not absolute, but which seeks to establish a denial through the presentation of supplementary facts (or **new matter**) which, if accurate, would render the allegations untenable. See 13 A. 2d 456. See **absque hoc; confession and avoidance.**

TREASON a crime involving "[a]dherence to the enemy and rendering him aid and comfort." 325 U.S. 1. "Treason against the United States is defined by the Constitution itself. . . . By this instrument, it is declared that 'treason against the United States shall consist only in levying war against them, or in adhering to their enemies, giving them aid and comfort." 26 Fed. Cas. 18, 21.

TREATY in international law, a compact made between two or more independent nations with a view to the public welfare, 107 F. 2d 819, 827; "an international agreement of the United States must relate to the external concerns of the nation as distinguished from matters of purely internal nature." Restatement 2d, Foreign Relations Law of the United States §40 (1965). Under the Constitution the President has the sole power to initiate and make treaties, which must be approved by the Senate before they become binding on citizens of the United States as law. Art. II, §2. An EXECUTIVE AGREEMENT is often substituted for a treaty and does not require the advice and consent of the Senate but such agreements can reach only narrower topics or be entered into pursuant to formal authority delegated by the Congress in particular legislation. See 69 F. 2d 44, 48. Trade agreements, for example, are often executive agreements rather than treaties. States may not engage in treaties of any kind, and once a treaty becomes law it is binding on the states under the **supremacy clause**. Art. I, §10, c. 1; Art. VI, c. 2.

TREBLE DAMAGES see **damages**.

TRESPASS at common law, a **form of action** instituted to recover **damages** for any unlawful injury to the plaintiff's person, **property**, or rights, involving immediate force or violence, 235 S.W. 2d 531, 532; also used today to signify the violent act itself which causes such an injury. See 266 A. 2d 175, 180-81. In modern parlance, the term most often connotes a wrongful interference with or disturbance of the **possession** of another, 69 So. 2d 724, 726, and is applied to **personalty** [things] as well as to **realty**, see 287 S.W. 2d 202, 204.

CONTINUING TRESPASS "where the defendant erects a structure or dumps rubbish upon the land of the plaintiff, the invasion is continued by a failure to remove it. In such a case, there is a continuing wrong so long as the offending object remains. A purchaser of the land may recover for the continuing trespass, and a transferee of the defendant's interest in the chattel or structure may be liable." Prosser, Torts §13 (4th ed. 1971).

TRESPASS ON THE CASE one of the two early English actions at **common law** dealing with **torts** (the other being **trespass**). Trespass on the case, or simply "case," afforded remedy against injury to person or property indirectly resulting from the conduct of the defendant. The action of trespass covered only directly resulting injury. "The classic illustration of the difference between trespass and case is that of a log thrown into the highway. A person struck by the log as it fell could maintain trespass

against the thrower, since injury was direct; but one who was hurt by stumbling over it as it lay in the road, could maintain, not trespass, but an action on the case." Prosser, Torts 29 (4th ed. 1971).

TRESPASS QUARE CLAUSUM FREGIT trespass "whereby he broke the close;" where the defendant enters upon the land of the plaintiff, he is subject to damages for such entrance under the common law. See 57 A. 2d 329, 330. See **quare clausum fregit**.

TRESPASS VI ET ARMIS trespass with force and arms, or by an unlawful means; a remedy for injuries accompanied with force or violence, or where the act done is in itself an immediate injury to another's person or property. 173 S.W. 2d 606, 613.

TRIAL an examination usually involving the offering of testimony, before a competent tribunal according to established procedures, of facts or law put in issue in a cause for the purpose of determining such issue. See 106 N.Y.S. 2d 933, 934.

TRIAL DE NOVO a completely new trial held at the appellate level in which the case is tried as if the original trial had never taken place. See 280 P. 1083, 1085. Trial de novo is most frequently encountered after trial in local courts of very limited jurisdiction, and in some kinds of administrative hearings. New testimony may be addressed or the matter may be determined de novo on the basis of the evidentiary **record** produced below.

TRIBUNAL an officer or body having authority to adjudicate matters. 75 F. Supp. 486, 487. See also **forum**.

TRIER OF FACT see **fact-finder**.

TRIPARTITE having three parts.

T.R.O. temporary **restraining order**.

TROVER an early common law **tort action** to recover **damages** for a wrongful **conversion** of **personal property** or to recover actual **possession** of such property. See 49 S.E. 2d 500, 504. Originally, the action was limited to cases in which **lost property** had been found and converted by the finder to his own use. See 28 A. 2d 334, 337.

Later the action was expanded to include property not actually lost and found, but only wrongly converted. At first, a fiction was created (when the facts revealed otherwise) that such property had been lost and found, but since the distinction was later abandoned, the use of such a fiction became unnecessary. See Prosser, Torts 79-80 (4th ed. 1971). Compare **detinue; replevin; trespass; unlawful detainer.**

TRUE BILL see **indictment.**

TRUST " 'a right of property, real or personal, held by one party for the benefit of another.' . . . It implies two interests, one legal, and the other **equitable;** the **trustee** holding the legal title or intrest; and the **cestui que trust** or **beneficiary** holding the equitable title or interest." 140 P. 2d 335, 338. The one who supplies the property or **consideration [res]** for the trust is the **settlor** [also called trustor or **donor**]. Trust also applies generally to any relationship in which one acts as a **guardian** or **fiduciary** in relation to another's property. Thus a deposit of money in a bank is a "trust," or the receipt of money to be applied to a particular purpose or to be paid to another is a "trust." See 18 A. 1056, 1058.   ⟍

CESTUI QUE TRUST *(sĕs'-twē kā)*—Old Fr: beneficiary; "one for whose benefiᵗ the trust is created . . . The property given in trust is called the subject matter, or trust **res** [or corpus]." 195 N.E. 557, 564.

EXPRESS TRUST [DIRECT TRUST] a trust created from the free and deliberate act of the parties, including an affirmative intention of the **settlor** [the one granting the property] to set up the trust, usually evidenced by some writing, **deed,** or will. See 13 N.W. 2d 749, 751. A **parole** [oral] agreement to create a trust cannot be enforced where the **statute of frauds** requires a written instrument. See 210 S.W. 2d 985, 987, 988. Trusts are generally classified as either "express" or "implied," the latter class including RESULTING TRUSTS and CONSTRUCTIVE TRUSTS. (See below) See 55 S.E. 377, 379. A valid express trust requires the cooperation of three parties: the settlor; the trustee [the

one who administers the trust and who holds legal title], and the beneficiary [for whose benefit the trust is created].

IMPLIED TRUST one which is inferred from the parties' transactions by **operation of law,** in contrast to an express trust which is created by the parties deliberate acts and/or expression of intent. See 189 P. 396, 398; 149 S.W. 2d 930, 932, 933. Implied trusts can be either "constructive" or "resulting." See 55 S.E. 377, 379.

CONSTRUCTIVE TRUST [INVOLUNTARY TRUST] one which is found to exist by operation of law or by "construction" of the court, regardless of any lack of express agreement between or intent on the part of the parties. When one party has been wrongfully deprived either by mistake, fraud, or some other breach of faith or confidence, of some right, benefit, or title to the property, a court may impose upon the present holder of legal title a constructive trust for the benefit of that party. See 219 S.W. 2d 282, 285. Thus in order to prevent the **unjust enrichment** of the legal holder, such person is deemed to hold the property as a trustee for the **beneficial use** of that party which has been wrongfully deprived of its rights. See 25 N.W. 2d 225, 228. Contrast RESULTING TRUST.

PRECATORY TRUST one frequently created by a **will,** arising from words of entreaty, wish, expectation, request, or recommendation which are expressed therein. Though they do not amount to actual instructions or directives, such words are effective to create a trust so long as they are not "so modified by the context as to amount to no more than mere suggestions, to be acted upon or not, according to the caprice of the interested **devisee.** . . ." 50 P. 578, 579. See **precatory.**

RESULTING TRUST a **trust** arising by implication of law when it appears from the nature of the transaction that it was the intention of the parties to create a trust. See 121 N.E. 621, 627. It is therefore to be distinguished from a "constructive trust" in that "a resulting trust is a status that automatically arises by operation of law out of certain circumstances, while a constructive trust is a remedy that **equity** applied in order to prevent injustice or in order to do justice." 89 C.J.S., Trusts §14. Thus a "resulting trust" involves the element of intent, which, though implied, makes it more like an EXPRESS TRUST. A constructive trust, in contrast, is sometimes found contrary to the parties' intent, in order to work equity or frustrate **fraud**. See 53 A. 2d 805.

TRUST DEED see **deed of trust**.

TRUSTEE one who holds legal **title** to property "in **trust**" for the benefit of another person, and who is required to carry out specific duties with regard to the property, or who has been given power affecting the disposition of property for another's benefit. "Trustee" is also used loosely as anyone who acts as a **guardian** or **fiduciary** in relationship to another, such as a public officer towards his constituents, a state toward its citizens, or a partner to his co-partner. See **use**. Compare **settlor**.

TRUSTEE IN BANKRUPCTY an officer, elected and approved by the **referee** or judge of a **bankruptcy** proceeding, who takes legal title to the property and/or money of the bankrupt and holds it "in trust" for equitable distribution among the bankrupt's **creditors**. See 65 A. 430, 431, 192 F. 830, 832, 99 F. 691, 694.

TRUST FUND **real** or **personal property** held "in **trust**" for the benefit of another person; the **corpus [res]** of a trust.

TRUSTOR one who creates a **trust**; more often called the **settlor**.

TRY TITLE to submit to judicial scrutiny the legitimacy of **title** to property. See also **quiet title**.

ULTIMATE FACTS facts said to "lie

in the area between evidence and a conclusion of law. They are the essential and determining facts on which the final conclusion of law is predicated. They are deduced by **inference** from evidentiary facts, which can be directly established by testimony or evidence," 74 N.E. 2d 563, 567. Compare **mediate data**.

ULTRAHAZARDOUS ACTIVITY an activity giving rise to **strict liability** which "necessarily involves a risk of serious harm to the person, land or **chattels** of others, which cannot be eliminated by the exercise of utmost care" and which "is not a matter of common usage." Restatement, Torts §§519, 520. Blasting is universally recognized as an ultrahazardous activity, and it should be noted that strict liability in this context means the duty owed cannot be **delegated**, e.g., an owner of property who hires an independent **contractor** to perform blasting cannot thereby escape liability for damage resulting from the blasting operation. See Restatement 2d, Torts §§423, 427.

ULTRA VIRES *(ŭl'-trá vē'-rāz)*—Lat: beyond, outside of, in excess of powers; that which is beyond the power authorized by law for an entity. The term applies especially to an action of a **corporation** which is beyond the powers conferred upon it by its **charter**, or by the statute under which it was created. See 79 S.W. 2d 1012, 1016. Ultra vires activities of a corporation may give rise to an action **quo warranto** by the state **attorney general** to forfeit the corporation's charter of incorporation.

UNCLEAN HANDS one of the **equitable** maxims embodying the principle that a party seeking equitable **relief** must not have done any dishonest or unethical act in the transaction upon which he maintains an action in equity; a court of conscience will not grant relief to one guilty of unconscionable conduct. See 171 A. 738.

UNCONDITIONAL DISCHARGE see **sentence**.

UNCONSCIONABLE so unreasonable to the interest of a contracting party as to render the **contract** unenforceable.

The common law rule rendering unconscionable contracts unenforceable was codified in the Uniform Commercial Code in §2-302. "The basic test is whether, in the light of the general commercial background and the commercial needs of the particular trade or case, the clauses involved are so one-sided as to be unconscionable under the circumstances existing at the time of the making of the contract." U.C.C. §2-302 Official Comment.

"Unconscionability has generally been recognized to include an absence of meaningful choice on the part of one of the parties together with contract terms which are unreasonably favorable to the other party.... Ordinarily, one who signs an agreement without full knowledge of its terms might be held to **assume the risk** that he has entered into a one-sided bargain. But when a party of little bargaining power and hence little real choice, signs a commercially unreasonable contract with little or no knowledge of its terms, it is hardly likely that his consent . . . was ever given to all the terms. In such a case the usual rule that the terms of an agreement are not to be questioned should be abandoned and the court should consider whether the terms of the contract are so unfair that enforcement should be withheld." 350 F. 2d 445, 449-50. See also **duress.**

UNDER COLOR OF LAW see **color of law.**

UNDER COLOR OF TITLE see **color of title.**

UNDERLEASE see **sublease.**

UNDERWRITE to insure the satisfaction of an obligation, such as an **insurance** contract or the sale of **bonds.** To underwrite an insurance contract is to act as the insurer for the life or property of another. See 69 N.W. 141. To underwrite a **stock** or bond issue is to insure the sale of stocks or bonds by agreeing to buy the entire issue if they are not sold to the public before a certain date. See 70 F. 2d 815.

UNDISCLOSED PRINCIPAL see **principal.**

UNDIVIDED INTEREST [UNDIVIDED RIGHTS] that interest or right in **property** owned by **tenants in common, joint tenants,** or **tenants by the entirety,** whereby each tenant has an equal right to make use of and enjoy the entire property. See 63 F. Supp. 220, 223. An "undivided interest" derives from **unity of possession,** which is essential to the above tenancies. "Undivided interests" in property are to be distinguished from interests that have been **partitioned,** i.e., divided and distributed to the different owners for their use in **severalty.** See 33 Mass. 87, 98. An undivided interest may be of only a fractional share, e.g., "an undivided one-quarter interest," in which case the holder is entitled to one-quarter of all profits and sale proceeds but has a right to possession of the whole.

UNDUE INFLUENCE influence of another which destroys the requisite free agency of a **testator** or **donor** and creates a ground for nullifying a **will** or invalidating an improvident **gift.** 32 A. 2d 371, 374. It is established by excessive importunity, superiority of will or mind, the relationship of the parties (e.g., priest and penitent) or by any other means constraining the donor or testator to do what he is unable to refuse. See 58 A. 2d 31, 33. The elements of undue influence are susceptibility of testator/donor to such influence, the exertion of improper influence, and submission to the domination of the influencing party. See 160 N.W. 2d 49, 50. The strong influence of affection, however, does not constitute undue influence. 159 N.E. 305, 309. Compare **duress.**

UNEXECUTED USE see **use.**

UNILATERAL CONTRACT see **contract.**

UNILATERAL MISTAKE see **mistake.**

UNITIES the **common law** requirements necessary in order to create a **joint tenancy,** or a tenancy **by the entirety.** A joint tenancy requires the "four unities" of "interest," "possession," "time," and "title," and in addition to the four unities, a tenancy by the entirety requires "unity of person." Tenants in common, as a result of the kind of estate they hold, have a unity of possession but no unity is required to create such an estate.

UNITY OF INTEREST the requirement that **interests** of the co-tenants in a joint tenancy or tenancy by the entirety be equal. An individual joint tenant cannot encumber his "share" by **mortgage** without destroying this unity; to preserve the joint tenancy the mortgage must be agreed to by all. Tenants in common are not subject to this unity of interest rule and may have unequal shares in the same property.

UNITY OF POSSESSION the equal right of each co-owner of property to the **use** and **possession** of the whole property. See 300 S.W. 2d 379, 383. Unity of possession is necessary for each of the three types of co-tenancies. See **undivided interest**.

UNITY OF TIME the requirement that the interests of the co-tenants in a joint tenancy or tenancy by the entirety must commence (or **vest**) at the same moment in time.

UNITY OF TITLE the requirement that all tenants of a joint tenacy or both tenants of a tenancy by the entirety acquire their interests under the same **title**; thus, such co-tenants cannot hold by different **deeds**. See 126 N.E. 2d 479, 480.

UNITY OF PERSON the common law requirement for the creation of a tenancy by the entirety that the co-tenants be husband and wife, based on the conception that marriage created a "unity of person." See 103 So. 833, 834.

UNIVERSAL AGENT one authorized to transact all the business of his **principal** of every kind. See 10 So. 304, 307. See **agent**.

UNJUST ENRICHMENT principle in law of contracts by which "a person who has been unjustly enriched at the expense of another is required to make **restitution** to the other." Restatement, Restitution 1. Restitution and unjust enrichment are the modern designations for the older doctrine of **quasi-contracts**, which are not true contracts, but are obligations created by the law when money, property, or services have been obtained by one person at the expense of another under such circumstances that in equity and good conscience he ought not retain it. See 209 P. 2d 457, 460. When one receives a benefit and his retention of it would be inequitable, the law will impose a duty to pay compensation in order to prevent unjust enrichment. Retention of a benefit without compensation will not be considered inequitable or unjust if the benefit was conferred without any reasonable basis of compensation and in no event should the compensation ordered exceed the compensation anticipated by the person who rendered the service or delivered the goods. But see **officious intermeddler**. See also **quantum meruit**.

UNLAWFUL ASSEMBLY a **misdemeanor** at common law consisting of "a meeting of three or more persons with a common plan in mind which, if carried out, [would] result in a riot; a meeting with intent to commit a crime by open force or execute a common design lawful or unlawful in an unauthorized manner likely to cause courageous persons to apprehend a **breach of the peace**." Perkins, Criminal Law 403-404 (2d ed. 1969). The right of people of this country "peaceably to assemble" is constitutionally guaranteed by the First Amendment. See also **conspiracy**.

UNLAWFUL DETAINER the act of holding **possession** without right, as in the case of a tenant whose lease has expired. UNLAWFUL DETAINER STATUTES often create a right to oust by summary process a **holdover tenant** and to determine speedily the right to possession of real property, thus avoiding the judicially disfavored remedy of **self-help**. The summary process determines only the question of possession and no ultimate determination of **title** or **estate** can be made in such a proceeding. See 173 P. 2d 343, 348. See **forcible entry and detainer**.

UNNATURAL ACT see **crime against nature**.

UNNATURAL OFFENSE see **crime against nature**.

UNREASONABLE RESTRAINT OF TRADE see **restraint of trade**.

USE the right to enjoy the benefits flowing from **real** or **personal property**. "Landowners resorted to the practice of vesting legal **title** in another, upon the understanding that the land would be administered for the use and benefit of the transferor or for the use and benefit of his nominee. **Equitable** protection of the interests of such person early developed to a point where it could be said that he had equitable ownership. Legal ownership might thus be separated from EQUITABLE OWNERSHIP— the 'use'   .," Burby, Real Property 7 (3rd ed. 1965). Uses, historically, have been created (1) by express provision in a valid **deed**; (2) by implication to the conveyor when **conveyance** is made without **consideration** [called a RESULTING USE]; (3) by **bargain and sale**; (4) by covenant to stand **seised**. Id. at 8. Under the **Statute of Uses**, the party in whom a use was created was deemed seised of a like **estate** as he had in the use, hence "A to B for the use of C for life" was operative under the statute to convey to C a life estate. It should be noted that not all uses were converted under the Statute to legal interests or estates. The Statute applied to PASSIVE USES, i.e., instances where the legal titleholder had no obligations with respect to the estate other than to hold title. Thus, A to B for the use of C created a passive use which the statute converted into a legal estate in C. Those not so converted, classified as UNEXECUTED USES, were: a use raised on a non-**freehold estate**, i.e. a **tenancy**, "A to B for 10 years for the use of C;" a USE ON A USE, "A to B for the use of C for life then to the use of D;" and ACTIVE USES, which constitute the modern **trusts**, i.e., where a person holds legal title but unlike the passive use the legal titleholder has duties and obligations to perform in connection with his holding. Thus, A to B to invest for the benefit of C creates an active use and legal title does not merge with C's use. See Moynihan, Introduction to the Law of Property 207-212 (1962).

An important effect of the Statute of Uses was the validation of **executory interests** (a species of **future interests**) which had heretofore been recognized only in equity. Two kinds of executory interests so converted into legal estates were the springing and shifting uses. A SHIFTING USE is a use which arises in derogation of another, i.e., "shifts" from one beneficiary to another, depending on some future contingency. A SPRINGING USE is a use which arises upon the occurrence of a future event and which does not take effect in derogation of any interest other than that which results to the grantor, or remains in him in the meantime. Thus, A to B and his heirs to the use of C and his heirs beginning at some future date creates a legal estate in B, a resulting use for the interim period in A, and a springing use in C when his use comes into effect. If A conveys property to B for the use of C unless a contingency occurs in which case D should have the use, C obtains an equitable estate but if the contingency occurs then the equitable estate shifts to D who has a shifting use. "A shifting use is one which cuts short a prior use estate in a person other than the conveyor; a springing use is one which cuts short a use estate in the conveyor." Id. at 178.

USE IMMUNITY see **self-incrimination**.

USUFRUCT in the **civil law**, the right to use and enjoy **property** vested in another, "and to draw from the same all the profit, utility, and advantage which it may produce, provided it be without altering the substance of the thing." 75 P. 698, 699. See **beneficial use**.

USURY an unconscionable or exorbitant rate of **interest**; an excessive and illegal requirement of compensation for **forebearance** on a **debt** [**interest**]; "a bargain under which a greater profit than is permitted by law is paid, or is agreed to be paid to a creditor by or on behalf of the debtor for a loan of money, or for extending the maturity of a pecuniary debt." Restatement, Contracts §526. A usurious contract is illegal and is therefore void. Id. at §§598, 607. Although universally deplored, it was not recognized as an offense at **common law**. See Calamari & Perillo, Contracts 560 (1970). The state legislatures today determine the maximum allowable rates of interest that may be demanded in any financial transaction. One exception is that **corporations** are in most cases immune from these usury statutes. While in many jurisdictions a usurious contract is a nullity and is hence unenforceable, in some jurisdictions a creditor may recover his **principal**; in others, principal as well as interest at the legally authorized rate.

UTMOST RESISTANCE that degree of resistance which a woman must offer her attacker in order to charge that she has been raped; it is a relative term and a woman is only expected to give that resistance of which she is capable. 149 N.W. 771, 772. The "utmost resistance" doctrine may not apply if the woman is put in fear of personal violence and so submits to avert serious bodily injury to herself. 143 S.W. 2d 288, 289.

UTTER to put forth, to execute; especially, to offer, whether accepted or not, a forged instrument with representations by words or acts, directly, or indirectly, that the instrument is valid. See 125 So. 793, 794.

The crime of uttering a forged instrument includes the element of fraudulent intent to injure another, see 101 P. 2d 860, 863, and is distinguished from the crime of **forgery**, by the requirement that the utterer pass or attempt to pass the forged instrument. See 419 P. 2d 403, 406. Mere showing of a forged instrument without an attempt to pass it as genuine is not uttering. See 29 N.W. 923, 925.

UXOR see **et ux.**

VACATE to render **void**; to **set aside,** as "to vacate a judgment." See **reverse.**

To move out; to render vacant as in "vacating **premises.**" See **abandonment.**

VAGRANCY a general term for a class of minor offenses such as idleness without employment, having no visible means of support, etc.; roaming, wandering, or loitering; wandering or strolling around from place to place without any lawful purpose or object. Vagrancy statutes developed following the breakup of the English feudal estates. The downfall of the feudal system led to labor shortages. The Statutes of Laborers, 23 Edw. 3, c.1 (1349); 25 Edw. 3, c.l. (1350) were enacted to stabilize the working force by prohibiting increases in wages and prohibiting the movement of workers in search of improved conditions. Later the poor laws included vagrancy provisions to prevent the movement of "wild rogues" and the "notorious brotherhood of beggars." See [1937] 1 K.B. 232, 271.

More recently, the vagrancy statutes have been used by the police as authority for arresting persons who are suspected of some wrongdoing but where **probable cause** for their arrest does not exist. However, these statutes have been open to abuse and have recently found disfavor in the courts. See 282 NYS 2d 739. Courts have declared them unconstitutional as unreasonable, violative of **due process**, and **void for vagueness.** See, e.g., 405 U.S. 156.

VALUABLE CONSIDERATION see **consideration.**

VARIANCE in procedure, a discrepancy between what is **charged** or **alleged** and what is proved or offered as proof; not every variance is fatal. 257 A. 2d 814, 817. A FATAL VARIANCE, is, in both civil and criminal cases, a material and substantial variance, and, in criminal cases, it must also tend to mislead the defendant in making his defense, or tend to expose the defendant to the injury of being put twice in jeopardy for the same offense. 237 P. 2d 162, 165. (See **double jeopardy**).

In zoning law, it is an exemption from the application of a zoning ordinance or regulation permitting a use which varies from that otherwise permitted under the zoning regulation. The exception is granted by the appropriate authority in special circumstances to protect against an undue hardship wrought by strict enforcement of the zoning regulations. See also **non-conforming use.**

VEL NON *(věl nŏn)*—Lat: or not; as,

"The question of his being guilty, vel non, is for the jury to determine."

VENDEE buyer; purchaser, especially in **contract** for the **sale** of **realty**.

VENDOR seller; especially person who sells **real property**. The word "seller" is used more often to describe a **personal property** transaction.

VENIRE *(vĕ-nē'rā)*—Lat: to come; refers to the common law process by which jurors are summoned to try a case. 46 A. 2d 921, 923.

VENIRE DE NOVO *(dā nō'-vō)* to come anew; refers to the summoning of a second **jury** for the purpose of proceeding to a second trial. Such a second trial is awarded where a **verdict** [by the jury] or finding [by the court] "is so defective, uncertain, or ambiguous upon its face that no **judgment** can be rendered upon it." 41 N.E. 383, 386. At early common law, the writ of venire de novo (or VENIRE FACIAS DE NOVO, which was the more proper term), issued only in response to a jury's verdict, Id., and only where the defect appeared on the face of the record rather than at some place extrinsic to it, 27 N.E. 448; but these technical limitations have been incorporated into the more modern procedure of granting a new trial, which serves the purpose of the old venire de novo. See, e.g., Fed. R. Civ. Proc. 59. The term is therefore sometimes used simply to denote generally a new trial. See 171 N.E. 585.

VENUE a neighborhood, a neighboring place; synonymous with "place of trial." It refers to the possible or proper place or places for the trial of a **suit**, as among several places where **jurisdiction** could be established. See 132 N.W. 2d 304, 308; and 257 F. Supp. 219, 224. "Jurisdiction deals with the authority of a court to exercise judicial power. Venue deals with the place where that power should be exercised. Jurisdiction over the **subject matter** cannot be conferred by the parties, and the lack thereof may not be waived. Venue, on the other hand, is bottomed on convenience, and improper venue may be waived." Green, Civil Procedure 51 (1972). Venue "is the right of the party sued

to have the action brought and heard in a particular judicial district." 249 A. 2d 916, 918. See also **forum non conveniens; removal**.

VERDICT the opinion of a jury, or of a judge sitting as a jury, on a question of fact. See 31 Ill. App. 325, 338. A verdict differs from a judgment in that a verdict is not a judicial determination, but rather a finding of fact which the trial court may accept or reject and utilize in formulating its judgment. See 446 S.W. 2d 243, 244.

COMPROMISE VERDICT a verdict resulting from improper surrender of one juror's opinion to another on a material issue. See 215 P. 887, 889-90. [See QUOTIENT VERDICT below].

DIRECTED VERDICT see **directed verdict**.

GENERAL VERDICT ordinary verdict declaring simply which party prevails, without any special findings of fact.

PARTIAL VERDICT in criminal law, finding defendant guilty of certain charges but innocent of others.

QUOTIENT VERDICT improper and unacceptable kind of compromise verdict resulting from an agreement by the jurors that their verdict will be an award of **damages** in an amount to be determined by the addition of all juror's computations of damages and its division by the number of jurors.

SPECIAL VERDICT one rendered on certain specific factual issues posed by the court. "Instead of a general finding for one party or the other, the special verdict requires the jury to make a specific finding on each ultimate fact put in issue by the **pleadings**. . . . The Court will then apply the law to those found facts." Green, Civil Procedure 183 (1972).

When a trial court in a criminal case directs that the jury answer specific questions and render special verdicts incident to its general verdict of guilty or not guilty as to particular counts of the indictment, it may operate to coerce a particular result by leading the jury to that conclusion. For this reason special verdicts have been held improperly ordered in criminal cases where rendered against the wishes of the defendant who, it is said, has a right to a general verdict free from the influence of the court's special interrogatories. See 416 F. 2d 165.

VERIFICATION confirmation of correctness, truth, or authenticity of **pleading** or other paper **affidavit**, oath, or **deposition**, 12 F. 2d 81, 83; an affidavit attached to a statement insuring the truth of that statement. See 105 P. 2d 59, 63.

VERTICAL PRICE FIXING see **price fixing**.

VESTED fixed, accrued, or absolute, see 170 S.W. 885, 888; not contingent; generally used to describe any right or **title** to something which is not dependent upon the occurrence or failure to occur of some specified future event (**condition** precedent). Although sometimes used to refer to an immediate possessory **interest** in the property, the more technically proper definition comprehends, as well, interests that will only become rights to actual **possession** of the property at some later time [**in futuro**]. See 344 P. 2d 16, 21. Originally applied in reference to estates in **real property**, it has come to be applied to other property interests. See, e.g., 24 N.W. 161, 170-171 (**personal property**); 156 S.W. 2d 146, 151 (**trusts**); 4 N.W. 2d 919, 920 (**alimony** and child support payments). Compare **contingent**.

VESTED ESTATE a property **interest** which will necessarily come into **possession** in the future merely upon the **determination** (end) of the **preceding estate**. Thus for there to be a "vested estate" there must exist a known person who would have an immediate right to possession upon the expiration of the prior estate. See 157 S.W. 2d 429, 436. At common law "vested estate" was one which could be **devised** or **alienated**, whereas a **contingent estate** could not. Unlike a vested estate, a contingent estate depends upon the occurrence of an uncertain event or the future ascertainment of presently unknown takers. The simple determination of the preceding estate is not a sufficient **condition precedent** for a "contingent estate" to become **possessory**. See 51 N.Y.S. 1038, 1043. Contingent estates can now be devised and alienated.

VESTED INTEREST "a present right or title to a thing, which carries with it an existing right of alienation, even though the right to possession or enjoyment may be postponed to some uncertain time in the future. . . ." 120 S.W. 2d 778, 781. See **interest**.

VESTED REMAINDER "[a **remainder**] which is limited to an ascertained person in being, whose right to the **estate** is fixed and certain, and [which] does not depend upon the happening of any future event, but whose **enjoyment** is postponed to some future time." 102 S.E. 643, 644. See **contingent remainder**.

VESTED RIGHTS in relation to constitutional guarantees, it is a broad shield of protection which consists of "a vested interest which it is right and equitable that the government should recognize and protect, and of which the individual could not be deprived arbitrarily without injustice." 65 N.W. 2d 785, 791. The term "is frequently used to designate a right which has become so fixed that it is not subject to [being] divested without the consent of the owner." 84 P. 2d 552, 554.

VEXATIOUS LITIGATION civil action shown to have been instituted maliciously and without **probable cause**, and one which may be protected against by **injunction**. See 11 N.Y.S. 2d 768, 772. See **litigious**; **malicious prosecution**.

VICARIOUS LIABILITY the imputation of **liability** upon one person for the actions of another. In tort law, if an employee, EE, while in the **scope of his employment** for employer, ER, drives a delivery truck, and hits and injures P crossing the street, ER will be vicariously liable, under the doctrine of **respondeat superior**, for injuries sustained by P. In criminal law, in some jurisdictions, if EE, who is employed by ER as a bartender, sells liquor to a minor, ER will be criminally liable for the offense of EE. See 110 N.W. 2d 29, 34. Sometimes this doctrine is called IMPUTED LIABILITY. Compare **strict liability**.

VICINAGE neighborhood; vicinity. Its contemporary meaning denotes a particular area where a crime was committed, a **trial** is being held, or the community from which jurors are called.

VIDELICET   see **viz.**

VI ET ARMIS   see **trespass** [TRESPASS VI ET ARMIS].

VILLEIN SOCAGE   see **socage.**

VILLENAGE   a menial form of feudal **tenure** in which the **tenant** [the **villein**] was required to perform all **services** demanded by the lord of the manor.

VIOLATION OF PROBATION   see **probation.**

VIS MAJOR   *(vĭz mä'-yôr)* — Lat: a greater force, superior force; it is used in the civil law to mean **act of God**, see 38 So. 873, 874, and has reference to an "irresistable natural cause which cannot be guarded against by the ordinary exertions of human skill and prudence." 121 S.W. 36, 43. "A loss 'vis major' (superior force) is a loss that results immediately from natural cause, without the intervention of man, and could not have been prevented by the exercise of prudence, diligence and care." 222 F. Supp. 299, 305. "The early authors treated [the phrase] as the equivalent to an **act of God.** Later authority seems to have broadened its meaning to include any insuperable interference." 77 F. 2d 614, 617.

VITIATE   to void or render a nullity; to impair.

VIZ.   *(vĭz)*—Lat: abbreviated form of the Latin word "videlicet," meaning namely, that is to say. It is a term used in relation to **pleadings** "to particularize or explain what goes before it. It may restrain the generality of a preceding word, but cannot enlarge or diminish the preceding subject-matter. In the former case it is merely explanatory of the language which precedes it, while in the latter it is repugnant to it." 48 A. 639, 642. "When any fact alleged in pleading is preceded by 'to wit,' 'that is to say,' or 'namely,' such fact is said to be laid under a 'videlicet,' " the purpose of which is to particularize or specify. 116 N.W. 2d 243, 244.

VOID   empty, having no legal force, ineffectual, unenforceable, 146 N.E. 2d

477, 479; incapable of being ratified. For example, one who has been adjudicated an **incompetent** and for whom a **guardian** has been appointed has no capacity to contract, and any **contract** he enters into is void. Compare **voidable.**

VOIDABLE   capable of being later annulled; a valid act which though it may be avoided, may accomplish the thing sought to be accomplished until the fatal defect in the transaction has been effectively asserted or judicially ascertained and declared. 152 N.E. 2d 813, 817. For example, an infant has no capacity to contract, hence any contract he enters into is voidable. It is not **void,** however, and until and unless **repudiated** by the minor it is binding on the **competent** party. The infant may ratify the contract and so be bound thereunder when his disability of infancy is removed, i.e., when he reaches the age of **majority.**

VOID FOR VAGUENESS   a criminal statute is constitutionally void for vagueness when it is so vague that men of common intelligence must necessarily guess at its meaning and differ as to its application. 269 U.S. 385, 391. A statute is void when it is vague either as to what persons fall within the scope of the statute, what conduct is forbidden, or what punishment may be imposed. "**Due process** requires that criminal statutes, administrative crimes, and **common law** crimes be reasonably definite as to persons and conduct within their scope and the punishment which may be imposed for their violation. In determining whether a legislative, judicial or administrative definition is void for vagueness, the following inquiries are appropriate: (1) Does the law give fair notice to those persons potentially subject to it? (2) Does the law adequately guard against arbitrary and discriminatory enforcement? (3) Does the law provide sufficient breathing space for First Amendment Rights?" LaFave and Scott, Criminal Law 83 (1972). Use of this doctrine as a constitutional attack is based upon an assertion that the meaning of the statute in question is so uncertain and unclear as to render it void. The due process clause of the Fifth Amendment requires that criminal statuts give reasonably certain notice that an act has been made criminal before it is committed. Every man should be able to know with certainly when he is committing a crime. See 341 U.S. 223, 230; 105 F. Supp. 202.

VOIR DIRE *(vwŏr dēr)*—Fr: to speak the truth. A VOIR DIRE EXAMINATION usually refers to the prospective examination by the court or by the attorneys of prospective jurors, to determine their qualification for **jury** service, to determine if cause exists for challenge (i.e. to excuse) particular jurors, and to provide information about the jurors so that the parties can exercise their statutory peremptory challenges (objections to particular jurors without the need for any cause to be stated). See Green, Basic Civil Procdeure 102 (1972).

A voir dire examination during the trial refers to a **hearing** out of the presence and hearing of the jury by the court upon some **issue** of fact or law that requires an initial determination by the court or upon which the court must rule as a matter of law alone. Thus, where a **confession** of the **defendant** is to be introduced by the state in a criminal **trial**, the trial court must conduct a voir dire examination to determine if the statements were voluntarily obtained in compliance with the **Miranda** requirements and thus constitutionally admissible. This determination must be made at least initially by the court before the jury is permitted to hear the confession. 378 U.S. 368; 385 U.S. 538, 543.

VOLENTI NON FIT INJURIA *(vō-lĕn'-tē nŏn fēt ĭn-jû'-rē-à)*—Lat: the volunteer suffers no wrong; no legal wrong is done to him who consents. 102 P. 2d 213, 218. In torts, it refers to the fact that one cannot usually claim **damages** when he consented to the activity which caused the damages.

VOLUNTARY APPEARANCE see **appearance**.

VOLUNTARY DISABLEMENT see **anticipatory breach (of contract)**.

VOLUNTARY MANSLAUGHTER see **manslaughter**.

VOLUNTARY WASTE see **waste**.

VOTING TRUST the "accumulation in a single hand, or in a few hands, of **shares** of corporate **stock** belonging to many owners in order thereby to control the business of the **company**." 152 N.E. 609, 611. "A voting trust as commonly understood is a device whereby two or more persons owning stock with voting powers, divorce the voting rights thereof from ownership, retaining to all intents and purposes the latter in themselves and transferring the former to trustees in whom the voting rights of all the depositors in the trust are pooled." 130 A. 2d 338, 344.

WAIVER an intentional and voluntary giving up, relinquishment, or surrender of some known right. In general, a waiver may either result from an express agreement or be inferred from circumstances, 200 A. 2d 166, 172, but courts must indulge every reasonable presumption against the loss through waiver of constitutional rights. 304 U.S. 458, 464. To be effective as a constitutional waiver it must be an "intelligent relinquishment or abandonment of a known right." Id. Courts will not imply waiver from a silent **record**, and thus to find a waiver of a constitutional right, the trial court should hold a hearing and make explicit **findings of fact** supporting a valid waiver. In criminal procedure, the defendant should personally participate in a decision to waive a constitutional right whenever his consent can practicably be obtained. 405 U.S. 504. Thus, he may be unable to participate in strategic trial waivers but he can give intelligent consent to whether or not to appeal his conviction. See **informed consent**.

EXECUTORY WAIVER one which affects a still unperformed duty of a contracting party, as in the excuse by A of **performance** by B of something which A has a right to exact. 318 S.W. 2d 456, 459. An executory waiver does not require **consideration** but may be retracted until there has been detrimental reliance upon it. See U.C.C. §2-209(5).

WANT OF CONSIDERATION see consideration.

WANTON grossly **negligent** or careless; extremely **reckless**, etc.; virtually synonymous with reckless. 5 So. 2d 41, 45. **Willful** implies intent or purpose, while wanton expresses a reckless disregard of consequences. 88 A. 895, 896.

WARRANT a written **order** directing the **arrest** of a person or persons, issued by a court, body, or official, having authority to issue warrants of arrest (See also **bench warrant**); also, a **writ** from a competent authority directing the doing of a certain act. 171 F. Supp. 393, 395.

WARRANT TO SATISFY JUDGMENT an authorization issued by the **judgment creditor**'s attorney to the clerk of the court directing him to enter a **satisfaction** of the **judgment** in the official court records.

SEARCH WARRANT an order that certain premises or property be searched for particularized items which if found are to be seized and used as **evidence** in a criminal **trial** or destroyed as contraband. See **search warrant**.

The word "warrant" is also used in commercial and property law to refer to the act of guaranteeing, assuring; creating an express warranty as to the quality and validity of what is being **conveyed**. See **guarantee; merchantability; warranty**.

WARRANTY an assurance by one **party** to a **contract** of the existence of a fact upon which the other party may rely, intended precisely to relieve the promisee of any duty to ascertain the fact for himself, and which amounts to a promise to **indemnify** the promisee for any loss if the fact warranted proves untrue. 155 F. 2d 780, 784. Such warranties are either made overtly (EXPRESS WARRANTIES) or by implication (IMPLIED WARRANTIES). See U.C.C. §§2-312 to 2-318.

A **covenant** of warranty in **real property** is a covenant **running with the land**, insuring the continuing validity of **title** and the **breach** of which occurs at the

time of conveyance and gives rise to an action by the last vendee against the first or any other warrantor. See 24 N.W. 333, 335.

WARRANTY OF FITNESS a warranty that the goods are suitable for the special purpose of the buyer, which will not be satisfied by mere fitness for general purposes.

WARRANTY OF HABITABILITY [more properly, an implied or express **covenant of habitability**] a promise by landlord that at the inception of the lease there are no **latent defects** in facilities vital to the use of the premises for residential purposes, and that these facilities will remain in usable condition during the duration of the lease. See 56 N.J. 130, 145.

WARRANTY OF MERCHANTIBILITY a warranty that the goods are reasonably fit for the general purposes for which they are sold. See U.C.C. §§2-314.

WASTE generally, an act, by one in rightful **possession** of land who has less than a **fee simple** interest in the land, which decreases the value of the land or the owner's **intrest** or the interest of one who has an **estate** that may become possessory at some future time (such as a **remainderman, lessor, mortgagee, reversioner**). Waste is "the deterioration or improper deterioration or material alteration of things forming an essential part of the **inheritance**, done or suffered by a person rightfully in possession by virtue of a temporary or partial estate, as, for example, a **tenant** for life or for years. The rightful possession of the wrongdoer is essential, and constitutes a material distinction between waste and **trespass**." 21 A. 2d 354, 358.

AMELIORATING WASTE a change in the physical structure of the occupied premises by an unauthorized act of the tenant which, though technically "waste" in fact increases the value of the land, e.g., where the tenant tears out all the cabinets in the kitchen and replaces them with new cabinets of better quality. Ameliorating waste is not ordinarily grounds for liability. See 162 N.E. 621, 622.

EQUITABLE WASTE "such acts as at law would not be esteemed to be waste under the circumstances of the case, but which in the view of a Court of Equity are so esteemed from their manifest injury to the inheritance, although they are not inconsistent with the legal rights of the party committing them." Story, Eq. Jr. §915 (13th Ed. 1886). Thus, conduct will be enjoined where the court finds it to be abusive and where the injunction is required **pro bono publico**. Id. Courts may be guided by the standard of "that which a prudent man would not do with his own property" in defining the limits of this equity power. See 62 N.E. 210, 214.

PERMISSIVE WASTE   injury to the inheritance caused by the tenant's failure to make reasonable repairs on the premises; e.g., A, life tenant or tenant for years, fails to cover a hole in the roof of the dwelling house on the leased premises and as a result the floors and ceilings are damaged by rainfall. A tenant is bound to make ordinary repairs. Id.

VOLUNTARY WASTE   "injury to the inheritance caused by an affirmative act of the tenant." Id. at 237.

In the law of Oil and Gas:

PHYSICAL WASTE   a production practice which in light of alternatives, reduces the quantity of hydrocarbons which may be produced from a reservoir.

ECONOMIC WASTE   a production practice which, in light of alternatives, reduces net value of hydrocarbons which may be produced from a reservoir.

WEIGHT OF THE EVIDENCE   a phrase which indicates the relative value of the totality of evidence presented on one side of a judicial dispute, in light of the evidence presented on the other side, see 109 So. 2d 375, 378; refers to the persuasiveness of the testimony of the witnesses. See **against the weight of the evidence; burden of proof.**

WHIPLASH INJURY   neck injury commonly associated with "rear end"-type automobile collisions; caused by a sudden and unexpected forced forward movement of the body while the unsupported head of an automobile occupant attempts to remain stationary consistent with the laws of physics, subjecting the neck to a severe strain while in a relaxed position. 320 F. 2d 437, 441. It is a favorite **claim** in **tort** actions arising from such collisions because it is difficult to medically prove or disprove.

WHOLESALER   middleman;   person who buys large quantities of goods and re-sells to other distributors rather than to ultimate consumers. Compare **jobber.**

WIDOW'S ELECTION   the right of a widow to elect or choose to acquiesce in the stipulations of her husband's **will,** or to object to the will (and thereby reject it) and demand that which is provided for a widow by statute. See 20 A. 714, 715, 1 P. 556, 559. Compare **dower.**

WILD'S CASE, RULE IN   see **Rule in Wild's Case.**

WILL   a person's declaration of how he desires his property to be disposed of after his death, which declaration is revocable during his lifetime, operative for no purpose until death, and applicable to the situation which exists at his death. A will may also contain other declarations of the party's desires as to what is to be done after he dies but it must dispose of some property. Atkinson, Wills 2 (2d ed. 1953).

The difference between a will and a **deed** is that by means of a deed, a present **interest** passes on delivery, while a will takes effect only upon the death of the **testator.** 20 So. 2d 71, 72. "Will" is generally used as synonymous with **testament,** 74 P. 2d 27, 32, but the latter is, technically, confined to the disposition of **personal property.** 54 F. 860, 865. LAST WILL AND TESTAMENT is an expression commonly used to refer to the most recent document directing the disposition of the real and personal property of the party. See **codicil; causa mortis.** Compare **gift; testamentary disposition.**

WILLFUL [WILFUL]   in civil proceedings, denotes an act which is intentional, or knowing, or voluntary, as distinguished from accidental. But when used in a criminal statute, it generally means an act done with a bad purpose; without justifiable excuse, stubbornly, obstinately, perversely. 290 U.S. 389, 394. See Perkins, Criminal Law 780 (2d ed 1969).

WINDING UP the process of **liquidating** a corporation. It "involves the process of collecting the **assets**, paying the expenses involved, satisfying creditors' claims and distributing the net assets usually in cash but possibly in kind, first to any preferred shareholder, according to their [sic] liquidation preferences and rights, then to any other shareholders with more than normal liquidation rights, and finally **pro rata** among the rest of the shareholders." Henn, Law of Corporations 614 (2d ed. 1961).

Liquidation procedures are usually prescribed and regulated by states. Partial liquidation is possible in which case the corporation would not be dissolved. Liquidation should thus be distinguished from DISSOLUTION, which refers to the termination of the legal life of the corporation.

WITHDRAWAL the removal of money or the like from the place where it is kept, such as a bank. In criminal law, it is the separation of one's self from the criminal activity; to be effective to terminate **liability** for subsequent acts of a continuing **conspiracy**, the withdrawing party's action must evince disapproval of or opposition to the criminal activities, and communicate timely to the other active members. 200 N.E. 2d 11, 14. Compare **renunciation**.

WITH PREJUDICE see **dismissal** [DISMISSAL WITH PREJUDICE].

WITHOUT PREJUDICE see **dismissal** [DISMISSAL WITHOUT PREJUDICE].

WITNESS one who gives evidence in a cause before a court and who **attests** or swears to facts or gives or bears **testimony** under oath, 183 N.Y.S. 2d 125, 129; to see the execution of, as that of an **instrument** and/or to sign one's name to it to authenticate it [attestation]. 294 N.W. 357, 362.

ADVERSE [HOSTILE] WITNESS one whose relationship to the opposing party is such that his testimony may be prejudiced. 313 P. 2d 684, 686. A witness declared to be hostile may be asked **leading questions** and is subject to cross-examination by the party that called him.

WITNESS AGAINST HIMSELF see **self-incrimination**.

WORDS OF ART words which have a particular meaning to a particular area of study; e.g., in law, **last clear chance**, **promissory estoppel**, **reliance** are all words of art because they have either no or different meanings outside a legal context.

WORDS OF LIMITATION words used in an **instrument** conveying an **interest** in **property** which seem to indicate the party to whom a **conveyance** is made, but actually indicate the type of **estate** taken by the **grantee**; e.g., in a conveyance from A "to B and his heirs," "and his heirs" are words of limitation, in that they delimit the estate taken by B, namely, a **fee simple**; and since a fee simple vests in B an absolute power to **alienate** the fee, B is under no obligation to give his heirs anything. On the other hand, WORDS OF PURCHASE are those which indicate the grantees or persons who take, as they would seem to indicate; hence, in the example above, "to B" are words of purchase.

WORKMEN'S COMPENSATION ACTS statutes which in general establish the liability of an employer for injuries or sicknesses which "arise out of and in the course of employment." Prosser, Torts 532-33 (4th ed. 1971). The liability is created without regard to the fault or **negligence** of the employer. Benefits generally include hospital and other medical payments and compensation for loss of income; if the injury is covered by the statute, compensation thereunder will be the employee's only remedy against his employer.

These statutes have had the effect of abolishing the notion that the hazards of a particular job or workplace are voluntarily encountered by the employee by virtue of his agreement to work there, and thus could not give rise to liability for negligence on the part of the employer. See 132 A. 2d 505, 511. Also contrary to the common law rule, the employer is generally not exempt from liability under these statutes when the injury is caused by the negligence of a fellow-servant. See Id. at §80. See **strict liability**. Compare **employers' liability acts**. See also **scope of employment**.

WORK PRODUCT that work done by an attorney in the process of representing his client which is ordinarily not subject to **discovery**; "work product can generally be defined to encompass writings, statements, or testimony which would substantially reflect or invade an attorney's legal impressions or legal theories as to a pending or reasonably anticipated litigation. An attorney's legal impressions and theories would include his tactics, strategy, opinions and thoughts." 34 F.R.D. 212, 213. The leading federal case is *Hickman* v. *Taylor*, 329 U.S. 495.

Where special necessity is demonstrated discovery may nevertheless be had; e.g., where "relevant and non-privileged facts remain hidden in an attorney's file and production of those facts is essential to the preparation of one's case." Id. at 511.

WORTHIER TITLE, DOCTRINE OF early common law rule whereby a **gift** by **devise** to one's **heir** which amounted to exactly what the heir would have taken by **descent** had his ancestor died **intestate**, was disregarded and the heir took instead by descent, which was considered as conferring a worthier, better title.

The rule has an **inter vivos** application as well, under which a grantor may not limit a **remainder** to his heirs. This has been recognized in many American jurisdictions, as a rule of construction in effectuating the intent of the grantor. Thus, a **reversion** in the grantor is preferred to a **remainder** in his heirs. See 122 N.E. 221. See generally, Moynihan, Introduction to the Law of Real Property, 149-162 (1962).

WRIT a mandatory precept issued by the authority and in the name of the sovereign or the state for the purpose of compelling a person to do something therein mentioned. It is issued by a court or other competent tribunal, and is directed to the sheriff or other officer authorized to execute the same. In every case the writ itself contains directions as to what is required to be done." See **peremptory writ; prerogative writ.**

WRIT OF CORAM NOBIS *(kôr'-äm nō'-bĭs)*—Lat: before us; in our presence, .e., in our court. The purpose of the writ "is to bring the attention of the court to, and obtain relief from, errors

of fact, such as . . . a valid **defense** existing in the facts of the case, but which, without **negligence** on the part of the defendant, was not made, either through **duress** or **fraud** or excusable mistake; these facts not appearing on the face of the **record** and being such as, if known in season, would have prevented the rendition and entry of the **judgment** questioned. . . . The writ does not lie to correct errors of law." 198 P. 2d 505, 506. This writ is addressed to the court that rendered the judgment in which injustice was allegedly done, in contrast to **appeals** or review directed to another court. 269 N.Y.S. 2d 983, 986. It is another name for "writ of error coram nobis." Sometimes it is referred to simply as "coram nobis."

WRIT OF ERROR an early common law **writ** issued out of "the **appellate court** and served on the trial judge ordering him to send up the **record** in the in the case. The one who sought the review, whether the plaintiff or defendant in the trial court, [is] designated as the 'plaintiff in error.' His opponent [is] the 'defendant in error.' . . . The only function of the appellate court [is] to review alleged errors of law. . . ." Green, Basic Civil Procedure 225 (1972). It is similar to a writ of **certiorari**, but a writ of error, unlike a writ of certiorari, is a writ of right and lies only where jurisdiction is exercised according to the course of the common law. See 29 N.E. 43, 45; and 67 Me. 429, 433.

WRIT OF EXECUTION a routine court order by which the court attempts to enforce the **judgment** that has been granted a **plaintiff** by authorizing a sheriff to levy on the property belonging to the **judgment debtor**, which is located within the county. See Green, Civil Procedure 197 (1972). See also **in rem; sheriff's sale.**

WRIT OF PROHIBITION a **process** or **writ** issued by a superior court that prevents an inferior court or tribunal from exceeding its **jurisdiction** or usurping **jurisdiction** with which it has not been vested by law. See 194 N.E. 2d 912, 914; 193 So. 2d 26, 29. "It is an extraordinary writ because it only issues when the party seeking it is without other means of redress for the wrong about to be inflicted by the act of the inferior tribunal. It is a **prerogative writ**." 179 So. 403, 404. Where the action sought to be prohibited is judicial in nature the writ may be exercised against public officers. See 208 S.W. 835, 839. Sometimes it is referred to simply as PROHIBITION.

WRIT OF RIGHT a **writ** generally issued as a matter of course or granted as a matter of right, in contrast to **prerogative writs** that are issued only at the discretion of the issuing authority.

Also the name of an ancient writ for the recovery of real property.

WRONGFUL ACT "[a]ny act which in the ordinary course will infringe upon the rights of another to his **damage**, unless it is done in the exercise of an equal or superior right." 73 N.J.L. 729, 744. Thus, the scope of the term is not limited to acts which are "illegal," but comprehends as well acts which are deemed immoral, anti-social, tortious, etc.

WRONGFUL DEATH STATUTE statutes which provide relief from the common law rule that the death of an individual can not be a **cause of action** in a civil **suit**. Every American state has a wrongful death statute. Prosser, Torts 902 (4th ed. 1971). "The statutes usually provide that the action can be maintained [by the executor, administrator or beneficiaries of the decedent] for 'any wrongful act, neglect or default' which causes death. They are therefore held to cover intentional, as well as negligent, torts." Id. at 903. See **survival statutes**.

YELLOW DOG CONTRACT an employment **contract** expressly prohibiting the named employee from joining **labor unions** under pain of dismissal. See 101 P. 2d 436, 443. Under most state constitutions the right to join a union and bargain collectively is guaranteed. See, e.g., N.J. Const. Art. 1, §19 (1947).

Federal and state statutes now generally declare that such contracts will not form the basis for legal or equitable remedies. 43 C.J.S., Injunctions, §138 at 693.

Z

ZONE OF EMPLOYMENT that physical area within which injuries to an employee are compensible by **workmen's compensation** laws; it denotes the place of employment and surrounding areas, including the means of ingress and egress, which are under control of the employer. 57 N.E. 2d 607, 608. Compare **Scope of employment**.

ZONING legislative action, usually on the municipal level, which separates or divides municipalities into districts for the purpose of regulating, controlling, or in some way limiting the use of the property, and the construction and/or structural nature of buildings erected within the zones or districts established. See 198 A. 225. Local zoning authority ordinarily derives from a state constitutional grant of power to the state legislature, which in turn by statutes defers or delegates it to municipalities. See, e.g., N.J. Const. Art. IV, §6, cl. 2 (1947) and N.J.S.A. 40:55-32. Zoning is said to be part of the state **police power**, and therefore must be for the purpose of furthering the health, morals, safety or the general welfare of the populace. See 283 A. 2d 353, 355.

Zoning decisions are subject to judicial review against arbitrariness and compliance with **due process**; zoning ordinances properly adopted are presumed to be valid, 181 A. 2d 129 (upholding exclusion of trailer camps from an industrial district), although equal protection considerations must be satisfied. See, e.g., 75 N.W. 2d 25. Aesthetics as such have been held insufficient to support a zoning ordinance but have been upheld if adopted with "a view of conserving the value of property and encouraging the most appropriate use of land." 29 N.J. 481, 494.

Other Barron's Titles Available

GUIDE TO LAW SCHOOLS
Elliott M. Epstein, Jerome Shostak, Lawrence M. Troy
350 pages $5.50 paper
Provides descriptions of ABA-approved law schools with information on admissions, financial aid, programs; lists law practice requirements by state.

HOW TO SUCCEED IN LAW SCHOOL
Brian Siegel
272 pages $4.50 paper
Step-by-step method that promotes an understanding of legal principles and provides a total organization and preparation for law school examinations.

BARRON'S NEW GUIDE TO THE LAW SCHOOL ADMISSION TEST (LSAT)
Jerry Bobrow
640 pages $6.95 paper
Intensive review and practice for all test sections, with 4 full-length examinations having fully explained answers.

HOW TO PREPARE FOR THE MULTISTATE BAR EXAMINATION (MBE)
Victor Schwartz
233 pages $5.50 paper
Thorough preparation on how to handle the MBE. Includes a test in each of the 6 subject areas, with fully explained answers.

BUSINESS LAW
Lowell Howard
596 pages $6.50 paper $10.50 cloth
Complete introduction to the fundamental principles of law. Precise yet easily understood reference for the businessman, student, lawyer. Includes the Uniform Commercial Code.

THE LAW, THE SUPREME COURT, AND THE PEOPLE'S RIGHTS
Ann Fagan Ginger
700 pages $7.95 paper $14.95 cloth
Comprehensive review of the controversial decisions of the Warren Supreme Court era. Brings alive the American human rights law.

At your local bookseller or order direct from *Barron's,* Woodbury, N.Y. 11797, adding 10% postage, plus applicable sales tax.